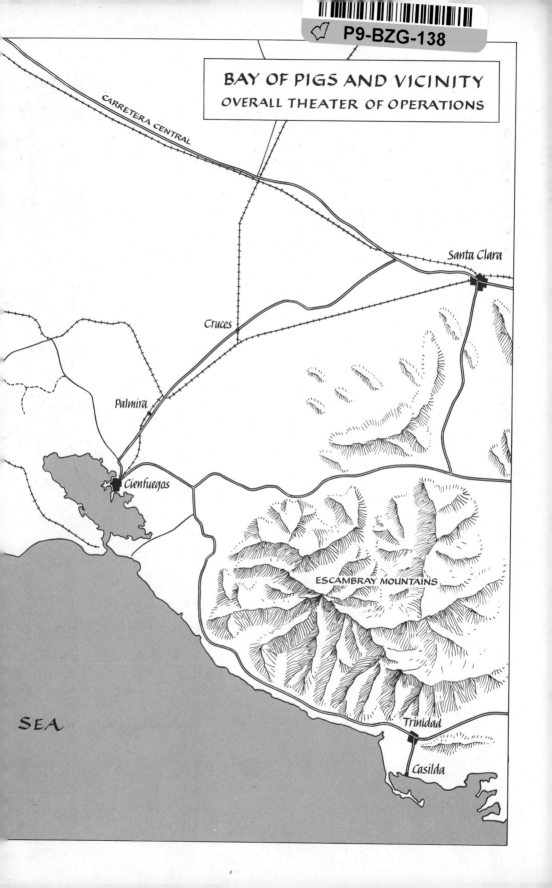

BAY OF PIGS AND VICINITY
OVERALL THEATER OF OPERATIONS

P9-BZG-138

CARRETERA CENTRAL

Santa Clara

Cruces

Palmira

Cienfuegos

ESCAMBRAY MOUNTAINS

SEA

Trinidad

Casilda

BAY OF PIGS

The Untold Story

PIGS

by Peter Wyden

SIMON AND SCHUSTER | NEW YORK

Photo editor: Vincent Virga
Designed by Irving Perkins and Jeanne Joudry
Manufactured in the United States of America

1 2 3 4 5 6 7 8 9 10

Library of Congress Cataloging in Publication Data
Wyden, Peter.
  Bay of Pigs.

  Bibliography: p.
  Includes index.
  1. Cuba—History—Invasion, 1961.   I.   Title.
F1788.W9   972.91′064   79–4188
ISBN 0-671-24006-4

Contents

KENNEDY   # "How could I have been so stupid...?"

No notable event in recent United States history remains as unexplained and puzzling as the Central Intelligence Agency's adventure that became known as "the Bay of Pigs." Now the fog can be lifted from this mystery with the help of the men who know—the eyewitnesses, men who have remained largely silent, the men who planned this supposedly ultrasecret operation, who directed it, who fought in it, not just on the beaches and roads and in the swamps of Cuba, but in Washington, Miami, Guatemala, Nicaragua, Puerto Rico, Havana, and at sea in the Caribbean. Especially in the meeting rooms of Washington.

The telling of this story is long overdue, because the Bay of Pigs is more than a skeleton in the nation's historical closet; more than the first blemish on the magic of the Kennedy name and reputation; more than the collapse of the largest secret operation in U.S. history. It is a watershed.

If the CIA, acting out of control and independently, had not escalated its plans against Fidel Castro from a modest guerrilla operation into a full-fledged invasion, President Kennedy would have suffered no humiliating, almost grotesque defeat.

If Kennedy had not been thoroughly defeated by Castro on the beaches in 1961, Nikita Khrushchev almost certainly would not have dared to precipitate the Cuban Missile Crisis of 1962—the crisis which, in the words of former CIA Director William E. Colby, pushed the world "as close to Armageddon" as it has ever come.

7

And if the reasons for the collapse at the Bay of Pigs had not been covered up, to remain substantially secret to this writing, the CIA might perhaps have been curbed, and the country could have been spared the intelligence scandals of the 1970s, the revelations of a government agency routinely, daily, committing unconstitutional acts against its own citizens in its own country.

The swamps of Cuba raise questions for today. Did too much secrecy make reasonable efficiency impossible? Did bureaucracy sabotage management control? Did the ambitions of leadership compound risks to an intolerable degree? Could it happen again?

Hindsight improves with the years. Right after the event, President Kennedy found it impossible to explain. He asked his special counsel, Theodore C. Sorensen, the central question still being asked around the world: "How could I have been so stupid to let them go ahead?"

CHAPTER ONE

Plot at the CIA

Deputy Director for Plans

Richard Drain was disgusted. Nobody seemed to care that he existed. He had completed a successful two-year tour of duty as chief of station (COS) of the Central Intelligence Agency's mission in Athens and had been due for home leave and reassignment to another post. He felt he needed a change of scene and had cabled the personnel office that he was willing to serve anywhere except in Greece.

When he returned to Washington, the CIA personnel people seemed surprised to see him and asked when he was going back to Greece. Drain, slight of build, punctilious, acerbic, a World War II tank commander with two law degrees, including one from Yale University, was annoyed. He said he wasn't going back to Greece. The personnel people suggested he go on leave. It was early August 1960. He took his wife and two sons to Colorado for a month.

In early September he showed up again at the personnel office, rested and eager. "Have you had your leave?" they wanted to know. He said he had. "Well, when are you going back to Greece?" Controlling his temper with some effort, Drain said he wasn't going back to Greece. The personnel people seemed surprised and told him to keep in touch. He did exactly that for a while, several times a week. They had no assignment for him.

Late in September he was puttering with repairs around his home in the Cleveland Park section of Washington, a ten-minute drive from CIA headquarters. He called his office again, but they still had no word for him. He said he was sick of being unemployed, but that he wasn't going to call again, and they could find him at home. Inwardly, he was

9

seething about the sluggish metabolism of the Washington bureaucracy. "Horseshit," he said. It was one of his favorite turns of phrase.

Shortly after 4 P.M. on October 1, he was finishing some work in his yard, when his wife called, "Dick, Mr. Bissell is on the phone!"

Richard Mervin Bissell, Jr., was the CIA's deputy director for plans. The title was the agency's gentle euphemism for chief of all covert operations, and Bissell was second in influence only to the director, Allen W. Dulles.

"Bissell," so the saying went around the agency, "is where the action is," and he and Drain had known each other for a long time. Bissell, a former economist with a Yale Ph.D., had been Drain's faculty adviser at Yale in the 1930s. He had straightened out Drain's freshman schedule and persuaded him that Economics 10 was "Coolidge economics" and a waste of time.

When Drain reached the phone, Bissell said in his usual crisp but low-key way, "I hear you've taken some leave of your own."

Drain agreed.

"I want you to see Jake Engler* about an assignment," Bissell said.

"Fine," said Drain. "I'll go to see him in the morning."

"No," said Bissell, "I mean now!"

A call from Dick Bissell was not taken casually in Washington, not even by the President. Outside the intelligence community, Bissell was all but unknown. Many Washington reporters had never heard his name. He was one of a handful of bureaucrats functioning silently just below the very top level of the government, doing much of its thinking, often able to shape decisions their own way. They were men of enormous power and autonomy. They showed the more visible officials like Allen Dulles which buttons to push. Often they did the button-pushing for their bosses. Their true power derived from their ability to get things done, and getting things done in Washington was the art of arts. Its mastery often eluded even presidents. They needed action men. Among the elite of these men Bissell had acquired the reputation of a virtuoso.

When Dulles gave Bissell his own old job in charge of "plans," he said, "The only thing I want you to plan is how to get more intelligence about Russia." Old-fashioned spying was becoming less effective. The contemporary superspy used technology, electronics. By luck, one of President Eisenhower's innumerable advisory committees, the Killian Committee on Surprise Attack, had recommended building a plane that could fly at more than seventy thousand feet and photograph Soviet defense installations, especially missile sites. Earlier, an engineering

*A pseudonym.

genius, Kelly Johnson of Lockheed Aviation, had suggested a similar airborne spy system.

Bissell took the job of building what became the famous U-2 plane. He worked with Johnson, who had turned out the first American jet fighter in World War II, the F-80, in just 141 days; and with E. H. ("Din") Land, the developer of the Polaroid camera. Three superlative minds—but it was Bissell who got the U-2 operational in two years; the normal Air Force time would have been eight. His secrecy was overwhelming even by CIA standards. Most communications were face to face. The ultrasecret safes containing plans were rarely opened.

No other task had ever given Dick Bissell greater personal satisfaction. Not only was its success the key to the safety of the nation. He relished the way he could get it done, keeping control centered in his own hands. His team was "completely compartmented in the interest of security and walled off." He was boss in name and in fact: "Allen Dulles knew less of what went on in that component of the agency than he did about any of them. He didn't see much of the cable traffic. There were an awful lot of details that never came to anybody else's attention." Secrecy meant more than security. It meant control. Control meant power. Power meant getting things done without a lot of kibitzing by outsiders.

The U-2 secret kept until May 1, 1960, when Gary Powers was shot down over Sverdlovsk. In Dulles' office, Bissell, who enjoyed taking risks, took a big one: he explained how it would have been impossible for Powers to survive the crash. Therefore, the United States should stick to its cover story that his aircraft was a weather plane from Turkey that had strayed off course. So Eisenhower lied. Powers lived. The Soviets went through the roof. The furor torpedoed an upcoming summit conference. But Bissell's intelligence triumph in building the plane—its cameras could pick up license plates of parked cars—was warmly remembered in government.* And in August 1960 his victory became complete when, again unknown to the public, the first intelligence reconnaissance satellite, its development again supervised by Bissell, delivered an even more explicit view of Soviet targets. The official Air Force report gave him credit for that enterprise.

The closed Communist society had become all but an open book. And at his desk, as he ordered Dick Drain to report for the operation to unseat Castro, Bissell was toying nervously with his favorite coffee mug. It was a present from a colleague in the U-2 operation. It carried the letters "RBAF"—Richard Bissell Air Force.

*More than a year after the Bay of Pigs, the U-2 possibly averted nuclear war when its cameras spotted the Soviet missiles that produced the Cuban Missile Crisis before the weapons became operational.

Bissell was not the prototypical CIA executive. He had no military, investigative or legal background. Unlike most of the principal intelligence officers of his generation, he had not shared the wartime brotherhood of spies in the Office of Strategic Services. Yet among his colleagues he moved as a marked man, an original, because of his energy and his mind.

Lean, stoop-shouldered, long-faced, with dark-rimmed spectacles, he looked professorial but did not act the part. His long legs made him appear even taller than his six feet three inches. He reminded Dick Drain of a great stork. He rarely walked. He loped. It was difficult for him to stay anchored to a desk. He had to pace and keep on pacing. He never dictated except on the move. Another of his assistants, Jim Flannery, always imagined that his coattails were flying as he kept striding, leaning forward as if bucking a wind, hands clasped behind his back, up and down his large rectangular office or on his almost daily outdoor walks to work off steam, an hour or two at a time.

Even at his desk he was in incessant motion. He toyed with a screw and a matching nut. He polished his glasses. He threw a toy tire into the air again and again and caught it. He picked up a nasal inhalator and sniffed to fight off a chronic catarrh. His hands mangled a paper clip with the right hand, then with the left, then with both. Then it went between his thin lips to be crushed and chewed by the teeth, again and again, then shifted from one side of the mouth to the other and back again. He picked lint off his slacks. He paced. And paced. The excess energy was all but visible.

His colleagues regarded Bissell with awe. Robert Amory, Jr., the agency's DDI (deputy director for intelligence), an elegant former Harvard law professor known for irreverence, thought of him as "a human computer" and "very spookish, a glutton for security." Drain, recalling the U-2, considered his former professor "one of the true heroes of our time" but "too bright for me." Flannery saw him as a perfectionist "who could drive you bananas," a "genius," sometimes "frightening to work around." His impact on people was "overwhelming."

His colleagues liked and admired Bissell, but they found him "eerie." He could race through a memo, holding each new page at the bottom between two fingers, scanning, flipping every few seconds, gulping the entire contents while others were struggling with the opening pages. He could recall almost any detail months later. If the telephone interrupted him while he was dictating, he could pick up later in midsentence.

When the independence movement was taking hold in Africa, Bissell once said he had half an hour to be brought up to date on that continent. The division chief and his deputy arrived for the briefing, and Bissell said, "To save time, why don't I tell you what I know and you take it from there?" He talked for ten minutes. Flannery thought, "It was the damnedest thing; they didn't have a thing to add." The performance was a Bissell characteristic: he could intimidate without intimidation; he only had to display the power of his mind.

Bissell's world was an elitist's possession divided between "decision-makers" and "technicians." If technicians seemed to labor sluggishly, his impatience could be incendiary. His face reddened and he shuffled his feet as if he wanted to stamp them. During the Bay of Pigs, Jake Engler, the project director, sometimes found that his head was the target for one of Bissell's well-sharpened pencils. Another eruption hit Cord Meyer, Jr., head of the agency's International Division, who frequently submitted thick reports to Bissell for concurrence shortly before they were due in Dulles' office.

One afternoon, caught with another Meyer report and an imminent deadline, Bissell phoned the author and shouted, "I'm going to tear it up! I'm going to tear it up!" He dropped the phone, tore up the report, picked up the receiver and shouted, "I just tore it up!" From then on, the reports arrived in time for his scanning.

Low-key salesmanship, combined with mastery of his subject, overcame many of Bissell's frustrations with bureaucracy. William P. Bundy, another of his Yale students, remembered how, as deputy administrator of the Economic Cooperation Administration, Bissell was "the real mental center and engine room of the Marshall Plan." He infused congressional committees with the confidence to vote billions of dollars for then revolutionary foreign-aid schemes. The requisite facts and figures poured out of Bissell's head, usually without reference to notes.

He acknowledged his impatience, his preference for "very direct kind of intervention," using power "just to get things done." During the Marshall Plan days he became "so thoroughly fed up" with French budget policy that he "wanted to cut off all aid to France." The fact that France was then one of America's stoutest allies made little difference. The French civil-service mentality was more frustrating than Bissell could bear. The State Department came to France's rescue; it was one of his many run-ins with the department and its maddeningly cautious ways. "I admire and believe in the use of power, when it's available, for purposes that I regard as legitimate," he said years later. Greater freedom for direct action made the CIA attractive to a man of Bissell's temperament.

No movie director would cast Richard Mervin Bissell, Jr., as an assassin. He was an elitist born. His father was president of the Hartford Fire Insurance Company and generally considered a millionaire. Dick's friends thought Mr. Bissell looked as if he had just stepped out of the frame of the oil painting of himself that hung in his board room. He seemed to address others from "two steps up from where you were standing." He was a symbol of the Hartford, Connecticut, establishment and always dressed for dinner. His authority was quietly exercised but unquestioned. When Mr. Bissell said, "Now I think we'll play bridge," no discussion was required.

Dick's mother was a Truesdale from Cleveland; her father had been president of the Delaware and Lackawanna Railroad. She ran a punctilious salon: the appearance of ashes in an ashtray was a signal for the nearest servant to whisk it away. She was "strong-willed" and "very interested" in her children's success.

Until Dick was nine years old, the family lived in the Mark Twain House near central Hartford, a brooding multigabled red brick mansion with five baths. The thickly paneled stairwell measured fifteen by twenty-five feet. Speaking tubes connected the six bedrooms with the servants in the kitchen. Mark Twain had written *Tom Sawyer* and *The Adventures of Huckleberry Finn* in these imposing surroundings. Eventually the house was turned into a museum.

Dick's home environment became more cosmopolitan when the family moved to suburban Farmington in 1918. In Avon, at the other end of "The Valley," lived the Alsops—Joseph, the columnist and friend of President Kennedy, became Dick's best childhood chum—and scattered on estates throughout the stately hills were families that traveled and read widely, argued passionately and had prized their ties to the Theodore Roosevelt administration. Bissell found it "a stimulating place to grow up." His parents took it for granted that he would go to Groton and Yale.

Bissell's drive for control emerged early. Joe Alsop found Bissell "a terrific dominator, possessive of his friends until he married. He ran their lives." His friends did not resent him for it. When they were together at Groton, stars of the long-remembered class of '28, Alsop was grateful when Bissell reconstructed his chaotic finances from bank deposit slips and drew up a budget. Another pal, Francis Sargent Cheever, never forgot how easily he passed his college boards in geometry because Bissell instructed him not to go through old exams but to bone up on axioms which were the basis for most of the problems. When a sizable contingent of the class was quarantined for six weeks in "the pest house" with whooping cough, accompanied by frequent vomiting, nobody considered it odd that it was Bissell who laid down rules for making it to the bathroom just in time.

All his life he was to exercise this benevolent dictatorship of the intellect. It was welcomed because it offered better solutions. He was a mover who could assemble pieces of a problem and move them forward against formidable obstacles of distances, time and physical impediments. When he was small and railroads were the principal instruments for massive movements, he memorized railroad timetables as other boys loaded up on pulp novels. At CIA staff meetings he delighted colleagues by recalling precisely how many hours and miles separated one point of the world from another. He could, also from memory, draw the main lines and principal branches of every railroad system in the United States and knew the gauges of all trains in Latin America and Africa and most of those in Asia.

His fascination with railroads dated back to sitting on his father's lap absorbing picture books of trains. Toy trains became his favorite preoccupation. He liked his maternal grandfather, the railroad president, and among Dick's earliest memories was a glorious ride aboard that formidable relative's private railroad car, the *Anthracite*.

Later, his interest expanded to maps and railroad geography, and, since he almost never did anything casually, he pursued this hobby with the single-mindedness of obsession. All his life, often during his hours of rapid walks, he mentally rerouted railroads or built new systems where none existed. These fantasies were invariably precise.

On the Union Pacific main line, for example, west of Cheyenne, he discovered a stretch of about a hundred miles that had been built "just plain in the wrong place, and any damn fool could have been able to see it when they built it." If the railroaders had followed the North Platte, they could have circumvented Sherman Hill, lowered the elevation of their highest grade by five hundred or possibly a thousand feet, and made the trip much shorter and easier. This ancient gaffe did not merely annoy Bissell. It offended him.

Never a team man, he was equally offended by organized sports and by secret fraternities. They had no sensible purpose. At Yale, he not only refused to be pledged himself; the day Gene Rostow was to be pledged, a rare honor for a Jew, Bissell took his friend for a long ride in the country to save him from temptation. Instead, Bissell became leader and spokesman of a group of intellectual rebels, "a brilliant coterie of iconoclasts, loud in speech, brutal in analysis, enthusiastically uninhibited in their attack on the old tribal gods."

From the gloomy Harkness Memorial Quadrangle, they issued *The Harkness Hoot*. On university issues they took elitist stands. "It is time to ring down the curtain on mass production," said an editorial by Bissell. "The proper cure for indifference is expulsion." On social issues, they railed against the Depression and the other injustices of their fathers' world. But Bissell and his band used a weapon that reflected their own forte.

"These rebels placed a special trust in the intellect," said one Yale historian. "They believed that by taking thought they could evolve a new and better world. Injustices should be righted, but by collective planning, not via the barricades."

Bissell's planning—against the economics of his father and much later against enemies of the United States from his power station within the CIA—never strayed from the system. As the Yale historian analyzed the wave-makers of the *Hoot:* "For all their criticism of private enterprise they betrayed an urgent wish of their own for security. They enjoyed the showers and other comforts of Harkness with scarcely a twinge. . . . They wanted to have the cake yet scold the cook." Nor did Bissell merely write for the *Hoot*. Together with his roommate Richard S. Childs, he owned it. Wealth could buy influence, even at Yale.

When Dick was a junior, he met a *Hoot* writer, a sophomore named Herman W. ("Fritz") Liebert, later the rotund and loquacious director of the Beinecke Rare Book and Manuscript Library at Yale. Their friendship would survive their twenty-year joint ownership of a fifty-four-foot yawl, the *Sea Witch*. Liebert became its cook—and the principal eyewitness expert on Bissell's career.

Fritz took issue with Bissell watchers who likened Dick's mind to a computer making series of small choices. Liebert regarded his friend as an innovator on the grand scale, in search of new patterns, new rules that he could frame personally. Bissell had "intellectual peripheral vision" and experienced "extreme frustration" when he encountered imperfection.

Sometimes Liebert helped him to laugh off the realities of human frailty. Together, they formed the Procrustes Corporation,* and whenever they encountered flawed products—oyster-cracker packages that couldn't be pulled open or a ship's engine that would not follow

---

*Procrustes was a legendary robber in ancient Greece who, impatient with individual differences and needs, stretched (or cut off) his victims' legs to adapt them to the length of a bed.

orders—they joked that the offending items had been manufactured by this fictitious company.

Even trivial frustrations could trigger a Vesuvian outburst in Bissell, "a release with the quality almost of an orgasm." If his wife made him fifteen minutes late for a dinner party or he suspected someone of having mislaid his wallet on his boat, this jarred the equilibrium of his world. It constituted disorder, and "Dick went wild." His body shook. He waved his fists. Whatever articles were in his way went flying through the air. Within moments the tantrums passed. Bissell was forever amazed that they filled witnesses with "terror."

These explosions were infrequent and fairly private. Among the Yale intellects, Bissell ruled with quiet urbanity. In discussions he would follow a pattern of his own. He led off by laying out many alternatives to solving a problem. Then he would encourage others to talk themselves out, rarely interfering unless someone went off in a direction he considered unusually foolish. Next he would push the solution of his own choice by saying, "Really this problem is . . ." Rarely would there be serious opposition, because Bissell's polish made him—in the words of McGeorge Bundy, another of his Yale students and a Bay of Pigs veteran—"a great expositor."

When Secretary of State Dean Rusk, reconstructing the White House sessions about the Cuba affair years afterward, called Bissell "a persuasive briefer," he did so with a meaningful wink. It was another characteristic of Bissell's winning manner: many of his peers felt he was a manipulator but liked him too well or were too awed by his persuasiveness to say so outright.

As a skipper of small boats—he always did act as the skipper—he operated the same way. If Liebert and the rest of the crew were discussing the destination of a cruise, proceedings remained "democratic up to a point." Dick suggested where to go, got out the charts and sat back. After hearing the others talk he said, "Of course you can see this is what we must do . . ." The crew always did see matters Dick's way, much as Dick's family back in Farmington followed his father's lead when Bissell Senior suggested playing bridge. There was one difference: Dick liked to buttress his views even after a "team decision." He then brought out one or two additional arguments that he had withheld before.

His pattern-making skills made him a fine navigator, yet in spite of his planning, or perhaps because of it, he often took needless risks. The "wives were terrified of Dick's chance-taking." Sailing down the Connecticut River near Old Saybrook, he concluded that the railroad drawbridge wasn't opened for his boat because his mast was low enough to squeeze through. In fact the bridge was closed because a train was coming. Bissell's mast came down, and he ran aground. It was not the first or last time. Stuck in harbor because of fog off the dangerous Nova Scotia coast, he got tired of waiting for the weather to clear and said, "Goddammit, we'll go out anyway"—and ran aground. The challenge of adverse conditions excited him. Caught in trouble, he always found room to extricate himself.

But not when he was climbing. Bissell's love of conquering heights, Fritz Liebert thought, was also in character. He usually did it alone, taking considerable risks. As an undergraduate, he clambered about the Neo-Gothic steeples of the Harkness quadrangle in the dead of night. Later, when he was an instructor, he fell off cliffs outside Farmington, sustained a concussion, and broke his collarbone.

Always there was the urge to search, to push beyond the frontiers of the known; to systemize the unorganized, to make order out of disorder, to explore ground where there were few footsteps, preferably none. At Yale, Dick became interested in economics but soon grew impatient with its lack of "discipline." He veered to mathematical economics before Maynard Keynes made it fashionable, before it was even a recognized field of study (though quickly becoming anathema to his father and other establishmentarians). Dick was not superior at mathematics; he used it "in search of a greater degree of rigor in economic theory," to make amends for the Great Depression.

He did not have to search for disciples; they rallied on their own, and they were formidable personalities too. When Bissell joined the economics faculty as a graduate student, McGeorge Bundy, later Kennedy's Special Assistant for National Security, took two courses with him. He found Bissell quick, clear, authoritative, rejoicing when he was questioned knowledgeably, never happier than when he was satisfied that nobody had beaten him in an argument, pacing, always pacing. Mac's older brother Bill, who would work on plans for the Bay of Pigs as Kennedy's Deputy Assistant Secretary of Defense for International Security Affairs, also studied with Bissell. The year Mac took the course, Walt W. Rostow, Mac's deputy on the National Security Council during the Bay of Pigs, graded papers for Bissell.

Rostow had met Bissell when he was in high school in New Haven, and Rostow's older brother, Eugene, later an Assistant Secretary of State, had worked for Bissell on the *Hoot*. Together the two student editors developed a plan for reviving the national economy. The scheme was widely discussed; its authors even defended it on a Boston radio station.

Walt Rostow gravitated naturally toward an unlisted "black market" seminar which Bissell gave on economic theory, afterward relishing the wide-ranging discussions in Bissell's living room in the Neo-Gothic building that housed Davenport College. It was a long room; Bissell paced up and down the middle, expounding, his listeners' heads bobbing back and forth as at a tennis match. Talk was mostly of getting the Depression economy moving again. Later in the evening everybody went out for hamburgers. Rostow remembered, "Part of my growing up was learning to articulate differences with this most articulate man that has ever been—temperately and precisely."

Bissell's personal qualities had worked well for him and for the CIA during the agency's 1954 coup to unseat the government of Guatemala. Now they would go to work on Cuba. It was Jake Engler's job to put the boss's ideas into action.

Plot at the CIA

Jake Engler thought Castro had to go. Engler had been CIA chief of station in Caracas, Venezuela, from 1957 to 1960, and had met many of the Cuban exiles who were plotting against right-wing dictator Fulgencio Batista. They had strong pro-Communist leanings. Some were now in Castro's Cabinet. When Castro visited Caracas in 1959, he received a hero's welcome. As he rode through town in an open truck, Engler was wedged in the cheering crowds. Impressed by the Cuban's charisma, he wrote Colonel J. C. King, chief of the CIA's Western Hemisphere division, in early December 1959, predicting there was going to be "a real problem in Cuba." If headquarters wanted him, he'd be happy to help. He was asked to come to a meeting in King's office the following January 18. None of the dozen men in the room had heard of a place called the Bay of Pigs, but at that meeting the operation that came to bear its name was born. The idea was to capitalize on the Cuban underground and organize a "typical Latin political upheaval." No more than thirty Cubans were to be trained in Panama to serve as cadre for the guerrillas. Engler was appointed project director. He got the impression that if nothing came of the project, it would be no disaster. This was going to be a relaxed venture.

Engler nevertheless set to work with characteristic enthusiasm. He was a husky man, handsome, well-muscled, with huge shoulders, very light blue eyes, bushy eyebrows, and inexhaustible energy. He looked commanding, like a military chief, and he had been one in World War II, working with guerrillas for the OSS in the Far East and later in

Georgia as chief of the CIA's own guerrilla training center. Before going to Venezuela, he had been Cuban desk officer and chief of station in Guatemala. Few were aware that Jake had aspired to be a singer and had a special love for oratorios. It was more generally known that he had been an accountant briefly after the war and had little affection for the "Yalies" who seemed to call the shots at the agency.

Affecting a fake accent, he liked to say, "Ve Dutch are not so dumb." Jake brought many qualities to the Cuba project, including his temper and a flair for the dramatic. Most especially, he called himself the "cement" that was supposed to hold the project's many elements together on behalf of the man who counted, Dick Bissell.

The start-up meeting in King's office on January 18 was no momentous occasion. About a dozen men assembled. Some, like Gerry Droller, who had been the Swiss desk officer and smoked a large, pungent cigar, lacked any Latin-American experience. Most, like Engler, were veterans of the CIA's 1954 coup in Guatemala.

The "Guatemala model" was on everyone's mind, especially Bissell's. In one week the CIA had overthrown the Guatemalan government. A force of 150 exiles, firing hardly a shot, and a handful of World War II P-47 fighters, flown by American pilots hired by the agency, were the overt weapons. CIA deception was the real one. The agency had used the same base it would activate for the Bay of Pigs: a two-story barracks of the largely abandoned U.S. Navy air base at Opa-Locka, in suburban Miami. Both of the agency's senior field operators, the elegant Tracy Barnes and the unconventional E. Howard Hunt, would occupy pivotal posts in the Cuba operation. Together they had recruited a propaganda chief for the Guatemala venture: the man who was to do the same job in Cuba, David Atlee Phillips.

Phillips had once been an actor. He looked as suave—and articulated as carefully—as when he was touring with road companies of *Junior Miss* and *You Can't Take It with You*. Charming and clever, he went to Chile to run a newspaper when Herman Shumlin and David Merrick would not produce a play he had written and they had optioned. The play was about his first intelligence experience—on the escape committee of his Air Force prisoner-of-war camp in World War II. In Chile, working under "deep" (i.e., legitimate) cover, he became a part-time CIA agent. Guatemala was his first full-time assignment.

For it, Phillips had created the Voice of Liberation, a rebel radio station in Honduras purportedly broadcasting from a jungle hideout in Guatemala. It managed to make itself believed through the ingenuity of its lying. When a well-known Guatemala fighter pilot defected with his plane, Phillips' operators got him drunk. Then they asked the aviator to tape a broadcast calling on his former colleagues to defect. The pilot declined. Phillips' men encouraged him to act out the kind of speech he would make if he had no relatives in Guatemala. The pilot obliged with a fervent recital—which the CIA operators taped and broadcast. After that, the Guatemalans would not trust any of their pilots to fly. Their Air Force was grounded.

Shortly before the CIA's handpicked President-to-be Castillo Armas rumbled across the border from Honduras in an old station wagon, President Eisenhower had had a breakfast meeting in the second-floor dining room of the White House with Allen Dulles; his brother, John Foster Dulles, the Secretary of State; members of the Joint Chiefs of Staff; and other leaders.

"Are you sure this is going to succeed?" asked Eisenhower.

The men around the table assured him it would.

"I'm prepared to take any steps that are necessary to see that it succeeds," the President said. "If it succeeds, it's the people of Guatemala throwing off the yoke of Communism. If it fails, the flag of the United States has failed."

When it was all over, Eisenhower was so pleased that he wanted a White House briefing. Allen Dulles and his operators, including Dave Phillips, made their presentations in the East Wing auditorium of the White House to the President, his Vice President, Richard M. Nixon, and much of his Cabinet and staff. To the dismay of Dulles and Tracy Barnes, even Mamie Eisenhower was there.

"How many men did Castillo Armas lose?" asked Eisenhower. He was told that only a courier had been killed.

"Incredible," said the old general. Leaving, he shook hands with Dulles. "Thanks, Allen, and thanks to all of you. You've averted a Soviet beachhead in our hemisphere." Eisenhower never forgot how the CIA bought him such dramatic gains for such a small investment. Neither did Bissell; nor did Engler and Dave Phillips.

Dave did not know why he was supposed to report to Quarters Eye, a one-time WAVE barrack off Ohio Drive near the Potomac in downtown Washington. It was one of the shabbiest of the World War II "tempo" buildings occupied by the CIA around the reflecting pool facing the Lincoln Memorial.

Inside, Jake Engler said he was in charge of a new project. "I'll give you three guesses," he told Phillips.

Dave replied, "Cuba. Cuba. And Cuba."

Engler said the project would eventually have forty officers. Phillips asked what the leaders had in mind. "The Guatemala scenario," said one of Jake's assistants. Phillips was to run the propaganda shop.

Dave was pleased to be working with the Guatemala crew again. Howard Hunt stuck his head in the door and said, "Welcome aboard, Chico"; it was a name Hunt used for people he liked. Dave felt like old home week.

He had spent four years in Cuba running a public-relations business for U.S. companies. Cubans would be a far more sophisticated propaganda audience than the Guatemalans. They were more worldly. They listened to Miami radio stations. They had their own TV with many American programs. And Castro was one of the great propagandists of all time. But Phillips felt optimistic. Leftist dictators rarely stayed in the saddle for long in Latin America. Repelled by executions and repression, the middle class seemed to be turning away from Castro. The middle class was crucial.

When Phillips called on Bissell at his office in K building, he was swept by a wave of depression. Vermin-ridden, K building was called "cockroach alley." The lighting was poor. The linoleum floors buckled. Paint was peeling off the wallboards. The cafeteria was as gloomy as a prison camp. Only the most senior executives worked in cheerier settings. The walls in Bissell's office were sparkling white. There were curtains and carpeting. And there was Bissell, the powerhouse, fidgeting, sniffling, getting up, pacing, sitting down, firing questions. Phillips felt better.

He told Bissell he would need a plane for leaflet drops before the invasion and on D-Day. Right now he needed a medium-wave radio station. Guatemalans were accustomed to short wave; its transmitter could fit onto a truck. Cubans would need a fifty-kilowatt medium-wave transmitter that filled several boxcars. Phillips wanted to camouflage the station as a commercial outlet and proposed broadcasting from the Florida Keys.

The State Department would never agree, said Bissell. The station had to be outside the U.S. In Guatemala, Phillips had done his work in six weeks. How long would it take to soften up the Cubans' will to resist? "Closer to six months," Dave estimated. Could he start in a month? "Absolutely impossible," said Phillips. Flashing a frosty smile, Bissell said he felt sure Dave could do it.

The only unattached 50-kilowatt transmitter Phillips and Bissell's assistant Jim Flannery could find belonged to the U.S. Army. It was aboard a train in Germany, shortly to be turned over to the Voice of

America. Phillips commandeered it with a few phone calls. He and Flannery called on an admiral in the Pentagon who remained unruffled when they explained that, while the station's studios were to be in Miami, they had less than thirty days to get the transmitter operating on the best politically acceptable site: Great Swan Island, a mile and a half long and half a mile wide, in the western Caribbean, off Honduras.

Consisting of guano—seafowl droppings—Swan Island (population twenty-eight) offered superb privacy. It had a total of three coconut trees and was all but overrun by lizards. The admiral had to send Seabees to put up a dock for unloading the transmitter. When Phillips' CIA crew arrived, they found that since 1863 both the U.S. and Honduras had claimed sovereignty over Swan. One Sunday thirteen Honduran students arrived, planted their flag and sang their national anthem. Phillips, tipped off by a Honduran broadcast, had a destroyer sent to Swan and instructed the CIA men on the island to stall the landing party unless it threatened to damage the transmitter. The CIA agents invited the invaders for beer. The Hondurans departed amicably, and "Radio Swan" started broadcasting thirty days after Bissell issued his edict.

Bissell was pleased when he got the report from Phillips, but when Dave told him of the studio setup in Miami and the experienced broadcasters he had rounded up from the exile community, the DDP started pacing. "Too professional," he said, "too American. Go back and put some rough edges on it. Make it more Cuban."

Phillips agreed, with admiration. He had been listening to Radio Swan from the basement of his new rented home near the Alban Towers Hotel off Massachusetts Avenue and was constantly trying to improve the quality of the announcers and the programming. Now he saw the error of his ways. He instructed his propagandists to stop worrying about their diction and to remove the rugs from the studio so that chairs could be heard scraping.

Unknown to Phillips, Engler or any of their colleagues in the project, Bissell was already working on "another string to our bow." He did not have a great deal of confidence that it would work, but even the possibility was attractive. It could make the military operation "either unnecessary or much easier." The extra "string" was the assassination of Castro.

The morality of the idea did not trouble him one bit. After all, "assassinations are as old as history." He recalled that Allen Dulles had played a role in the generals' plot to kill Hitler on July 20, 1944, which almost succeeded. It seemed to Bissell far more humane to take the life of one dangerous, charismatic leader than to start a military effort in which hundreds or thousands might die, not to speak of the risk of civil war in Cuba.

So Bissell was not surprised or shocked when he read a memo from J. C. King to Allen Dulles recommending that "thorough consideration be given to the elimination of Fidel Castro." Needlessly, King added, "Many informed people believe that the disappearance of Fidel would greatly accelerate the fall of the present government." It was this kind of belaboring of the obvious that caused many informed people to take the colorless ex-colonel less than seriously. Already Bissell had decided that King would have no operational hand in the Cuba project. King administered his papers meticulously. Having spent twenty years representing the Johnson & Johnson pharmaceutical interests in São Paulo and Buenos Aires, he retained a concern about the fate of U.S. corporate holdings in Latin America. Unfortunately, he lacked flair.

Bissell penciled his concurrence onto the King memo, as did the director. It was routine. Bissell felt King was probably thinking of "eliminating" Castro only by "incapacitating" him; an assassination might be arranged "if we can't do anything else." For the present, only "thorough consideration" of Castro's removal was authorized, nothing else.

President Dwight D. Eisenhower knew none of this and for good reason: he never gave Cuba high priority. When Allen Dulles asked for an appointment to discuss moves against Castro, the President was sympathetic, but his interest was routine. Dulles had brought along a photo of a Cuban sugar refinery. He explained how it could be put out of commission by guerrilla saboteurs, but the two men agreed that most such damage could be too speedily repaired. Something more was needed. The President said that if Dulles and his people really wanted to mount a greater effort, they should come back with a "program."*

It was the invitation that Bissell had been maneuvering for. By early March, the CIA had drafted a top-secret policy paper, "A Program of Covert Action Against the Castro Regime," and had it approved by the committee of all committees in Washington: the Special Group.† It

---

*When someone at a subsequent National Security Council meeting spoke about a "plan" against Castro, Eisenhower sternly objected. There was no "plan," he said. There was only a "program." To him, nothing called a "program" was fully hatched. When he insisted in a September 10, 1965, interview that "there was no tactical or operational plan even discussed" with him while he was in the White House, he was technically correct.

†This group, also known as the 5412 Committee—because covert operations were operated under authority of National Security Council Directive NSC 5412/2—consisted of only a Deputy Under-Secretary of State, the Deputy Secretary of Defense, the Director of the Central Intelligence Agency, and the Special Assistant to the President for National Security Affairs. It was the most secret operating unit of government.

called for four steps: (1) creation of a "responsible and unified" Cuban government in exile; (2) "a powerful propaganda offensive"; (3) "a covert intelligence and action organization" in Cuba, to be "responsive" to the exile opposition; and (4) "a paramilitary force outside of Cuba for future guerrilla action."

The document also called for "a small air supply capability under deep cover as a commercial operation in another country," to be operational in two months. The creation of the entire "capability will require a minimum of six months and probably closer to eight." The news that the CIA hoped to be ready for the overthrow of Castro perhaps as early as September was perhaps most appreciated by one of the men who was present when Ike authorized the CIA program: Richard Nixon, who was running for President in November.

On March 10, a long meeting of the full National Security Council discussed ways to "bring another government to power in Cuba." The official minutes showed that the big, bluff Admiral Arleigh Burke, Chief of Naval Operations, took a particularly militant role:

> Admiral Burke thought we needed a Cuban leader around whom anti-Castro elements could rally. Mr. Dulles said some anti-Castro leaders existed, but they are not in Cuba at present. The President said we might have another Black Hole of Calcutta in Cuba and wondered what we could do . . . Admiral Burke suggested that any plan for the removal of Cuban leaders should be a package deal since many of the leaders around Castro were even worse than Castro.

On March 14, the Special Group considered the fate of the Cuban leaders again. The minutes reported:

> There was a general discussion as to what would be the effect on the Cuban scene if Fidel and Raúl Castro and Che Guevara should disappear simultaneously. Admiral Burke said that the only organized group within Cuba today were the Communists and there was therefore the danger that they might move in control. Mr. Dulles felt this might not be disadvantageous because it would facilitate multilateral action by the OAS Organization of American states. Col. King said there were few leaders capable of taking over so far identified.

Assassination was not discussed, but Dulles and Bissell now knew they were not alone in wishing Castro off the scene. Then, on March 17, President Eisenhower approved the agency's four-point military plan. The Cuba project was officially in business.

Revolutionary in Washington

Fidel Castro had been in power less than a week when three newspaper editors started their pre-luncheon martinis in the upper room of New York's expensive "21" restaurant and considered their problem. One of them, George Healy of the *New Orleans Times-Picayune,* was the 1959 president of the American Society of Newspaper Editors. The others, Don Maxwell of *The Chicago Tribune* and Alicia Patterson of *Newsday,* were members of his program committee for the society's annual convention in April, less than four months away.

They needed a headline speaker and began trying out names on each other. They had just disposed of Harold Macmillan when Healy and Maxwell, almost in unison, said, "What about Castro?" It would have been a brilliant scoop at any time. At this stage of Castro's career public curiosity about him was particularly intense.

The editors at "21" had not risen to the top of their profession for nothing. They scented a good story in Castro and good publicity for the ASNE convention. Don Maxwell phoned his Cuba correspondent, Jules Dubois, on the spot. Dubois said he'd go to work on the idea. Toward 3 P.M., Maxwell and Healy arrived in the East Eighty-first Street apartment of another member of the program committee, Turner Catledge, executive editor of *The New York Times,* who was confined to home because of a gout attack. He thought the Castro idea was "wild" but liked it. He had barely poured his old cronies a drink when Dubois called from Havana to report that Castro had accepted.

The eleven-day "unofficial" visit was a personal triumph for Fidel from the moment his turbo-prop Britannia touched down two hours late at Washington's National Airport. His beard, battle fatigues, warm grin, and youthful vigor (he was thirty-two) fascinated and charmed almost everybody. Here was a revolutionary who looked and acted like one. The crowds shouted, "Viva Castro!" and "Hi, Fidel!," and he created huge traffic jams. He kissed babies, signed autographs and ignored his guards. When a small boy pulled his beard, he chuckled. He never seemed to stop talking. Turner Catledge thought he "made Hubert Humphrey look like Silent Cal Coolidge."

He was a guest who told everybody what they wanted to hear. At the ASNE convention luncheon, where the demand for tickets had been the greatest since General MacArthur returned for his final farewell, the applause was scattered when he began his two-hour session. He took up to fifteen minutes to answer a single question. At the end he received an enormous hand. He told the editors he was for a free press, "the first enemy of dictatorship."

Later he told the Senate Foreign Relations Committee he would not expropriate U.S. property. He told the audience of NBC-TV's *Meet the Press* that he opposed Communism and would side with the Western democracies. In Washington's Meridian Hill Park he told a student he stood for "Cubanism," not socialism. He laid wreaths at the Lincoln and Jefferson monuments and commented that Jefferson "understood what revolutions should do." Republican Congressman James G. Fulton of Pennsylvania thought the U.S. had a *nuevo amigo* and said, "I think we should help him all we can."

The applause was not unanimous. Senator George A. Smathers, Democrat of Florida, grumbled that Castro had Communists "peppered throughout his government." *Time* magazine noted that firing squads in Cuba had shot twenty-eight more Castro opponents the preceding week, bringing the total executions to 521.

The most influential comment on the visit, however, came in a secret memorandum from Richard M. Nixon. It was the seed that grew, two years later almost to the day, into the Bay of Pigs.

Vice President Nixon was a politician with a problem. Its name was Eisenhower. The genial general was the folk hero of a generation; Nixon was the Communist-hunter—many said witch-hunter—with the perpetual five-o'clock shadow. In foreign policy, Nixon had not only been overshadowed by the war hero President. The ailing John Foster Dulles, going into retirement the week Castro arrived in the capital, had been Ike's hard international hand for eight years. Nixon was given such greeter's chores as representing "the American people" at an American National Exhibition in the Soviet Union the following July.*

The announcement of Nixon's mission to Moscow, also released during the week of Castro's tour, came from "the temporary White House" near the golf links in Augusta, Georgia, where Eisenhower was enjoying one of his frequent vacations. The vacation was timed to insure that Ike would not have to meet this odd leftist upstart from Cuba. That chore too was left to the ambitious Vice President.

It was scheduled for Sunday afternoon to insure minimum attention from the press. The rules were unusual. No staffs were to be present. No photographs were to be taken. The scene was the Vice President's large office on the west side of the Capitol with its magnificent view of the Mall. It was used almost exclusively for ceremonial occasions. On Sundays it was all but deserted.

"It seemed to me," Nixon wrote later, "that until he demonstrated some intention of modifying his anti-American stand he should not be

*Nixon made the most of it. The exhibit became the scene of his famous "kitchen debate" with Nikita Khrushchev.

accorded the same treatment I would give to other visiting foreign officials."

Sunday, April 19, was a warm but rainy spring day. Nixon was in no mood to go to the office. Yet he was intrigued by the opportunity to size up Castro on behalf of the President. Fresh from his success on *Meet the Press*, Fidel appeared on Capitol Hill in his fatigues, smiling. Nixon found him "striking." He noted the visitor's compelling, intense voice and "sparkling black eyes." Castro "radiated vitality." He was "intelligent, shrewd, at times eloquent." Nixon thought Fidel gave the appearance of sincerity but felt this was belied by his "almost parrotlike" answers to questions which the Vice President had discussed with "many Communist leaders."

When Nixon asked Castro why he didn't hold free elections—so the Vice President reported later to President Eisenhower—Castro said, "The people of Cuba don't want free elections; they produce bad government." When he was asked why he didn't give fair trials to his opponents, Castro said (Nixon reported), "The people of Cuba don't want them to have fair trials. They want them shot as quickly as possible." Asked whether he wasn't afraid that the Communists in his government would eventually seize it, Castro said, "I am not afraid of the Communists; I can handle them."

(To Castro, Nixon seemed unimpressive. He felt in the presence of a very well-dressed, remarkably young man, almost "a teenager," not in appearance but in behavior. The Vice President was "a bit superficial," certainly not "a heavy man." He seemed to say little. Castro was trying to impress him with his country's poverty, illiteracy, unemployment, the need for agrarian reform. He spoke about these problems at length. Nixon was "not hostile." He just would not discuss the subjects of interest to Castro. "He simply listened.")

The discussion lasted three and a half hours. Nixon told Eisenhower he could make "no headway" with his attempts to convince Castro that Communism was more than a political and economic idea and that its agents were enormously skilled at infiltrating and seizing governments. He told Ike he saw in Castro "that indefinable quality which, for good or evil, makes a leader of men." In his four-page secret memo to the President, Secretary of State Christian A. Herter and Allen Dulles, Nixon concluded: "Castro is either incredibly naïve about Communism or is under Communist discipline."

The wording was needlessly hedged. Nixon considered Castro anything but naïve. From the moment the Vice President left his office at sunset that Sunday he was, as he wrote later, "the strongest and most persistent advocate for setting up and supporting" a covert military effort to unseat the man who had kept him working that afternoon.

Nixon's Push

The usual midsummer humidity and heat brought the usual vacation lethargy to the capital, but in Nixon's office in the cavernous, high-ceilinged old State, War and Navy Building next to the White House the activity—and the political heat—were rising sharply. "The boss," as his staff called Nixon, was running hard for President, and Castro was increasingly becoming an election issue.

General Robert E. Cushman, Jr., was not yet accustomed to political heat. A huge, bluff career Marine (he graduated from the U.S. Naval Academy in 1935) with piercing brown eyes and a booming bass of a command voice, he had become Nixon's executive assistant for national-security affairs on the recommendation of Admiral Burke, the Chief of Naval Operations.* "You can hire and fire, just don't make anybody mad," Nixon had told Cushman.

It was the general's "first brush with politics." He was comfortable preparing Nixon's daily intelligence briefing from papers delivered at sunup by a CIA man. He was not quite so at ease with the pressure that the boss was exerting about the Cuba operation. Cushman knew that Nixon had repeatedly urged speed on Eisenhower. The Vice President regarded the operation as a major political asset. He was eager for the Republican administration to get credit for toppling Castro before the election.

"How are the boys doing at the Institute?" he asked Cushman, always careful not to discuss sensitive matters openly, even in the office. "Are they falling dead over there? What in the world are they doing that takes months?" Often Nixon issued reminders by memo. ("You didn't go banging into his office.")

Cushman grew less and less fond of the project. Even when he got away from Nixon's prodding, it was no fun. One weekend he found himself on a small CIA plane with Director Dulles. They were going to Palm Beach to meet William S. Pawley, the archconservative former diplomat and friend of Nixon. There was a scheme afoot to print up some Cuban bonds, presumably to jar the Castro economy. Pawley was

---

*In 1969, President Nixon appointed Cushman deputy director of the CIA. It was he to whom Howard Hunt turned for the famous wig and electronic devices that Hunt and his fellow burglars used in their Watergate operations. In 1971, Nixon made Cushman Commandant of the Marine Corps.

supposed to help. Cushman was supposed to be his liaison. Nothing ever came of the project. On the way to Florida the plane was hit by lightning. Crockery scattered all over the walls and the ceiling. Cushman was delighted to be back at his desk, where he merely had Nixon to contend with.

Dutifully, Cushman kept phoning Jake Engler at "the Institute." Engler, who knew where the heat was coming from and why, refrained from telling Cushman that Howard Hunt was having trouble with the faction-ridden Cuban leaders in Miami. Soon, Nixon was nudging Cushman again: "How the hell are they coming?" Cushman did not tell the boss what he was thinking. He felt that Nixon thought of the operation as "mostly rifle training" and did not wish to be bothered with details. Nixon did not understand the military complexities and perils. Ike did.

Bissell was uneasy about Eisenhower's casual attitude. The old general "did not seem troubled by moral doubts about the propriety of clandestine operations." Ike had shown in the case of Guatemala and other successful covert CIA operations that he felt no "squeamishness" about them and "wouldn't be worrying about the moral rightness or wrongness" of such intervention. But he displayed no "vigorous activism" in the Cuba project, which could have used it.

Bissell was relieved when the President finally approved a $13-million budget at an August 18 Cabinet meeting. At least some of the operation's long-incurred bills could be paid. "Use of Department of Defense personnel and equipment" was also approved, at least in principle. "No United States military personnel were to be used in a combat status."* Bissell could live with that. The problem was: would Ike make a "go" decision if the operation had to be made in his term of office? What if, as seemed increasingly likely, the Cuban exile force would not be ready until later? Nixon could be counted on. Kennedy was an unknown factor. He might be influenced by the old soldier's enthusiasm or lack of it, and so far Ike was unenthusiastic.

Gordon Gray thought so, too. He was Eisenhower's assistant for national-security affairs, a dignified former North Carolina newspaper

---

*This language comes from the so-called Taylor Report, which was not declassified until May 1977, and then only in part and in slightly expurgated form. The report was the work of a board of inquiry formed immediately after the Bay of Pigs by President Kennedy and chaired by General Maxwell D. Taylor, later Chairman of the Joint Chiefs of Staff. It was classified "secret" as well as "eyes only" and "ultra-sensitive." In 1961, only one copy was made. The report was regarded so touchy that General Taylor had it hand-carried to each member of the Joint Chiefs in turn. The messenger was a general, David W. Gray. He was instructed to sit in each of the chiefs' offices while each four-star general read it and to make certain that nobody took notes. The board called itself the "Green Study Group."

publisher with a thick Southern drawl, the quintessential member of the board. He noted how often Ike asked Dulles, "Where's our government in exile?" Dulles hinted that the CIA found Cuban politicians hard to harness.

As the months dragged by, Ike displayed impatience. "Boys," he told Dulles and Bissell, "if you don't intend to go through with this, let's stop talking about it." Gray raised his enormous bushy eyebrows. He felt that the operation might eventually come off. He also felt that, for the present, the CIA kept bringing it up because it wanted Eisenhower's "involvement recorded." The value of the general's imprimatur was great.

Bissell faced other crucial problems. He knew that the operation was not getting the pick of the agency's best brains. The CIA was a closed bureaucracy of its own. Whenever a temporary operation sprang up, every chief in the conventional departments clung to his best Indians, especially if the head chief would not take the chiefs into his confidence about the special project. Dick Drain, who wound up in the operation because he didn't want to go back to Greece, was disgusted. Seven or eight times Dulles had ordered all top agency executives to give this project highest priority. Still, when Drain went recruiting, "a helluva lot of people were looking out the window." "You'll get a certain number of people that their supervisors let you have with crocodile tears because they are quite happy to get rid of them," Bissell said later.

Gearing Up

Of all the unlikely operators to be placed in charge of CIA diplomacy with the exiled Cuban leaders in Florida, Gerry Droller ("Frank Bender") was the most improbable. He was recruited by Tracy Barnes. Jake Engler was appalled. The German-born Droller had worked for OSS during the war behind the lines in France. In the CIA he was a Swiss-desk officer. He knew nothing of Latin America. He spoke no Spanish. His English was so heavily accented that sometimes his Spanish interpreters had trouble with it. So did others. He often said "Yo." Sometimes it meant "yes" and sometimes "no."

Slight and balding, Gerry chain-smoked cigars. The ashes landed on his jacket. He was deferential to colleagues and supervisors and called them "Popsy." Underlings found him less congenial. With the Cubans he posed as a steel tycoon with arrogance to match. He liked to tell them that he carried the revolution in his checkbook. The liberal Cubans hated him more than did the conservatives, but none of them liked the famous "Mr. B." Engler had to bawl him out constantly. Jake learned that the agent hailed from a long line of Eastern European circus clowns and observed that Gerry could have made a fortune in show business but should never have gone into the agency.

When Barnes brought in Howard Hunt to help Droller, old agency men shook their heads. It was like sending Rosencrantz and Guildenstern to tame the Eskimos. Hunt spoke Spanish and posed with charm as "Eduardo" with the Cubans. His performance, however, was known to be uneven. Except that, as Flannery liked to say, Hunt was consistent in his judgment: "always wrong."

Dave Phillips, the chief of propaganda operations, remembered working with Howard on the Guatemala project. Even then an old-timer warned him, "Be careful of Howard. Listen to his music, but not his lyrics." Phillips found out what that meant when Hunt insisted on playing host to a group of visiting Guatemalan conspirators in Miami's biggest nightclub. Expectably, they all had their picture taken by the club photographer, and Phillips had to buy back the negative for twenty dollars.*

It hardly helped that Droller and Hunt got along no better than the rival Cuban factions they were supposed to bring into line. A graduate of Brown University and a prolific writer of pulpy espionage fiction, Hunt felt he outranked Droller in status. But mostly he hated Gerry's chutzpah. He cringed when Droller addressed him as "boychick." Eventually Hunt got him banned from Florida except by "specific invitation."

Droller came to Miami anyway. Once he met a Cuban contact, without Hunt's knowledge, at a motel near the airport. The connecting door to the adjoining room allowed a vacationing secretary to listen to the intriguing conversation between two accented voices. The secretary had a brother in the FBI. She took notes in shorthand. The FBI sent them to the CIA. Droller was reprimanded and Hunt regaled their Washington colleagues with the tale.

Hunt teamed up amicably with Bernard L. Barker, who took pride in his code name "Macho." Bernie was born in Havana of American parents. He served in the U.S. Air Force and eventually became a CIA

*When Hunt organized the celebrated break-in at the Democratic National Committee in the Watergate complex in 1972, his efficiency had not improved. He provided the investigators with the first sensational link between the White House and the burglars. One of them, Eugénio Rolando Martínez, a fearless CIA skipper of infiltration missions in Bay of Pigs days, had left his flip-top telephone directory in the gang's hotel command post. It listed "Howard Hunt"; next to the phone number it noted "W. House." Another burglar was Hunt's Bay of Pigs assistant Bernard L. Barker, whose small black address book held an entry for "H.H." with a number marked "W.H." It turned out to be Hunt's phone in the Executive Office Building.

informer in Cuba. Bernie was dedicated to Hunt. "I was not there to think," he said later. "I was there to follow orders."

Together, Howard and Bernie wheeled and dealed with the exile politicians. They mediated squabbles and started others. They played political favorites, which was easy because they gave out considerable CIA money. Hunt carried as much as $115,000 in his briefcase.

When he had so many visitors at his home in the Bricknell Point Apartments that neighbors told the landlady he must be a bookie, Hunt tried to negotiate for a lavish house with indoor swimming pool, facing Biscayne Bay. The deal fell through because Hunt could not disabuse the owner of the notion that he was a major racketeer. The agent settled for an ample home on Poinciana Avenue in Coconut Grove. There the nearest neighbor was a widow with a beautiful blond daughter who modeled in TV commercials in New York. Howard had so many nocturnal male visitors that the widow thought he was homosexual, but she was eager to fix him up with the daughter anyway. It was not a bad life.

No tears were shed at CIA headquarters when Hunt and Droller reported to the Cuba project. But eyebrows went up when Richard M. Helms stayed out. As director of operations in the directorate for plans, Dick Helms came as close to being Bissell's deputy as Bissell would permit. Elegant, his hair meticulously slicked down, educated in Switzerland, Helms joined the agency in its infancy in 1947. He knew the performance record of every operator in the clandestine service and was respected as a punctilious administrator. "His incomings were out by five o'clock every day," said Bob Amory, head of the CIA's intelligence-gathering apparatus. Cautious and exceedingly ambitious,* Helms had a nose for incipient failures.

When Helms attended early planning meetings of the Cuba project, Bissell and his men noticed he remained unusually quiet. Dave Phillips, the propaganda chief, thought it "incredible" that Helms wasn't asking penetrating questions. Soon Helms stayed away altogether. Relations between him and Bissell, always civil but cool, became even more remote. They almost never spoke about Cuba. "An unspoken division of labor" developed: Bissell ran the project, Helms tended the rest of the clandestine store. Bissell could tell that Helms liked it that way. It was his distinct impression that "this was not the kind of operation Dick

---

*Director of Central Intelligence from 1966 to 1973, Helms became a controversial figure during Watergate. President Nixon tried to keep him in line by threatening to "blow" historical skeletons buried with the Bay of Pigs. Helms always said he knew of no skeletons. In 1978 he remarked, "I don't know to this day what he was talking about." Neither did anybody else.

Helms wanted to be connected with," that Helms didn't think it "appropriate for the clandestine service."

Bissell was right. Helms wanted to "distance" himself from the project. His attitude was a career gamble. He knew Dulles was "gung-ho for this." If the operation succeeded, Bissell would be the unquestioned hero of the agency's most ambitious success. But Helms thought the project entailed excessive risks. It was being pushed with too much enthusiasm, inadequate weighing of the odds, not enough realistic, skeptical contingency planning. If it went wrong, it could destroy the agency, certainly the top people connected with it.

At first he stayed in touch. Three times Jim Flannery briefed him on progress. Flannery thought Helms would be a great asset. He would have been effective with the Cubans and would have understood their ways. One quiet Saturday afternoon, Flannery even suggested to Bissell with utmost diplomacy ("I took my heart in my hands") that Helms be brought aboard. Bissell declined. Eventually Helms asked for no more briefings. When he happened to learn some operational details, he dismissed them as "harebrained." And when one of the supply drop planes crash-landed in Jamaica and Helms had to call Dick Drain about it he kept saying, "I've had nothing to do with this operation, I hate to intrude . . ."

Finally Drain interrupted, "You've said this three times. I'm sorry you don't have anything to do with it. We could sure use your talent!"

A potential voice of caution within the agency had been stilled—had stilled itself.

Robert K. Davis thought his assignment was going to be no trouble. His title was First Secretary of the American Embassy in Guatemala City; actually, he was the CIA chief of station. He was an experienced hand in Latin America and spoke fluent Spanish. He had operated in the area for the FBI back in World War II. In 1954 he had been part of the CIA's Guatemala team, setting up the logistics for the overthrow of President Jacobo Arbenz Guzmán. One of his closest co-workers had been Jake Engler, the project director for the Bay of Pigs. Jake had preceded him as chief in Guatemala. The men had become good friends. Whenever Davis was in Washington, he stayed at Jake's home and caught up on office scuttlebutt.

Since its last coup, the CIA had found it pleasant to work in Guatemala. President Miguel Ydigoras was strongly anti-Communist, eager to enjoy the good graces of the United States and its $50-million-a-year aid program. Bob Davis liked "the Guats," a term he used fraternally, not with disdain. He was popular with them. He was a loud, cheerful, animated man who loved good food, drink and cigars. Wide-shouldered, hawk-nosed, extroverted, he gestured much as the Latinos did, laughed a lot and had a large repertoire of emphatic grimaces to help sell whatever he was selling.

He was a superb salesman, but he needed no persuasion to get his end of the new Cuba project started. It required only lunch with his old friend Roberto Alejos. Roberto had already heard about the project from his brother Carlos, the Guatemalan ambassador to the United States. He was happy to help. "What do you have to do?" he asked Davis.

The CIA chief said he needed a secure place to train twenty or so Cuban radio operators, that was all. "I got the perfect place," Alejos said. As a child, Roberto used to peddle candy that his mother made at home. He had once been Arbenz' secretary. Now he was close to Ydigoras. His political connections and his coffee plantation had made him very rich.

The plantation, Helvetia, was where Alejos took Davis. It covered five thousand acres in the Sierra Madre mountains at altitudes from four thousand to eight thousand feet. It was crisscrossed by sixty miles of private roads. The nearest village, San Felipe, was fifteen miles from the *finca*'s residence with its swimming pool and servants. Some two thousand Indians worked in the fields, at the hydroelectric power plant and the coffee-packing factory. A still-active volcano, Santiaguita, loomed nearby.

Alejos said he needed only a few extra refrigerators to accommodate the Cubans. They could live in the guest house and get their instruction in one of the ninety-yard-long barns where his workers usually selected and graded coffee beans. The working places were separated by individual partitions. Davis agreed it was the perfect setup for training radio men. The CIA would furnish the refrigerators. His job was done. So he thought.

Assembling the Cuban Exile Fighters

José Basulto was assigned identification number 2522 in the Cuban force. It made him proud and very happy. The CIA wanted Castro's intelligence to think that the force was much larger than it was, so the numbers began with 2500. Even years afterward, the men with low numbers were the elite among patriots; the lower your number, the more honored was your badge of courage.

Basulto was impatient for important action. A devout Catholic, he had left Boston College, where he majored in physics, in January 1960 to return to his native Havana so he could join the Federación Católica, the Catholic underground organization. He found only great confusion in the underground and no action. Basulto wanted to be part of something big. He was twenty, wavy-haired, handsome, with a sense of humor that appreciated the ridiculous. He had style, even something of a swagger. He knew that his brains made him special, and he liked being special.

Now it was May 21, and a power boat with a crew of American civilians was taking him from Fort Myers, Florida, to tiny Useppa Island, a resort off the southwest coast. He was one of twenty men who were going to be trained as radio operators to be infiltrated into Cuba. He did not trust all the other men, because some were known Batista supporters. When the Americans frisked the group, the Batistanos all had guns that they had to surrender. Basulto did not carry a gun. He thought the Americans would keep the Batista people in line. Besides, they were all going to be infiltrators, a dangerous and important mission. If caught, they would be shot as spies. And if infiltrators were special, the radio men were particularly special. They carried code books, and, unlike the ordinary infiltrators, they were not considered expendable. They were the lifeline between the resistance and the Americans. Basulto loved the role.

Nobody mentioned the CIA. The deserted island, where José and the other infiltrators were comfortably settled into a rustic golf club, was supposed to have been leased by a "wealthy" Cuban from Miami, Freddie Goudie. When the amiable little Goudie, who operated a travel agency and sometimes did errands for the CIA, appeared on Useppa to play his millionaire role, Basulto told his friends, "Bullshit, he can't pay for this." Besides, there were too many American professionals around. "Carl," who was in charge, had a military bearing and walked with a limp. He was a retired Marine and knew all about guerrilla warfare. "Max," the psychiatrist, gave Basulto a lie detector test, made him fill out "kilometers" of psychological tests and asked him about his fantasies every day for a week. José felt like a "psychiatric guinea pig." He thought it was hilarious.

The radio training was run by businesslike American instructors. Basulto was initiated into the intricacies of cryptography and worked with two types of radios. They were more complicated and lower-powered than modern units and supposedly more difficult to detect. The Cuban operators were told that when they went into action, each man's call signs would be unique and would be changed every hour. José's training would continue for more than nine months. It wasn't exciting, but it was clearly leading to something important. José enjoyed every minute.

Bob Davis, the CIA station chief in Guatemala City, began to realize that he had not heard the last of the new Cuba project when Washington instructed him to get barracks ready for another fifty men, then for another 150. As yet there were no appropriations for the construction. He was to push ahead anyway. Alejos was agreeable. A survey was made. New roads were laid out. On volcanic soil a thousand feet below Helvetia, a spot was found for the barracks that became known as Camp Trax. Then, toward the end of May, Davis was astounded to get a message instructing him to build an airport.

Again, the Guatemalans agreed. A group of Air Force officers arrived from Washington and estimated that the project could be built at Retalhuleu, below Helvetia, for $350,000. Unfortunately, they were not experienced construction men. Davis enlisted the help of an American firm already active with heavy equipment in Guatemala, Thompson-Cornwall, Inc. When the experts went to work, the initial payment—Alejos signed the contract—was $450,000. The full Thompson estimate was $1 million. The ultimate cost for all air facilities was $1.8 million.

Davis was ordered to report to Washington to see Bissell, whom he knew and was fond of. He was familiar with Bissell's temper and had known how to handle it in the past. This time the DDP was all but out of control. He "began screaming." When David recited the basis of the first cost estimates, Bissell yelled, "That was stupid!" He jabbed a pointed finger at Davis and warned him not to let the project get out of hand.

Davis let the boss's temper burn itself out. "All I know is what Thompson tells me," he said.

The airport was built in ninety days, instead of thirty, as Bissell had demanded, but Davis never forgot to watch the CIA's money. When the full invasion brigade began to assemble, he even had the men's fatigues manufactured in Guatemala City. It was cheaper than having American uniforms flown in.

José Basulto, the radio operator infiltrator, arrived in the Guatemala camp on the Fourth of July, but there was no holiday. It rained "like mad," and his first job was to help dig ditches around the barracks. They lacked foundations, and the rain threatened to collapse them. The downpour kept up for weeks, but drinking water was very short, and no showers were built until October. The four-hole outdoor latrine was the social center. A single tattered issue of *Playboy* was the camp library. Three of the trainees were growing their own marijuana, and another was said to have developed a sexual affinity for a mule.

José's cryptography and radio classes continued daily, and he made friends among the men who kept arriving from Miami. One turned out to be a convicted murderer. Another was severely retarded. José loved them all: "The common cause made us brothers."

Conditions in the camps did move José and the other radio operators to develop their own crypto code so they would be able to communicate with each other wherever they would be. They "just didn't trust the CIA."

Bob Davis was summoned again from Guatemala to receive the news from Jake. The Brigade was to grow to at least four hundred. He groaned. Then he "raised hell." He yelled, "I'm not going to go back and tell Ydigoras we're going to bring an army in there! You do it!"

The Washington chiefs told Davis they were sure he could handle the "Guats," and he did. It turned out to be easier than Davis had anticipated. Ydigoras was conditioned to the CIA's escalating demands. He had been gentlemanly beginning with the accommodation of a mere twenty communications men. He knew he could count on the backing of Nicaragua's President Somoza and several other Latin-American dictators whom he consulted privately and regularly. And he liked the CIA's quid pro quo: if he let them train a brigade of four hundred, the Americans would give the same training to four hundred of his toughest soldiers. Ydigoras could gain comfort from such a private army. But his political opponents did not like it. How long could the Guats afford to let Bissell's force stay?

Plotting Castro's Assassination

On the night of July 20 the CIA duty officer in Washington was called at home. He was asked to come to headquarters at once. A cable, just arrived from the Havana station, reported that a Cuban volunteer agent would probably be in contact with Raúl Castro soon. What intelligence information should the agent try to get?

The duty officer contacted Colonel J. C. King and Tracy Barnes and asked what they wanted to reply. Barnes was nominally Bissell's deputy, but Bissell once complained to an associate that his inability to work with a true deputy—someone authorized to exercise as much control as the boss when the boss was absent—was his greatest failing.

Bissell had a strong need to retain control himself, and he knew it.

Barnes did not mind. He was content to play second fiddle to Bissell's intellect. It had been his role, off and on, since he had been a class behind his mentor at Groton and Yale. Barnes was a follower, considerate, respectful of old-school-tie loyalties, eager not to upset anything. When Bissell ruffled a colleague's feathers, Barnes took the victim to lunch and made him feel good again.

Tracy had a cheerful, casual, elegant Ivy League air. Women liked him. He had money, and his wife, Janet, was an Aldrich. He had charm and social contacts. His clothes were correctly cut. He could open any door and knew how to draw together people who didn't like each other. He was a chronic optimist and a team man. At Yale he served on the hockey team, the rugby team, the baseball team, and managed the glee club.

Barnes was no fool. He graduated from Harvard Law and practiced with Carter, Ledyard & Milburn on Wall Street. In the OSS he worked with Dulles in Switzerland, parachuted into occupied France and won the Croix de Guerre twice—once with palm, the other time with star. He admired men who were "civilized" and "decent," two of his favorite words. He loved being liked, and he was—even by people who did not respect him very much, either for himself or for being senior legman to Bissell, a role which was to become crucial at a turning point of the Cuba operation later.

Shortly after midnight on July 21 a cable went to Havana: "Possible removal top three leaders is receiving serious consideration at HQS." Was the Cuban sufficiently motivated to risk "arranging an accident" for Raúl Castro? The station could "at discretion contact subject to determine willingness to cooperate and his suggestions on details." The Cuban agent was to be offered $10,000 payable "after successful completion." No advance payment was permitted, because the Cuban might be a double agent. The signature was, "By direction, J. C. King."

When the Cuban's case officer in Havana read the cable, he "swallowed hard." It was "quite a departure from the conventional activities." When he talked to the agent, he avoided the word "assassinate." He asked about an "accident to neutralize this leader's influence." The Cuban agreed after the case officer assured him his sons would get a college education in the event of his death.

When the CIA man returned to his office, he found another cable from Washington: "Do not pursue ref. Would like to drop matter."* It

*Even Senator Frank Church's intelligence investigations committee could never determine why the assignment was canceled. Testifying in 1975, Bissell remembered nothing about this incident. He assumed the cancellation was ordered by Dulles, perhaps because he considered it "altogether too risky and technically not sufficiently likely of success."

was signed by Tracy Barnes. The case officer cursed. His agent had already left to see Raúl Castro. Everybody was relieved when the agent found no way to arrange an "accident."

Efforts to undermine Fidel Castro's charisma by sabotaging his speeches also aborted. The agency's Technical Services Division (TSD) considered spraying his broadcasting studio with a chemical that produced erratic behavior, much like LSD. This plan had to be abandoned because the chemical proved unreliable. TSD impregnated a box of cigars with a chemical that produced "temporary disorientation" and hoped—in vain—that Castro could be tricked into smoking one before delivering a speech.

The division also hoped to dust his shoes with thallium salts, a strong depilatory, hoping that Fidel's beard would fall out so his image would be damaged. The salts were to be administered during a trip when the planners hoped Castro would leave his shoes outside his hotel room to be shined. The depilatory was satisfactorily tested on animals, but Castro canceled his trip. Another box of Castro's favorite cigars was contaminated with botulism toxin so potent that he would be killed as soon as he put one in his mouth. No one knows whether the cigars ever reached Castro.

Bissell's impatience kept rising. The building of the airfield in Guatemala was slowed by torrential summer rains. Howard Hunt and Gerry Droller made no headway coralling an exile government in Miami. The Technical Services Division had botched its job to neutralize Castro with depilatories and poisoned cigars. The outcome of the Presidential election clouded the future of the entire project. It was very frustrating for a man with a strong drive to move, to get on with the job.

In August, Bissell got a call from Colonel Sheffield Edwards, director of the agency's Office of Security. Bissell had a high regard for "Sheff." He was a sophisticated security man who didn't see Communists everywhere. He was "really outstanding" and got things done. Edwards declined to mention over the phone what was on his mind. He would say only that he wanted to see Bissell.

In Bissell's office the two men weighed ways to "eliminate" or "assassinate" Castro. Edwards said he thought the job needed to be done by Cubans, but not the sort of Cubans the agency was dealing with in the Brigade. He proposed that the assassins be hand-picked by the American underworld, specifically syndicate interests who had been driven out of their Havana gambling casinos by the Castro regime.

Bissell liked the proposed alliance. The gangsters would be deeply motivated, having been cut out of a "very profitable place." This gave them "their own reasons for hostility." Their use would be "the ultimate cover" because "there was very little chance that anything the syndicate would try to do would be traced back" to the U.S. government. Bissell attributed high standards of efficiency to the Mafia. Its reputation for silence would be an asset. Its experience with successful "hits" was unquestioned. Sheff's idea showed imagination. It was so outrageous that it just might work, although Bissell didn't give it more than one chance in ten. He instructed Edwards to proceed and left the details to the trusted security chief.

Edwards assigned the mission to James O'Connell, a former FBI man, the chief of his Operational Support Division. When it came to recruiting someone "tough enough" to handle the CIA's contact with the Mafia, they decided on Robert A. Maheu.

Maheu, also a former FBI man, headed Robert Maheu & Associates, private investigators, in Washington. One of his clients was the reclusive and eccentric Howard Hughes. Another was the CIA. Since 1954, the agency had paid Maheu a monthly retainer of five hundred dollars for jobs in which it "didn't want to have an agency person or a government person get caught."*

He had once arranged to place a listening device in the room of a businessman who held a contract that could have given that man almost complete control over the shipping of all oil from Saudi Arabia. Maheu had also arranged production of a film in Hollywood that purported to show a "foreign leader" dallying with a woman in the Soviet Union.

O'Connell had been Maheu's case officer over the years; they had become close personal friends. When O'Connell first asked Maheu to contact an underworld figure named John Rosselli† to ask "if Mr. Rosselli would be inclined to help in a program for removing Mr. Castro from the scene or eliminating him in connection with the invasion of Cuba," Maheu was reluctant. The money which he was to offer Rosselli, $150,000, seemed adequate. So was the cover story. Maheu was supposedly representing businessmen who regarded the elimination of Castro as the first step toward the recovery of their investments in Cuba. But Maheu did "not want to lose" his wealthy new client, Howard Hughes. Hughes was making increasing demands on Maheu's time.‡

*Maheu said in 1975 that he accepted no money for his work against Castro because "I didn't particularly enjoy this assignment."

†Maheu testified that it was O'Connell who suggested Rosselli.

‡Later, when Hughes phoned Maheu personally and pressed him to come to the West Coast, Maheu told him that the project that was keeping him busy "was on behalf of the United States government." He disclosed "that it included plans to dispose of Mr. Castro in connection with a pending invasion."

Maheu finally accepted the assignment because he felt he owed it to the agency and because "we were involved in a just war."

Maheu had known Johnny Rosselli since the late 1950s and considered him well qualified to finger an assassin for Castro. Tall, silver-haired, elegantly dressed, Johnny looked like an actor's agent. He had started out under Al Capone in Chicago. In the 1930s he was the mob's man in Hollywood and served three years for participating in a plot to extort $1 million from movie companies. He had run the syndicate's Sans Souci casino in Havana and served as its top representative in Las Vegas. Maheu knew that Johnny "was able to accomplish things in Las Vegas when nobody else seemed to get the same kind of attention."

When Maheu met with Rosselli at the Brown Derby restaurant in Beverly Hills in early September, he decided to forget the cover story. Maheu told the dapper mobster that "high government officials" needed his "cooperation" to recruit Cubans who would eliminate Castro. Rosselli was "very reluctant." He was working at becoming respectable. He had even been sponsored by George Jessel, the comedian, as a member of Hollywood's prestigious Friars Club.* He finally agreed to help because he considered it "patriotic." Also, he faced deportation for having entered the country illegally as a youngster.

He did insist on confirming his patriotic mission with a representative of the government, and on September 14 Maheu and Rosselli met with O'Connell at the Plaza Hotel in New York. There was no problem. Rosselli knew O'Connell. They had met previously at Maheu's home in Washington.

The timing of the meeting at the Plaza was an interesting coincidence. The New York papers were full of preparations for guarding Castro's life during his upcoming visit to the United Nations.

Edward Spatz, the owner of the sedate Shelburne Hotel at Lexington Avenue and Thirty-seventh Street in the Murray Hill section of New York's East Side, had ulcers. They were acting up. One of his guests, Fidel Castro, had saddled him with an entourage of eighty *barbudos* (bearded ones), more than two hundred suitcases, and pickets who marched outside shouting, "Fidel, Communist, Fidel!" Castro was in town for a United Nations summit meeting. He had also brought along a bad temper and refused to post a ten-thousand-dollar bond for possible damage to the hotel.

The following day at 7:20 P.M., after shouting at UN Secretary General Dag Hammarskjöld that he and his men were mountain people

---

*In 1968 Rosselli was convicted of swindling members of the Friars, including Zeppo Marx and Phil Silvers, the comedians, out of about $400,000 by cheating at card games.

who could camp out in Central Park, he showed up at the Hotel Theresa, the "Waldorf-Astoria of Harlem," at 125th Street and Seventh Avenue. He had been planning to be lionized by the curious Harlem crowds right along; the day before, his emissaries had paid $840 cash for their first day's stay at the Theresa, more than twice the Shelburne's charges. During that day the Cubans ran up an additional bill of $1,700 for room service.

The beards and the dungarees were the same that charmed Americans during Castro's first visit the previous year. Little else was. This time *Life* magazine chided Castro for "boorishness." There also was no longer any doubt about Fidel's sympathies. Nikita Khrushchev's limousine speeded to Harlem so that the Russian Premier could give Castro a bear hug. The following day, Castro kept Khrushchev waiting from 6:56 to 7:38 P.M. on the front steps of the Soviet UN Mission at 680 Park Avenue, where the two leaders had dinner. During the week, Castro participated by telephone in a meeting of his Cabinet in Havana, which recognized Communist China and North Korea. Cuba was the first nation in the Western Hemisphere to do so. While Fidel was many things, he was hardly, as a congressman had said the year before, a *nuevo amigo*.

Dulles was still unaware that his agency had retained the underworld to kill Castro. In late September, Bissell decided that he and Sheff Edwards should brief the DCI and General Charles P. Cabell, the deputy director (DDCI), in Dulles' office.

The discussion was "circumspect." Edwards did most of the talking. Very deliberately, he avoided any "bad words." He talked about "an intelligence operation." He described his channel as moving "from A to B to C." He used no names. By "A" he meant Maheu. "B" referred to Rosselli. "C" was "the principal"—the assassin in Cuba. Dulles only nodded. Sheffield and Bissell came away with the firm impression that Dulles knew exactly what he had approved.* There was no discussion in the National Security Council or the Special Group. The operators were in charge.

Johnny Rosselli was registered at the Kenilworth Hotel in Miami as "John Rawlston" and told his Cuban contacts that he represented Wall Street financiers who had "nickel interests and properties around in Cuba." Maheu was with him. In mid-October, O'Connell joined them briefly, using the name "Jim Olds." Together they met at the

---

*During his 1975 investigations, Senator Church asked why the CIA men talked "in riddles to one another" even in privacy. Bissell said, "I think there was a reluctance to spread even on an oral record some aspects of this operation."

Fontainebleau Hotel with the two men on whom Rosselli intended to rely. Rosselli introduced them: "Sam Gold" was to be "back-up man"; "Joe" would be courier to Cuba and make arrangements there. Both men were short and balding and had thin, tight lips.

Maheu and O'Connell did not know the real identities of these men, but shortly afterward Maheu phoned O'Connell in Washington and asked him to look at a current magazine article. It was about the FBI's ten-most-wanted-criminals list. Embarrassingly, there they were. "Gold" was Momo Salvatore Giancana, the Mafia chief of Chicago. "Joe" was Santos Trafficante, former syndicate chief in Havana. By that time, Bissell already knew whom he was doing business with. On October 18, the FBI had sent him a memo reporting that Giancana had told "several friends" that he was involved in an assassination attempt against Castro. This breach of security was not to be Bissell's last disappointment with the efficiency of his gangster helpers.

Regrettably, their sex lives intruded in their business. The FBI discovered that Rosselli and Giancana shared the time of an attractive brunette, Judith Exner, who liked parties. At a party in Las Vegas that winter she met President-elect Kennedy and developed a close personal relationship with him as well. The possibility of leaks or blackmail troubled the law enforcement men, especially after they found records of seventy phone calls between Mrs. Exner and the White House.*

Another close friend of Giancana, Phyllis McGuire, the singer, proved time-consuming to the team that the CIA had deputized to eliminate Castro. O'Connell felt trapped in a "Keystone comedy act." Maheu was annoyed because much of the time he spent with Giancana and Rosselli he had "to hold their hands." This became necessary because Giancana kept threatening to fly to Las Vegas to check up on his friend Phyllis. He thought her attentions might be drifting elsewhere. In his absence from Miami, his CIA business would suffer neglect.

When Giancana asked Maheu to bug the room of Dan Rowan, the comedian, in Las Vegas, Maheu recommended to O'Connell that the CIA handle the installation. O'Connell went to Edwards, who said the CIA could not do the job but would pay for it if it was done by a private detective. Maheu hired a detective. He was worried. He wondered "whether Giancana had told his girl friend about the assassination plot, and whether she was spreading the story."

The bug was installed and soon discovered by a maid. The Las Vegas sheriff arrested the private detective, whose bail was paid by Rosselli.

*The Kennedy-Exner relationship continued until March 22, 1962, when FBI Director J. Edgar Hoover had a private luncheon at the White House with the President. The White House logs showed that the last phone contact between the President and Mrs. Exner came a few hours after that luncheon.

When Giancana heard that the tap had been discovered, he thought it was hilarious. Rosselli would always remember "his expression, smoking a cigar, he almost swallowed it laughing."

Security, Security, Security

To Dick Bissell, secrecy continued to be a vital element of the operation as it grew. He thought security was attainable. There were precedents. The CIA's sponsorship of the Guatemala putsch did not leak for years. Neither did word of the U-2 reconnaissance overflights. Now was not the time to dwell on the circumstance that Guatemala had been a small rumble in a backwater; that the U-2 involved only a handful of American professionals tucked into secure factories and bases. Or that there were other differences: Cubans never did anything quietly; the Cuban project involved thousands of men in dozens of places; and most of these sites were visible to nosy outsiders who believed it was their job to keep the public informed of what their government was doing, especially reporters, editors and publishers.

The CIA's first serious security scare started in August. As a practical joke, some American youngsters tossed firecrackers into a Cuban training camp in a farm area near Homestead, south of Miami. (The camp was oddly public. Nearby residents heard drill orders transmitted by loudspeakers and saw Cubans marching.) The trainees thought they were under attack from Castro agents and burst out with rifles firing. An American youth was wounded. Several Cubans were arrested. The city desk of the *Miami Herald* became interested when it heard that the cases were dropped because of a "confidential request from federal authorities." It asked the paper's energetic Washington reporter, David Kraslow, to find out why.

After weeks of checking sources at the FBI, the State Department and the White House, Kraslow pieced together a remarkably complete 1,500-word account. It revealed that the CIA had organized not only the Homestead camp but a much wider recruiting effort; that the Justice and State departments were unhappy over this violation of the Neutrality Act and were pressuring President Eisenhower to move all such CIA training operations out of the country; and that the exiles were to be spirited into Cuba for guerrilla warfare against Castro.

Herald editors Lee Hills and George Beebe agonized over the story. Would they tamper with national security if they published it? Unsuccessfully, they attempted to get guidance from officials, including James C. Hagerty, the President's press secretary. Eventually, Kraslow and his bureau chief, the crusty Ed Lahey, were received by Allen

Dulles and related what they had found. Dulles said that publication of such a story "would be most harmful to the national interest." The *Herald* then decided not to print it. Kraslow, who had been troubled by doubts all along, was disappointed. However, he was not critical of his management: "it was a very tough call to make." When it came, it preserved Bissell's secret. But not for long.

Bissell's security curtain was beginning to leak badly. On October 30, Clemente Marroquín Rojas, a journalist well known in Guatemala and director of the newspaper *La Hora*, published a story disclosing that the CIA had built a heavily guarded $1-million base near Retalhuleu to train Cuban counterrevolutionaries for landing in Cuba.

The disclosure was ignored by American media, but at about the same time Dr. Ronald Hilton, director of the Institute of Hispanic-American Studies at Stanford University, visited Guatemala and heard that the existence and purpose of the base were "common knowledge." His discovery found its way into an editorial in the November 19 issue of the political weekly *The Nation*, entitled "Are We Training Cuban Guerrillas?" "If the reports as heard by Dr. Hilton are true, then public pressure should be brought to bear upon the Administration to abandon this dangerous and hair-brained [*sic*] project," it said. The reports "should be checked immediately by all U.S. news media with correspondents in Guatemala."

Again there was no reaction. Even the editors of *The New York Times* did not spot the brief editorial in the little weekly—not until a reader sent it to the paper, along with a letter to the editor, asking whether the allegations were true and, if so, why they hadn't been reported in *The Times*. The letter landed on the desk of Clifton Daniel, the assistant managing editor. His interest was aroused, and Paul P. Kennedy, the *Times* man in Central America, based in Mexico City, was dispatched to Guatemala. Bissell's curtain was about to tear.

Bissell's secret stood exposed on top of the front page of the January 10 *New York Times*. The three-column headline said: "U.S. Helps Train an Anti-Castro Force at Secret Guatemalan Air-Ground Base." The subhead said: "Clash with Cuba Feared" and "Installations Built with American Aid." The dispatch was by Kennedy, who had penetrated two miles into the training area. It was accompanied by a map.

"Commando-like forces are being drilled in guerrilla warfare tactics by foreign personnel, mostly from the United States," the article said. "The United States is assisting this effort not only in personnel but in material and the construction of ground and air facilities."

An ad in the *Times* the same day announced a series of articles about to be published in the *Daily News*. "Castro's Black Future," said the headline. It went on: "Over 35,000 saboteurs ready to strike from within, 6,000 Cuban patriots poised to swarm ashore."

Reaction was mild or nonexistent. Guatemalan authorities insisted that the training operation was defensive; it was supposed to meet an expected assault from Cuba. President-elect Kennedy was busy at Harvard. He was meeting with the Board of Overseers and with fellow members of the class of '40. More than a thousand students greeted him in the bone-chilling winds of Harvard Yard. "I'm here to go over your grades with Dr. [Nathan M.] Pusey [president of Harvard]," he said, "and I'll protect your interests."

Nobody seemed much concerned about Bissell's secret.

Everybody in the operations office at José Martí International Airport in Havana thought it was a fine joke. Eduardo Ferrer, one of the Cubana Airlines captains, was getting ready to fly Flight 480 to Santiago de Cuba with stops at Varadero Beach, Cienfuegos, Santa Clara and Camagüey. He was thirty, tall, exceptionally broad-shouldered, gregarious, with a mobile face, expansive hand gestures and a booming deep voice. He smiled and joked a lot. He was immensely popular: everybody loved Eddie. That morning, July 27, he seemed in particularly good humor. Right in front of the security guards with their Czech-made submachine guns he inquired of a pilot friend when he would be leaving the country for Miami.

While everybody chuckled, the friend said, "I'm not leaving. Are you?"

"I'm leaving right now," said Ferrer.

He was grinning, but he wasn't joking. It was his way of puncturing any suspicions about his loyalty to Castro. At the bottom of his brown flight bag was a 9-millimeter Browning pistol. It had been given to him in his suburban Miramar apartment by a CIA agent who called himself "John." Ferrer was leaving for Miami to fly for the Brigade. John had suggested that he go there by hijacking his own plane. Behind his smile Eddie was very tense. A tough armed guard was stationed on every Cubana flight. Ferrer's airplane theft had been carefully prepared, but nobody could predict how the three other crew members would act in midair. The reaction of five of the fourteen passengers was predictable. They were part of the plan.

In Cienfuegos, Ferrer watched impassively as his friend Alberto Pérez boarded with his "family" and took seats in the rear. The "wife" was a woman whom Pérez knew only as a recent recruit for the escape scheme. She looked pregnant. In actuality, the bulge in her stomach was a pillow. Under it nestled a .45-caliber pistol. Her two daughters, who accompanied her, had been coached to call Pérez "Daddy."

In Santa Clara, one of the new passengers who came aboard was Pepe Vergara. Ferrer greeted him like an old friend, which he was. The men hugged each other as if their meeting was an accident, which it was not. Fifteen minutes after takeoff, Ferrer and Vergara went to the rear, where the security guard was keeping an eye on everyone. They told the co-pilot they were going to have coffee. As Ferrer stuck his Browning at the guard's face and said, "Don't move or I'll kill you," Vergara moved behind the man and disarmed him. Pérez kept the others in line with his woman companion's pistol.

It was over within seconds. Half the passengers asked for asylum in Miami. One of them could hardly contain himself. Over and over, he said he felt as if he'd won the lottery. For six months he had been trying to think of a reliable way to quit Cuba. Now Ferrer, Pérez and Vergara had landed him exactly where he wished to be. Within days, all three hijackers joined the Brigade.

Ferrer was more than impressed. He was awed. One of his old Cuban pilot friends who had preceded him to Miami told him to go to an apartment house on Segovia Street in Coral Gables, where two Americans named "Bill" and "Jack" had turned eleven apartments into offices. They obviously had military backgrounds, and they asked knowledgeable questions about Ferrer's flying experience. More than forty other Cuban pilots were also being questioned. A few had flown for the Cuban Air Force, some for the Navy, some for Expreso, a cargo airline.

The Americans were close-mouthed: "They didn't say who they were. They asked questions; they never answered one." Ferrer felt uncharacteristically subdued. He was new in the United States, which he considered "the great tiger of the world." He felt "just like a little mouse. Who's going to dare ask questions?" The rumor was that the Americans were from the CIA. The ebullient Eddie never questioned it.

For four days, ten hours a day, he took tests, most of them psychological. They came in soft-cover books, usually about fifteen per day. He was also tested about his technical knowledge of planes and flying. They were standard U.S. Air Force tests. That "tickled" Eddie. It made his efforts seem official. He felt he was joining "the greatest air force in the world."

On the morning of the fifth day an American doctor asked him additional personal questions: What didn't he like about the Castro regime? Why did he want to fight? The "whys" continued until they "got on your nerves." Then the doctor told him to report at 2 P.M. to Room 8. There three men attached wires to his chest and asked more questions for the benefit of a lie detector. He was asked his name and age, and then:

"Are you a Communist?"

"No."

"Are you a homosexual?"

"What?"

"Have you had relations with other men?"

Ferrer laughed so hard he could barely say, "Hell, no." Evidently, homosexuality was almost as serious a menace to the Americans as Communism.

Three days later there were more questions in a big house at Twenty-seventh Avenue and Tenth Street Southwest, the office of the Frente, the loose, constantly feud-ridden exile political leadership. Ferrer learned he would be paid $175 a month plus $50 for the first child and $25 for each additional child. For a moment he felt like a mercenary. Then he told himself his reaction was silly; the money could barely house and feed his wife, María, and their two small sons once he could get them out of Cuba.

The Frente building was teeming with infantry recruits for the Brigade. Ferrer ran into his fellow hijackers, Pérez and Vergara, who had received orders to leave for the training camp that night. They had no idea where it was. Eddie hugged them goodbye. That night he got through to Havana on the phone and talked to María. He told her he was "going on a long trip very soon." María said, "I love you, God be with you."

Three days later, on August 29, shortly after 1 P.M., Ferrer and forty-five other pilots reported back to the Frente house. They were issued khaki shirts and pants, a baseball cap and a bedroll. Each man was handed a manila envelope and was asked to surrender driver's license, pilot's license and all other personal articles except watches. Ferrer received a round metal tag with a neck chain. The legend said, "Eduardo Ferrer, 2492, Alerg. Peni. [allergic to penicillin]."*

The pilots boarded two canvas-covered trucks that were followed by a civilian car, all without markings, all driven by Americans. The trip

---

*Subsequently, Ferrer was issued "pocket litter"—phony papers—including a Cuban driver's license in the name of Eduardo Kent Gonzales of Miramar Avenue, Havana. On his combat missions he carried identifications with both names. Nobody explained why. Ferrer thought this was "crazy," but he did not question it. By that time, many of his other experiences seemed equally irrational.

seemed endless. Ferrer, in the rear of one of the trucks, faced an old friend, Gustavo Ponzoa, also a former Air Cubana pilot. They kept asking each other, "Where the hell are we going?" Peeping through openings in the canvas, they applied their expertise in navigation. Spotting Venus to the west, Eddie announced, "We're traveling south." Half an hour later Ponzoa said, "I got Venus on the other side, we're traveling north."

After three and a half hours they found themselves at the abandoned Navy airfield of Opa-Locka. Without zigzagging for security, the trip would have taken forty minutes. The airport was totally blacked out. Ferrer could not even spot runway lights. They got aboard an unmarked C-54 operated by three men with heavy European accents. The windows were painted black. Black masking tape covered the edges. They flew for nearly seven hours, destination still unknown. They scratched a little paint off the windows. The very deep shades of green below indicated they were over Central or South America. The pilots agreed they were probably headed for Panama.

When the door opened after they reached the ground, they saw two buses and a jeep with Guatemalan license plates. They were in San José, south of Guatemala City—and puzzled. A Guatemalan colonel told them in Spanish that they were going on a three-hour ride. If there was any occasion for anyone to talk to anybody in any of the villages en route, they were to speak only English and say they were construction engineers who had come to help finish the air base in Retalhuleu.

Instead, they traveled to Robert Alejos' plantation, Helvetia, and moved onto canvas cots in one of the unused coffee-grading barns. The first meal, mostly an amalgam that was announced as scrambled eggs, was so bad that Eddie gave it all to the hungry Indian youngsters who hung around begging. (He lost twenty-five pounds while serving in the Brigade.) There were no showers; the pilots could soap off in the Alejos swimming pool with its icy mountain water. The summer rains kept everything moist; the men covered the canvas on their cots with cardboard. Eddie Ferrer was no longer awed by American efficiency.

He naturally expected to fly, but the base was not finished. The pilots spent most days unloading trucks of supplies for the infantrymen at nearby Camp Trax. Then they went through a period of marching and calisthenics. Ferrer never lost his sense of humor. When the pilots were asked to give each other military haircuts, he picked up the clippers and worked on Gus Ponzoa—who was known as "the silver fox" because of two proud silver streaks in his hair. Eddie left Gus almost bald but with a long V-shaped island that made him look like Mephistopheles.

Ferrer's morale did not even leave him when he had to have a severe toothache treated by a local dentist in Retalhuleu, who tried to extract the offending tooth with pliers until the crown broke; the roots had to be pulled by instruments that looked to Eddie like a hammer and chisel. So they made him morale officer. He hung battle pictures of World War II on the bulletin board and scrounged milk shakes and ham-and-cheese sandwiches nightly for men who could not stand the regular suppers. He had "never been so motivated."

Dr. José Almeida, the Brigade's first physician, arrived at Trax base on September 8 around 2 P.M. and was immediately commandeered to help search for Carlos ("Carlay") Rodríguez Santana, who had just fallen two thousand feet off a cliff on a training hike. Rodríguez' Brigade number was 2506. Shortly after 9 P.M., Dr. Almeida and his search team found his body. The Brigade honored him by using his number as its name.

The doctor was not discouraged. He was twenty-six and looked younger. Enthusiastic, boyish and bubbly, he was a classmate and close friend of the psychiatrist-turned-politician Manuel Artime, who had recruited him for the operation. They had gone to medical school together in Havana. Almeida had just finished his internship at Mercy Hospital in Toledo, Ohio. He was not the type to be depressed by anything.

The health conditions in the camps did give him pause. The hills were full of poisonous snakes. He asked for the proper antidote. It never came. He asked for Band-Aids, bandages, penicillin and other basic supplies. He asked again. And again. The supplies arrived three months later. Dr. Almeida shrugged. "We're Cubans," he said to himself. "Whatever we get is fine."

José Basulto, the happy-go-lucky radio operator-infiltrator, did not even gripe when his pocketknife closed on his right little finger while he was peeling an orange—the cut was so deep that the bone stuck out—and Dr. Almeida, known behind his back as "Dr. Coricidin," had nothing but a narrow bandage for closing the wound.

One morning the doctor was called to see a soldier who had turned yellow all over his body. All he could do was hope that it wasn't infectious hepatitis and try to get the man evacuated for tests. He was told that the man could not be moved, because of "security." Five days later an American doctor arrived, examined the patient and said, "OK, let's get him out of here." It turned out that the man suffered from an intestinal obstruction. By luck, the Brigade had been spared an epidemic.

Bob Davis, the CIA station chief, was leaving Guatemala City on one of his reporting trips to CIA headquarters. As usual, he had dinner beforehand with Alejos and President Ydigoras in the Presidential Palace and asked them about any problems he should discuss in Washington. Over cigars, the President brought up a topic that had long worried all of them. Cuban trainees had been going AWOL, usually for a couple of days at a time, to visit prostitutes near the Retalhuleu base. Despite an increase in the number of security guards and the strengthening of fences, this had been a custom since the camps began. Now it was getting out of control. The Cubans managed to leave in ever larger numbers. Some even tried to reach Mexico. Training was seriously disrupted. The Guatemalan Army could no longer keep rounding them up. There was no telling how much intelligence information the trainees gave away to the women.

"You've got to do something," Ydigoras said. "They're Latins. I don't blame them. That's all it is, it's women. What we've got to do is control it. We've got to set up some system where they will be allowed to do certain things if they behave themselves. I wish you'd bring that up in Washington."

At dinner with Dick Bissell and Tracy Barnes a few days later, Davis said, "I got one big problem from the President."

"What is it?" asked Barnes.

"Women."

Barnes's nose wrinkled with distaste, and he shifted nervously in his chair. He looked like a man who knew he was about to be told more than he wanted to know. But he plunged on. "What do you mean?"

"Well, frankly," Davis said, waving his cigar and making one of his emphatic grimaces, "we're going to have to get some whores for these guys."

"Oh, you can't do a thing like that," said Barnes. "You can't use American taxpayers' money for anything like that."

"I'm not asking you to use any taxpayers' money, but we're going to have to say OK."

Barnes got up without a word and left the table for several minutes. This was Bissell's decision, and he didn't want to have to admit to anyone later that he knew what the DDP had ruled.

Bissell had been following the dialogue with amusement. Now he laughed. "I don't want to hear any more about it. Your job is to get things done down there."

That was precisely what was worrying Davis. His chiefs in Washington kept pressing him to push all kinds of projects without specific authorization. It bothered him especially to sign contracts for constructing buildings, roads and airport facilities before appropriations were available. Now he was supposed to authorize a whorehouse. If any of this were to leak to Congress or to the press, there was "only one guy it's going to come back on," and he knew who that was.

Ydigoras understood that problem, too. Davis reported the Washington reaction to him. The President said to leave it to him. Within a few days he told Davis, "It's all done."

Davis made it a point not to inquire about the details. Eventually he learned that Ydigoras had recruited girls from El Salvador and Costa Rica. For security and political reasons, he preferred not to get Guatemalans involved. The brothel was set up outside the Retalhuleu base. Davis was never told how many women were recruited, but there were enough so that the AWOL problems disappeared almost entirely. The house was well organized. There were two shifts daily, one for men with red coupons, the other for customers with green ones. Anyone with a good disciplinary record was entitled to a coupon at reasonable intervals. Ydigoras financed the project with local funds. Alejos and Davis "didn't want to know anything about it." Alejos didn't want stories to get back to his wife. Davis wanted none to reach Bissell.

Nobody understood this better than Bissell. To him, the see-no-evil, hear-no-evil technique was standard for dealing with unpleasant realities.

Setting Up in Guatemala

By September, Eduardo Ferrer, the ebullient Cubana Airlines pilot who had hijacked his jet to Miami, felt happier than ever about the operation. The Brigade air force's morale officer, he was assigned to a C-46 squadron. The airfield at Retalhuleu in Guatemala was now operational. Eddie and the other pilots were settled in livable barracks. Visitors from Camp Trax called them "the Hilton." The food was improving. Training began, mostly takeoffs, landings and procedures for dropping supply bundles to guerrillas. Eddie's American trainers, "Hoyt" and "Jack," he learned much later, had both been naval officers. (He never found out their real names.) The B-26 pilots trained in planes with Guatemalan markings, but the C-46s and C-54s were unmarked and in excellent condition. Ferrer found them "shining, beautiful." Most recently they had seen service on Formosa. Ferrer discovered this from the Chinese letters in the cockpit of an aircraft. The lettering had remained there because of sloppy "sanitizing."

The flying began poorly. One of the older pilots, training with an American instructor, hit the runway so hard that the landing gear of his C-46 was smashed. The Cuban sustained a herniated diaphragm and had to be sent to the United States for surgery. The left wing tip of a C-54 hit a mountain. Part of the wing fell off, and the plane had to be abandoned after a forced landing on a deserted beach near Champerico. Early in October, a C-54 flying the first supply drop over the Escambray Mountains found enemy fire waiting instead of guerrillas. One of the engines was lost, and the captain barely managed to land in Mexico.

It saddened Ferrer to watch the American advisers lose confidence in their Cuban charges. He wondered how much the accidents had to do with the increasing frequency with which the Americans, after belting a few drinks in their bar, grumbled about "the fucking Cubans." This hurt Eddie, especially since the Americans, whom he admired so extravagantly, also had other ways to treat the Cubans as second-class citizens on the base. The door to the bar had a sign, "Classified Personnel Only," so no Cubans were allowed. Some of the Americans with Southern accents were especially scathing when they dealt with Cubans. Eddie's colleagues became resentful in return. It was not an easy time to be morale officer.

After breakfast on November 5 Eddie looked at the smallest of the blackboards in the operations shack, the one with the red lettering, "Missions." It had not been used since the first supply drop ended in Mexico. Now a new mission was scheduled. Ferrer was only to be navigator, but he didn't care. Here was another chance to show the Americans that Cubans could do a job right.

The 5 P.M. briefing in the control tower was given by the American air operations chief, who called himself "Billy Carpenter." The Cubans called him "Barrigón" (potbelly). Ferrer later learned that Carpenter, which was not his real name, was an Air Force colonel. For the present, Eddie was concerned only because Carpenter was hard to understand—he mumbled so much. Ferrer was eager to absorb every word; his congenital optimism was not helped by what he heard.

The flying instructions for his mission over the Escambrays, code-named "Mad Dog," were easy. It was a lot more difficult to swallow Carpenter's orders for what to do in case of trouble. If they encountered ground fire, they were "under no circumstances" to land in the American naval base at Guantánamo Bay. "If you do so, you will be turned in to the Cuban authorities," Carpenter said. "Goddammit," Ferrer said to himself, "instead of one enemy I have two." For a moment he felt that way strongly.

If the aircraft landed on unfriendly ground, Carpenter continued, the crew was to shoot into one of the gas tanks and blow up the plane. If they had to ditch at sea, they were to pick a deep place to be certain the aircraft would sink; at night they were not to ditch near any light. That amounted to suicide.

Later, in their barracks, Ferrer and his crew argued hotly. "This son of a bitch is crazy," someone said. "He's full of shit," said another man. But the prevailing view was what the Cubans had told themselves about the Americans many times: "They know what they're doing." Ferrer felt that way. He kept telling himself he was "dealing with the Central Intelligence Agency of the greatest country in the world, a country that's putting a man in space—that is no bullshit." Whenever he gave himself this historical reminder, his spirits revived. Besides, what choice did he have? Who else would help him liberate his beloved Cuba?

Ferrer and his crew, taking off for the 1,680-mile mission at 6:30 P.M. the next day, were determined to deliver their 11,500 pounds of food and weapons to the right hands at the right time. They flew over the Cuban coast at five-hundred feet to avoid detection by radar. Over the drop zone at eight-hundred feet they looked for the signal they had been told to expect: seven flashlights forming an L—four heading north to south and three heading east to west. They saw nothing. Captain Juan Pérez began a five-mile 360-degree turn. Nothing. He circled again. Nothing. During the third turn five lights flashed up, not seven. They did not form a pattern that looked anything like an L.

The captain told the parachute-drop officers (PDO's) to make the drop anyway. They completed it in ten seconds, but nobody ever learned whether the guerrillas received any of the cargo. Back at base the crew reported exhaustively to Billy Carpenter, who taped all the information and instructed the men not to mention a word to their comrades about the missing L. They were to say that the drop was successful.

Comparatively, it was. During Ferrer's eleven drop missions between November and the following March he saw the drop zone only twice. Usually, he dropped his cargo "just by navigation. Maybe there's somebody over there." His performance may have been better than the overall record. Of sixty-eight missions flown, seven were rated successful, and even those were not always appreciated by the recipients. Ferrer kept hearing that the guerrillas complained about rice being dropped in 150-pound sacks instead of smaller units. How could a man climb a mountain with a 150-pound sack? The guerrillas also reported that they frequently made it to drop zones at great risk and then failed to find the promised planes.

To Eddie Ferrer, the key was obvious. Instructions for drops came from Washington. Instead, the guerrillas should have been in direct radio contact with the planes. He did not reckon with the security-conscious ways of the CIA, nor with the suspicion that some guerrilla units had probably been infiltrated by Castro agents. Better contact between the patriots on the ground and those in the air might have led to more aircraft losses. As it was, there were plenty of emergency landings in Jamaica and on the Cayman Islands.

By December, morale among Ferrer's pilot group hit its low. The men were upset about the failure of the supply missions. Many thought that such instructions as emergency ditching in deep water were "childish"; they wondered whether the CIA was really going to back them up when trouble came. Ethnic resentment against the Southern advisers grew. Training went into a lull. Supply drops were few. The men were bored. Some sneaked to a swimming pool at a motel near the base. Ferrer was ordered to bring them back. He did so—after they invited him for a wonderful dinner which he enjoyed with them.

Finally, thirteen pilots "resigned." Ferrer heard they were kept in a camp until after the invasion. Almost at once, the Americans became much friendlier. The trainees were no longer "the fucking Cubans." The "Classified Personnel Only" sign disappeared from the bar; the Cubans were invited. Julie London records, especially her rendition of "If I Am Lucky," were heard in the barracks. The movie *Pal Joey*, in particular its stars, Kim Novak and Rita Hayworth, set off so many erotic fantasies that it was shown seven times in two weeks. When one of the once hated Southern advisers was ordered replaced, Ferrer and several of his friends went to the airport and sang, "For he's a jolly good fellow."

When Antonio de Varona and Dr. Antonio Maceo of the Frente leadership, escorted by Howard Hunt, toured the camps in January, Varona was struck by the lopsided arithmetic of the operation: how could the Americans really expect the little Brigade to do its job? He decided to question the American camp commander, "Colonel Frank," while they were riding in his jeep. The colonel was driving. Maceo and Hunt sat in the back. Maceo was translating.

"You'll have only a few hundred men," said Varona, who had a son and two brothers in the Brigade. "How can you win? Castro has two hundred thousand!"

The colonel, radiating cheer and confidence, said he would confide a military secret. While the landings were in progress, pamphlets would be dropped to tell the Cuban population that it would be dangerous to use railroads or highways. This would paralyze ground traffic. For the air, complete control was assured. "We'll protect the invasion with an umbrella," he said. "The air will belong to us. No car can travel without being bombed. We don't need more men." The reassuring word "umbrella" would come up again often.

Tracy Barnes, Jake Engler, Bender and Hunt met with Bissell as soon as Hunt returned from escorting Varona and Maceo through the camps.

"I took some photographs at the camps that show formations, drills and committee members with Brigade officers," Hunt announced. "I think they ought to be published."

"Why?" asked Bissell.

"Stimulate recruiting," said Hunt, "and demonstrate graphically that rapport exists between the Frente and the Brigade."

"No," said Jake. "They'll tell Castro too much."

"I like the idea if it can be done securely," ruled Bissell.

Hunt offered to black out some of the faces on the pictures and said he would distribute the photos "anonymously." Bissell told him to go ahead. Hunt handed the rolls of film to Bender and ordered large glossy prints, about a dozen each. It was becoming more difficult to be sure how much of the operation was really supposed to be secret.

When Tony Varona returned from the camps and opened the Miami newspapers the next day, he couldn't believe his eyes. He had been instructed to tell absolutely no one that he was going to Guatemala and hadn't even confided his destination to his secretary. Yet here were pictures in all the papers showing him inspecting the Brigade in the camps. It was "crazy." He was furious.

New men meanwhile were constantly arriving at Camp Trax from Miami. Eager to expand the Brigade so that it could bring off a frontal assault on beaches, the CIA had stepped up its recruiting drive. As the Brigade grew—there now were five hundred men in training—the Byzantine political complexities of Miami spilled over into the Guatemala camps. The Americans in charge, all officers borrowed by the CIA from the armed services, became vexed, then frantic. No military operation could work unless people followed orders. The Cubans didn't bother challenging orders; they argued about who should have the right to issue orders in the first place.

Rodolfo Nodal joined the debate with fervor. He was an attorney, twenty-six, earnest, opinionated, highly articulate. His father had once been Cuban Defense Minister. In Cuba, Rodolfo had worked in one of the many squabbling anti-Castro underground groups. At Trax he quickly became communications officer of the Second Battalion.

Like all the Cubans, Nodal knew that the Americans were indispensable to his cause. But, watching how the camp commander, "Colonel Frank," and the U.S. command of thirty-eight "advisers"* lorded it over the Brigade from their hilltop residence, "like mandarins over a Chinese province," Nodal seethed. Control should not be in "the hands of foreigners, however friendly." It should rest with the Frente and its own designated "general staff" in Florida. They, not the Americans, should appoint the Brigade commanders. Hopefully, they also would not condone the recent CIA relaxation of recruiting standards and allow Batistanos into the brigade.

Focal point of the debate was the American-appointed commander, Pepe San Román. He had worn the yellow Batista uniform but had organized a revolt against the dictator in his own army and had been imprisoned until Castro came to power. The Americans had picked him because he was what the Brigade needed most: a professional soldier, a graduate of Cuba's military academy, trained at Fort Benning, Georgia, and Fort Belvoir, Virginia, which meant that he had learned to follow orders. To Nodal and the other dissidents, Pepe symbolized total submission to the Americans, not only for the present but for the future in Cuba when Castro would be deposed.

As the debate heated up, training all but stopped. Cliques formed and argued. Fist fights erupted. Friends stopped speaking to each other. "Strategy meetings" assembled, conspired, broke up and re-formed. Messages to and from the Miami exile factions passed back and forth. As the controversy grew, men were promising each other positions in ministries of postvictory governments in Havana.

For Nodal, the crisis point arrived when two officers who were supposed to represent the Miami general staff were sent home for "playing politics." The Americans, suspecting that the Frente was fomenting trouble, asked all trainees to hand in their rifles, pistols and submachine guns. Tension mounted. Nodal and his friends hid eight .45-caliber pistols "to shoot it out, if necessary." They stayed up all night to guard their arsenal.

Instead, there was a mutiny. Some 230 men "resigned," including all of the Second and Third battalions. Whereupon San Román resigned to join up as an ordinary soldier. His resignation statement said the Brigade belonged to no one but "to Cuba, our beloved country."

With Colonel Frank away, his superior, another American officer named "Bernie" and known as "Sitting Bull" because of his squat appearance, assembled the Brigade in formation and announced from a wooden platform, "I am boss here, and the commander of the Brigade is still Pepe San Román."

*These instructors were "sheep-dipped"—i.e., military men posing as civilians.

He told Pepe to step up and resume command. San Román asked that those men willing to fight with him and to "forget about political things" step to the right. The others should stand fast. About a hundred stood still, including Nodal, who had been elected one of five leaders of the dissidents. They demanded that the Frente be allowed to visit the camps. The Americans agreed. But Nodal found himself under arrest in tents normally occupied by the Brigade's tank units. He was one of twenty men who were considered the principal troublemakers and he was apprehensive.*

Assembling the CIA Pilots

Everything about Major General George R. (Reid) Doster was outsized: the leonine head with its craggy face on his six-foot-one frame, the quarterback shoulders, the bellow in his voice, his enthusiasm for hunting, fishing and flying, his restlessness when he was bored. He was very bored that morning in October when a CIA man, a quiet little fellow with a Southern accent, dropped in at his office at the Sumpter Smith Air National Guard on the east side of Birmingham, Alabama, municipal airport.

Reid Doster was commanding general of his state's Air National Guard, and when the CIA man said, "We need your help for a mission for the United States government," Doster eagerly volunteered answers for everything the man from Washington wanted to know. The visitor was especially interested in the availability of pilots with experience on the old B-26 medium bomber, along with maintenance and armaments specialists. The CIA man said secrecy was mandatory. He hinted that the mission's goal was to unseat Castro.

Doster was delighted. The headlines about Castro's successes had been making him angry. The dictator was "a threat to the whole hemisphere." The fact that he was only ninety miles away was "an insult." He "had to be gotten rid of" before the Soviets would use him as a "steppingstone for something bigger."

At once the general began to assemble a CIA air force that eventually numbered eighty Americans. He was the ideal recruiter; his men called him "Poppa" and were correspondingly loyal. A few of the pilots whom he approached turned him down because they did not want to disrupt

---

*Nodal's fears were not unjustified. He was given a lie detector test, threatened and interrogated "like an enemy." Along with fellow dissidents, he was spirited by seaplane and canoe to a camp in the Petén, a mountainous, almost inaccessible jungle in northernmost Guatemala. It was guarded by four Americans and twenty-five Guatemalans. The prisoners were issued thin slippers to discourage escapes. Nobody tried to get away. Two weeks after the invasion, Nodal was flown to Miami and released. He phoned his family at 3 A.M. They did not know he was alive.

their civilian careers. Most of his prospects reacted like the Air Guard's flight surgeon, Major Theodore C. Marrs, a pediatrician in Montgomery.

When Doster phoned, the doctor had an officeful of patients. "I've got a T-33 waiting for you," the general said. "I want you up here in thirty minutes."

The doctor arrived within the hour.

"Ted, we've got something that's really important for the country. It'll take a hundred twenty days and you might get shot at."

"When do we leave?" Dr. Marrs asked.

John O. Spinks, a gunsmith by trade and long a senior master sergeant on the Guard's permanent staff, was another early recruit. He looked like a sleepy farmer in a Norman Rockwell magazine cover, but he had a delicate touch with aircraft guns, rockets and bombs. He was at first puzzled when General Doster asked him into his office for a "strictly confidential" talk.

The general took no time for preliminaries. "Would you like to kick the hell out of Castro?" he asked.

"Sure!" said Spinks. He knew that the United States had for years supplied Cuba with weapons, and now these guns were being turned on the American donors. He felt double-crossed. But he wondered, "How can we kick the hell out of Castro?"

Doster gave few details. Indeed, Spinks never heard of a place called the Bay of Pigs until after he returned to Alabama from Nicaragua six months later with stomach ulcers. For the moment Doster said, "There are some Cubans down south that need to be trained." Spinks would get fake papers identifying him as coming from Atlanta. He was to tell his family that he was off to a "secret school" and would be gone at least forty-five days. He would take a polygraph test and get a hundred dollars to buy work and sports clothes and a raincoat. All had to be new so that they wouldn't have telltale laundry marks. Then he'd report in Miami for a "black" flight to Guatemala.

Doster called Air Guard units in Arkansas and other Southern States for specialists he couldn't produce in Alabama, especially men who could mix napalm bombs. In Little Rock he was pleased to turn up a colonel with flying experience in Cuba. The colonel had trained Cuban pilots to fly T-33 jets that the United States had given the Batista regime.

The CIA gave Doster forty-five days to get ready. It took a little longer, but not much. The general worked almost around the clock. The mission sounded foolproof to him, although he had been told next to nothing except that his part of the operation would be "just a small cog."

He "had confidence" and "had to assume that the logistics were available and the planning had been done." His briefings convinced him that the surprise invasion would throw Cuba into turmoil. The population "was supposed to be waiting for this" and would gladly join the men of the Brigade "as they landed." And he did his best to measure up to the CIA's intense feelings about secrecy. Every new recruit received a Doster blast: "If you open your goddamned mouth, I'll have your ass."

Despite General Reid Doster's admonitions about security, word was getting around among the pilots at the Birmingham airport that a military operation was in progress. Flight personnel kept disappearing. Rumors circulated that the men were going someplace exotic south of the border. Albert C. ("Buck") Persons was not surprised when Riley W. Shamburger took him aside in January and said, "Reid is getting up some four-engine pilots for a job out of the country. It's legitimate. Do you buy it?"

Persons and Shamburger were beer-drinking buddies. Shamburger was a test pilot for Hayes Aviation, which repaired and modified planes for the Air Force. He was a muscular, 209-pound six-footer with a good memory for jokes and a reputation as a superior pilot. He was also operations officer for one of the Alabama Air National Guard squadrons. The talkative, politically sophisticated Buck Persons was the nephew of a former Alabama governor. He had enlisted in the Royal Canadian Air Force in September 1939, "thirty minutes after the war began," and had relished the combat experience. Now he was a bit bored flying a DC-3 for a construction company. Doster's job sounded intriguing. He went to see the general.

Doster was vague. He preferred pilots without current military ties. They were going to fly combat missions. Although he didn't say where, Persons had no trouble guessing. He knew that Cuban exiles were flooding Miami and that Castro was accusing the United States of planning an invasion. He happily agreed to attend a further briefing in Doster's office.

Close to twenty pilots assembled for the 8 A.M. meeting, where a civilian called "Al" said he represented some wealthy "foreign nationals" who were planning, well, an invasion down south. They had been using "foreign national crews" to drop supplies to some guerrillas, and some of the pilots had been dropping their cargoes in the ocean instead. American guts and expertise were needed. Any pilot who was interested should pick himself a new identity and home town and come to the next briefing. Nobody in the room doubted that Al and his associates represented the CIA. Otherwise, how could they be sitting in the Air National Guard headquarters?

Persons said he wanted to pick Washington as his fake home town because he knew the city well. A civilian named "Jake," who was in charge of the men's cover stories, said this wouldn't be a good idea. Persons then picked New York. He hardly knew the city; he figured that if he was shot down and questioned the city was so big he could make even a rather general story believable—if it mattered, and he didn't think it would matter at all in that situation. A man named "Hoyt" said they would be paid $2,800 a month, including $600 expenses. In case of death the widows would get a $550-a-month indemnity for life.

At the next meeting Hoyt opened an attaché case filled with hundred-dollar bills. Each enlistee could draw up to one month's pay, and one pilot did. Persons asked for five hundred dollars and instructed Hoyt to send the rest to his bank. He went over his cover story with Jake and was asked to fly by commercial craft to Miami and register in his new name at the McAllister Hotel. No more than two of the aviators were to take the same flight. When Persons got to the Birmingham airport, ten of his group of four-engine C-54 transport pilots, flight engineers and radio men were already there. By coincidence, they had all booked the same flight. Five B-26 bomber pilots had left earlier.

Amused, Persons and his group decided they could do with a little less security. They did not try to create the impression that they did not know each other, either on the flight to Miami or at the hotel, which turned out to be in the busiest part of the downtown area. The bar was one of Miami's most popular rumor mills, incongruously close to the small room where the fliers were told to report, one at a time, for lie detector tests. The civilian with the polygraph did not say he was with the CIA. He said, "I'm employed by your employers."

When Persons and his colleagues were told to get new, unmarked work clothes, they all trooped to Sears. When they were told to report to the municipal airport at Fort Lauderdale for refresher training, they went together in rented cars and took apartments in the same neighborhood. In the daytime, they trained on an ancient unmarked C-54 parked at the Mackey hangar. Nobody had a problem except one man who found himself a Turkish belly dancer in a nightclub and sometimes was so fatigued in the morning that he had to be helped into the airplane. At night the group went to an abandoned Air Force field in the Everglades and "shot" landings with just a couple of small flare pots outlining the runway.

After a month, Persons' contingent reported to a Travelers' Motel on Thirty-sixth Street in Miami, were loaded into the usual rental truck and driven via the usual circuitous route to nearby Opa-Locka airfield for the usual "black" flight to Guatemala. Buck Persons was comfortable. He felt part of an American military operation. He was convinced it had been meticulously "planned at the Pentagon." It never occurred to him that it might conceivably falter.

The Alabama Air National Guard contingent was not altogether happy training the Cuban pilots. General Reid Doster felt out of place in his sandals and khaki shorts. It was difficult to be "Poppa" to the Cubans, even when you could understand their English. Their moods were remarkably mercurial; they were in tears one minute and cracked up laughing the next. It was hard to get them organized. Many had less than a hundred hours of flying experience. Doster felt uneasy about that; nobody with less than three hundred hours should be sent into combat. The CIA's secrecy curtain was less than impenetrable; all identifying marks were supposed to have been removed from the B-26s, but when Doster scraped a bit of paint off one steering wheel with his fingernail he found a familiar number: he had flown that plane before, in the States, in saner days.

Master Sergeant John Spinks, the armaments specialist, didn't mind staying up all night mixing napalm and loading five-hundred-pound bombs onto planes with a forklift that kept breaking down, but sometimes he thought the Cubans would never get the hang of the guns. They kept coming back from practice flights complaining that the machine guns wouldn't fire. Sometimes Spinks found that the pilots were loading the weapons improperly. More often they failed to turn off one or more of the three safety switches. The Cubans' morale was nevertheless superb. They treated Spinks like a close friend and invited him to the "big party in Havana" where they would celebrate victory after it was all over.

Buck Persons, the C-54 pilot, bored with confinement at the Happy Valley base, was grateful when the Nicaraguan camp commander, a Captain Cardona, flew him and three other American pilots to Managua for a weekend and checked them into a hotel. On Sunday, Cardona vanished. The Americans did not have enough cash to pay the hotel bill. They sat around the lobby for hours in their T-shirts and work pants, knives stuck in their belts, feeling all too conspicuous among the tourists. They decided to try a telephone number that they had been given for emergencies. It turned out to be President Somoza's palace. The Americans hung up, embarrassed. Persons thought it was hilarious—like being unable to pay the bill at the Mayflower Hotel in

Washington and calling the White House to be bailed out. Eventually, Cardona reappeared and settled the bill.

Billy ("Do Do") Goodwin, a B-26 pilot from Birmingham who had been a test pilot at Hayes Aviation, like Riley Shamburger and some of the other Alabama fliers, thought the Happy Valley base was just fine. He didn't mind "millions and millions" of flies or the humidity and the heat, often a hundred degrees or more. He had brought no personal belongings except five packs of his favorite razor blades, but he lacked nothing. Busch Bavarian beer was free, and there was plenty of it. Whiskey was a dime per shot, two cartons of cigarettes a week were furnished without charge, movies were shown on Sundays. The excellent boiled local shrimp were daily fare; Billy never tired of them. While he didn't gamble, one of his friends, Leo Francis Baker, a flight engineer who had also worked at Hayes, won three hundred dollars in a poker game.

Goodwin was only twenty-eight. He was a six-footer, very skinny, spoke softly with an unusually thick Southern accent, and had a courtly manner. He had flown with the Alabama Air Guard in his spare time. According to his CIA cover story, he was supposed to be from San Angelo, Texas; he had been stationed there when he was in the Air Force. He worried because his Cuban pilot trainees rarely hit their targets during bombing practice over a deserted lake. He also wondered whether the invasion would really set off a civil revolt within Cuba. Without it, he "couldn't see how the thing would work." He consoled himself that he was "just a little pilot." The men above him had to be better informed. He trusted Reid Doster and the CIA men he had met. They knew what they were doing.

CHAPTER TWO

Escalation

Cuban Shadow Over the U.S. Election

It was close to 9 P.M. on October 19, and the statement had to be released quickly to make the morning papers. Kennedy's campaign staff was red-eyed, rumpled, near exhaustion. Sleep came mostly in catnaps between crises. That evening they were working in poorly lighted rooms at the Hotel Commodore on Forty-second Street and Lexington Avenue in Manhattan. Two of the principal campaigners, the rotund press secretary, Pierre Salinger, and speech writer Richard Goodwin, twenty-eight, pockmarked, brilliant and abrasive, were addicted to large, heavy cigars. Their smoke fogged the air.

Goodwin, an attorney, a former clerk for Supreme Court Justice Felix Frankfurter but new to politics, took the statement out of his typewriter and showed it to Sorensen and Salinger. "We must attempt to strengthen the non-Batista democratic anti-Castro forces in exile, and in Cuba itself, who offer eventual hope of overthrowing Castro," it said. "Thus far, these fighters for freedom have had virtually no support from our government."

Goodwin had reason to respect Cuba as an election issue. On the plane between campaign stops he had been studying the question cards collected from audiences at the candidate's rallies. Usually there was time to deal with only a handful of questions; in their entirety, the cards were good indicators of the issues that were arousing the electorate. Goodwin made a remarkable discovery: "Castro was bigger than Khrushchev." The country seemed to regard the Cuban leader not only as the principal enemy in the Western Hemisphere; he personified the confrontation between Communism and Americanism.

Nixon obviously had the same impression. Two days previously, at the American Legion annual convention in Miami, the Vice President had announced that his patience with Castro was over; it was time to eradicate this "cancer" from the American hemisphere "to prevent further Soviet penetration." The government was already planning "a number of steps." Now Nixon proposed an all-out "quarantine."

The Kennedy men at the Commodore felt under the gun. Many politicians and voters considered their candidate a lightweight, a rich man's playboy son. At the last Gridiron dinner, Washington correspondents had staged a skit to the tune of "My Heart Belongs to Daddy." They changed the words to "Just send the bill to Daddy." The Senator fell in with the joke. He read a purported wire from his father: "Dear Jack: Don't buy a single vote more than is necessary—I'll be damned if I'm going to pay for a landslide."

The candidate was also being attacked as "soft on Communism." The Cuban issue unquestionably was important, perhaps critical. Kennedy conformed to the black-and-white mind-set of the Cold War. He wanted Castro unseated even though the two men had much in common: youth, vigor, charisma, bright dreams of the future. Castro was a Communist, and Kennedy was determined to become President. The fourth and final of the candidates' TV debates was only a day away. It would focus entirely on foreign affairs. A new statement on Cuba now would help.

Kennedy was at his favorite hotel, the elegant Carlyle on Madison Avenue. Shortly after nine o'clock the staff tried to reach him by phone. He had gone to sleep, dead tired. Nobody felt like waking him. The staff men wondered: Should they release a statement without his OK? They had never done so. But Goodwin's words broke no new ground. Kennedy had been attacking the Eisenhower administration for allowing Communism to come to flourish "eight jet minutes from the coast of Florida."

The term "fighters for freedom" had no specific meaning for Goodwin and the others. They did not know about the CIA godfathering a Cuban brigade. Goodwin, who enjoyed coining phrases and was good at it, considered his words "political rhetoric." Later he said it was "just an issue like Chiang Kai-shek," the venerable head of Nationalist China, who was forever being "unleashed" against Mainland China, a vision so absurd that it was turning into a sour joke. So Goodwin's statement was handed to reporters.*

---

*After the incident blew over, Kennedy told Goodwin, "If I win this election, I won it. If I lose, you lost it." Later, shortly before the Bay of Pigs, in the President's Oval Office, Kennedy put his arm around Goodwin's shoulder in front of the glass door to the Rose Garden. They stood on the wooden mat bearing cleat marks of Eisenhower's golf shoes. "Well, Dick," the President said, "we're about to put your Cuba policy into action."

When Nixon saw the newspapers the next day, he went into a "rage." *The New York Times* ran Goodwin's rhetoric as the lead story on the front page. The headlines said: "Kennedy Asks Aid for Cuban Rebels to Defeat Castro, Urges Support of Exiles and 'Fighters for Freedom.'" Later Nixon wrote: "I could hardly believe my eyes." He sent for Fred Seaton, a senior aide, and asked him check with the White House whether Kennedy had been informed about the Cuba project during the intelligence briefings which Eisenhower had ordered Dulles to give personally to the opposition candidate. Within half an hour, Seaton reported that Kennedy had been briefed.*

For the first and only time in the campaign, Nixon "got mad at Kennedy—personally." He felt "like a fighter with one arm tied behind his back." He was certain "that Kennedy, with full knowledge of the facts, was jeopardizing the security of a United States foreign policy operation." He was advocating what was already the policy of the Eisenhower administration, covertly, thereby drawing support from voters who favored stronger moves against Castro. The voters could not know that a very strong move was quietly in progress.

Despite his fury, Nixon felt that "the covert operation had to be protected at all costs." The only way to do this, he said to himself, was: "I must go to the other extreme: I must attack the Kennedy proposal . . . as wrong and irresponsible because it would violate our treaty commitments."

In the debate, Nixon called Goodwin's campaign rhetoric "the most shockingly reckless proposal ever made . . . by a presidential candidate." He felt frustrated at his inability to say why he felt so strongly. In defending his position, in which he did not believe and which had no foundation in fact, he made a prediction of the future which proved uncannily correct months later under totally new circumstances: If the United States were to back the Cuban freedom fighters, it would be "condemned in the United Nations" and "would not accomplish our objective." It would be "an open invitation for Mr. Khrushchev . . . to come into Latin America and to engage us in what would be a civil war

---

*Precisely how much Kennedy had been told by Dulles during a briefing on July 23 at Hyannis Port on Cape Cod will probably never be known. The men met for two and a quarter hours at Kennedy's summer home. When Dulles later told the National Security Council that he had briefed the Senator on Cuba, he said he had done so in general terms but had included such details as the CIA clandestine radio operations. As the meeting broke up, Nixon "exploded," according to Robert Amory, Jr., who was present. Under no circumstances, said the Vice President, should Kennedy have knowledge of the invasion. Dulles placated him. On March 20, 1962, the White House denied that Kennedy had been told about the secret plans before the election. Dulles backed up Kennedy and said there had been an "honest misunderstanding" by Nixon. Since there were no "invasion" plans in July 1961, only plans for guerrilla infiltrations and air drops, Kennedy probably did not learn of *major* military plans against Cuba until he was briefed by Dulles and Bissell in Palm Beach after his election.

and possibly even worse than that." He again suggested his "quarantine" plan.

The public thought Kennedy won the debates. How much Nixon's softer stand on Castro may have contributed to the Republican defeat at the polls cannot be known. Goodwin was impressed by what he had inadvertently accomplished. He always hated Nixon passionately. For once, the two could agree: the Cuba project led men down tortuous byways.

Herbert G. Klein, Nixon's press secretary, had been briefed by the Vice President about the Cuba operation. They often talked secretively about "our Nicaraguan friends." Klein expected the overthrow of Castro perhaps still in October. He was deeply involved in the difficult presidential campaign. A successful Cuba operation would have been "a major plus," indeed "a real trump card." He knew that Nixon kept urging Eisenhower on. He worried that no move might come until November. If it had to be November, he would have been grateful if it were to be November 1 rather than closer to the election on the eighth.

His colleague, General Cushman, who knew more, worried more. The project was becoming so big that "everybody in the world would know the U.S. is behind this." The operation "looked pretty hairy" to him. He thought it would require standby U.S. forces, and "if it failed, they should jump in." As a Marine, he felt the Marines would be right for the job. He did not say so. He was "supposed to have a purple suit on"—meaning that in his job with Nixon he was supposed to be above rivalry between the military services.

Ike continued to be wary. If he felt pushed by Nixon, he never showed it. He kept pressing Dulles about the missing Cuban government in exile. Dulles and Bissell assured him that the CIA was making progress. Eisenhower was skeptical. "I'm going along with you boys," he said, "but I want to be sure the damned thing works."

Escalation

Allen Dulles and Bissell traveled to Palm Beach on November 27 to brief Kennedy, the new President-elect, in his father's home. The meeting lasted less than an hour. Bissell did most of the talking. Kennedy did not seem surprised. Only the scope of the operation seemed to give him pause. He did not indicate any wish to change course. Before the CIA men left, Dulles and Kennedy chatted briefly while walking in the garden. They obviously wanted to be alone. Bissell did not think this in the least unusual. His boss was master at steering projects past presidents and bureaucracies. It was a pleasure to watch him work his way, step by step, never faster than necessary, never slower.

Dulles chose not to brief President Eisenhower on "the new paramilitary concept" until two days later, even though the escalation toward a greatly expanded operation had been long in progress. The CIA chief received an "indication" that the outgoing President wanted the operation "expedited."

The ultrasecret Special Group did not consider the supposedly "new" concept—it called for a landing by 600 to 750 men preceded by air strikes—until December 8. Bissell and his men were "encouraged" to continue "development" of the force. Someone remarked that the presence of a "U.S.-backed" force in Guatemala was already "well known throughout Latin America."

The big decision was "internal." The word was Bissell's. It referred to the move to escalate the Cuba project radically. When it grew from a series of guerrilla-infiltration-air-drop jabs into a concerted military effort, the Special Group, the National Security Council and the President were not consulted. The change, Bissell thought, was "internal really to the people involved in the operation." Even at the CIA there were no meetings about it. No "formal recording" of this pivotal shift existed. Mostly it came down to Bissell personally.

Even in his own mind, the change was all but imperceptible, almost unconscious. He could see that present methods were "not going to get us anywhere." Castro was tougher than expected. Since nothing was working, more had to be done. There was no thought that the agency might be starting to operate out of control. Bissell was responding to the facts. His "desire to respond" was strong. And with Bissell, "strong" was what others called "relentless."

For a frontal beach assault a military commander with amphibious experience was now needed. Dulles thought it should be a Marine. The Marine Corps suggested Colonel Jack Hawkins. Bissell found him "an ideal choice." It was "hard to see how there could have been a better selection."*

Hawkins was a six-footer, lean, with wavy brown hair and an ascetic face. Jake Engler, who liked this old soldier instantly, thought he looked

---

*After the invasion, Hawkins' qualifications were questioned. Bob Amory, the DDI who was not consulted about the operation, had fought in twenty-six assault landings during the war in the Pacific, many of them as small as the Bay of Pigs. Hawkins, he said, "had made one in his whole goddamn life, and that was Iwo Jima, which was three divisions abreast. He was a very able soldier and Marine, but he just didn't know beans about what a small, self-contained beachhead would be like."

"like a typical movie Marine." During World War II, Hawkins fought at Iwo Jima. During the Korean War, he saw much of his command killed at Yalu. For two years he was behind the lines in the Philippines and acquired guerrilla action experience. He had a reputation as a scholar of military science, and everybody soon heard he was on the Pentagon list for promotion to general.

Even Bissell, never eager to warm up to new personalities, "liked and admired" the dedication and precision of Jack Hawkins.

As the escalation from guerrilla operation to invasion took hold, the importance of air power increased enormously, and Bissell brought one of his favorite disciples into his inner circle: Colonel Stanley W. Beerli, with whom he had worked for four years in the famous "Richard Bissell Air Force," and who felt "affection" for Bissell that was "boundless."

The head of the Air Operations Division was quiet, intense and almost skeleton-thin. His round little balding head was birdlike, its skin stretched so tight it looked shrunk around its bones. A perfectionist like Bissell, he shared the boss's devotion to secrecy and precision. Beerli was proud that even some of his office security guards were college graduates. He knew that tight planning could make up for an operation's smallness; that smallness—"reducing the numbers"—was essential to covertness; and covertness was his business.

He had learned that business not in the Air Force, where he had been a reconnaissance specialist and from which he was still on detached duty, but with the CIA's U-2 project. Bissell had personally hired Stan Beerli as commander of the U-2 detachment at the critical supersecret base in Turkey. Now Bissell needed another private air force for his Cuba project. The colonel was assigned to assure "air superiority"— but there was a string attached. He was to do the job with the least possible number of planes. At the same time, he received the similarly contradictory order—which also came to apply to the expedition's ships, its arms, and its command and control—to make the CIA's best professional efforts look sufficiently amateurish and shabby so they could be passed off as Cuban. The American sponsorship was supposed to be deniable. "Plausible denial" was the intelligence jargon for the applicable doctrine of clandestinity.

Beerli decided that World War II–vintage B-26 bombers would be the operation's work horses because they had been sold as surplus all over the world. The Alabama Air National Guard was the best source for personnel to train Cuban pilots and crews, because it had been the last American unit to fly B-26s, and some of its personnel had been cleared for security during earlier CIA projects. The fleet of retired Air Force planes mothballed outside Tucson, Arizona, contained more B-26s than anybody could ever use, and CIA technicians were ready to "sanitize" them—that is, remove all identifying numbers and insignia.

Beerli's principal obstacle turned out to be his supposed colleagues in the Pentagon. He found them "reluctant." They placed him "in a begging position" where he "had to fight for every damn airplane, everything we wanted, every bit of the way." They "put a price tag on everything"; the CIA could not borrow the equipment but had to transfer government funds from its budget to the Defense Department.

Beerli felt as if he were negotiating on behalf of some odious foreign government, particularly when he had to wrestle with his most unpleasant adversary, L. Fletcher Prouty, an Air Force colonel in charge of liaison with the CIA out of the Defense Secretary's office. Prouty, who hated the CIA, not only treated Beerli like the representative of an alien power. "He would try to pry information" out of the CIA man. He kept asking such questions as "Why do you want this?" or "What are you going to do with that?" Beerli, following his CIA rules, would not tell him.

He wondered whether the Defense Department was perhaps "jealous" of the CIA. More likely, he thought, the powers in the Pentagon were worried that the project might "go down the drain," and they therefore wanted as little to do with it as possible. Beerli concluded, "They were very concerned, and the less they became involved, the less the blame would be on them."

Dick Drain also was given cold treatment when he asked for the loan of twenty-seven sergeants from the Army Special Forces ("Green Berets") to help train the Brigade's infiltration teams. The Army would not release the sergeants until the case was carried all the way to President Eisenhower. When a presidential authorization reached Secretary of the Army Wilbur Brucker, the trainers were still not released. "If I'm authorized," said Brucker, "that doesn't mean I'm directed." Another appeal had to be made to the summit of the government.

Beerli and Drain were correct in their suspicion that they were not merely shadowboxing with foot-dragging Pentagon underlings. It was the top of the defense establishment under President Eisenhower that had no stomach for the Cuban project. The case of the twenty-seven sergeants crystallized the opposition, and the man who shaped the topside pessimism was one of the most colorful of the post–World War II military heroes, Colonel (later Major General) Edward G. Lansdale.

When the colonel appeared in the office of James H. Douglas, the Under Secretary of Defense, to bring up the issue of the twenty-seven sergeants, Douglas was automatically interested because of Lansdale's long-demonstrated expertise with guerrilla warfare and with difficult civilian populations in Southeast Asia. It was generally known that Lansdale was a real-life character in the best-selling novel *The Ugly American*.

Lansdale told Douglas that the CIA was planning an "over-the-beach" invasion of Cuba for which it estimated it would need three thousand men, although it had only seven hundred. He thought the landings were not going to work. Far more people, more supplies and more solid planning were needed. The logistics weren't consistent with the goals.

Douglas said he would recommend release of the sergeants but would make it plain that "the Defense Department in no way approved the plan or the general feasibility of such a plan."

At a meeting with the President and Dulles, Douglas brought up the sergeants, along with the Pentagon's "observation that the project appeared impractical." He wanted to "disassociate" the department "to avoid any misunderstanding that making Army training personnel available to the CIA in any way implied approval of the project." In fact, "there was never in my mind a present proposal to be taken seriously," and this was in line with the belief of Thomas S. Gates, a smooth Philadelphia investment banker who was Eisenhower's Secretary of Defense.

Gates also felt that the landing force was "wholly inadequate," and he was concerned because the invaders lacked a leader who would have "national appeal."

While Eisenhower responded to the Pentagon's frosty attitude by mildly requesting better coordination between the CIA, Defense and State, Lansdale considered the CIA scheme so quixotic that he spoke up against it again in December at a meeting of the Special Group.

He had just started on the project's lack of military know-how when Dulles interrupted: "You're not a principal in this!"

Douglas came to Lansdale's rescue. He felt grateful for the "good education" he had received about the project from the colonel and wanted to be on record to avoid giving the next administration the impression that "this tentative CIA project" was "something that had been approved" by the Defense Department under Eisenhower. He asked that Lansdale be permitted to continue.

The colonel reminded the Special Group that it was being asked to believe that the Cuban people would arise in the face of the landings. He said this was "extremely doubtful." At least there were not enough facts to substantiate the hope. Castro was executing opponents of his regime and getting away with it. "What's the political base for what you're going to do?" Lansdale asked Dulles. "How popular is it going to be?"

There was no memorable CIA rejoinder except that Dulles took Lansdale aside after the meeting and suggested that, for old times' sakes, he hoped the colonel would be more discreet.

The colonel's discretion, never one of his greatest virtues, would not be tested again on this issue. At the turn of the year he left on assignment to Vietnam, and he did not return to Washington until after the Bay of Pigs had failed.

In the Eisenhower State Department, the growth of the Cuban operation was most closely monitored by the Under Secretary, Douglas Dillon, a brisk executive blessed with versatility, a formidable intellect, and an incisive air of command. An investment banker, he had been ambassador to France and now, given his boss's travel schedule, was Acting Secretary of State more than one third of the time. *

Dillon was not a total admirer of Eisenhower's administrative practices. Describing Ike's Cabinet meetings to intimates, he would recall, "We sat around looking at the plans for Dulles Airport. They had a model and everything, and we would say, 'Why don't you put a door there?' and they would explain why they didn't. It was great fun if you didn't have anything to do."

Dillon developed a great respect, however, for Eisenhower's military philosophy. He agreed with the general "that one did not ever use military power unless you were prepared to use it to the full extent necessary to achieve whatever the objective was that you started for." The idea was to use military muscle liberally "so there would be no fight, [or] so it would all be over quickly."

Dillon knew the Pentagon felt "skittish" about the plans for Cuba, and was certain the military would never approve a plan without standby combat support by U.S. naval air strength "to see that the plan was successful if it was actually launched." That was "very definitely" his assumption "all the time" through the summer, the fall and into the winter of 1960. He took his cue from Eisenhower, who thought the operation was in its infancy. The President maintained "a certain skepticism until such time as the [Cubans'] training was completed, and then a willingness to look at it."

---

*After Dillon became Kennedy's Secretary of the Treasury and the only Republican in the Cabinet, it was widely reported, possibly because he became friendly with the new President and his brother Bob, that he attended JFK's meetings on the Bay of Pigs and approved of the landings. In fact, Dillon attended no meeting about the project during the new administration and was never consulted. Kennedy thought of him purely as an adviser on economic problems.

One State Department functionary who gave the Cuba project intensive attention was Thomas C. Mann, a career foreign service officer who became Assistant Secretary for Inter-American Affairs just before Kennedy's election. Brusque in manner and somewhat Lincoln-esque in his spare and glum appearance, Mann had a reputation as a conservative who liked to dot his i's painstakingly. To him, the first and most urgent question was whether "intervention" in Cuba was legal.

Closeting himself in his office for several weeks, he worked on almost nothing else, because "there was nothing more important in my mind." He "didn't tell anybody" what he was doing, because he "was always very security-conscious." He asked State's legal department for a definition of "intervention." The answer only frustrated him further; "it evaded the question."

In due course, he composed a memorandum. Following security regulations, he made sure no copies were made. The memo "opposed the expedition because it would be a violation of our treaty obligations." That was how he initially interpreted the charter establishing the Organization of American States. But his conscience would not let him drop his researches. The legal intricacies continued to intrigue and trouble him, because "when a sovereign state has chosen its policy, and if that policy threatens the security of the United States, at what point does the United States have the right to exercise its unilateral right of self-defense?"

Mann returned to the wisdom of his books. None of the authors had faced the problem in a way that satisfied his conscience. He felt he was on his own. He considered the Marxist-Leninist theory of expansion by revolution. He reviewed James Monroe's original statement of 1823, warning against foreign incursions in Latin America, and how it was broadened by subsequent presidents. He pondered the right of nations to lead their own internal lives and the need of the U.S., as a nation of laws, to conduct itself lawfully in its dealings with other countries. In the end he convinced himself that Cuba was, in fact, a Soviet satellite, and that the degree of Communist danger "is in direct proportion to the geographic proximity of a country to the U.S."

Now alarmed, he became disgusted when he found that nobody useful was available to hear the news that he had changed his mind about the Cuba project. Kennedy had been elected. Clearly, there was no point in sharing his private deliberations with anyone from the outgoing team. And he had been advised that Eisenhower and Kennedy had decreed a "flat prohibition" against men of his rank discussing current problems with anyone from the incoming administration.

In violation of this ruling, Mann "attempted to talk with several people to tell them that this was a very serious matter and needed immediate study because it could not be decided with the back of your hand." He even tried to penetrate the privacy of Dean Rusk, the Secretary of State designate, who was walled off in a little office in the State Department's basement until Inauguration Day. He was unable to obtain a hearing. Even later he never could decipher whether Rusk favored or opposed the venture ("It's not Rusk's nature to be very talkative").

Infiltrators Move In

On February 5, the young ex-collegian José Basulto and fourteen other infiltrators who had completed special training in Panama were assembled for a "mission briefing." The instructions were disappointingly vague. The men were told they would be spirited into Cuba to gather intelligence and train saboteurs. Their personal instructions were even less specific. One of Basulto's friends was simply ordered to "raise hell in Havana." José was to proceed to Oriente province. He gathered that "they wanted just to have an agent in Oriente." As his base he picked the main city, Santiago de Cuba, where he had friends and relatives.

The security precautions were formidable. Escorted by "Carl," the men were flown in a chartered DC-3 to Virginia. They landed in what appeared to be a Navy base and were issued civilian clothes with all labels removed. A twin-engine Aero Commander took them to Baltimore, where Basulto met his case officer, "Tom," in a downtown hotel. Together the two men flew to Boston on a commercial flight. The idea was to build a cover story for José: he was to be able to document that he was kicked out of Boston College. Tom visited school officials, who said they would cooperate, and then instructed José to fly to New Orleans, where he had relatives. The Mardi Gras was on, and José had a marvelous time. Eventually he flew to Miami and boarded a Cubana Airlines flight to Havana. His story was that he was going home to continue his studies because he was fed up with the American priests in Boston. Nobody even questioned him.

Maybe "Carl" had been too pessimistic, after all. José kept thinking about how the CIA operative had shaken his head gloomily in Baltimore and said, "If this goddamned operation comes off, it'll be a goddamned miracle." So far, though, the CIA had been meticulous and clever. If José had been picked up and tortured, he could have revealed little of value to the enemy.

Jorge Recarey, a high-strung former University of Havana student, did not make it to Cuba so easily. He and about twenty other infiltrators were taken from Panama to an abandoned motel near the Air Force base at Homestead, Florida, where they waited for more than a month. Twice a day they jogged and fell out for calisthenics and push-ups under the supervision of three CIA men. They were not allowed to leave the grounds. The confinement bored them, and the waiting increased their tension. They worried especially that the clothes the CIA would issue them for landing in Cuba would give them away.

One morning at two o'clock, Jorge and two of his friends, all in their teens, sneaked out, walked three miles to a private residence, and were given permission to use the phone. They called friends in Miami and asked them to bring clothes that would look inconspicuous in Cuba. Jorge wound up with recognizably American slacks, shirt and underwear, but he hoped they might be sufficiently neutral to escape detection. His friend Edgar Sopo got a complete outfit of Cuban clothes, including a windbreaker. While they waited, Jorge called his mother, who had immigrated to Arizona, and told her he was about to leave for Cuba. The CIA men at the motel would have been furious if they had known about his massive breach of security, but they never found out.* By four o'clock, Jorge and his friends sneaked back into their quarters and hid their new clothes.

In mid-February, Jorge was given two thousand Cuban pesos, a fake driver's license and a fake work permit, both under the name of Julio César Blanco, and was driven with four other infiltrators to a dock at Key West. A tall American gave them Dramamine against seasickness—it was cold, and the water could get very rough at this time of year—and they boarded a V-20 speedboat captained by Eugénio Rolando Martínez.† It was the first of Jorge's seven attempts to reach Cuba.

He knew he was in good hands. Martínez, only a little over five feet tall, was known as "Musculito" because he was so strong. He moved fast and talked in rapid staccato bursts. He had run a hotel in Cuba and had no boat experience when he signed up with a CIA recruiter named "Clarence" to run the *Riffer*, a twenty-six-foot racing prowl out of the Safe Harbor Marina, which was guarded by sheriff's deputies. In all his

---

*The CIA was not only concerned about the Castro agents who were known to be swarming all over Florida. The presence of Brigade members on U.S. soil violated several laws, so the agency was equally nervous about the State Department, the Justice Department, and the FBI, which wanted all the CIA Cubans kept outside the country.

† This was the Martínez who was ultimately convicted as one of Howard Hunt's Watergate burglars. During the Bay of Pigs period, Martínez knew Hunt only by reputation as the legendary "Eduardo" who represented the American presence to the Cuban exile community in Miami. Hunt and the exiles knew Martínez as a daredevil captain, a hero who skippered innumerable infiltration trips. Martínez himself did not know how many. He was amazed when a CIA man told him many years later that records showed he had made 354 trips between 1960 and 1969.

many trips, Musculito had never been caught. He always got to his rendezvous points in Cuba at dusk, well before the arranged hour. Professional fighters and boatmen did not impress him. "You can't fight a war of liberation with professionals," he said. Motivation. That's what counted.

It didn't prevent slipups, however. On Jorge Recarey's first four trips, Musculito missed the signals of the local farmers who were supposed to receive them but were still inexperienced at the task. Another time, everybody aboard passed out, because the wind was blowing carbon monoxide fumes under the canvas where the men tried to protect themselves against the cold; at the last minute they were rescued by the U.S. Coast Guard. On still another trip, Captain Martínez fell overboard in the high seas; miraculously the boat found him in the dark five minutes later, when he had already taken off all of his clothes. On the sixth trip Martínez' boat capsized just off the Cuban coast. He swam ashore and, despite the risk of discovery by the wrong people, built a huge bonfire. It was the kind of gutsy, almost mad maneuver that endeared him to his passengers. Friendly fishermen rescued him while Jorge Recarey, on an accompanying boat, decided it would be best to try landing still another time.

When Recarey finally made it on the seventh try, the farmers who met his boat in rowboats, stripped to their underwear, were so happy that they cried. Every night for more than two weeks they had risked their lives and waved flashlights on the beaches. Finally the very first team of the Brigade had landed. They were at Arcos de Canasi, where La Habana and Matanzas provinces meet on the north coast. The infiltrators named it Punto Fundora in honor of Jorge Fundora, a local landowner who met the many infiltration missions that landed there—and was executed for his efforts.

Building a Navy

When the time came for the CIA to shop for a navy, the logical source was the García Line Corporation with offices in Havana and at 17 Battery Place in New York City. The twenty-five-year-old shipping company was the only Cuban line still running rice and sugar out of Havana, and its six freighters provided perfect cover. They were suitably unmilitary: small (2,400 tons), slow, old, less than perfectly scrubbed and not in the best of repair. Their captains were Spaniards who had no love for Castro. Neither had the owners, Alfredo García, then eighty-three, and his five sons. The family's political sympathies had been tested. Despite the great risks, one of the ships, the *Río Escondido,* had been "exfiltrating" anti-Castro leaders whom the CIA wanted to spirit out of Cuba.

The company's most active and enterprising partner, Eduardo García, was summoned to a meeting with two CIA agents in an East Side New York apartment. It was the first of many such encounters for Eduardo in many apartments in New York and Washington and, once, in a public park. The government men never identified themselves except by first names and warned him never to discuss anything over the telephone.

The agents told Eduardo they wanted to charter his ships. The vessels were to go to New Orleans, Mobile and other American ports to be loaded with ammunition, aviation gasoline and other supplies, then to an unnamed Central American port to take on men and then to an unnamed Cuban port. Eduardo listened quietly. He was a heavyset, dark-skinned man, filled with contempt for Castro and Communism, a young Sydney Greenstreet, nimble on his feet and with his speech. He had a puckish sense of humor that he liked to hide. When Eduardo listened to a business proposition, he was totally without expression and sat as impassively as an immovable round Buddha.

Eduardo was fascinated by the CIA men's proposition and decided he would not hold out for a profit. He did not, however, want his ships sunk. He kept his face impassive and said he would not make his ships available unless he knew how the landings were going to be protected. He sounded as if he meant it. His briefers then revealed that there would be "air cover" and destroyers with guns of twenty-mile range. The planes would be "American combat" craft. All Castro planes would be destroyed. An "American Navy ship" would bring landing craft to pick up the troops from the García freighters and carry them to the beaches. The CIA men were "very enthusiastic" and pointed out that no landings staged by Americans had "ever failed."

Eduardo was convinced. He agreed to furnish his ships for "direct operating costs" of six hundred dollars per day per ship, plus the cost of fuel, food and personnel. No papers were ever signed to document the deal. Eduardo and his family did not think this was necessary, because they were dealing with the United States government in a "tremendous undertaking." Eduardo liked the agents he was dealing with and "trusted implicitly their word."

In line with Bissell's "spookish" ways, the Joint Chiefs of Staff were left in the dark about the CIA's expansion into the navy and amphibious-warfare business. The Chairman, General Lyman L. Lemnitzer, soft-spoken and known for conciliatory board-room diplomacy, had heard vague rumors about a "most highly secret" operation and made it his business not to inquire about clinical details. This remained his policy even after the Commander in Chief Atlantic (CINCLANT), Admiral Robert Dennison, roared at him across the scrambler phone from Norfolk, Virginia, fleet headquarters, "Lem, I want to tell you a story!"

Dennison, whose scraggy, scarred face and bulbous nose were in keeping with his choleric temper, had been influential in the White House as President Harry Truman's naval aide and was not easily pushed around. The story he told Lemnitzer had made him furious.

Two civilians had just called on Commander Romolo Cousins, the captain of the U.S.S. *San Marcos,* a 450-foot LSD (landing ship dock) anchored at Vieques Island, the naval base off Puerto Rico. The civilians wanted to requisition the vessel for the CIA so that it could be loaded with some landing craft to be taken to a rendezvous off Cuba. The vice-admiral who reported this visit to Dennison thought he'd better release the LSD.

"The hell you are!" Dennison had told him.*

Lemnitzer refused to let the story upset him. "I'll get hold of Allen Dulles and Cabell and get them to brief you," he said.

More than a month later, Bissell appeared in Dennison's office and gave the admiral a sketchy outline of the project. Dennison was "appalled." He wanted to know what the Cuban civilian reaction was likely to be. What about his own responsibilities to protect the U.S. Naval base at Guantánamo? What about evacuating U.S. nationals from Cuba? Bissell was so noncommittal that Dennison suspected the CIA had never considered such details. His fury did not abate, and on December 20 he sent Washington 119 questions about the operation. Only twelve were answered.

At that, Dennison knew more than his boss, the Chief of Naval Operations, Admiral Burke, known as "Thirty-Knot Burke" because he liked to operate his ship at top speed when he was a destroyer captain. With his heavy, lumbering walk and his pipe emitting clouds reminiscent of a battleship smokestack, the trumpet-voiced admiral still looked and acted the part of the fearless skipper. He had known that the CIA was supporting guerrillas and landing supplies in Cuba, but in November his own intelligence people reported particularly "strange" activities in Guatemala. It looked as if quite a few people were involved, including possibly Americans.

*The LSD was finally released February 10, 1961, by a request from the Joint Chiefs.

Burke asked his spies to spy on the CIA spies, because the idea of a big operation struck him as "odd." His men found out that the CIA was indeed involved, but Burke could not learn "in what."

Eduardo García was having second thoughts about his ships. His father had given permission to use them for the invasion, but the old man was still in Cuba and did not want to leave his homeland. Eduardo and his brothers told him they would withdraw their offer of the ships unless Alfredo agreed to join the rest of the family, who by now were all safely in exile in Miami. Finally the old man relented. Eduardo sent him a Teletype message to provide him with a cover to make the trip. The message said that the line was about to acquire another ship and he was needed in Miami on January 17 to sign the papers.

Eduardo also had renewed worries about his ships' safety. At a meeting with his CIA friends in a "secure" apartment in the northwest section of Washington, he was again reassured that "the beaches would be protected by American planes" and that an aircraft carrier would be part of the operation. Eduardo was impressed, but he had other men to think about, too.

"I'm a practical man," he said, "and I have respect for my people. Some of them have worked for us for twenty years. They're merchant marine people. They like it quiet and easygoing, that's why they picked that life. I want machine guns on the bridges, bows and sterns of all the ships."

The CIA men laughed. Who, they asked, was going to attack a fleet protected by American sea and air power?

This time Eduardo could not be moved. "We're going to have all that gasoline stored on deck," he said. "Even if a Piper Cub comes along with a twenty-two gun, the whole thing can go 'boom!' "

Eventually, the agents agreed to have machine guns installed for Eduardo's "peace of mind."

The ship owner mentioned that he needed gunners to man his defenses. Obviously, this was a job that his merchant seamen were not qualified to do. The agents said he should make his own arrangements with former Premier Miró Cardona, of the Frente. Eduardo met with Miró, who said he would not make gunners available just for ships. Whereupon García produced a very personal solution that pleased his sense of political justice and allowed him to play a joke on Miró, the anti-Batistano.

Which exiles, he asked himself, were most fiercely motivated to fight Castro and most wanted by him as arch-"criminals"? Why, men who had worked as executioners for Batista! So Eduardo hired some thirty men of precisely the background most shunned by the CIA and by Miró, and appointed them to be his defense force. After all, they were experienced marksmen, they were "entitled to a chance to fight," and Miró "didn't have a monopoly on the revolution."

Miró and García also disagreed about the ships' crews. The Frente leader did not wish to entrust his fleet to merchant men. He wanted the crews to be selected from the Brigade.

"Get other ships!" García snapped.

Miró was furious, but Eduardo insisted that military people wouldn't "take care" of his ships. His own captains would be the only ones allowed to operate them. Miró had no choice but to concede.

Nobody questioned that Eduardo was coming along with the expedition. "I'm going to be in charge of my ships," he said.

An elite group of specialists converged for training on an isolated beach near the U.S. naval base on the island of Vieques, off Puerto Rico. Andy Pruna, nineteen, had come from Martinique. He wanted to be an artist. He admired Gauguin and had decided, like the master, to paint on the Leeward Islands. Lean, handsome, six feet two, Pruna had done well in national swimming competition in his native Cuba and was also an accomplished diver. He was financing his painting by diving for archaeological relics when he heard rumors of infiltration and sabotage operations against Castro. He headed for Miami and ran into José Alonso, who had been clerk of a criminal court in Cuba and had qualified for the swimming team of the 1960 Olympics. Alonso had volunteered to assemble a UDT (underwater demolition team). He was forty-one, elderly for a diver, but looked ten or even fifteen years younger. Together he and Pruna recruited ten other frogmen and started practicing for the invasion in a Miami swimming pool.

Pruna "didn't even know what the hell the CIA was." The $150-a-month pay seemed like a lot for what he "wanted to do for nothing anyway." Nobody in his group minded the many endless forms they had to fill out, the lie detector tests or the psychological interviews administered by American civilians who seemed to have no names. Arriving on Vieques, they saw U.S. Navy planes bombing a beach, Marines storming ashore from sleek landing craft, helicopters whirring overhead.

"Jesus Christ, they got everything!" Pruna said. He and his teammates felt certain they were about to become part of the military muscle they were watching. They were very excited. To their amazement, they were driven to a beach which was deserted except for a few tents, some coconut trees, and "off limits" signs. They were told the American forces were forbidden to come near them. The U.S. exercises were routine maneuvers and had no connection with the Cubans' mission. The frogmen were confined to training on their separate beach, their contacts limited to "Jimmy," "Wolf," a few other CIA operators, and some fifty Cubans who were getting acquainted with three LCU's (landing craft utility) and four LCVP's (landing craft vehicle and personnel). The little craft looked ancient and woebegone to Pruna and his friends. Their euphoria evaporated.

The landing craft were commanded by Silvio Pérez, a fourteen-year veteran of the Cuban Navy, short, wiry, round-faced, with curly red hair and a sunny disposition that seemed never to desert him. He had worked in a Miami fiberglass factory until he volunteered at Cuban naval headquarters in the Arrowhead Motel on Twenty-seventh Avenue. One night he and his crews were driven in an unmarked rental truck to a dock on the Miami River to board an antique converted LCI (landing craft infantry). Two men promptly jumped ship because they "weren't going to go to Cuba to get killed." Pérez thought that perhaps they had inside information; nobody had told *him* where they were headed.

That night they went nowhere, because the LCI developed engine trouble. A week later they set off for Vieques, where they practiced daily, with and without the frogmen: sailing formation at night, landing on the beach, placing markers on landing sites. The trainees slept on the ships. A Cuban officer from Miami came with Cuban flags for the little craft and even the Cuban national anthem on tape recorders. He also brought three officers who were to replace the commanders of the LCU's. The arrivals had once been friendly to Castro. The crews had mostly been Batista sympathizers and refused to serve under the new men.

"We kill those guys," they said. The offensive officers were flown back to Miami.

Pérez thought his fleet was shaping up. There was room for thirty-six infantrymen on each of the LCVP's. The wider LCU's could accommodate the Brigade's five tanks, the trucks, jeeps, one bulldozer and three thousand gallons of gasoline each. Fifteen tank and truck drivers arrived to take charge of the vehicles. Pérez' ships were unarmed, however, and eventually a spokesman for the crews told him, "We won't go to Cuba without guns."

Pérez so informed "Wolf" and the other American trainers. They insisted the ships didn't need guns. "You'll have all the air support you need," they said. Pérez took this view back to his men, who said, "We won't go!" The CIA men watched the confrontation from a distance.

Eventually each LCU was equipped with two .50-caliber machine guns, and the LCVP's got some .30-caliber machine guns.*

Suddenly these preparations ceased and all the Cubans on Vieques were blessed with an unexpected ten-day vacation in Miami. Newspapers had reported that Cubans were being trained in Puerto Rico, a violation of U.S. law. Pérez and his men were told to clean up their beach, pick up every scrap of paper and remove every trace of human presence. While the men enjoyed their leave, the press was escorted around. Pérez thought the respite came just in time. Even the proximity of a cow near the beach had been arousing sexual interest among his sailors.

Once the men returned to their beach, training continued all but around the clock. The frogmen were in the water four hours every morning, two or three hours in the afternoon, and another two or three hours starting at 2 A.M. They practiced landing on rubber rafts. They learned about C-3 and C-4 underwater explosives and 02 underwater breathing equipment. They made practice raids on the LCU's and learned to make "kitchen explosives" whose principal ingredients were charcoal and urine. They practiced with machine guns, submachine guns, grenades, magnetic mines, and knives.

The CIA trainers were not always in agreement. "Bob" taught them how to throw knives. He was replaced by "Steve," who said a knife must never be thrown "because if you don't hit the guy, he's going to kill you." Pruna asked him, "What do you think our chances are?" Steve said, "You're not killers, you'll probably all get killed."

Assembling a Paramilitary Command

Unconventional warfare was Grayston Lynch's profession. An oil driller's son from the tiny town of Victoria in South Texas, "Gray" had enlisted in the Army at fifteen by lying about his age. He landed with the Normandy invasion on D-Day, received his commission without benefit of Officer Candidate School and then found his home in Special Forces, specializing in covert amphibious landings and guerrilla operations. When he retired as a captain late in 1960, to join the CIA with a six-month contract at ten thousand a year, the transition was "practically no change at all"; he had just returned from Laos, where he had operated in unfriendly territory wearing civilian clothes.

---

*In 1977, Pérez, now a lieutenant commander in the U.S. Navy, said, "Nobody would be alive today without the guns."

He looked the part of the "PM" (paramilitary). When he entered a room, he seemed to fill it, though he was only six feet tall. His wide, round head was anchored via an almost equally wide neck to a wide, round body that suggested pure muscle. Aboard the LCI, where he was to become the principal American presence at the Bay of Pigs, he could barely squeeze through the stairway. Yet he moved well, cursed sparingly, observed and remembered everything in sight. He felt comfortable following orders but had learned to improvise when he was on his own and never hesitated. It had not been planned that way, of course, but Gray became the closest thing to an on-the-spot military commander that the Cuban operation ever had. Hollywood could not have cast a better personality. Gray suggested what the operation needed most: indestructibility.

He revered Hawkins, his new boss. To him, the colonel was "a brilliant man, a brain." Gray considered him "just the easiest man to talk to, quiet, confident, a leader." He was particularly impressed by qualities that he lacked himself: "Hawkins was a very handsome gentleman with a beautiful command of the English language. His writing was beautiful, like poetry. His choice of words was fantastic. If you wanted to go into an operation and visualize the leader you would want, you couldn't ask for anybody better."

Hawkins introduced Gray to William ("Rip") Robertson,* and the two men became instant blood brothers. Rip revered nobody. To him, headquarters was "city hall"; its functionaries were "feather merchants." Another Texan, he had played football at Vanderbilt University and had come out of the Pacific battles of World War II as a Marine captain. Transferring to the CIA, he worked with its miniature exile force during the Guatemala coup of 1954. There he sent a pilot to bomb a Soviet ship, but a British ship was sunk instead. Lloyds of London was upset, and it cost the agency about $1.5 million to settle the claim. Ever afterward, Rip was a black sheep in the eyes of J. C. King, head of the CIA's Western Hemisphere Division. He drifted into gold mining in Nicaragua, became friendly with the reigning dictator, Anastasio Somoza. When the CIA needed a staging base in that country for the Bay of Pigs, Rip was smuggled back onto the agency's payroll behind King's back.

Anyone could tell at a glance that he was a less conventional unconventional warrior than Gray. He was taller, six foot two, also of massive build, his sun-drenched skin so wizened that the Cubans would call him "the Alligator." His clothes were permanently wrinkled, too. He liked loud Hawaiian shirts and such informal headgear as baseball

*Robertson died in 1970, apparently from the aftereffects of malaria contracted in Vietnam.

caps or wide-brimmed straw sombreros. To men under his command, he rarely talked; he bellowed, and they loved it. Ambling around in his slouch, he punched them playfully but not gently in the belly and was ever available for hand-to-hand-combat practice with a knife or any other handy weapon.

Orders from Washington were not sacred to him. When his CIA bosses instructed him not to step on Cuban soil during gun-running missions to the underground, Rip operated ashore anyway. Questioned about such breaches of etiquette, he grinned and said, "Oh, we're just training, just training."

At Quarters Eye, Hawkins told Gray and Rip in vague terms about amphibious operations against Cuba, but not about an invasion. Once Gray had finished training the frogmen outside New Orleans, he and Rip were to pump massive quantities of weapons quickly into the Cuban underground. The CIA strategists felt rather desperate about this mission. The supply runs by Cuban exiles having mostly failed, the agency wanted to make up for lost opportunities and get the job done professionally and on a bigger scale, this time by Americans working out of a secret CIA base in Key West.

Gray and Rip were pleasantly surprised by the scope of their Florida station. The CIA had taken over the large corrugated-metal warehouse, docks and terminal of the defunct ferry that used to run cars and passengers to Havana, and it named the enterprise Mineral Carriers Limited. According to the cover story, the company was drilling for oil in the Marquesas keys (a legitimate oil company actually was exploring there). Its two converted World War II LCI's, the *Blagar* and the *Barbara J.*, were supposedly engaged in hydrographic and geological research. The State Department was unaware of this illegal operation on U.S. soil, but Gray soon realized that "all the people in the Keys knew exactly what was going on."

The ferry warehouse sheltered enormous stockpiles of small arms and ammunition in watertight fifty-man and 100-man packs, along with radios and demolition equipment, all "sanitized" (identifying markings removed). With Gray taking charge of the *Blagar* and Rip of the *Barbara J.*, the ships kept circling around all of Cuba, dropping off their cargo. To Gray it was a boring routine, "almost like United Parcel, the delivery service," but the ships' crews troubled him.

They had once been all-Cuban, including the captains, but their performance was impaired by imperfect seamanship and political squabbling, so the CIA had superimposed American crews and captains on each ship. Each had a Cuban and an American cook who prepared separate menus. The duplicate effort worked well in the kitchen.

Elsewhere, relations between the two nationalities were strained. Gray, however, was worried by a more ominous built-in weakness.

Feeling uneasy about assigning either Navy or civilian seamen to the American crews, the CIA had compromised and hauled in personnel from the Military Sea Transportation Service, an obscure arm of the Navy that transports cargo. These were competent sailors, but they were men of peace. They liked the serenity of predictable schedules. The safety of their ships was the captains' highest concern. Hostilities were not part of their world. They had been told they would be shuttling around Cuba but would stay in international waters—three miles off the coast at that time.

Rip quickly encountered difficulties with his American captain. The closer this merchant man sailed toward danger zones, the more he smelled of alcohol. His speech became so slurred that his orders were not always unmistakable. When the ship made a side trip to knock out the power station for Santiago de Cuba (Rip demolished only one leg of the power tower because of faulty intelligence, and the power went off only briefly), the captain refused to sink the damaged catamaran that had been used for the final approach and was now slowing the *Barbara J.* down. He eyed the little boat proudly. "It's part of history," he insisted. After that trip, the Cuban crew went on a hunger strike to protest the captain's drinking, so Rip got him fired, and the first mate, George, an Irishman from Brooklyn, took over.

Gray liked his own captain, Sven Ryberg, but he felt sorry for this easygoing sailor of Scandinavian descent. Sven, who had one glass eye, had no idea what he was getting into. Gray realized that he and Rip were about to join some sort of amphibious operation involving the Brigade training in Guatemala. He felt that the four .50-caliber machine guns on the *Blagar* were inadequate. He wanted twelve. The captain said, "I don't think we should, it makes the crew nervous." Gray could tell that Ryberg was talking more about the American sailors than about the Cubans. He had the guns installed anyway, and factory crews from RCA outfitted both LCI's with five separate radio systems. That made *him* a good deal less nervous.

Enter the Joint Chiefs

When the Joint Chiefs decided to appoint a committee "to study in general hypothetical terms what might be done to unseat Castro" it had no knowledge of the plans already in motion. The committee was run by Brigadier General David W. Gray, chief of the Joint Subsidiary

Activities Division of the Joint Chiefs. Gray called it the "ash and trash section." It maintained liaison between the chiefs and the CIA, the FBI and other agencies about hush-hush matters, including paramilitary operations.

Gray was the prototype of a superior staff officer. He had planned amphibious operations in World War II, had parachuted into Lebanon and had been an associate professor at West Point. He had a bulldog face, with matching pugnacious manner and voice. His mind could order complexities quickly and easily. He would stay at the Pentagon until 2 A.M. to help the secretaries collate important papers and kept meticulous notes on just about everything he said or heard.*

The committee produced a paper, JCSM-44-61, outlining six alternatives: (1) economic warfare, (2) blockade, (3) infiltration of a guerrilla force, (4) a guerrilla force with United States back-up, (5) air and naval warfare with no invasion, (6) all-out invasion. It concluded that nothing less than step No. 4 would work. The study remained a "white paper," which meant it was an internal working document that "didn't turn green"—i.e., it was not put on green paper like official JCS documents.† It recommended the formation of an interdepartmental group to study all alternatives so that the President could decide on an overall plan.‡ It was the kind of systematizing that the military called "S.O.P." (standard operating procedure) and the CIA and the incoming innovators of the Kennedy administration scorned as "red tape." Red tape meant bureaucratic delay, and that was not in the Kennedy lexicon.

On a snowy Sunday, January 22, two days after President Kennedy's inauguration, Gray was asked to brief top officials of the new administration on the JCS study. Rusk, Robert McNamara, Robert Kennedy, Chester Bowles, Dulles and Lemnitzer were present. So was John Connally, the Secretary of the Navy, who stuck out his hand at Gray and announced, "I'm Connally." Gray presented the study in the form of charts. It was clear that getting rid of Castro was high on the new administration's priority list. Yet the meeting broke up quickly. The men were "not happy" when they heard that American forces were considered necessary.§

*After the Bay of Pigs, General Gray personally destroyed all his notes on the operation in his office shredder on order of General Lemnitzer.

†The next and highest grade of JCS paper was the "red stripe," which meant that it was an approved document; each page bore a diagonal red stripe.

‡According to the Taylor Report, "this recommendation reached the Secretary of Defense but appears to have been lost in the activities arising out of the change in administration."

§At an all-morning transition meeting in the Cabinet Room of the White House on the 19th, the top echelon of the incoming administration had been handed the project with a much more militant sendoff by Eisenhower, the old warrior. The only participant who made notes throughout was the stately Clark M. Clifford, special counsel to President Harry S. Truman and later Secretary

On January 28, at a full meeting of the National Security Council, President Kennedy ordered for the first time that the chiefs review the CIA plans. Admiral Burke felt uneasy when he heard that the military were only to "advise," that they were not to become "involved" and that they were "specifically forbidden to talk to subordinates." He did not dwell on the fact that under Eisenhower the operation had grown for a year without any military appraisal. He felt the inexperienced new politicians were proceeding with excessive secrecy which would take "a great deal of expertise away from the operation." He liked operations to be "staffed." The new men seemed to distrust the military's ability to keep secrets, and the admiral resented that.

Almost immediately, General Gray heard from an old friend, Lieutenant General Earl ("Buzz") Wheeler, who was director of the JCS's own staff. Gray was ordered to form a committee with four other officers and study the CIA plan on behalf of the chiefs. There was an army colonel who had won the Congressional Medal of Honor in World War II and was a specialist in tactics; a Marine colonel knowledgeable on logistics; an Air Force colonel who had flown B-26s; and an Army intelligence specialist who had served in Cuba.

Gray thought the committee was "awfully small" for such a job, but he understood about the secrecy. They all "had to swear up and down you wouldn't tell anybody anything," not even within the JCS staff. Gray's own executive officer became upset when he found his boss was not "cutting him in" on something big that was afoot.

The committee went to Quarters Eye and "expected to be handed a plan thick with documents and appendices." Instead, they met six very friendly CIA men who wore civilian clothes but looked and sounded like former military officers. Gray paid no attention to their names, because he was certain they would be "pseudonyms." The CIA men brought not a single piece of paper into the room except for a map of Cuba, devoid of any markings.

Despite his frequent dealings with the agency, Gray was "surprised and shocked" to get nothing more than "a verbal rundown." Apparently the agency men had never assembled their ideas in one place. The team from the Joint Chiefs "had to pull it out of them." They spent one afternoon at it, sitting around a conference table, scribbling furiously

---

of Defense under Lyndon B. Johnson. Sitting at the head of the table, close to the door of the Oval Office, Eisenhower, with Kennedy on his left, made it clear that the project was going very well and that it was the new administration's "responsibility" to do "whatever is necessary" to bring it to a successful conclusion.

Clifford detected no "reluctance or hesitation." Indeed, he reminded Kennedy in a memorandum on the 24th that Ike had said "it was the policy of this government" to help the exiles "to the utmost" and that this effort should be "continued and accelerated."

into stenographers' notebooks. When they returned to the Pentagon, they pooled their notes, "wrote a plan" for themselves covering some twenty-five double-spaced typewritten pages, and started studying it all but around the clock. They were told their task was "very urgent" because the rainy season was approaching, Cubans were being trained as MIG pilots, and tides made landings possible only on certain days.

They had received what came to be known as the "Trinidad plan," calling for a landing at dawn at Trinidad, a shore city in southern Cuba reputed to be a hotbed of opposition to Castro. The committee was told that the Brigade was really "a cadre," that every platoon leader could lead a company, every company commander could handle a battalion. With the help of local volunteers, the CIA expected the Brigade to double in size within four days. Airborne troops would blow up bridges over the deep gorges leading into the area. In the nearby Escambray Mountains, established guerrilla troops would be ready to help.

Gray's group concluded that the Brigade could last for up to four days, given complete surprise and complete air supremacy, which meant to Gray that the enemy couldn't have "any airplanes, period." Success would depend on uprisings in Cuba, and the committee felt it had inadequate data to judge how significant these would be or how quickly they would materialize.

When Gray reported his findings to Buzz Wheeler, the two friends had "a heated discussion."

"You've got to have an overall evaluation of success," Wheeler said.

"I don't know what to say," Gray responded.

Wheeler kept pressing him for some idea of the "overall" prospects. Gray remained reluctant.

"What about 'fair'?" asked Wheeler.

"All right," said Gray.

When they discussed what "fair" meant, Gray said he thought the chances were thirty to seventy.

"Thirty in favor and seventy against?" asked Wheeler.

"Yes."

But no figures were used in the Gray committee's report.*

When General Gray briefed the chiefs on his findings on January 31 he found the reception friendly. They had read his report and asked few questions. He emphasized the need for air strikes and pointed out all key locations on a map which he brought along in a case equipped with

*In 1977, General Gray was still severely troubled about his failure to have insisted that figures be used. He felt that one of the key misunderstandings in the entire project was the misinterpretation of the word "fair" as used by the Joint Chiefs. At the time, it never occurred to Gray that lack of figures might lead to a misunderstanding: "We thought other people would think that 'a fair chance' would mean 'not too good.' "

an especially secure lock. It was decided that the committee's report should "turn green." It was not "red striped" because it was considered too sensitive to be entrusted to the chiefs' filing system.

On February 3, the chiefs sent the White House and the CIA the cagily worded JCSM-57-61, "Military Evaluation of the CIA Paramilitary Plan—Cuba." It advised that "the likelihood of achieving initial military success" was "favorable" but "that ultimate success will depend upon political factors, i.e. a sizable popular uprising or substantial follow-up forces." It also said: "This plan has a fair chance of ultimate success and, even if it does not achieve immediately the full results desired, could contribute to the eventual overthrow of the Castro regime."

The chiefs left themselves another large loophole: "Assessment of the combat worth of assault forces is based upon second- and third-hand reports, and certain logistic aspects of the plan are highly complex and critical to the initial success. For these reasons, an independent evaulation of the combat effectiveness of the invasion forces and detailed analysis of logistics plans should be made by a team of army, naval and Air Force officers."

General David M. Shoup, the Commandant of the Marine Corps, "spent a lot of sleepless hours over this", because there was no plan "if there was something unforeseen, an act of God or something." Barring that, he felt the force could "accomplish their objective" *if* there was air superiority and *if* there were popular uprisings. He told his colleagues, "If this kind of an operation can be done with this kind of force, with this much training and knowledge about it, then we are wasting our time in our divisions; we ought to go on leave for three months out of four."

The general was not being sarcastic, and the other chiefs were not overly startled. Shoup had a reputation. He had strong dovish inclinations, but was a combat hero of stature; he had won the Congressional Medal of Honor at Tarawa. He was a feared disciplinarian, but also an intellectual. He read books that generals usually pass up, and he wrote poetry.

To him, uprisings were not part of the mission. They *were* the mission. No "military man would ever think that this force could overthrow Castro without support. They could never expect anything but annihilation." The distribution of weapons to dissidents was the key. Shoup was persuaded of the operation's viability when he learned that the chance of uprisings was "increasing" and that arms packs for thirty thousand men were part of the buildup.* The planners "wouldn't be

*Packs for fifteen thousand men were actually on ships and headed for the beaches on D-Day, along with recoilless rifles, mortars, jeeps, and trucks.

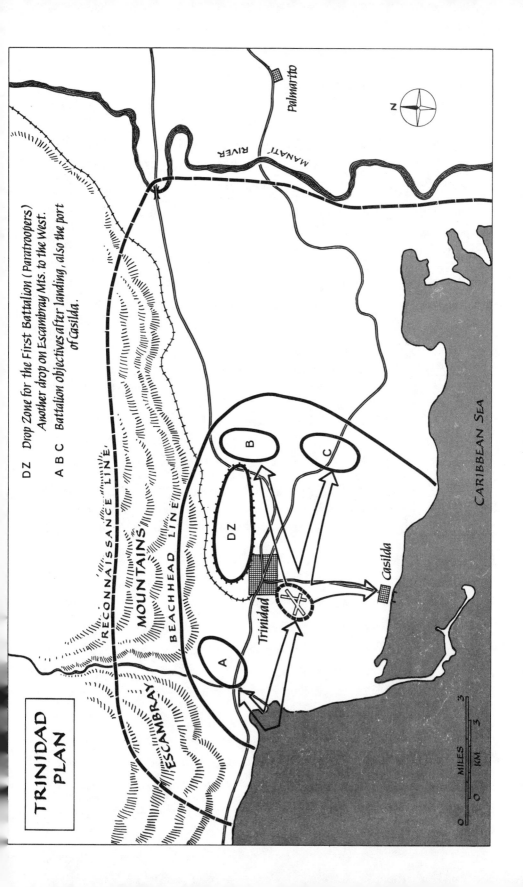

TRINIDAD PLAN

DZ Drop Zone for the First Battalion (Paratroopers)
     Another drop on Escambray Mts. to the West.

A B C Battalion objectives after landing, also the port
        of Casilda.

N

RECONNAISSANCE LINE

ESCAMBRAY MOUNTAINS

BEACHHEAD LINE

MANATÍ RIVER

Palmarito

DZ

B

C

A

Trinidad

Casilda

CARIBBEAN SEA

MILES 0 3
KM   0 3

taking thirty thousand additional rifles if we didn't think there was going to be somebody to use them." He believed CIA assurances that Cubans were waiting, even pleading for arms.

In his own mind, Admiral Burke was less sanguine. He thought that the CIA proposal, as pieced together by General Gray and his colleagues, was "weak" and "sloppy." There was no telling who was going to do what, because there was "no logistics annex." Burke had little faith in a military concept that came from men who had no military command experience. And he greatly resented having to be his own file clerk for his Cuba papers. Nobody else was supposed to touch them. After a while, there were so many that the admiral could not keep them straight or retrieve a paper when he needed it.

The President was briefed on the chiefs' appraisal in the Cabinet Room of the White House. Dick Bissell did the briefing—then and at the subsequent White House meetings. General Gray, seated on a chair against the wall behind General Lemnitzer, who was at the Cabinet table, thought that Bissell's briefing technique was "very peculiar." He seemed to address himself to specific items out of context. "He never said, 'This is the plan.' He never walked through it step by step." General Gray was distressed. He would have preferred "a well-rounded discussion."

The President's all too evident lack of enthusiasm also bothered Gray. As the meeting broke up, Kennedy said to Bissell, "Dick, remember I reserve the right to cancel this right to the end." General Gray felt that the President's reserved stance took some steam out of the Pentagon effort. "If he had said, 'We're going to go,' a little more intensity would have gone into it."

CHAPTER THREE

Reappraisal and Momentum

Conflicting Assessments

The CIA was of a divided mind about the power and popularity of Castro's revolution. On January 27, Sherman Kent, as chairman of the CIA's Board of National Estimates, sent Dulles a memorandum entitled "Is Time on Our Side in Cuba?" It was classified "secret" and—without his knowing it, since Kent and his board were not "witting" to the invasion plans—supported the argument that the project should be expedited or abandoned. It concluded: "Castro's position in Cuba is likely to grow stronger rather than weaker as time goes on."

The board—again without knowing it—argued against the project operator's hope that the Cuban population was eager to stage an uprising against Castro: "While Castro will probably continue to lose popular support, this loss is likely to be more than counter-balanced by the regime's effective controls over daily life in Cuba and by the increasing effectiveness of its security forces for maintaining control."

Bissell had known Kent for twenty-six years. When Bissell taught economics at Yale, Kent was in the history department. Over the years they had become "very close friends." Yet Bissell did not feel odd about withholding all information on the Cuba operation from an intimate who also was cleared to receive national-security information of the greatest delicacy. The operation was sealed off, and that was that. In its isolation, it marched to the tune of a different drummer. It took hope from such fragments as CIA internal Information Report No. 00-A3177796, distributed January 30: "A private survey made recently in Cuba showed that less than 30 percent of the population is still with Fidel. In this 30 percent are included the Negroes who have always followed the strong men in Cuba, but will not fight. . . ."

Bissell would have done better reading the newspapers. Senator-elect Claiborne Pell, a former Foreign Service officer and a friend of President-elect Kennedy, had just visited Cuba and reported in the *New York Herald Tribune*: "The people of Cuba that I saw and spoke to during three or four days of quiet observation were not sullen or unhappy or dissatisfied . . . they were still tasting the satisfaction of Castro's land reform, of his nationalization of United States companies and of the other much-touted reforms put into effect by Castro. The dispossessed and disgruntled were in jail or in exile."

Persuading Kennedy

Allen Dulles was laboring diligently to generate more presidential enthusiasm. The Yale-OSS-old-boy-network connection between the holdover CIA operators and many of the incoming New Frontiersmen was not all that endeared him and his spooks to the Kennedy administration. Dulles, the consummately skillful survivor of bureaucratic skirmishes, moved quickly to build his bridges to the new White House. He adopted precisely the most rewarding tactics.

It was the perfect opening for the old man, troubled by gout and in the waning days of his career, to bask in his own right at the summit of government, out of the shadow of his forceful, even more prestige-encrusted brother, Foster. It was hard to think of Allen Dulles as a deferential kid brother, but the highest officials on the inside during the Eisenhower days knew that the sibling relationship frequently left Allen on the sidelines. Time and again, these men heard Allen say at National Security Council meetings, "Yes, Mr. President, that's a tough question, but really it's up to the Secretary of State to answer it." Eisenhower would go along. John Foster Dulles was his right arm. Ike felt comfortable saying, "All right, Foster, well, what do you think?"

No more. With the elder Dulles and the general gone, the way was clear for Allen finally to make the most of his status. He was, after all—in Kennedy's phrase—"a legend." Dulles had gloried in being, with J. Edgar Hoover at the FBI, among Kennedy's first job appointments. And the new administration was not three weeks in office when he reserved the private dining room of the Alibi Club for a very intimate dinner. The Alibi Club was so exclusive that most Washingtonians had never heard of it. The occasion was jolly and broke important ice.

Dulles led a delegation of the CIA's top ten people. From the White House came some twelve men of the new inner council. Ted Sorensen was there. Bob Amory, head of the CIA's intelligence-gathering apparatus, sat next to Larry O'Brien, the political operator who had become Postmaster General. Almost everybody (except for Sorensen, a teetotaler) had three cocktails before dinner. Afterward Dulles asked each of his operators to introduce himself and describe his work.

Bissell stopped the show. "I'm your man-eating shark," he said.

Amory thought the remark set exactly the right note for a "good hair-down" meeting. No wonder Kennedy considered Bissell "probably one of the four or five brightest guys in the whole administration." And Dulles had certainly judged correctly that the new crowd preferred to hear "a New Yorkerish type of précis" rather than a stuffy briefing. The congeniality was the ideal door-opener: "Everybody got pleasantly acquainted." From then on, Amory could phone any staff man at the White House and get a hearing just by saying, "This is Bob."

The freshly anointed White House counselors were intrigued and asked a lot of questions ("What went wrong in Indonesia in 'fifty-eight?"). The dinner did not break up until 1 A.M. Amory left thinking what a pleasant way this was to get "a head start on State," where every piece of paper was pushed around "for three days in a messenger cart" to collect clearances.

Quick response paid off with the new President. Soon Mac Bundy told Amory that the President had said, "By gosh, I don't care what it is, but if I need some material fast or an idea fast, CIA is the place I have to go. The State Department takes four or five days to answer a simple yes or no." This was music to the ears of Amory and his colleagues, and they reciprocated: "People were willing to come in at three o'clock in the morning, because they knew damn well that what they produced was read personally by the President immediately."

Eisenhower's cumbersome coordinating committees were scrapped. The intelligence business was fun again. And for Bissell, in particular, the stakes were suddenly soaring.

For a man of means (his father had left him a fortune which friends estimated to run well into six figures) Bissell was relatively ambitious. Never temperamentally compatible with the niceties of bureaucratic give-and-take, he was eager to "make policy," to be less vulnerable to second-guessing. With Allen Dulles nearing retirement, there was a chance he might be in line for the directorship. Agency insiders were not at all sure he would inherit the mantle. "He had Dick Helms and Lyman ["Kirk"] Kirkpatrick [the agency's inspector general] breathing down his neck," said one.

Bissell's chances had received an unexpected boost when another Yale man ('24), Chester Bowles, became Under Secretary of State and wanted Bissell to take the "very crucial" job of Deputy Under Secretary for Political Affairs. The men had known each other since the 1930s. For several summers the Bowles family chartered Bissell's boat in Connecticut. When Bowles became director of the Office of Price Stabilization, Bissell was one of his assistants and mediated battles between the OPA and the unyielding Treasury Secretary, John W. Snyder.

Bissell was intrigued. Perhaps he had reached his peak at the CIA. Bowles's job definitely was the policy-making kind. It might be fun to join the enemy in Foggy Bottom, the State Department, and show them how to make foreign policy move, especially under an impatient, activist young President.

Bowles felt that Bissell could handle the old-timers at State. The CIA man "knew Washington much better" than he did himself—a polite way of saying that Bissell was more incisive at cutting through bureaucratic feathering. Bowles talked to Dulles, who didn't want Bissell to leave. They argued on the phone and then argued some more. Bowles felt that "Dick wanted to get out. He was really eager to come." Finally, over lunch, Dulles agreed. But the deal was vetoed.

Kennedy phoned Bowles. Bissell, a Democrat, had come to see Kennedy the previous fall and offered campaign help on economic issues. Now Kennedy said to Bowles, "I hear you're trying to get Dick Bissell."

"I hear you're trying to get Dick Bissell."

"That's right."

"You can't have him," said the President-elect.

"Why not?"

Kennedy said, "He's going to take Allen Dulles' job on July first."*

This was how Bissell learned of his impending rise. He liked the prospect. It went without saying that he also knew he had to make good on Cuba, the new President's first major enterprise.

Arthur Schlesinger, Jr., wanted to feel his way into his new job slowly, cautiously. He had barely been named one of the several "special assistants" to the President. His duties were vague. He had taught history at Harvard, and professors carried little weight among Kennedy "pragmatists." His principal political experience had been as a speech writer in Adlai Stevenson's bid for the presidency, and the

---

*When Bowles later incurred the displeasure of the Kennedys and was shunted aside as ambassador to India, he told Bissell, "If you'd taken that job, I'd have saved you and you'd have saved me."

Governor stood—slightly suspect—to the left of Kennedy. Finally, Schlesinger's research had convinced him that government was best run by its departments, not by White House brain trusters who "threw their weight around."

Slowness and caution came hard to Schlesinger. Small of stature and owlish behind spectacles, he had quickly outgrown the sobriquet "Little Arthur" (his inevitable lot for growing up in the shadow of his distinguished historian father, Arthur Senior). Young Arthur won his first Pulitzer Prize at twenty-nine.* He was known as a phrase-maker with a vast ego, irrepressible energy and caustic wit, and as an untiring party-goer.

When Kennedy summoned him in early February and dispatched him to pay the President's respects to the presidents of six Latin-American countries, Schlesinger wanted to do a quiet, efficient job. Almost incidentally, Kennedy asked him to sound out the Latinos on how they would feel if some Cuban exiles unseated Castro. The CIA was involved in such an effort, said the President. Schlesinger should get the details from Dick Bissell.

When Castro visited Harvard two years earlier during his first and triumphant tour of the United States, Schlesinger had been impressed with Fidel's "fluent harangue" and a "disarming ability to make jokes in English." He was struck by the delight of the students and thought they saw in Castro "the hipster who in the era of the Organization Man had joyfully defied the system, summoned a dozen friends and overturned a government of wicked old men."

Bissell told Schlesinger "nothing" of the CIA plans. The two men were "old friends." They had known each other since Bissell was with the Marshall Plan in the 1940s. That was no reason to violate security. Schlesinger was "embarrassed" to question Bissell too insistently. He got the impression it would get him nowhere. Besides, as an ex-corporal in OSS during World War II, he did not qualify as a military expert.

Yet even before he left for Buenos Aires, he sent Kennedy the first of a series of memoranda cautioning against "this first dramatic foreign policy initiative." He predicted: "It would fix a malevolent image of the new Administration in the minds of millions."

---

*Schlesinger's credentials as a historian of the presidency could hardly have been more impressive. His first Pulitzer was for *The Age of Jackson*. The series *The Age of Roosevelt* was widely praised. His second Pulitzer came for the brilliant *A Thousand Days*, the Kennedy biography—1,087 pages written in fourteen months. It contains the up to now most comprehensive history of the Bay of Pigs.

Doubters

It was a time for doubts, for second thoughts.

As a meeting of the new administration's top intelligence officials was breaking up, Allen Dulles, at the head of the table and enveloped in the usual cloud of pipe smoke, turned to the man next to him and started on a subject that had never been brought before this very select group and mused, "Gee, Roger, I don't know . . ." With an air of indecision, he said he was wondering what to tell the President about unleashing the Cuban Brigade against Castro.

Roger Hilsman, a West Pointer who had known Dulles since his own OSS days as a lieutenant serving with Merrill's Marauders in China-Burma, didn't know what to say. Hilsman had become director of intelligence and research in the State Department and might be expected to know about the plans. In fact he knew almost nothing more than was in the newspapers. Alerted by Dulles' rumination that the Brigade might soon see action, he became alarmed. From his military experience he knew that an invasion of hostile shores was the most difficult of operations. If a handful of exiles were to bring down the Castro regime, the assumption had to be that the population would revolt. Was there enough evidence that this would happen?

He asked Rusk for permission to have his department's experts study the question. "I'm sorry," Rusk said, "but I can't let you. This is being too tightly held." A source of potential opposition was eliminated. Hilsman could only console himself by evidence that others, closer to the action, shared his fate. "I want you to know I'm with you on this," Bissell's man Dick Helms told him shortly afterward, "but I've been cut out."

Reappraisal

On the question of Castro's internal strength, the usual conflicting views were available within the CIA. On March 2, its "Supplement to the Current Intelligence Digest" was cautiously optimistic:

> The fact that at least some of these outbreaks [of skirmishes between Cuban guerrilla bands and government forces] involve personnel who defected from the armed forces or other government entities is indicative of a situation that could in the long run become a threat to the [Castro] regime.

On March 10, CIA internal Information Report No. CS-3/467,630 sounded a stronger note of hope:

Many people in Camaguey believe that the Castro regime is tottering and that the situation can at any moment degenerate into bloody anarchy. . . . The opposition forces in the Escambray are enjoying great popularity. Residents must line up to get small pieces of soap and so-called detergent, which is made up mainly of ashes.

But on the same day, Sherman Kent, chairman of the CIA's authoritative Board of National Estimates, sent Dulles an updated "secret" memorandum that was far less reassuring. Again titled "Is Time on Our Side in Cuba?" it again affirmed that Castro was "likely to grow stronger rather than weaker as time goes by." It again warned against attaching too much importance to the internal resistance.

To be sure [it said], the regime's once overwhelming popular support has greatly diminished in recent months and various instances of guerrilla opposition, sabotage and economic dislocation have arisen to plague it. However, we see no signs that such developments portend any serious threat to a regime which by now has established a formidable structure of control over the daily lives of the Cuban people.

The Pentagon was equally ambivalent. From February 24 to 27 the Guatemala bases were inspected by three colonels of General Gray's review committee. They wore sports clothes and were not spotted by the Cubans as Pentagon emissaries. The air expert returned with a prophetic warning: if even a single Castro aircraft with .50-caliber machine guns survived the preinvasion air strikes, it could sink most or possibly all the invasion force.

Nevertheless, the Joint Chiefs pronounced again that the Trinidad plan "could be expected to achieve initial success. Ultimate success will depend on the extent to which the initial assault serves as a catalyst for further action on the part of anti-Castro elements throughout Cuba."

The chiefs hedged further. They expressed continuing restlessness about the operation's fragility and recommended that "a military instructor experienced in operational logistics" be sent to the Brigade base immediately. This reflected a new very specific worry that had arisen in General Gray's mind. He wondered whether the invasion ships would be loaded to minimize losses in the event of unexpected attacks on the fleet. A Marine colonel was dispatched to the staging area in Nicaragua to check the logistics on the spot.

When would the President make up his mind? The signs pointed to a White House meeting on March 11. Arthur Schlesinger found the assemblage in the Cabinet Room "intimidating." The President was there, looking preoccupied, along with the Secretaries of State and

Defense, three Joint Chiefs of Staff in uniforms and decorations, and numerous assistants. Schlesinger "shrank" into a chair at the far end of the room, an act that his friends and enemies would have enjoyed watching. It took a lot to shrink the voluble Arthur.

Dulles sounded a note of urgency. "Don't forget that we have a disposal problem," he said. "If we have to take these men out of Guatemala, we will have to transfer them to the United States, and we can't have them wandering around the country telling everyone what they have been doing." Demobilization in Guatemala would be worse. The Cubans might resist being disarmed. If they were successfully dispersed they would spread word all over Latin America of how the United States turned tail. This could trigger Communist takeovers elsewhere in the hemisphere.

Without enthusiasm, the President agreed it might be best to let the exiles go to the destination of their choice: Cuba. After all, Ike had urged him to go ahead and the retired President was more than a revered general. He and his party commanded powerful political support. If Kennedy cancelled the project, the Cuban exiles would be loudly furious. The Republicans would call him chicken. The political repercussions would be nasty. Anyway, the first move was to persuade the exiles to set up a more representative, more liberal political front—the achievement was still eluding Howard Hunt and Gerry Droller.

Bissell then presented a CIA paper entitled "Proposed Operation Against Cuba." It recommended the Trinidad plan: an amphibious/ airborne assault at Trinidad with concurrent (but no prior) tactical air support; seizure of a beachhead contiguous to terrain suitable for guerrilla operations if necessary; landing of a provisional government as soon as the beachhead was secured.

The President rejected the plan as "too spectacular." He said, "This is too much like a World War II invasion." He preferred a "quiet" landing, preferably at night, with no basis for any American military intervention.

Tom Mann agreed on behalf of the State Department. To avoid anti-American reaction in the United Nations and Latin America, he wanted American sponsorship thoroughly concealed. He particularly opposed Trinidad because its airstrip could not handle B-26s; there would be no way to maintain the fiction that the planes operated from Cuban bases.

General Lemnitzer felt that the putative origin of the air sorties was "an important consideration." Mann was "gravely concerned." He "hammered at the point repeatedly." General Gray was also impressed by Mann's insistence. He thought the Assistant Secretary was trying to get the entire venture killed.

The President listened closely. Summing up, he said the problem seemed to be: the smaller the political risk, the greater was the military risk, and vice versa. The two risks should be brought into better balance.

After the meeting Mac Bundy prepared National Security Action Memorandum No. 31:

> The President expects to authorize US support for an appropriate number of patriotic Cubans to return to their homeland. He believes that the best possible plan, from the point of view of combined military, political and psychological considerations has not yet been presented, and new proposals are to be concerted promptly. Action: Central Intelligence Agency with appropriate consultation.

Bundy did not say much at meetings, but he was very influential with the President, and he felt Castro was dangerous. As dean at Harvard, Mac had been Fidel's host at a rally of eight thousand students on the football field. Bundy had never forgotten the occasion. He found Castro surrounded by bright young Cuban advisers who were graduates of Harvard Business School. Castro displayed himself as a "master of the political situation but closed in the sense of any real discussion." Bundy's judgment then: "A man with a plan." His judgment now: it was good to have a plan against that man.

When Jake Engler heard in Quarters Eye that Trinidad was out, he seriously thought of resigning from the project. It was getting out of control. Schlesinger was somewhat more hopeful than he had been before the meeting: perhaps the President would drop the invasion after all.

An intensive hunt for a substitute location began instantly. Colonel Hawkins and his paramilitary staff worked through the night. Late on the morning of March 14 they suggested three alternatives to General Gray's Pentagon Review Committee: the Preston area on the north coast of Oriente province; the south coast of Las Villas between Trinidad and Cienfuegos; and the eastern Zapata swamps adjoining Cochinos Bay*—the Bay of Pigs (see front endpapers).

The next day the Joint Chiefs agreed with Gray's group and decided that of the three possibilities the Bay of Pigs was the most feasible, because its airstrip could accommodate B-26s and its few access roads

---

*They did not know that the swamps were Castro's favorite fishing spot or that his revolution had greatly improved life in the area.

would make it difficult for Castro's forces to rush in. Bissell and Hawkins liked the Bay of Pigs better than Trinidad. Trinidad had great advantages. It was more distant from Havana with its troop and plane concentrations. It had only one access road and that could be blocked by blowing up one bridge. The population of eighteen thousand was friendly and had been supporting guerrillas in the Escambrays. The mountains were proven guerrilla territory and very close. The port of Casilda had docks. In Girón and the Zapata, there were supposed to be almost no people—and no militia or police or communications whatever. There were no docks, but the airstrip was overriding. Later it turned out that the photo interpreters had made a mistake—the runway was 4,100 feet, not 4,900; but it could make air strikes "look Cuban," and the Miró Cardona provisional government could be flown there.

Admiral Burke thought that the Zapata plan's chance of success was "less than fifty percent," but the Joint Chiefs were relieved there was no more talk about a suggestion from Dean Rusk that the expedition use Guantánamo as a base and retreat there if necessary. The idea of endangering the base had startled and appalled them. They reported to Secretary of Defense McNamara that they still considered Trinidad best. For some reason this preference was not transmitted to the President, to whom the plan for the Bay of Pigs was presented the same day.

The President listened gravely and asked for changes. He wanted the CIA to "reduce the noise level" of the landings. Could they make certain that all ships would be unloaded at night? Again Kennedy said he reserved the right to call everything off twenty-four hours before D-Day.

On March 16, Bissell and his men were back at the White House for approval of modifications in the plan. The parachute drops would come at first light, not the previous afternoon, as first planned. The ships could unload and withdraw by dawn. The President told Bissell to proceed with the plan. He still withheld formal approval.

At none of these meetings—nor at the subsequent briefings—was the President made to realize that in approving the new plan he had, in effect, lost what he considered so important and what the military and the CIA knew he deemed vital: the guerrilla option for the Brigade. The President was left with the belief that the men could "melt into the mountains." Nobody pointed out that the mountains were now too far away (see back endpapers).

His principal advisers remained equally ill-informed. Mac Bundy was left "with the clear impression" that "a substantial portion of the force would almost certainly be able to survive for a prolonged period in guerrilla operations." McNamara thought that if there were no civilian uprisings the Brigade "would be split up into a guerrilla force and moved into the Escambrays."

The Joint Chiefs made no study of the "guerrilla option." They relied on CIA assurances that "a group of a hundred guerrillas were operating in this area and there was lots of small game." Nobody pointed out until after the event that no guerrillas had operated in the Zapata during the twentieth century and that even trained guerrillas find it hard to escape helicopters.

Castro's Expectations

With Eisenhower leaving, Castro assessed the risks of Kennedy's New Frontier. He found the outlook disquieting. It was hopeless to think the youthful new President would change the U.S. attitude toward the youthful Cuban revolution; Kennedy had committed himself too strongly against it during the presidential campaign. If anything, the great divide between East and West was widening. The new man wanted to look tough. He was swept up in the "emotional state" of the Cold War.

No strategist was needed to grasp the essentials of defending Cuba. It required only one look at a map of the crescent-shaped island and its almost two thousand miles of coastline with its bays, keys, coves and enormous stretches of unpopulated brush, weeds, swamps and beaches. It was an invader's utopia. There was no way to watch every vulnerable spot, much less defend it. Even such rudimentary technical resources as radar did not yet exist anywhere.

Help was on the way; it was much slower than Castro wished in the light of his assessment of the American timetable. No matter what U.S. intelligence thought, it would take many months before some fifty green Cuban MIG pilots could finish training in Czechoslovakia. Soviet field artillery and Czech antiaircraft guns were pouring into Cuba, but only a handful of Russian and Czech technicians had arrived to train gunnery crews. Castro was convinced he had almost no time left.

Frustrated at the sight of guns without gunners, he called a meeting of his artillery personnel in training and asked, "Can you teach people in the evening what you learned in the morning?" They could and did. It was a critical move, and just in time. Almost overnight, thousands of militiamen acquired great firepower.

Castro had taken for granted right along that innumerable plans existed to assassinate him. Assassination attempts were part of the way of life for leaders in Caribbean and Latin-American countries. No matter how ineffective the Cuban counterrevolutionary groups were throughout 1960, there were many of them; he supposed they all had assassination ideas.

He knew he was vulnerable. Traveling to receptions, public meetings and factories, he felt "like a dove." His staff took security measures with his food and cigars. He shrugged them off. They were not specialists in that sort of business. Anyway, living with assassinations became "habit." Besides, he did not think attempts by counterrevolutionaries would be too dangerous. A counterrevolutionary would be too cautious. He "does not want to die. He's waiting for money, for a reward, so he's on guard, he takes care of himself." A fanatic would be something else: "No one could escape a fanatic or a mentally ill person."

Eventually he began to suppose that the CIA was plotting an assassination, too. It was inevitable. But they would be using counterrevolutionaries. Poisoned food was a likely method, especially since it was known that he liked to snack at cafeterias in the Habana Libre Hotel (formerly the Hilton) and elsewhere. Once when he asked for a chocolate milk shake, he was served by a man who had poison in the refrigerator. He was planning to kill Castro. But he became nervous. He never poured the poison into the milk shake and was arrested later. Counterrevolutionaries were just inefficient assassins.

Castro was lucky in another respect. In November, he and Félix Duque made a careful inspection of the Bay of Pigs, quite fortuitously. Duque had fought with Fidel, his Commander in Chief, for two years in the Sierra Maestra. Félix had been captured, talked his way free, and risen to major, then the highest rank in the guerrilla army. He was Fidel's kind of man: a farmer, thirty, five feet three, with a full beard, short-cropped hair, the fierce broad face of a bantamweight Ernest Borgnine, and inexhaustible energy. Duque (pronounced Dew-kay) got things done. Barking and kidding, he got people moving. Fidel had placed him in charge of the agrarian reform movement in the area around Cienfuegos, near the coast east of Girón.

Driving in Castro's large unmarked American black car, they had come to Girón to look over one of Fidel's pet projects: the 180 concrete bungalows and the bathhouses, motel and recreation center going up on the east side of the mouth to the Bay of Pigs. Hooded twelve-foot lights on silver metal poles in concrete foundations had been installed throughout the new community; work was progressing day and night.

Still, the project was way behind schedule. In his usual green fatigues and cap, chewing on a cigar, and with two more unwrapped cigars peering next to the fountain pens out of his left breast pocket, Fidel was stalking about, questioning foremen and workers. Why hadn't the deadline for the motel been met? Why were so many bungalows unfinished? The foremen said materials didn't come on time. There weren't enough technicians.

Castro put Duque in charge. A resort wasn't agrarian reform, but Duque would get things done. He always did.

Duque was not surprised at the Commander in Chief's personal push for the Girón project. Fidel's affection for the area was widely known. Its wilderness appealed to what he called "my guerrilla mentality." He used to go trout fishing in nearby Laguna del Tesoro—named not for conventional treasure but for the priceless religious objects which the Indians threw into the water to hide them from the Spanish colonists, and which were never recovered.

Castro spent many weekends in a bungalow on what became known as "Fidel's key." Not long before, lounging on his bed, he had announced, "We're going to build a Tahitian village here!" Now a five-mile canal was being dredged to thirteen tiny islands in the lake. Japanese-style hanging bridges connected them. Forty-four thatched-roof octagonal resort units were going up on stilts, each hut with Soviet television set, air conditioning and private boat mooring. Hut No. 33 was getting special attention. Fidel would stay there.

Anywhere in Cuba, this resort village, Guama, would have been a showplace. In the middle of the Zapata swamps it was a miracle. Here was Cuba's largest peninsula—1,172 square miles—a place that time forgot. A little over a year previously, before Castro came to power—Cubans referred to this milestone as "before the triumph of the revolution" as if it separated B.C. from A.D.—there had been no roads, no schools, no electricity. More than eight thousand people, all but cut off from the rest of Cuba, lived here in conditions much like those reported by Columbus when he discovered the area in June of 1494.

Like Castro, Columbus found it fascinating. He decided it was "the mainland at the beginning of the Indies," and polled his crewmen so that they might attest to this, which they did. He saw naked Indians carrying "in their hand a burning coal, and certain weeds for inhaling their smoke." He had just discovered tobacco. Within the Bahía de Cochinos—thirteen miles long with an average width of four miles and named for the local *cochinos cimarrones,* pigs so wild that they often attacked humans—he discovered subterranean streams. Their water was "so cold, and of such goodness and so sweet that no better could be found in the world." He also found so many keys that years later even the knowledgeable Cortes got lost in them.

Over the centuries, fishermen's huts appeared at Playa Larga (Long Beach), at the foot of the bay, and at Playa Girón, at the entrance—named in honor of Gilbert Girón, a French captain defeated by a Spanish captain who carried away Girón's head as evidence of victory. Most natives lived off the fish, the pigs, the sweet meat of the plentiful alligators and whatever they could collect from supplying the *filibuster-os,** the local pirates. In the nineteenth century, revolutionaries managed to survive in this jungle during two wars for independence. The Spaniards did not dare enter this redoubt. The mosquitoes, the poisonous guao plants and the wall-thick marabu bushes with their inch-long thorns were less than inviting.

Talk of draining the swamps began in 1854. In 1912, a group of Americans organized the Zapata Land Company and retained a New York engineering firm, Barclay, Parsons & Klapp, to get started. They hired a tall, fierce-looking Cuban engineer, J. A. Cosculuella, to survey all 505,000 acres. He found them as inaccessible "as Stanley's Tenebrosa Africa . . . a place of fogs and deaths where alligators are absolute masters."

Charcoal-making was a major industry, and Cosculuella marveled at how its practitioners, the *carboneros*, sometimes subsisted all day on sugared water and slimy sea snails. It was intricate work. Forever blackened by soot, the men hatcheted mangrove branches to a length of about two feet. The branches were lined up, vertically and close together, around a teepee-shaped *horno de carbón*, a charcoal oven, made of straw and earth, hollow at the center. When the center was set afire, the wood smoldered, eventually turning into pungently sweet-smelling charcoal. With the help of soot-covered children, the smoking oven had to be watched around the clock. At the critical moment it was "drowned" with water. Nobody cooked with anything but charcoal, though few could afford a sack at a time. The *carboneros* sold as little as two cents' worth. The ashes were used for kitchen scrubbing.

Cosculuella's land company ran out of money—he reported that the project would be more difficult than draining Lake Okeechobee or the Everglades—and when Castro came to power the area was still impassable. Mothers with sick children had to wait for days for the boat to Cienfuegos to see a doctor. *Carboneros* still staggered into town with

*The word comes from *vrijbuiter*—Dutch for freebooter or pirate. It was first used in the United States during the 1850s to describe gunrunners to revolutionists in Cuba and other Central and South American countries. In 1853, a Congressman was first to criticize the excessively long-winded speech-making of his opponents for "filibustering against the United States."

charcoal sacks on their back. The *cagaleche* ("milk shitter") birds still owned the beaches. People still said, *"Está usted en su casa"* ("You are in your house") when a visitor arrived, and *"Esta es su casa"* ("This is your house") when he left. Only the alligators had been hunted into near-extinction. Castro ordered them rounded up for breeding. "When we have millions of them, we'll have an industry," he said.

Meanwhile, he had three highways built of hard-packed limestone. In Havana they would have looked like country roads. In the Zapata they looked like turnpikes. (Almost twenty years later they still stood empty, even on weekends, except for swarms of crabs scurrying across.) But the brand-new schools were filled. More than two hundred teachers from the national literacy campaign arrived. Cayo Ramón got a hospital. And then there was Girón, ah, Girón! There still was no telephone for fifteen miles around, but in this setting the pastel-colored cement tourist bungalows looked palatial, even in their half-finished state. The kidney-shaped swimming pool was going to be hard to believe. The airport with its own control tower and 4,100-foot runway would look out of another world altogether. Fidel and his "guerrilla mentality" had come this far in two years. No wonder he was urging the construction crews on to finish building the dream.

Fidel had experience with making a dream come true. It was called *la revolución*. Cubans felt about it the way Americans would feel about the Declaration of Independence if it had been signed within recent memory. When Fidel holed up in the Sierra Maestra with twelve men in December 1956, the revolution had been even less than a dream. It had been fantasy.

All the men started growing beards. (For Castro it was more than a trademark and a convenience; he liked hiding his double chin.) Hunted by tens of thousands of Batista soldiers, they never spent two nights in the same spot, never slept under a roof. Castro personally issued each bullet to each man.

Slowly, the *barbudos* force grew. On February 15, 1957, when Castro gave an interview to Herbert L. Matthews of *The New York Times*, mostly to counteract reports that he was dead, Fidel had to crouch on the ground and whisper into the correspondent's left ear in a "hoarse, impassioned whisper" because they were surrounded by the enemy. Matthews found Castro "overpowering."

The *barbudos* emerged from the mountains on January 1, 1959, after Batista fled the country. In triumph, they marched from city to city. For two weeks, Castro moved toward Havana, though not always on foot; he covered many stretches by helicopter, relishing it like a toy ("It's mine!

It's mine!" he exulted). Along the route the signs said, "*Gracias*, Fidel!" In the capital there were tears of joy. World War II news correspondents could remember no such a jubilant scene since the liberation of Paris. And when Castro spoke, it sounded as if Robin Hood had just been made a field marshal.

Now the revolution was gravely threatened. Castro was certain "an aggression" would come soon. He wondered only precisely when and, even more particularly, where. He had gone into the Escambray Mountains to help round up "bandits" who were trying to operate much as he used to harass the Batista regime from the Sierra Maestra. Documents were captured that hinted of landings near the town of Trinidad. He strengthened his defenses there. He thought the U.S. might occupy a nucleus of Cuban territory to "establish a puppet government, as in Taiwan." The Isle of Pines, not too far from Havana, seemed a likely spot. Its large prison full of "counterrevolutionaries" might explode. The Cuban Navy and Air Force might be too small to dislodge an occupation. He moved more forces to the island.

No matter: the aggression was inevitable. It was of a piece with the U.S. policy that cut off Cuban oil supplies and sugar markets; the diplomatic maneuvers to isolate him from the rest of Latin America; the smuggling of arms and saboteurs into his country in arrogant disregard of Cuban sovereignty. It was part of the U.S. "style" demonstrated in Guatemala. Before that, there was the long record of intervention in Mexico and other Caribbean and Central American nations.

He only wished for better intelligence. He knew about the Guatemala training camps. Yet he felt his intelligence service was poor. It was too inexperienced. So were his armed forces. They were not even organized in regiments. There was no defense ministry. He would have to do better—in a hurry. He thought the invasion might strike about New Year's. Perhaps the Republicans wanted to show the Kennedy men they could still finish what they had started. The oppression by the self-centered American bully nagged at him. It obsessed him and his people, even the children.

In the hot tropical sun youngsters no longer played cowboys and Indians. The popular game was "Cubans and Yankee invaders." It was difficult to keep going; few kids wanted to play Yankees, because they were invariably defeated.

Troops and the militia were on twenty-four-hour duty. Castro announced that the "Yankee invasion" was imminent. It would certainly come before January 20. Hundreds suspected of being "counterrevolutionists" were being arrested. The radio was filled with appeals for blood donations as well as for food for the militia "in the trenches."

Contract on Castro's Life

Castro was right. The CIA had not neglected the other string in Bissell's bow. After consulting Bissell, Sheff Edwards and the Technical Services Division, O'Connell, Edwards' chief for the Operational Support Division, was directed to plan a "gangland-style killing." Castro was to be gunned down by a Cuban assassin to be hired by the CIA's hired mobsters, Sam Giancana and Johnny Rosselli.

Giancana objected. He said it would be too difficult to recruit an "asset" for such an operation. It was too dangerous. He suggested poison. Rosselli passed along the request for something "nice and clean, without getting into any kind of out-and-out ambushing."

Bissell and his assistants asked Technical Services to develop a pill to slip into Castro's drink. Sheff Edwards had to reject the first batch of pills; they would not dissolve in water. A second batch, containing botulism toxin, was tested on monkeys and "did the job expected of them." O'Connell received the pills in February. He was assured they were lethal and gave them to Rosselli.

Rosselli reported to O'Connell that the pills that were supposed to poison Castro had been delivered to a Cuban official who was close to Castro. O'Connell inferred that the Cuban had probably received kickbacks from the Mafia gambling interests. Weeks later, the Cuban returned the pills because he had lost his position and access to Castro. Rosselli and O'Connell thought the official had just lost his nerve.

There was one last attempt to place the pills. Rosselli told O'Connell that Trafficante, the former Mafia chief in Havana, believed that one of the leaders of the Cuban exile movement might be able to get the job done. The CIA eventually concluded that this leader probably received money from Trafficante and other racketeers who wanted "gambling, prostitution and dope monopolies" in Cuba once Castro was overthrown. The Cuban leader said he had a contact in a restaurant frequented by Castro. He wanted cash and a thousand dollars' worth of "communications equipment."

In Bissell's office, O'Connell received fifty thousand dollars cash from J. C. King, the head of the agency's Western Hemisphere Division. The money was to be paid if the Cuban actually killed Castro. Bissell also authorized O'Connell to give the Cuban the requested equipment. (Years later, Bissell did not recall the meeting.)

O'Connell received the equipment from the CIA's communications office and turned it over to Maheu in Miami. Maheu delivered an automobile containing the equipment to an empty lot. The pills and an advance payment of ten thousand dollars were delivered to the Cuban leader at a meeting with Maheu, Rosselli and Trafficante in a suite at the Fontainebleau Hotel. At least that was the way Rosselli recalled it. Maheu

> opened his briefcase and dumped a whole lot of money on his lap . . . and also came up with the capsules and he explained how they were going to be used. They couldn't be used in boiling soups and things like that, but they could be used in water or otherwise, but they couldn't last forever. . . . It had to be done as quickly as possible.

John Shimon, a friend of Rosselli and Giancana,* had a different memory. He remembered that he and Maheu went to the third Patterson–Johansson world heavyweight championship fight in Miami on March 12. Maheu told him the CIA had given him a "liquid" to assassinate Castro; it would be put into Castro's food. Castro would get ill and die within two or three days, and an autopsy would not reveal what killed him. According to Shimon, they met Rosselli and the Cuban leader outside the Fontainebleau's Boom-Boom Room. After Rosselli left with the Cuban, Maheu told Shimon, "Johnny's going to handle everything; this is Johnny's contract."

A few days later, Shimon had a call from Maheu. "Did you see the paper?" Maheu asked. "Castro's ill! He's going to be sick two or three days. Wow, we got him!"

They didn't, because Castro had stopped eating at the restaurant where the "asset" was employed. Nevertheless, at about the same time another CIA man, William Harvey, was assigned to set up a "general capability" within the CIA for disabling foreign leaders, including assassination "as a last resort." The capability was called "Executive Action." Its cryptonym was ZR/RIFLE. Bissell's "string" would play on for years.

Meanwhile, reports of anti-Castro activity in Cuba sounded encouraging in Washington.

CIA internal Information Report No. CS-3/468,320 said:

---

*Five days before Rosselli testified about these matters before Senator Frank Church's Senate Intelligence Committee in June 1975, Giancana was assassinated by seven .22 bullets. They were fired into his neck and face at close range in his home in suburban Oak Park, Illinois. He was scheduled to testify before the same committee. Rosselli's decomposing body was found by fishermen in Dumfoundling Bay off North Miami Beach in August 1976. It was sealed in an empty fifty-five-gallon oil drum weighed down by heavy chains. Neither murder has been solved.

Many members of the militia are harassing physicians to obtain certificates to exempt them from military duties. . . . In Las Villas Province, large numbers of militiamen have refused to fight . . . Public attendance at government-organized events in the cities has dwindled . . . Popular support of the government among the rural population has also diminished.

A U.S. Air Force intelligence report of March 17 had this from "two clandestine sources in Cuba who have furnished reliable information in the past":

The military situation in Cuba is a chaotic system which is boiling with hatred and passions, and which lacks discipline . . . The Rebel army at the present time can consider some 75 to 80 percent of its personnel in disagreement with the political system now controlling the government. . . . A great percentage of the officers are believed ready to rebel against the government at a given moment, taking their troops with them. . . .

To Jorge Recarey, the ultranervous Brigade infiltrator, the situation looked different. During the two months before D-Day he almost never spent two nights in a row in the same house and never stopped taking Benzedrine. Wherever his jobs took him, he was always shepherded into secure houses with local people who put him up and were never indiscreet; safe cars with safe drivers took him anywhere. This was the network built up since 1959 by a twenty-eight-year-old engineer, Rogelio Gonzales Corso, whose code name was "Francisco," and who seemed never to sleep at all.

Recarey met Francisco in the bedroom of the Havana home where Fundora had taken him. He handed the leader a sealed envelope which he had been given by one of the CIA men in Florida. Francisco looked at the contents and told Recarey to go to the city of Matanzas and organize the resistance there. It was the only order he received during his career as an infiltrator.

Through Fundora, as the weeks went by, Recarey received large quantities of weapons that kept arriving from Florida: three tons of explosives, hundreds of submachine guns, rifles, pistols, and cash. The mix-ups were maddening. One huge shipment of detonator caps arrived without any explosives. The .45-caliber pistols reached him with .30-caliber ammunition. None of the several announced air drops of weapons materialized. His radio operator was ambushed and shot as he tried to rescue his equipment (seventeen years later the man was still in prison).

When $2 million worth of pesos came ashore in four jute sacks that had gotten wet, the sacks were leaking blue, red and green liquid, but the underground workers were only mildly annoyed. They knew that the CIA was sending them counterfeit money; that the printing and the paper were excellent but the ink was so unreliable you could usually wipe it off with saliva. The counterfeit money, tens and twenties, was used by middlemen who bought expensive items—such as cars—from people they hoped never to see again. The currency supplied to the infiltrators for their own use was authentic; at least its ink did not run.

Moving from house to house in Matanzas, Recarey kept up a breakneck pace. He organized several demolition teams, and every time a man was arrested he made certain that the surviving team members would vanish to other cities. He hid caches of weapons in numerous safe locations. He trained five team leaders who trained other leaders until eventually he commanded a knowledgeable army of 180 saboteurs and more than fifty houses where they could be hidden. He would cut Cuba in half by blowing up one key railroad bridge and cutting the telegraph and telephone lines. He got a civil engineer to prepare precise drawings of the bridge; several of his men repeatedly walked across and under it so they would know where to place explosives.

In March, much bad news depressed him. Francisco was betrayed when he insisted on attending a large meeting that included several suspicious types; he was executed soon afterward. Some of the supply ships dropped their weapons in the water off Punta Fundora and steamed away. The CIA sent Jorge a replacement radio operator by parachute, but the man had never made even one training jump; when he landed and could locate only a frightened farmer instead of his assigned reception group, he asked to be sent back to his base.

In his eagerness to excel at the first job he had ever held, Recarey decided to support the invasion of his friends in Guatemala in ways the CIA had never taught him. One day, a former Hungarian freedom fighter turned up among his resistance workers. The man had been an army colonel in Hungary and knew all about street fighting. He showed Jorge how to make his own superfast "tanks" by placing two machine guns on the platforms of construction trucks and surrounding them with sandbags.

Through visitors who went to see political prisoners in the Matanzas prison, Recarey contacted five leaders and sent word that he would open the prison doors on D-Day. How many inmates would really fight? The prisoners claimed that eight hundred of the fifteen hundred men would join the guerrillas. Jorge thought five hundred would be a more likely figure. Through the visitors, he sent technical information into the prison so that the new recruits could occupy themselves by learning how to fire rifles, pistols and bazookas.

Edgar Sopo, one of the infiltrator friends from his Florida training days, came visiting from Havana to talk about his troubles. Sopo had been assigned to supply weapons to a guerrilla force of sixteen hundred men in the countryside on the north coast of Las Villas province, but he got only fifty pistols, and that was weeks ago. Nobody knew when and why the operation was scrubbed. Sopo did not mind. Las Villas was flat, with almost no places to hide, and the mission had struck him as crazy from the start. Sopo and Recarey recalled how the Americans often dreamed up crazy schemes. Usually the infiltrators ignored these ideas. Nobody, for example, followed the CIA instructions to tie a grenade to the inside of the upper thigh. In case of capture, you were supposed to escape torture by asking to go to the bathroom and blowing yourself up testicles first—hardly the *macho* Cuban way to die.

Sopo told Recarey he kept busy teaching crash courses in the art of demolition. Every night, five or six recently recruited resistance men were sent to his safe house, where Sopo demonstrated step by step how to fashion plastic explosives into bombs. The rest of the time, he said, he was preparing for his D-Day mission: seizing CMQ, the biggest radio station in Havana.

His radio operator, an infiltrator whom Sopo had known in Miami, had taken him to the back of a garage in Havana where Sopo found his backpack, which he had been asked to hide near the beach where he landed, and enough submachine guns and grenades to equip a team of twelve men. They were to take over the station and start broadcasting on behalf of the anti-Castro troops.

Unhindered, Sopo had walked through the station three times and familiarized himself with the layout. Several times he lunched in a little coffeehouse across the street and watched the movements of the guards. In his hideaway room he drafted the text of his first broadcast. He was very excited. He tried to be brief. It took several rewrites before he thought he had hit upon the wording worthy of a historic proclamation.

"The day of liberation has come at last," he wrote. "We are fighting the final battle against Fidel Castro, who has betrayed the true Cuban revolution, which was not a Communist revolution but a revolution based on social justice. . . ." Every day he rehearsed his solemn declaration, waiting, waiting to hear D-Day had come.

Cubans are not good at waiting. In Havana particularly, people were talking openly in the streets about a coming invasion and an internal uprising. The big El Encanto department store was set afire with explosives from Jorge Recarey's stocks. The Brigade infiltrators could not be certain how much longer they could maintain control over the resistance fighters they were training, arming and assigning to dozens of missions.

Organizing the Exile Leaders

By mid-March the Cuban government in exile, which Eisenhower had first started asking about nine months earlier, was still unborn. Howard Hunt, the CIA's principal negotiator with the exile politicians in Miami, kept stirring up dissension among the competing revolutionary groups by pushing his friend Manuel Artime, the flamboyant psychiatrist turned politician. He dismissed other leaders with important constituencies as dangerous radicals. He could not get along with his chief assistant, Droller, the famous "Frank Bender" who called everybody "Popsy" and couldn't get along with Cubans of any stripe. Even Cuban CIA agents coming back to Washington from Miami asked, "What the hell is going on? Who is this guy?"

Jim Noble* the last station chief in Havana, was listening to the tales from Miami with growing distaste. He had been assigned to sit in on staff meetings in Quarters Eye to keep up-to-date for his next job: he was to return to Cuba as station chief in the wake of the invasion. This made him very popular around headquarters. Everybody seemed to know that he had started to recruit his new staff, and agents were stopping him in the corridors to volunteer for duty in sunny Havana.

Jim sympathized with Droller. He knew the Cuban politicians as "the greatest bunch of prima donnas in the world." Still, Droller's open contempt was "going to screw everything up." Jim felt "they may have deserved it, but you don't get along by showing it." His own contempt was reserved for Hunt, who was getting nowhere, even though he had been given instructions to "knock their heads together and kick them in the ass, anything at all."

Jim also found himself "shattered" by the ignorance in Washington about the backgrounds and personalities of the influential Cubans on the American side. Nobody seemed to know who was who. On one embarrassing occasion, the U.S. planners were even unacquainted with one of their fellow planners from the White House.

Jim was attending a meeting in the State Department run by Bissell and Adolf A. Berle, Kennedy's Latin-American specialist at State. Colonel King, the CIA's Western Hemisphere man, was there. Bill Bundy represented Defense. At the end of the table sat a small

*A pseudonym.

dark-haired pockmarked newcomer puffing on a large cigar. Bissell turned to the men he knew and said suspiciously, "Who is this?"

"I'm Richard Goodwin from the White House," the small man spoke up. "President Kennedy sent me over here to monitor this meeting."

Bissell was not satisfied. He sent an assistant to phone the White House and did not start the meeting until he was assured that there was indeed a Goodwin on the White House staff and, yes, he was supposed to attend the meeting.

Finally Berle said, "Well, whom do we have who could become part of the Cuban committee?"

King turned to Jim, who said, "Well, there's Tony Varona."

"Well," said Berle, "give us a rundown on him."

Jim said that Varona was a former Vice-President of Cuba and head of the Cuban Senate. He then mentioned other exile leaders. The men at the table seemed to know little or nothing about any of them.

"Why don't we get together four or five of these people and name them?" asked Berle.

Jim said, "Gee, can I make a suggestion? There must be a couple of hundred thousand Cubans in the Miami area to give this thing some substance. Couldn't they have a convention down there? Maybe we could get a few thousand of them together. Whatever it is, at least you would have some basis of popular support."

"We have no time for consulting the Cubans on this," Berle said.

Noble was "shocked." He remembered Berle from his own OSS days. Berle had been a "bright boy from Harvard," a Brain Truster of Roosevelt's New Deal. He thought this was "the reverse of democracy in action. If I'd just thrown in Joe Blow's name and made up a fictitious background for him, he could have been named to the government, too."

At another meeting, this time in Quarters Eye, Jim asked when the Cuban underground would be notified.

"We're not going to advise them at all," Colonel Hawkins said. "With those dumb bastards over there, it'll be all over town. If we tell them it's going to be on a certain day, the whole goddamn island will know about it."

"The whole goddamn island knows about it now," Jim said, "and every newspaper in the United States knows about it. Why should we keep in the dark the guys whose heads are going to be on the block?"

"Well, I don't trust any goddamn Cuban," the colonel barked.

"Jack," Jim taunted, "why the hell are we mounting an invasion in Cuba? Why don't we mount an invasion in Denmark? They're real nice people over there, and I think you'd love it! You'd trust the hell out of them. Don't let's fool around with these Cubans."

Time was running out for arguments and indecision. So was Bissell's patience. The landings were now scheduled for early April. He called Jim into his office and said, "I want you to go down to Miami. You're replacing Howard Hunt. You know these people. I want them together. They've *got* to be together. We've only got a week to put them together and then another week when this thing is going to take place. You go down there and do whatever is necessary." As his assistant, Jim was to take along Will Carr, a New York engineer who had spent much of his life in Mexico, spoke Spanish without accent and had shown skill when he ran delicate free-lance errands for the agency in Latin America. Bissell knew Carr as "quite a persuader."

Noble and Carr flew to Miami and checked into inexpensive motel rooms. Noble told Hunt that he was through and was to return to Washington. Then he talked to Tony Varona, Artime and, particularly, the popular Manuel Ray, a former Interior Minister and now head of the MRP, whom Jim had known in the underground and had helped smuggle out of Cuba. Ray's views were somewhat left of center. Hunt had tagged him as a "Communist." Jim told him, "Manolo, there will be no committee without you."

When Droller heard that Jim was trying to recruit Ray, he told his new boss, "I'll have nothing to do with that goddamned Communist!"

Noble said, "I'm sure he's not a Communist, and whether you have anything to do with him or not has nothing to do with this." He was tired of low-echelon field men setting up veto powers for themselves. Droller was taken aback and kept quiet.

When the Cubans' heads still proved too stubborn to knock together, Jim composed a two-minute ultimatum in Spanish. It reminded the leaders that while they were enjoying the comforts of Florida, polishing their "selfish little aims and petty differences," their friends in Cuba were being hounded and killed. Unless they formed a truly representative committee on the spot, the United States government would close down the entire project.

Jim Telexed his text to Washington for approval, which arrived within twenty-four hours. On March 18, the leaders were summoned to the Skyways Motel. This time they were not confronted by Droller, his bluster and his German accent, but by Carr with his elegant Spanish and Jim's unequivocal script. Jim told Carr to tell the Cubans, "If you don't come out of this meeting with a committee, you just forget the whole fuckin' business, because we're through!"

Nobody found the Cuban politicians easy. Annette Aaron experienced them as clients. British-born and birdlike, she had become accustomed to frenzy and secrecy during proxy fights and political campaigns. Her boss, Lem Jones, had done public relations for Wendell Willkie and Twentieth Century–Fox. In her status as all of the "associates" in the New York PR firm Lem Jones Associates, Inc., Miss Aaron found herself in the middle between the Frente and the CIA.

The Frente hired Jones because the newspapers had been ignoring it. When Jones listened to the Cubans' problem, he could see why. Their latest press release ran thirty pages—in Spanish. To be certain he was not getting himself into trouble, Jones called a friend in the CIA and asked him to check out the names of some Frente leaders. His friend called back quickly. He told Jones he was onto something very big. Another man would call in half an hour and say he wanted to meet Jones alone.

So Jones met Dave Phillips, Bissell's propaganda chief, sometimes in hotel rooms, often in Grand Central Terminal. Phillips was curious about what the CIA-financed Frente was up to. Once Phillips came into Jones's one-room office on the twelfth floor of 280 Madison Avenue and said, "I want to see you alone." Miss Aaron rose and went to the hairdresser at Arnold Constable nearby. She thought "it was the ladylike thing to do."

The previous September, while Castro was in New York, Miss Aaron had escorted a protest demonstration from Miami to New York. Invented by the CIA, it was called "caravan of sorrow." It was a busload of Cuban exile women, six of them pregnant and suffering from morning sickness. When the driver, exasperated by the frequent rest stops, briefly refused to take the bus "another inch," one of the women threatened to shoot him. She indicated she had a gun in her handbag. "Give me the gun," said Miss Aaron. It turned out the woman didn't have one, and Annette got the caravan photographed by the leading papers at the Liberty Bell in Philadelphia and then, in prayer, at St. Patrick's Cathedral in New York. She had been on easier assignments, yet there were compensations. Much of the work on the Cuban account was done with firm assistance from Washington.

The Frente was issuing more frequent press releases forecasting liberation from Castro. It would come soon. The Cuban exile leaders did not have to write the ringing phrases. They came from Phillips. The phone would ring in Lem Jones's public-relations office. Annette Aaron would answer it. "Hello, Annette, this is Dave. Take this down." It was Dave Phillips with another Frente declaration. Annette would take it down in her Pitman steno, type it up on a stencil and run off copies on Jones's temperamental A. B. Dick Mimeograph. It had to be inked frequently, which was invariably messy. With the particular loyalty of a foreign-born citizen, Miss Aaron sighed and said to herself, "My country, right or wrong."

Dave Phillips no longer had trouble keeping Cuban "rough edges" on his Radio Swan programs. The Frente leaders saw to that. Some transmissions were becoming too authentic. The leading exile groups had been allowed to buy time on the CIA station with CIA funds furnished by Hunt and Bender—the agency never objected to a little extra bookkeeping to keep up a neat front. The factions preferred to trumpet their own political horns, rather than Phillips' party line. They squabbled right on the air. Some sounded nostalgic about the Batista days.

Phillips flew to Miami and lectured the leaders in the offices of the Gibraltar Steamship Corporation, the CIA's cover. He reiterated that Batista was taboo. They were to unite behind the agency's propaganda theme: the Castro regime was the revolution betrayed. Castro should not be attacked. He was to be viewed with sorrow, not anger, for betraying the revolution.

The admonition helped. Havana jammed Radio Swan. Castro denounced its spokesmen as "hysterical parrots." Still, Phillips was troubled by his lack of control. He began purchasing time on legitimate stations throughout Latin America and broadcast propaganda without disclosing its CIA origin. Even more worrisome was word from Bissell that there could be no leaflet drops over Havana and other major centers. It would be too provocative to suit State Department.

Jay Gleichauff often wished he could duck in and out of Miami like Phillips and the other visiting dignitaries from Washington. Gleichauff was entitled to sixty days' leave for 1960 and 1961. He took only four. His wife was furious. It couldn't be helped. He was director of the CIA field office in Miami. Cuban refugees were arriving at the rate of seventeen hundred each week, on seventeen flights. Eighteen government agencies dealt with their reception. Gleichauff's office pumped the arrivals for intelligence information.

The Cubans talked and talked. Little of what they said had value, but you never knew when you might hit a golden nugget. It was Gleichauff and his men who tipped off Washington that about fifty Cuban pilots were training in Czechoslovakia to fly MIG's for Castro, and that the Soviets were about to supply him with high-speed Komar patrol boats to guard the Cuban coast against intrusions.

Gleichauff had a list of almost seven hundred anti-Castro groups conspiring in the Miami area. The infiltration and exfiltration boat traffic grew so "you really needed a traffic cop on Biscayne Bay." The Coast Guard did its best. They could not always be sure whether they were nabbing a "sponsored operation" financed by the CIA or just "wild Cubans." When in doubt, they woke up Gleichauff, often around 3 A.M.

As Bissell's operation grew, the complexities generated new complexities. A fleet of rented cars and trucks was needed to shuttle recruits and other supposedly secret operators. The CIA organized a subsidiary of an established car rental business so it would not have to account for the movements of the vehicles. Gleichauff dispersed them in lots all over town and made sure their license numbers did not run too closely in sequence.

The dozens of CIA "safe houses" generated so many not-so-stealthy Cuban callers that neighbors kept complaining to the police. Gleichauff liked the Cubans. He had served in Latin America and spoke Spanish. But his charges were undeniably noisy. "Get three of them talking about the weather, and it sounds like a riot."

The need for secrecy had been drilled into the CIA man. But what was he supposed to do about the newspapers when they ran photographs of Cubans lined up at the recruiting stations and sightseers flocked to Opa-Locka nightly to watch the steady flow of blacked-out planes leaving for Guatemala? You couldn't "put a cork in everybody's mouth." Inevitably, the operation became "as secret as Christmas Day."

Jim Noble's efforts to unite the Cuban exile leaders or suffer the loss of U.S. support had paid off. The Cubans caved in, and at a press conference at the Commodore Hotel in New York they flexed their new muscle. The splashy details that they revealed made Bissell and his men shudder. Tony Varona announced, "We have the forces necessary to overthrow Castro"; they had been trained in camps "in the Western Hemisphere." Former Premier José Miró Cardona, president of the new Cuban Revolutionary Council, said the group would be transformed into a provisional government once it had gained a military foothold in Cuba. It would have been difficult to hand Castro a more complete script of events to come.

In Washington, the smart set smiled knowledgeably when Bob Amory, the CIA's deputy director for intelligence, appeared at a costume party dressed up as Fidel—fatigues, beard and all. When Dulles heard about it, he was not amused.

More Doubters

Some vehement opposition to the venture developed within the Kennedy administration, but much of it was never allowed to surface to the President's level. When it did, Kennedy discounted it because it came from the thinkers of the Democratic Party, the eggheads, the card-carrying liberals of whom the President liked to say that they, unfortunately, lacked "balls."

Under Secretary of State Chester Bowles had begun to hear in late January that "a raid of some kind" was being planned against Cuba. Though it did not sound like a major military action, he objected to it in principle. Bowles's crew cut and button-down shirts were his exterior trademarks, but ideologically he had nothing in common with the quintessential Madison Avenue type that one would expect the co-founder of the Benton & Bowles advertising agency to be. He thought in idealistic global terms. East–West tensions were as much America's fault as the Soviets', and that applied to Cuba too. "Our mistakes had helped create Castro," he argued, through "our own mistaken support of the reactionary Batista."

Late in March, while Rusk attended a SEATO conference in Bangkok, Bowles, still in the dark about the real invasion preparations, sat in for his boss at one of the meetings in the Cabinet Room. When he heard about the scope of the operation, he was horrified. It made no sense to him at all. He "marveled that they even considered" anything like it. There was "no damn excuse for spending valuable time arguing about such a proposal, much less doing it." When Allen Dulles suggested the scheme to the President, "he should have been thrown out of the office." Now Bowles could hardly believe his ears when he heard his old Connecticut sailing companion Bissell brief the policy-makers about the military details.

But he said nothing. He did not wish to undercut Rusk. Besides, Rusk would be back shortly. Bowles thought he could persuade the Secretary to oppose the plan strongly and that would end it.

It was a plausible strategy and prudent office politics. Bowles had been the first in the liberal establishment to support Kennedy for the presidential nomination, but that was many political crises ago. At one time rumors had been floated that Bowles was in line for Secretary of State. The reality had always been otherwise. Ever since the presidential campaign the former Governor of Connecticut had lost influence. He was considered too utopian in his views, too wordy in his ways. No matter how short the question, he invariably had a long answer.

Whatever the subject, he might allude to the starving masses of India or the Henry Ford five-dollar-a-day minimum wage of decades past. The Kennedy pragmatism seemed alien to him.

After the White House session, Bowles discussed the Bay of Pigs with a carefully limited handful of close associates. Leonard Meeker, Rusk's assistant legal adviser, among others, was against it. Bowles was further encouraged by a private luncheon in the Pentagon office of Deputy Defense Secretary Roswell Gilpatric, where they were briefly joined by Defense Secretary McNamara. Bowles wanted to know where the military stood and steered the conversation to the Bay of Pigs.

"Will this work without American troops?" he asked.

"It would be very doubtful," said McNamara.

Shortly after Rusk got back to his office on Friday, March 31, Bowles handed him a memorandum reporting that "on Tuesday, April 4, a meeting will be held at the White House at which a decision will be reached on the Cuban adventure." The memo said that Bowles considered the plan "profoundly disturbing" and "a grave mistake." It would violate "high principle" as well as the Act of Bogotá which established the Organization of American States. Nor did it seem pragmatic:

> Those most familiar with the Cuban operation seem to agree that, as the venture is now planned, the chances of success are not greater than one out of three. This makes it a highly risky operation. If it fails, Castro's strength and prestige will be greatly enhanced. The one way we can reduce the risk is by commitment of direct American military support. . . . I realize that this operation has been put together over a period of months. A great deal of time and money has been spent and many individuals have become emotionally involved in its success. We should not, however, proceed with this adventure simply because we are wound up and cannot stop. If you agree that this operation would be a mistake, I suggest that you personally and privately communicate your views to the President. It is my guess that your voice will be decisive.

When Bowles gave this memorandum to Rusk, he made it clear that he was ready to carry his opposition to the top. "I think you can kill this thing if you take a firm stand on it," he told the Secretary. "But if you can't, I want to see the President. I mean, here are the reasons I think it's crazy."

The President never saw Bowles's memo, but coincidence and his own social grace happened to deal Kennedy at least one other valuable player with useful cards that he did consider—and then ignored.

Senator J. William Fulbright, Democrat of Arkansas and chairman of the influential Senate Foreign Relations Committee, had not been informed of the impending invasion but had been reading the newspaper coverage of the Cubans' training and shaking his head over Howard Hunt's photographs with growing alarm. During the last week of March, the President chanced to ask Fulbright casually, "What are you going to do for Easter?"

When the Senator said he was flying to Delray Beach, Florida, where his wife, Betty, had a very old aunt, the President invited Fulbright, under whom he had until recently served on the Foreign Relations Committee, to fly along aboard the presidential plane, *Air Force One*. The President was headed for Florida, too.

Fulbright, an owlish, bushy-browed scholar-politician who spoke with a deceptively quiet and folksy Ozark drawl, was considerably more than a senior personage on Capitol Hill. Oxford-educated, he had become president of the University of Arkansas at thirty-four. On the Hill he was known as a brilliant—if sometimes verbose—thinker, the intellectual in residence. President Truman used to call him "that overeducated Oxford s.o.b." Kennedy watchers believed that if Bill Fulbright had not signed an anti-desegregation declaration known as the Southern Manifesto, he almost certainly would have become JFK's Secretary of State.

Assured of access to the President's attention in the relative privacy of the plane and "offended" by Kennedy's "obsession" with Communism, Fulbright asked Pat Holt of his committee's staff to draft a memorandum setting out all the reasons why the Senator judged an invasion of Cuba to be a terrible idea. The two men reworked the memo until it became a 3,766-word all-out broadside. Fulbright handed it to Kennedy shortly after they boarded the plane on the morning of Friday, March 30.

Calling the rumored venture "ill-considered" and already "an open secret," the memo predicted that it would become impossible "to conceal the U.S. hand" that manipulated this "brainchild and puppet"; that the Frente leadership was a weak, unrepresentative "shotgun marriage"; that an invasion would violate several treaties and American law, specifically Title 18, United States Code, Sections 958–962 and Title 50, Appendix, Section 2021, which "prohibit the enlistment or recruitment for foreign military service in the United States, the preparation of foreign military expeditions, the outfitting of foreign naval vessels for service against friendly powers . . ."

Fulbright also warned against the action on moral grounds: "To give this activity even covert support is of a piece with the hypocrisy and cynicism for which the United States is constantly denouncing the

Soviet Union in the United Nations and elsewhere. The point will not be lost on the rest of the world—nor on our own consciences."

The Senator even issued a prescient view of the expedition's outcome:

The prospect must also be faced that an invasion of Cuba by exiles would encounter formidable resistance which the exiles, by themselves, might not be able to overcome. The question would then arise of whether the United States would be willing to let the enterprise fail (in the probably futile hope of concealing the U.S. role) or whether the United States would respond with progressive assistance as necessary to insure success. This would include ultimately the use of armed force; and if we came to that, even under the paper cover of legitimacy, we would have undone the work of thirty years in trying to live down earlier interventions. We would also have assumed the responsibility for public order in Cuba, and in the circumstances this would unquestionably be an endless can of worms.

Instead of invasion, Fulbright advocated a policy of toleration and isolation toward Castro. "The Castro regime," he concluded, "is a thorn in the flesh; but it is not a dagger in the heart."

Kennedy, the successful graduate of a speed reading course, read the memo immediately and rapidly but offered no reaction. The Senator wondered whether he should invite a discussion on the plane, but decided that it would be rude to take the initiative. Besides, he was under the impression that the President had strong doubts of his own about the venture. He felt that with the memo he had done all he could.

Like Fulbright, John Plank knew nothing about an invasion. And like the Senator, he thought it was time to warn the White House. Plank's fascination was Latin-American politics. He lectured on the subject to his government classes at Harvard and had attended the 1960 meeting of the Inter-American Bar Association in Havana. He spoke excellent Spanish and, after talking with a lot of Cubans, felt he had accurately gauged the political temperature. He was convinced that most Cubans were "quite happy with the Boy Scout atmosphere" created by Castro. They thought "the new world lay just around the corner" and loved land reform and the other new liberalizing laws.

As he studied the pronouncements of the Cuban exiles from New York and listened to his newspapermen contacts, it became evident to him that the United States was encouraging some sort of imminent upheaval in Cuba. He didn't like what he read and heard. Most revolutions tended to fail, especially those inspired from outside. And he wanted Castro to "have a chance" because Batista had been "altogether despicable." Under him and American gamblers and gangsters like Meyer Lansky, "Cuba was the whorehouse of the Western Hemisphere." The exile leaders' politics suggested that the Batista ways might be coming back.

By late March he was sufficiently disturbed to phone Arthur Schlesinger. Plank had shared an office with the historian at Harvard. He told Schlesinger that he had discussed his concern with Bill Barnes of the Harvard Law School. "We don't think this thing is going to go, whatever it is," Plank told Schlesinger. "We'd like to come down and brief you."

Schlesinger asked the two professors to come at once. He happened to be working on a government white paper on Cuba. The President had instructed him that *if* there was to be an invasion—and the emphasis was Kennedy's—he wanted the world to know that it was not to mean a return of the old order. "Our objection isn't to the Cuban revolution," he told Schlesinger. "It is to the fact that Castro has turned it over to the Communists."

To Schlesinger here was an opportunity to make history, not just to record it. Closeting himself for several days, he composed a document mixing eloquence ("The people of Cuba remain our brothers"), humility ("We acknowledge past omissions and errors in our relationship to them"), and toughness tempered with flattery: "We call once again on the Castro regime to sever its links with the international Communist movement, to return to the original purposes which brought so many gallant men together in the Sierra Maestra and to restore the integrity of the Cuban Revolution."

Plank and Barnes (who went to Yale with the CIA's Tracy Barnes but was not related to him) arrived during Schlesinger's labors. Schlesinger immediately assigned them an office in the West Wing of the White House. The academics worked through the night and produced a written appraisal of Castro's strength. It predicted that efforts to unseat Castro would fail because the last thing Cubans wanted was the return of politicians who went into exile with the Lanskys and other forces of corruption.

Schlesinger read it and said he would show it to the President. Meanwhile, he arranged for them to see Tracy Barnes and Paul Nitze of the Pentagon. Barnes gave them a charming dinner at his home but no comfort for their ideas. Nitze did not even seem to pay much attention. The next day Schlesinger reported that he had shown the professors' document to the President, but that it was too late to stop the move against Castro.

Plank and his friend went back to Harvard, certain they were right, galled by the futility of their efforts to change events: "We had access to the top of power, and there was nothing we could do to stop it."

Assembling U.S. Naval Support

Rear Admiral John A. Clark thought the operation might succeed because of its "sheer brazenness." A tiny, birdlike figure with very light blue eyes and an urbane, gentle manner, "Johnny" Clark was hard to picture as a senior military commander when he was not in uniform. He had acquired a reputation as a smooth operator commanding Hunter Killer Force Atlantic, a branch of the Navy that never went to peace. Year after year, always two weeks at sea followed by two weeks ashore for maintenance, he had run an aircraft carrier and a group of destroyers sweeping the Atlantic for Soviet submarines, his jets patrolling overhead. It was exacting duty and made a man forget that the rest of the world did not normally live poised for nuclear trouble.

In the last week of March, Clark was summoned to the office of Admiral "Denny" Dennison on the old hospital grounds of the naval base in Norfolk, where a captain from Washington briefed him about Eduardo García's little navy and its mission. Clark thought the details were "rather sketchy." In fact he was entrusted with as much relevant information as anyone was given at the time.

He and his staff were to board the carrier *Essex*. The carrier was to take aboard a special crack squadron of AD-4 Skyhawk jet attack fighters. Along with five destroyers, the *Essex* was to escort five of García's ships close to a rendezvous point outside the Bay of Pigs. The hull numbers of the destroyers were to be painted out. All were assigned separate courses so they would remain out of sight of each other and so that their movements would not appear coordinated. The carrier was not to venture as far as the rendezvous point, but two of the destroyers would meet the García ships there and take them into the Bay of Pigs and Cuban waters. Clark's job was to make sure that the Cubans got safely to the beaches. His task force was to guard them against possible enemy interference. This would be highly unlikely to create problems, because Castro's air force would be destroyed. He was not to allow a shot to be fired by an American vessel or aircraft unless absolutely necessary in self-defense.

Johnny Clark listened to this intricate script "a little bit nonplussed," his head slightly cocked. Then he asked Dennison, "You mean I'm to go down there armed to the teeth, but I'm not supposed to do anything?"

Dennison, annoyed as ever about the entire venture and its messy, unmilitary ways, was trying hard not to show his feelings. Grimly he said, "Yes, my darling daughter, don't go near the water."

A dozen doubts flooded Clark's mind, but he was given his "top-secret" eight-page operations order and found himself silenced by its two-page "intelligence annex." It was "simply hypnotizing." It "just oozed confidence" to a degree that made the operation look like a folk festival. As soon as "the first shot was fired," the populace of several provinces would arise, especially in western Cuba. The political prisoners incarcerated on the Isle of Pines would be released and join the invading Brigade. Castro's own troops would defect and "jump aboard." Whoever composed this intelligence estimate was totally convinced that the operation could not fail. The optimism was infectious.

Much of Clark's briefing was devoted to impressing him with the requirement for absolute secrecy. Tight security was normal in the admiral's life; for this operation, the secrecy criteria went beyond anything he had ever heard. Fake reports of the ships' movements were to be filed with the Atlantic Fleet Movements Report Center. Record-keeping was to be limited to the absolute minimum. Whatever operational records became unavoidable during the mission were to be destroyed afterward. For the time being, Admiral Clark was to discuss no aspect of the operation with anyone. Not with anyone at all.

Clark did not protest, but he clearly needed immediate assistance. Somebody had to plan the routes and transit times for the ships and arrange schedules of meetings with the oiler that had to refuel the vessels. The *Essex* was not equipped to operate Skyhawks. New spare parts had to be brought aboard. The carrier's catapult fittings had to be changed so they would be compatible with faster aircraft. The admiral could not possibly accomplish all these preparations alone. He decided to read his second in command into the operation: Captain Edward R. Fickenscher, Jr., the chief of staff, known as "Deacon" since his Naval Academy days in the class of 1940.

In Admiral Dennison's office, Deacon was introduced to a CIA agent who wore a commander's uniform. The CIA man said he was confident that "the whole Cuban nation was ready to rise up and throw Castro out, and all that was needed was somebody to come and help them." Fickenscher thought "he made it sound pretty good." Deacon also was struck by the impression that nobody had "a clear picture of what we were supposed to do down there." He did come away with the clear intent that "if these Cubans would get into trouble, we would help them out."

Dennison told Clark and Fickenscher, "If we have to do it, we can only hope that men of goodwill around the world will know why we're doing it." Perhaps all the naval power that was heading for the Bay of Pigs would be more than a professional escort service, after all. This possibility had now been forecast by no less than the Commander in Chief of the Atlantic Fleet. To the task force commanders it made immediate good sense to be prepared for orders to do more than guard duty. Throughout the operation, the idea of such a change in orders would never leave their minds.

Deacon Fickenscher promptly set about plotting his ships' routes. He got new catapults installed. He personally briefed the captain of the oiler about when and where to rendezvous for refueling. He made sure that the Movements Report Center would "file and forget" the customary route which he told them the task force would take. For the records, it was headed for antisubmarine operations in the area of "Point Pete" in the Atlantic near Bermuda. In actuality, the force would take the new jets aboard some two hundred miles due east of Jacksonville and then head into the Caribbean. It would move in radio silence, highly unusual in peacetime.

Captain S. S. ("Pete") Searcy, Jr., the skipper of the *Essex*, was "personally pleased" that his ship had been chosen to play a key role in an American effort to "wipe out Castro and Company." He was a steely, laconic old sailor and former combat pilot, Naval Academy class of '33, with large, piercing brown eyes, a grave face and a strong resemblance to Eric Sevareid. He did not, however, share the commentator's liberal outlook. Pete Searcy thought of himself as a practicing patriot, a conservative and a fervent anti-Communist. His distaste for Castro was profound. So was the loyalty of the carrier's 3,200 men to their skipper. His officers said that if Pete Searcy had told them to line up and march over the side of the ship, they would not question the order.

Searcy's orders were to take the *Essex* from its base at Quonset Point, Rhode Island, to Norfolk. He thought this was strange because he had no CarDiv (carrier division) commander aboard at the time. In Norfolk he felt better when Clark and Fickenscher joined the ship and Admiral Dennison handed Searcy a sealed brown envelope. There was no discussion. Searcy was merely told that the envelope contained his operational order; that it was top secret; that only thirteen copies existed; and that he was to take it back to the ship.

Searcy opened the envelope in his in-port cabin and was "completely surprised." He liked the idea of the operation, but wondered why the document was relatively brief. It did not contain the intelligence annex.

It reduced the Bay of Pigs project to a naval traffic order of unusual complexity but left nothing to the imagination. He decided it was time to call in his executive officer, the navigator, the chief engineer and the air operations officer.

When his men filed into the cabin, each was given his turn to read the order while the others waited. For nearly half an hour, the silence in the cabin was broken only by an occasional "Holy cow!" and a "Jesus Christ!" The ensuing discussion was brief and matter-of-fact. No one decided to raise the obvious question: Was the United States going to war in Cuba?

Captain Robert R. Crutchfield received his assignment from Admiral Dennison at about the same time but was never shown a word in writing. A division commander of the five-ship destroyer force, he was called "Commodore" and was going to be the senior U.S. officer closest to the beach. He would be most vulnerable to any unexpected developments arising from the combat situation, yet the absence of written orders didn't trouble him. Indeed, he liked it. It reminded him of Lord Nelson calling his skippers together in his cabin and telling them, without going through the traditional minuets of formal procedure, what they were all going to do.

Crutchfield, a burly, thin-lipped, florid-faced Virginian, had the musculature of a farmer or a boxer. He looked immovable, a man whose word had best not be questioned, and had the reputation of a tough, taciturn taskmaster. His speech was soft but wary, deliberate, with faint remnants of a drawl. Eventually he would become an admiral even though he did not attend the Naval Academy and many others who held key spots in the Cuban operation found that it ruined their careers.

Crutchfield had a flair for improvisation, and nobody who improvised made admiral unless he was improvising to follow his orders better. Crutchfield's orders were to protect the Brigade convoy with his fast little ships but never, never to fire unless this was absolutely indispensable. Before his briefing ended, he realized that the old manual searchlights on his ships could become a critical handicap. They were fine for long-range signaling. In this operation, with his own forces and the Brigade flotilla ordered to observe radio silence, he had to identify possible enemy ships visually, at night. His searchlights needed automatic controls and had to be linked to the radar in the Combat Information Center so that possible targets could be illuminated when they were spotted.

Within two days, the lights on the destroyers were hooked to radar via sound-power telephones. The lights had no markings to indicate the various directional bearings, so Crutchfield and his men drew bearing circles on their decks with chalk. It was "very, very crude," but for two nights en route to their meeting with García's navy Crutchfield, on the *Eaton*, practiced on his fellow-destroyer *Murray*, and vice versa, until they "got pretty good at it."

It was good for the *Eaton* to be working closely with the *Murray* anyway, because the *Eaton* would lead the Brigade ships into the Bay of Pigs. The *Murray* would guard them from the rear. There was no telling what surprises Castro might prepare for them.

The hull number of the *Eaton* was 510. She was known by her crew as the "Five and Ten." Like many old dime stores, she was fast but tired. When her skipper, Commander Peter Perkins, a thoughtful, international-minded six-footer, a member of the United World Federalists, heard that he was going on an ultrasecret operation, he fell to worrying seriously about the condition of the ship.

He was told next to nothing about the mission except that Commodore Crutchfield would be aboard and knew all about it. The antisubmarine capability of the ship was going to come in handy (later, Perkins thought this was mentioned only as a ruse). It was all "real vague, very vague," yet such "great secrecy" prevailed that he at once said to himself it "smells like combat," and here he was running a nineteen-year-old ship "limping along."

It troubled Perkins that his ship might not measure up to what was obviously a touch-and-go expedition. The destroyers of the *Eaton* class were exceptionally fast—up to thirty-nine knots per hour—but the engines were so unreliable that Perkins never knew whether they would last for the entire length of the usual two-week antisub exercise. He had "never been happy with the reliability of the ships. Nobody was."

There was more to be concerned about. The *Eaton* had been receiving so many new men that Perkins could not gauge how well the crew would operate as a team. He hadn't fired his guns for such a long time that he was worrried about their accuracy, especially since it did sound as if they possibly "were going to have to shoot." Quickly, he had his men build a floating target. They practiced firing their five-inch guns at the float for a day en route to Cuba (not that Perkins was certain that this was where he was headed). They also practiced going to general quarters often, night and day. They were the division flagship, after all. Nobody else had a commodore aboard. Perkins knew Crutchfield liked a tight ship. He was going to do his damnedest so the boss wouldn't have to transfer to another destroyer.

Aboard the *Cony*, another of the destroyers assigned to shepherd the Brigade fleet, the skipper, Commander Frank C. Dunham, cheerful, talkative, smooth of face and manner, thought he was headed for "Point Pete," to hunt submarines, as always. An hour before under-way time, he was called aboard the *Waller*, which was also headed for the mission. The captain of the fifth destroyer, the *Conway*, was already there.

The skipper of the *Waller*, Commander Gilven Slonim, said, "Gentlemen, I called you over at this late moment to tell you that when we depart this morning for ASW operations, we are not heading for Point Pete." When the captains raised questions, Slonim repeated, "Gentlemen, all I can tell you now is that when we depart Norfolk, we are not going to Point Pete." Then he added, "We're probably going to be gone longer than our normal two weeks. I forbid you to call home to tell your wives what I've just told you. You have authority to tell one other person in your ship what I've just told you. I imagine that will be your exec. Godspeed, goodbye."

Dunham and the other captains returned to their ships "absolutely mystified." Dick Bissell would have been pleased if he could have seen their puzzled faces. Here was one bunch that wasn't going to blab his secrets about.

Commander William J. (Jim) Forgy had been planning to take some leave and thought there was "something really screwy" about his sudden new mission. He was executive officer of VA-34 fighter squadron, the "Blue Blasters," based at Cecil Field Naval Air Station, outside Jacksonville, and the orders were to fly the squadron's twelve AD4-2 Skyhawk jets aboard the Aircraft Carrier *Essex* on April 4 "for ASW [antisubmarine warfare] exercises." Their equipment was to be airlifted to the *Essex* immediately "COD" (carrier onboard delivery).

Neither Forgy nor anybody else in the squadron could figure out what the orders were really all about. They had just returned February 25 from the carrier *Saratoga* in the Mediterranean, and they were combat-ready. Planes never went to sea for "exercises" so soon after lengthy overseas duty. When they did go aboard a carrier, they didn't fly to it; the planes were lifted aboard in port—it was easier and less risky. And if the *Essex* was going on antisub patrol, why was it sending away half of its regular complement of Grumman S-2 propeller-driven craft that were specifically designed to hunt, track and kill submarines?

Whatever was happening evidently required the fastest, most versatile available fighter. That description fit the Skyhawk, known as "Heineman's hot rod," in honor of the Douglas Aircraft engineer who designed it. It cruised at three hundred knots, speedy for its time. It was an attack aircraft, superior for supporting ground troops, but somebody must have thought the squadron might see air-to-air combat too. Lieutenant Sam Sayers, the weapons training officer, was sent scrambling to calculate how far ahead of an airborne target the pilots should aim their rockets and machine guns. They had not done that kind of firing before.

When the squadron arrived aboard the *Essex*, the mystery deepened. Admiral Clark, the task force commander, visited the pilots in the ready room and said that they were going on "some sort of operation" in the Caribbean, but that he couldn't "find out anything" about it. The ship's navigator would not tell the aviators where they were, much less where they were going. Although no aircraft was ever supposed to be launched without at least one "bingo base" where it could be diverted in case of emergency, the pilots' repeated requests for "divert bases" were ignored. The push was on for plenty of practice flights to get used to the new carrier and "to get that ordnance ready." Somebody expected that the squadron was going to do some shooting.

At whom? Sam Sayers thought the operation might involve Haiti or the Dominican Republic, maybe even Cuba. He thought "it was kind of exciting" to put his training to use, to be "doing our thing for the first time." And there still was opportunity for relaxation. At sea, it turned out to be Sam who made the 103,000th landing aboard the *Essex* in his jet, No. 301; the occasion was commemorated in front of the ship's photographers in the wardroom with the cake-cutting ceremony that followed every thousandth landing.

Rendezvous in Nicaragua

Jake Engler visited the Key West maritime base and asked Gray and Rip to step out into the parking lot where nobody could hear them. He told them that the Brigade was going to invade Cuba, but not where or when. To Gray, Jake's instructions sounded unremarkable.* They were to sail their ships to the beaches, land two teams of six frogmen each, make sure that the Brigade got ashore and give the invaders any help they could. Gray's *Blagar* was to be the command vessel and carry arms for one thousand men, Rip's *Barbara J.* for five hundred. As soon as the beachhead was firmly established, they were to withdraw and be available to drop off their cargo at whatever locations the Cuban underground could best use them.

Ordered to leave the next day, they almost didn't make it. Both of the eighteen-foot catamarans which the LCI's needed for the frogmen had

---

*As late as 1977, Bissell insisted that Gray and Rip were not told to accompany the invasion, that they decided to go along on a whim of their own.

been damaged on earlier operations. Replacements were being trucked nonstop from Texas. By the time they arrived and the outboard engines were mounted, it was 11 P.M. The ships sailed for Nicaragua at one in the morning.

It was a noisy journey. The Cuban crews had never fired a machine gun before; the CIA planners felt there would be no enemy targets for them to shoot at. Gray and Rip were not so sure, so they had cleaned out a Key West toy store of all the kites it had in stock. The kites came in several gay colors. The CIA agents covered them with luminous paint, which turned them into fine targets when searchlights were played on them during extracurricular gunnery practice at night.

Andy Pruna was still feeling terrific about being part of the frogman team. To look special, all twelve had grown beards and called themselves "the twelve apostles." On March 10 a blacked-out plane flew them to New Orleans. They were met by Gray and Rip, who gave them more commando training in a deactivated naval ammunition depot some twenty miles downstream and across the Mississippi.

Once they got a day off in New Orleans. Pruna found it a mixed blessing. Agents followed them "everywhere" and "were so goddamned obvious it was insane." Several of the men shook off their guards. Nobody was supposed to make phone calls, and Pruna refrained from calling his parents in Miami, though he was very tempted. One called his wife and gave away where he was. Pruna told him he was a "motherfucker." He wanted the frogmen to be model fighters.

At the ammunition depot, they kept up their water training in a filthy swimming pool. They met and trained with the infiltration team, who were "really great." But they resented having to make up beds in preparation for a group of older men led by Nino Díaz, a controversial politician; they looked "really terrible, all out of shape," and their morale was poor.

Finally the frogmen were taken to the García Line's *Río Escondido*, at anchorage on the Mississippi, and introduced to the captain, Gus Tirado, a merry little Spaniard, a bachelor who had been working with "the company" for more than a year. He had "exfiltrated" such resistance leaders as Nino Díaz and Manolo Ray out of Cuba and had great confidence in the CIA. Its agents had invariably performed well for Tirado. They even got him his mascot, a German shepherd which the captain had trained to attract the attention of guards and customs officials while he smuggled his high-level stowaways aboard.*

---

*When the dog, Aitor, died of heart failure, the CIA replaced it with another German Shepherd, Ciclon, just before Tirado left for the Bay of Pigs.

Now Tirado carried a critical load for the invasion: the communications van that was supposed to become the command lifeline between the Brigade and Washington; large quantities of ammunition; 54,000 gallons of aviation gasoline in tanks below deck and another two hundred 55-gallon drums topside.

His voyage began poorly and ended in catastrophe. Shortly after he started down the Mississippi at 3 A.M., the ship shuddered. From the bridge, Tirado called the engine room: "We hit something! How's the engine going?" The chief engineer said, "We have more revolutions than usual; everything seems to be fine." By noon, the vessel was doing only four knots per hour instead of the usual ten. Tirado decided something had to be wrong with the propellers and asked the frogmen to dive and look.

Alonso and Pruna found the propellers entangled in wires and lumber. Only one of the three portside propellers was not bent. The divers cleared the props, but the ship never overcame its limp. It made only six knots per hour and arrived at the Nicaragua staging base two days late. The radio operator had not been trained on the ship's new equipment, and the *Río Escondido* was unaccounted for. It troubled Tirado that nobody bothered to send a plane to look for him.

En route to Nicaragua, word finally seeped through to the crew that the ship was not, as they had been told, delivering supplies to the Nicaraguan government but was headed for a full-fledged invasion of Cuba. Given a chance to bow out of the mission, they went to Tirado en masse and asked him if he was going. When he said, "Yes, I go," they said, "We all go." Tirado was naturally pleased by this, but not by much else. The ship got new radios, supposedly to communicate only with other sets in the immediate area, but they picked up voices of cabdrivers in California. The 180 men of the Sixth Battalion who came aboard seemed cheerful enough, but there were no life jackets for them.

It wasn't until Eduardo García's ships arrived in Puerto Cabezas that the other crews were told they were headed for Cuba. They had been led to believe that their arms, fuel and ammunition were destined for the government of Nicaragua and would be unloaded in that country. They had not been told that they were about to take an army aboard. While nobody had questioned Eduardo's Batistano gunners, the CIA had screened the captains and the crews for political reliability. Now the merchant men were given a chance to bow out of the venture. Six, including one captain with relatives in Cuba, declined to make the trip and were detained in Nicaragua until the operation ended.

Eduardo, wearing khaki pants and a ship officer's white shirt, watched over the loading of his fleet. He was pleased to see the cargo, which included cases of whiskey and candy.

"These Americans really think of everything," he told one of his men.

Not quite. The Americans were still so positive that the ships would never come under attack that they could not be bothered to install the .50-caliber machine guns that were to be mounted on the decks as Eduardo had insisted in Washington. When he kept reminding the CIA men of their promise to mount the weapons, the Americans delegated the job to Nicaraguan soldiers. The Nicaraguans were inexperienced at this work. They were also so slow that some of the guns, including all of those on the *Houston,* had to be installed at sea by Eduardo's own people. On the *Río Escondido* the weapons had to be mounted without welded plates by the ship's mechanic, and they "shook like crazy." The fragility of his defenses worried even the easygoing Tirado, because "our ship was one bomb"; it wouldn't require much of a fuse to set it off.

When Gray and Rip arrived with their LCI's in Puerto Cabezas on April 1, they did not know of the switch from Trinidad to Zapata, but the base was in a state of emergency. At Trinidad, the Brigade would have landed on two adjoining beaches—really one beach divided by a creek. The Zapata plans called for three beaches sixteen miles apart. The original landing fleet of three LCU's and four LCVP's was suddenly insufficient, but by now Bissell and his men were accustomed to improvising. They had quickly purchased and flown in thirty-six eighteen-and-a-half-foot dark-gray aluminum boats with brand-new untested outboard motors that had to be mounted. Working almost nonstop in 100-plus degree heat, Rip and Gray and their ships' crews barely got the little fleet outfitted by April 10 when a Constellation arrived with six or eight senior CIA and Pentagon brass to inspect the troops and brief the leaders.

Rip, Gray and all the ships' captains were briefed in a tent with wooden floors at an isolated end of the Retalhuleu airstrip in Guatemala. American security men guarded all four corners of the tent. No outsiders were allowed within earshot. Maps of the invasion area covered the canvas walls. Each man received a reddish-brown manila file with a string tied around it. Inside was a precise hour-by-hour plan of the landings in English and Spanish.

The briefing was conducted by Norman Imler, the chief of paramilitary maritime operations under Colonel Hawkins. A lieutenant commander in the Naval Air Reserve, Imler was another six-footer, quiet, speaking slowly with a slight Midwestern drawl, bald, extremely thin, imperturbably cheerful, a bland personality with no distinguishing characteristics except a prominent Adam's apple.

He seemed to have plenty to be cheerful about. Castro, he explained during the five-hour session, had only sixteen operational aircraft. These would be knocked out on the ground by three air strikes: on D minus two (Saturday, two days before D-Day); D minus one; and D-Day. Two U.S. Navy destroyers would escort the Brigade flotilla close to the landing area. A Navy LSD (landing ship dock) would carry the LCU's and LCVP's to rendezvous with the García fleet off the beaches.

As a graduate of the armor school at Fort Knox, Gray was knowledgeable about tanks and knew that Castro had the "tremendous" Stalin III tanks. He was delighted to hear that these would become "sitting ducks" for the rockets of the Brigade's B-26s. The tanks had only three roads to the beaches. These would turn into "shooting galleries": they were forty-foot causeways built up from fill and dirt of the surrounding swamps, with no way to get off them.

It sounded open-and-shut: the Brigade had only to carve out a bridgehead large enough to keep Castro artillery fire off the Playa Girón airstrip where the Brigade B-26s would quickly start operating. Eventually, doubled or tripled in strength by the underground and defectors, the CIA force would simply "walk out." It all made excellent sense to Gray . . . if . . . the Brigade air force could operate as planned.

It was a big if. The operation's most critical element, air power, had first become controversial in January with a CIA memorandum entitled "Policy Decisions Required for Conduct of Strike Operations Against Government of Cuba." It recommended air preparation of the landing area to commence no later than dawn before D-Day (D minus one) and that a "maximum" number of aircraft be used. "The Cuban air force and naval vessels capable of opposing our landing must be knocked out or neutralized before our amphibious shipping makes its final run into the beach," the memo said. "If this is not done we will be courting disaster."

It was the overture to an intense bureaucratic battle. The CIA wanted maximum air power. The State Department wanted it kept at a minimum so that the planes could ostensibly originate in Cuba. The lines were drawn at a meeting of the Special Group in January. The State Department representative protested strong air power as too "spectacular." He especially warned against the use of jets because it could not be claimed that these were based on the island. The argument continued until D-Day and beyond.

"Look, Imler," Gray Lynch said, "everything is on our planes. Are they going to be able to do the job?"

"Well, as long as we have air superiority we'll be able to take care of this," Imler replied, agreeing that control of the air was "the key factor."

Captain Ryberg of the *Blagar* was named "naval commander," which worried Gray and Rip. Gray, in particular, was suspicious of the freighter-crew mentality: "When you say 'invasion' to those people, they don't know what the hell you're talking about." It was the less diplomatic Rip who, once they confronted Imler alone, asked that Gray and he be named commanders of the invasion fleet.

"Well, now," said Imler, "you know the captains of these ships are very funny. They don't like people intruding on their prerogatives. You'll have to work this out among yourselves. The captain will listen to you. You'll make suggestions, and don't put it in the way of an order." Nobody was truly in charge.

Gray and Rip were to scout the beaches with the frogmen, mark them with landing lights and "expedite" the unloading operations. "Expedite" was Imler's favorite euphemism, and he kept repeating it.

It occurred to Gray that there might be more to "scouting" than merely taking a look around, especially at his landing site, the principal one, Blue Beach, where most of the ships were to be unloaded and the Brigade command was to go ashore. He pointed out to Imler that his frogmen had never been in combat. What if the beaches were heavily defended? Imler told him not to worry, there would be no defenses. In the event that there were, Gray was to have the frogmen "back out."

"This is very, very important," Gray said. "I'm going to have to make a decision right there on the whole landing. I want to know whether or not those things are defended. I want to *know*, not assume. Let me tell you now: if I have to, I'll go ashore myself to check to be sure."

Gray had been cut off from news reports and did not know of President Kennedy's order that no Americans were to participate in Cuban military operations. Imler said nothing about this. "OK," he told Gray, "do whatever you have to do."

Pleased with the outcome of the briefing, Gray set to studying the U-2 reconnaissance photographs that Imler brought along from Washington. They pictured the entire landing area and the surrounding countryside in impressive detail. Gray paid special attention to Blue Beach. The more closely he peered, the more obvious it became that a dark mass extended under the water just offshore. He kept looking at that dark mass. It seemed suspicious. He said to himself, "Coral reefs!"

He mentioned his suspicion to Imler's men, and they sent him to the

air section. In a specially secured area within the section there was a
CIA photo interpreter, working with sensitive technical equipment.
Gray had to get special permission to enter this tiny domain. He had
seen only prints of the photos. The photo specialist had the negatives.
He placed one on a glass surface that was lighted from beneath.
Considerably more detail became visible.

"I want to know about this stuff under here," Gray said, pointing at
the dark mass.

The photo interpreter looked at the spot carefully.

"Seaweed," he said.

"Well, are you sure?"

"Oh yeah. That's seaweed all along here. You won't have any
problem."*

Elsewhere near the runway, in a clearing of the piney woods, the
Brigade commanders and doctors were briefed by Colonel Frank. The
men sat on benches, some on the ground. The aerial photos were
displayed on makeshift plywood easels. As the colonel pointed out
various landing sites and initial objectives, Dr. Juan Sordo, a Brigade
doctor who had been a surgeon in Havana, looked closely at some
ripples and shadows in the tidewater off Blue Beach. He was an avid
fisherman and a sport pilot and had once done aerial photography
elsewhere along the same coast for an American company. Similar
shadows in his own photos had turned out to be reefs, so he spoke up:

"Listen, those are coral heads in there. How are you going to get the
landing craft in?"

"I beg to differ with you," Frank said. "Those are clouds."

"I beg to differ with *you*," Dr. Sordo said. "They are not clouds, they
are coral heads. I know them, and I have seen them, and I have taken
pictures of them. It's going to be stupid to try to get landing barges in
there, because you won't have more than two or three feet of water over
those coral heads, and that's going to stop you!"

Calmly but unequivocally, Frank suggested that Dr. Sordo worry
about the expedition's medical services instead. "You're going to get in,
Doctor, you're going to get in," he said.

Dr. Sordo "decided to shut up because he was so positive."

Gray too had been reassured about his suspicions, but, en route from
Nicaragua to the beaches, when the aerial photos were spread out
before all the Brigade commanders and the frogmen in the little mess

*While aboveground objects, even license numbers on cars, could be deciphered from such
photographs, accurate interpretation of objects below water was extremely difficult, especially
when wind ripples were present.

hall aboard the *Blagar*, José Alonso also pointed out the ripples at Blue Beach. He told Gray that this meant the water was extremely shallow. Gray said the experts had told him the water level was OK.

"Well, look again," Alonso said.

"These are experts, honcho," Gray said.

"I don't care," Alonso said. "This is my land, and I know this is a coral reef, and there's no way for us to get there. That photo has been interpreted in the wrong way."

"We got reasons to believe that those photos are OK," said Gray.

Alonso shook his head and said, "Well, we'll do the best we can."

The Brigade doctors had been promised that a hospital ship would accompany the invasion fleet. When they arrived in Nicaragua, they were told that, instead, a field hospital with 120 beds had been crated and was being loaded aboard the *Houston*. That sounded satisfactory. Dr. Sordo inspected the crates, and they contained everything that was likely to be needed.

Additional doctors had arrived from Miami, but more had been promised. Six more did arrive shortly before the sailing date. They said they had been assigned to a hospital ship. When they learned that there was none, Dr. Almeida faced "kind of a rebellion." The new doctors were "disgusted." They said they would serve only aboard a hospital ship and went back to Miami.

CHAPTER FOUR # At the Watershed

Awaiting the Decision

On March 29 Arthur Schlesinger noted in his journal that a "final" decision would have to come April 4. He felt "the tide is flowing against the project."

There had been another meeting in the Cabinet Room that day. Delightedly, Schlesinger found the President "growing steadily more skeptical." Kennedy was concerned that the landing could handicap the chances of a settlement with the Soviets on Laos, another crisis spot that threatened to erupt in warfare. The "noise level" of the invasion also continued to trouble him.

"Do you really have to have these air strikes?" he kept asking Bissell. The CIA man said his group would work further to insure maximum effectiveness for minimum noise from the air.

Was the CIA really certain that enough Cubans on the island would join in an uprising? Bissell continued to be reassuring. Eventually, he and Dulles said that 2,500 to 3,000 Cubans belonged to resistance organizations, some 20,000 more sympathized with the underground and, once the Brigade was settled in, the "active support" of one fourth of the population was likely.* They mentioned requests of arms drops from the resistance. There was no talk about the countless attempted arms drops that had failed month after month.

The Zapata plan had a D-Day of April 5. It was obvious the deadline could not be kept. The President now advanced it to April 10. He still

---

*The White House advisers unanimously expected uprisings in Cuba. So did the Joint Chiefs. In 1963, Allen Dulles wrote in *The Craft of Intelligence:* "I know of no estimate that a spontaneous uprising of the unarmed population of Cuba would be touched off by the landing." This statement must be read with emphasis on the words "spontaneous" and "unarmed."

139

withheld approval. Bissell was relieved that the operation was not further reduced or canceled.

The CIA's intelligence from within Cuba continued to sound cheery. Information Report No. CS-3/469,391 reported:

> Opposition to the Castro regime is becoming more open; grumbling about government policies is becoming more audible. The lower classes are now actively opposed to Castro. In front of the G-2 [secret police] offices the lines of those detained are made up of the poorer classes . . . The shortage of basic food and household items, felt by all levels of society, is causing increasing dissatisfaction . . .

The CIA's "Current Intelligence Weekly Summary" said on March 30:

> Sabotage and organized resistance activities evidently are continuing to increase throughout Cuba despite a presumably steady gain in the strength of the government's instruments of repression. Accounts of attempted sabotage of industrial and agricultural installations are becoming increasingly frequent, and anti-Castro terrorists are exploding bombs daily in Havana— twelve in a single day. . . .

For the presumably more reliable technological detail, Bissell thought he could depend on Arthur Lundahl.

Lundahl did not just love his work. He relished it as few men do. Small, gregarious and infinitely patient, he had taught geology at the University of Chicago. In 1940, infectiously enthusiastic, he plunged into the new science of photogrammetry and pioneered in the techniques for interpreting aerial photos—drawing from them information about sizes, shapes, "trafficability" and other details of objects on the ground. During World War II he analyzed potential invasion sites for the Navy. "The photo interpreter is like a Pied Piper," he liked to say. "He can lead the decision maker right over the cliff."

In 1953, Bissell recruited him to set up a Photo Intelligence Division with thirteen men. Lundahl said, "I don't want any cloak-and-dagger crap crawling around some border." He would unlock technology for spying, and he did.*

Lundahl was never told details about the Cuba project. The more he was drawn into it, the more he wondered whether the United States was

---

*When Lundahl retired in 1973, his division numbered two thousand people. He worked with Bissell on the interpretation of the revolutionary U-2 and satellite photographs and briefed President Kennedy on the aerial photos that set off—and helped settle—the Cuban Missile Crisis. The British knighted Lundahl, and the CIA awarded him the National Security Medal.

"suddenly going to break a Pearl Harbor of its own." But he was very fond of Bissell, trusted him totally, and Bissell said, "Art, make no mistake about it. This is the most important thing on your plate."

Lundahl set up a special crew of four—later twelve—specialists who worked on draftsmen tables in a separate laboratory crammed with optical equipment. The door was marked "Off Limits." Into this room flowed films of Cuba made from seventy thousand feet during twenty U-2 flights over seven weeks. Mostly Bissell wanted lengths, widths, gradients and other details of various beaches and their surroundings.

When the Trinidad plan was scrapped, Lundahl went to Quarters Eye to brief Bissell and his men on the Bay of Pigs. The special war room of the Cuba operation was on the first floor. Its windows were permanently blacked out. Only Bissell wore the red badge that authorized unlimited access to any CIA office, but even he could enter this room only if someone opened from within or if he knew a special combination of numbers that changed at irregular intervals. The numbers had to be punched on knobs that surrounded a buzzer. If the right numbers were punched and then the buzzer button, the door opened.

Within, two walls were covered with maps and the plastic overlays on which the tactical details were drawn. Lundahl was asked about the airfield at the Bay of Pigs. He displayed a sixteen-by-sixteen print and pointed to obstacles on the unfinished runway, evidently sand or gravel. "We do not believe an airplane can survive without cartwheeling," he said.* Bissell was "very upset."

Dave Phillips, the propaganda chief, was even more distressed when he weighed the implications of the change in landing sites. He learned of it by walking to the largest map and finding a red cross marked over Trinidad. "Trinidad is out," Colonel Hawkins, the military commander, told him. "Now we are going to land here." He pointed to a spot on the coast some one hundred miles west of Trinidad. Phillips squinted to read the tiny print: "Bahía de Cochinos." Even after five years in Cuba, he had never heard of it. He laughed. Somebody had to be kidding. How on earth could his propagandists persuade Cubans to join the Brigade at a place with such a vile name?

Hawkins was uninterested in psychological warfare. "That's the new plan," was all he said.

"But it's too far from the mountains," Phillips protested. He might have been talking directly at the swamps.

---

*Even this negative intelligence turned out to be wrong (or at least obsolete) by the time of the invasion. The Brigade found the airfield cleared and serviceable.

Dick Goodwin, the Kennedy speech writer who had become the White House specialist on Latin America, was attending a meeting in Adolf Berle's office in the State Department.

"Why do you think the Cubans will rise up?" he asked Bissell.

Bissell chose not to reply directly. "Don't we have an NIE [National Intelligence Estimate] on that?" he asked one of his assistants.

"Yes," said the assistant.

The discussion shifted to what might happen if the Brigade ran into desperate trouble anyway. At worst, the CIA men said, the invaders could disappear into the mountains.

Keeping the Cover On

Bissell thought that "a fig leaf" of secrecy still covered vital parts of his operation. President Kennedy knew otherwise. On March 31, he received a memorandum from Schlesinger, who reported on a visit from Howard Handleman, a reporter for *U.S. News & World Report*. Handleman had just spent ten days in Miami. His knowledge of the operation was remarkable.

Cuban exiles had told him an invasion was "about to be launched," he told Schlesinger. There had recently been a "great increase" in recruitment for the training camps. He described the Brigade's training and planes. Schlesinger asked how the exiles thought they were going to "beat the vastly superior forces of Castro." Handleman said they expected a "mass uprising" but "that the logic of the situation will require the U.S. to send in Marines to make sure that the invasion is a success."

Schlesinger listened deadpan. He was pleased that Handleman understood "the delicacy of the situation" and did not plan to reveal all the details he had uncovered. But Schlesinger was jarred. "Obviously," he wrote the President, "if an enterprising magazine writer could pick up all this in Miami in a couple of weeks, Havana must be well posted on developments."

A few days later there was an even closer call. Gilbert Harrison, the publisher of the *New Republic*, sent Schlesinger galleys of a pseudonymous article called "Our Men in Miami." He asked whether any reason existed for not publishing it. Schlesinger found it "careful, accurate and devastating." Feeling "defeated by the moral issue" of whether the government could properly ask an editor "to suppress the truth," he handed the galleys to the President. Kennedy read them on the spot and said he hoped the article could be stopped. Harrison "accepted the suggestion and without question." Schlesinger felt this was "a patriotic act." It did leave him "oddly uncomfortable."

Ten days before the invasion its fig-leaf shelter essentially fell away—because Tad Szulc was on vacation.

Szulc, swarthy, voluble and indefatigable, had been the *New York Times* man in Rio de Janeiro. En route to New York for reassignment, he stopped off in Miami to visit friends. He was an unusually gifted reporter, even for the *Times*. His boss, Turner Catledge, the managing editor, loved him because he seemed "news prone." Wherever Szulc went, news began to break. He spoke fluent Spanish. His cronies and contacts were spotted all over Latin America, and he had covered its upheavals for years.

Szulc was staying at the unfashionable McAllister Hotel in crowded downtown Miami. It was his first night in town. He was in the bar waiting for a friend when he spotted an acquaintance, a former follower of Castro whom he had met in Cuba the year before. "What're you doing in Miami?" the man asked. "You probably heard about the training."

Szulc had indeed heard about it, but he was wary. Refugees always spun schemes to invade their old homelands. "Is it serious?" he asked. "Can I meet more people?"

The following day, he did. He was told that the traffic to Guatemala had increased. Cuban leaders had been told to be ready to move on short notice. CIA people were mentioned. At a party, a friend took him aside and said, "This is one of our top American people—Eduardo," and introduced him to Howard Hunt.

Excited, Szulc called Catledge in New York. He said he had run across a big story that he didn't want to discuss on the phone. That same afternoon he was in Catledge's office on the sixth floor of the Times Building on Forty-third Street in Manhattan. Sensing the sensitivity of the story, Catledge had taken a rare precaution. He had asked the publisher, Orvil E. Dryfoos, to come down from the fourteenth floor to listen to the details.

Szulc was told to consider himself stationed in Miami and arrived back there the same day. En route, he stopped in Washington and briefed *the* Washington correspondent of the *Times*, James (Scotty) Reston. Plump, pink and quiet, Reston had come to the United States from Scotland as a young boy. He started as a sportswriter. Over the decades he had become the best-informed and most influential newspaperman in the capital. Presidents, including Kennedy, often took him into their confidence—up to a point.

Reston knew about an invasion. It was to be the first big move of the Kennedy administration, which made it all the more significant. Kennedy was trying hard to minimize the American role. He had pointed out to Reston that all the weapons were in the hands of the men who were going to do the fighting. The invasion, the President argued, was not dependent on any action of the United States. After listening to Szulc, Reston made use of his legendary access to top officials and called on Dulles at his home on P Street, off Wisconsin Avenue in Georgetown. Two CIA agents were watching in the entrance hall.

In the library, Dulles seemed enormously at ease. The scene struck Reston as "very English." He almost expected to come upon "the late George Apley reading eighteenth-century novels." Reston asked about the CIA's involvement in the Cuban invasion. Dulles pooh-poohed it. Reston thought "he was lying like hell." He was becoming increasingly disturbed. His column on the *Times* editorial page was supposed to see the Washington scene in historical perspective. So far, everything he had heard about the plans to depose Castro went against the principle of nonaggression which the United States said it championed.

In Miami, Szulc, pumping Cuban exile leaders for more details, also felt uneasy. He thought there was "no acceptable reason" for an invasion. Worse, he was convinced it would not work. Over and over, the exiles told him the landings would trigger a general uprising. He "knew Cuba well enough to know that they were kidding themselves." And if they weren't really counting on a revolt, how could a little brigade overthrow Castro? The whole thing did not make sense.

Later, convinced that the invasion was imminent, Szulc worried about how to cover it. Assuming that the CIA would never permit reporters to hit the beaches with the Brigade, he hoped someone in government would at least arrange for press briefings in Miami.

During a quick trip to Washington, he called an old friend, Donald M. Wilson, a long-time *Time-Life* correspondent who had just been appointed deputy director of the United States Information Agency. Wilson was a logical contact for Szulc. The USIA operated the Voice of America and other propaganda efforts. It had to know what was going on and would have to keep abreast of the landings' progress.

When Wilson met Szulc for breakfast at 8 A.M. on Wednesday, April 5, in the Georgetown home of Tad's uncle, a retired U.S. ambassador, it immediately became apparent that Wilson knew "zero." The USIA man was "shocked." Even his top-secret daily briefing book from the CIA had mentioned nothing about an invasion. It was almost unbelievable. Yet Szulc related so many convincing details that it had to be true. Not only were the landings a reality; they would clearly break very soon.

Wilson rushed to his office at 1776 Pennsylvania Avenue, picked up the phone and told his boss, Edward R. Murrow, that he had to see him "instantly." Murrow had been an inspired choice as director of the USIA. His pinched face with its arched forehead and his inevitable cigarette were household phenomena. TV watchers followed him on *See It Now* and *CBS Reports*. His crusade against McCarthyism was well remembered. Ever since his doleful World War II radio voice announced, *"This is London . . .,"* Ed Murrow had been a symbol of integrity.

He was "very upset" at his deputy's news. He picked up the phone, got Allen Dulles on the line and said he and his deputy wanted to come right over to see him on "a matter of great importance."

Shortly before 10 A.M. Murrow and Wilson were ushered into the director's office. Dulles was smiling comfortably behind his pipe smoke, at ease, the picture of the country gentleman, as always.

"I've received very disturbing information," said Murrow solemnly, and he invited Wilson to repeat Szulc's story.

The smile never left Dulles' face. It was a matter of great regret to him, but he simply was in no position to discuss the subject. The situation was unfortunate. He was just not authorized to do anything about it. Murrow and Wilson left in less than fifteen minutes.

The USIA men agreed that the director had done "a beautiful job" of dodging. They were "sore as hell," but not at Dulles. He had performed "so engagingly." As experienced reporters, they knew that Dulles had, in effect, confirmed the Szulc story. If the information had been wrong, the CIA chief would have denied it.

Shortly afterward Murrow had a call from Mac Bundy, asking him to stop by the White House after lunch. Bundy told Murrow about the operation in general terms. Murrow listened quizzically and said it was about as terrible an idea as he could think of. He said it wasn't right for the United States to commit an act of aggression against a small nation; "using" Cubans for such a sneak attack was unworthy of America; and the role of the U.S. could never stay hidden.

Bundy said that Murrow's objections were not without validity, but nothing could be done about them. The operation had gone too far to be stopped.

Murrow and Wilson picked up the signal. They were to act as if they knew nothing, as if the United States were not involved. They thought the lack of guidance for the government's official information outlet was "deplorable." But they had no choice. They decided to be "good soldiers" and "went along." Their news operators would have to get the word about the landings from the commercial wire services—which had to rely largely on Lem Jones, who got the word from Dave Phillips and Howard Hunt, the propaganda operators in Quarters Eye.

Consensus to Go Ahead

Senator Fulbright had booked seats for a commercial flight from Florida back to Washington and was pleased when the President invited him to return on *Air Force One* on Tuesday, April 4. On the way back, Kennedy again said nothing about Fulbright's lengthy Cuba memo, but shortly before the plane landed at 4:25 P.M. at Andrews Air Force Base outside Washington—it was chilly and everybody wore topcoats—he told the Senator that he was holding a meeting later that afternoon at the State Department about Cuba and asked the Senator whether he would like to attend.

The meeting—which Schlesinger considered "climactic" even though it still produced no presidential "go" order—was held at the State Department for security reasons. Secrecy was still considered crucial; the President had to be in Foggy Bottom for duties that were of such low priority that interest in his movements was certain to be at a minimum.

At 5:32, JFK, accompanied by Secretary Rusk, Fulbright and Roger Tubby, the State Department press spokesman, officiated in Room 1410, where the President, smiling and in blue pinstripes, was presented a gold shovel by one Douglas Hill, representing Archie Gubburd, Governor of South Dakota. Then the Chief Executive attended the swearing-in ceremony of Anthony J. Drexel Biddle as ambassador to Spain. And at 6 P.M. the President, Rusk and Fulbright ducked into a small conference room behind the Secretary's office and took their places around a round conference table.

Some of the men had been waiting for a considerable period because they had been asked, again to keep the occasion inconspicuous for security reasons, not to arrive all at one time. The press was told the meeting was about "Laos and other problems." In fact Laos was the pressing issue that day. A cease-fire was being negotiated. The situation was delicate. British Prime Minister Harold Macmillan had arrived to confer with Kennedy about it. Rusk had just rushed in from greeting the Prime Minister at the heliport on the grounds of the Naval Observatory. Cuba was an intrusion on the day's real business.

Nobody in the tiny, drab meeting room knew what to expect. Within minutes, all were acutely uncomfortable—but, like the characters in *Rashomon*, all had differing perceptions of what was happening.

The President motioned Fulbright to a chair on his right. The Senator was "taken aback by the size and formality" of the occasion. More than a dozen men were jammed into the cramped space. As he listened to Dick Bissell bringing the President up-to-date on the combat preparations, Fulbright's amazement increased. He had considered the invasion "a very serious matter," but didn't realize how grave and immediate a decision was required. He had not expected the plans to be so large, so complex—or so far advanced. Questions started flying around the table. How motivated were the Cuban troops by now? How was their training going? What could be done if the Brigade had to be disbanded after all? Bill Fulbright hardly listened. He was "very tense." Since it was evident that no one but the President knew of his memorandum, the Senator restated its main points without notes. He did not regard himself as so important that the President would have staged the occasion just to sell the Senator on the invasion concept. Rather, Fulbright believed the President was using him "to voice his own doubts."

Without eliciting discussion on Fulbright's specific points, the President started going around the room and asking various men, "What do you think?" He wanted an overall judgment on whether he should let the invasion proceed. His manner was not forbidding, but he made it clear that he wanted "yes" or "no" answers. When Adolf A. Berle, the venerable State Department specialist in Latin-American affairs, began a ruminative reply, JFK cut him off and said, "But, Adolf, you haven't voted!" Whereupon this gung-ho, "hard liberal" survivor of Franklin D. Roosevelt's New Deal wars snapped, "I say, 'let 'er rip!'"

Secretary Rusk also remained unmoved by Fulbright's many arguments. His feelings were more pragmatic. He thought that success in irregular warfare was "self-legitimizing," the way it had been for Castro when he came to power. And Rusk liked to remind himself that if our forefathers hadn't succeeded in the American Revolution, "they'd have been hanged as traitors."

To the Secretary, the meeting was mostly another upsetting example of the new President's "very informal sense of administration." He thought of that phrase frequently but without satisfaction. This latest gathering annoyed him very particularly. He felt he had been herded together with a crowd of young people and that the Secretary of State had been reduced in status to become just one head in the herd. The other officials in the room operated at greatly varying levels of responsibility; here, all of a sudden and for no apparent reason, they were all elevated to the level of Cabinet members, with each holding one vote. It irritated the Secretary greatly, especially since the

President didn't turn first to him, the senior member of the Cabinet.

Rusk was proud of his practice not to explain his views to the President while they were in "a significant group." He thought this was discreet and in keeping with his status as a most senior presidential adviser. His experience in helping to plan guerrilla operations as an infantry colonel in the China-Burma theater during World War II had convinced Rusk that, for the Bay of Pigs operation, "the chances of succeeding were near zero." But he was eager to "close ranks with the President" and did not say so. When it came time to vote, Bissell thought that Rusk stayed "closer to abstention than to a ringing affirmative." Schlesinger felt Rusk limited himself to "mild disclaimers."*

Tom Mann was present because his teeth were in less than good repair. He had ceased to be Assistant Secretary of State for Inter-American Affairs on April 1 and was about to leave for his new post as ambassador to Mexico. His departure was delayed because of the dental work he needed to have finished, so he was asked to make a special trip to the department.

He too found the meeting frustrating. He thought it was "very indecisive," "very unsatisfactory." It should have been setting policy. Instead, the policy-makers were talking past each other like "ships passing in the night." He thought Fulbright's objections were far-fetched, that there should have been a really penetrating discussion to pinpoint the precise difference between "intervention" and "self-defense."

Clearly, this meeting was not the time or place to penetrate anything. The President was impatient and pushing for adjournment. So Mann did not raise his previously voiced concern about the lilliputian size of the invasion force. And to his thinking, the Bay of Pigs was a much *more* promising landing site than Trinidad "because it wasn't based on the false premise that ninety percent of the Cuban people were going to come out with their muskets and start shooting."

He confined himself to saying that he would have opposed the landings at an earlier stage, but that Castro was a direct threat to the security of the United States, and he thought this was the one overriding factor. He voted for the plan.

Of the civilians present from the Pentagon, Paul Nitze, a craggy-

*In 1977, nobody who had been in the room could remember anyone except Fulbright speaking up against the operation. Rusk remembered he "didn't take a flat position" and remained "very noncommittal." Testifying before the Taylor Committee on May 4, 1961, he said, "I believe that I was the only one that didn't approve." The counsel he gave President Kennedy privately will not become known until the Rusk papers in the Lyndon B. Johnson Library at the University of Texas are opened in 1990. Meanwhile he says: "I served the President badly by not going to him and forcing him to ask the Joint Chiefs: 'What would you need if we were to do this [invasion] with American forces?' "

faced, impassive international lawyer who had just become Assistant Secretary of Defense for International Security Affairs, felt a particularly "deep unhappiness." He had been overloaded coping with a crisis in the balance of payments, a crisis in Laos, a crisis in the Congo. When he had heard about the Cuba operation, he turned it over to his deputy, Bill Bundy, a former CIA man. Nitze believed that the odds were less than fifty-fifty for an early success of an invasion. The assumption that the Cuban people might arise made the project more palatable: "It was not implausible."

But he was disgusted with the way the meeting was being run. He felt Fulbright was trying to force it into a fruitless theoretical argument over whether the invasion was moral. "The real issue was: would it succeed? It was assumed that it would succeed; it wasn't discussed." He remembers that when JFK asked him to vote, "I was unhappy with myself. I should have had the guts to give a complicated answer." He too wanted to close ranks for the President, who, so Nitze believed, merely "wanted to be polite to Fulbright, and the rest of us were part of it." He voted for the plan.

To Bill Bundy, tall, slender and elegant, the presence of Bill Fulbright turned the meeting into a "charade." Bundy thought that political considerations were by now irrelevant. "Dammit to hell," he said to himself, "these are bridges we crossed long ago." Worse, the setting didn't strike him as proper for members of the Executive Branch of the government to be frank. He felt they were honor-bound to stand with the President against Fulbright's arguments, to back up the presidential effort at "rallying the troops" to deal with the lone nay-sayer.

When JFK asked for a vote, Bundy thought, "This is not the right way to do it." The yes-or-no format was too broad-brush for him and certainly "not designed to elicit the response 'Mr. President, now that you mention it . . .' "

Like a good team player, he voted "Yes."

The military leaders in the room felt almost as if they were listening in on deliberations about a problem that was none of their business. General Lemnitzer, the Chairman of the Joint Chiefs of Staff, was not unsympathetic when Fulbright pointed out how difficult it would be to disavow U.S. sponsorship of the operation, but the general noted to himself that disavowal was not his trade, and that he could make no contribution on the subject. Admiral Burke, the normally outspoken Chief of Naval Operations, thought that so much time had been given to presentations by Messrs. Bissell and Fulbright that none was left for more military details. When the President again expressed concern that the operation would look too much like a World War II invasion, General Gray, sitting on his left, assured him that the landings had been shifted from daytime to night and that there would now be relatively small assaults spread over four separate beaches. This seemed to make the President feel easier. Otherwise, contributions to the meeting by the military were minor. Secretary McNamara merely cast an affirmative vote.

The meeting broke up as inconclusively as it began. "Gentlemen, we'd better sleep over it," the President said.

Curiously, the two men who held the most rigidly fixed positions, Fulbright against the operation and Bissell in favor, both felt somewhat relieved. Fulbright was pleased that he had been given a respectful hearing. Nobody had attacked him or his views. Doubts—presumably much the same as the President's—had been solemnly aired before the top-level audience that mattered. And the final decision could still be "No," even though none of the President's advisers had joined Fulbright in speaking out against the plan.

To Bissell, the meeting sounded like excellent news: "There was much more of a sense of decision-making in that meeting than in most, much more of a sense of finality." Bissell had previously rated the odds favoring a "go" order at three to one; he now believed them to be even more favorable. Whether or not some of the President's advisers had merely wanted to show the Chief Executive's flag against Fulbright's challenge out of the Legislative Branch was of no consequence. The point was that all the advisers present were on record as wanting to go ahead.

All but one. As the advisers left the room, the President called back Arthur Schlesinger, who, along with several other junior advisers, had not been asked to vote. When the President asked for Schlesinger's opinion, the young historian said he opposed the operation. Quickly, he tried to summarize why. The President listened and nodded once or twice. Schlesinger thought he was doing a disorderly and too hurried job, and as he left, worried, he began to think of setting out his views in detail and in writing.

Rusk returned to his office and was joined by Bowles, who asked whether the invasion had been canceled or whether he should see the President. Rusk assured him that there was no need to take any further action.

"Don't worry about this," he said. "It isn't going to amount to anything."

"What do you mean, 'amount to anything'?" asked Bowles.

"Well, it just won't amount to anything."

"Will it make the front page of *The New York Times?*" persisted Bowles.

"I wouldn't think so," said the Secretary.

Bowles's memo of March 31 was returned to him without comment. In the upper-right-hand corner appeared the handwritten initials "D.R." The letters were so tiny that they were all but invisible.

The next morning Schlesinger was at his office at six-thirty, organizing his thoughts about the operation. He wanted his memorandum on Kennedy's desk before the President's daily routine began. He had been "thinking about little else for weeks." He was certain the project was a "terrible idea." But the President seemed ready to go along with it now that Bill Fulbright alone had spoken out in opposition. At the voting meeting, the President had not even called on Schlesinger to express his view openly.

The historian was in a bind. If he only raised "a few timid questions," he might appear to be going along with the project. If he objected openly and continually, he would become "a nuisance." He was a college professor, new to government. What right did he have "to interpose his unassisted judgment in an open meeting against that of such august figures as the Secretaries of State and Defense and the Joint Chiefs of Staff, each speaking with the full weight of his institution behind him?" The advocates also had a "rhetorical advantage." They could "strike virile poses" and speak of such tangibles as air strikes. To oppose the venture, he had to "invoke intangibles"—morality, reputations and other idealistic notions.

He could see no way out but to confine himself to memoranda that appealed to logic and foresight.* Fortunately, the encouragement of an exile effort to oust Castro did not bother him; there was historical precedent for backing refugees against dictatorships back home. The reactions in Moscow and Latin America could be overcome. And Schlesinger felt he could not "question the military premise advanced by CIA and endorsed by the Joint Chiefs that the Brigade would be able to establish itself on the shores of Cuba." It was the likely developments after successful landings that troubled the historian.

He wrote the President: "If we could achieve this by a swift, surgical stroke, I would be for it." However, "a) no matter how 'Cuban' the equipment and personnel, the U.S. will be held accountable for the

---

*In his memoir *A Thousand Days* (Boston: Houghton Mifflin, 1965), Schlesinger acknowledged that his memoranda were "the easy way out" for him. After the operation, he "bitterly reproached" himself and suffered "feelings of guilt" for "having kept so silent during those crucial discussions in the Cabinet Room." His conclusion: "One's impulse to blow the whistle on this nonsense was simply undone by the circumstances of the discussion."

operation, and our prestige will be committed to its success," and "b) since the Castro regime is presumably too strong to be toppled by a single landing, the operation will turn into a protracted civil conflict."

What if the invasion succeeded but the rebellion faltered? Schlesinger predicted that the rebels would call for U.S. armed help. Congress would take up the cry. "Pressures will build up which will make it politically hard to resist the demand to send in the Marines." Sending them would not solve the problem. The Fidelistas would fight fiercely—in mountain retreats, if necessary. "The Russians would enlist volunteers in José Martí and probably even Abraham Lincoln Brigades and seek to convert the conflict into another Spanish Civil War." The United States would be branded as an aggressor in the United Nations. Castro was not really a sufficiently "grave and compelling threat to our own national security" to warrant triggering such a chain of events.

The President read the memorandum almost immediately and told Schlesinger, "You know, I've reserved the right to stop this thing up to twenty-four hours before the landing. In the meantime, I'm trying to make some sense out of it. We'll just have to see."

Schlesinger was very doubtful that the President would call off the operation. But he was clearly still trying to scale it down. "We seem now destined to go ahead on a quasi-minimum basis," the historian noted in his journal after another meeting, "a large-scale infiltration (hopefully) rather than an invasion." But there still was no presidential decision. Some time for further argument remained.

Keeping Adlai Stevenson in the Dark

Another key official who would normally have been informed of what was in the wings but was also left deliberately in the dark was Adlai Stevenson, the United States ambassador to the United Nations, who later told Pierre Salinger, Kennedy's press secretary, that the Bay of Pigs had given him the most "humiliating experience" of his years in public service.

Clayton Fritchey, Stevenson's public-relations adviser and a weathered political hand from Washington, had been following the stories about Cuba in *The New York Times*. He placed some phone calls to cronies in the press and became convinced that a major operation was about to be "pulled off."

One evening about two weeks before the invasion, he asked Stevenson, over cocktails, whether the ambassador had been "holding out" on him about Cuba. Fritchey thought his boss might have been secretly informed of whatever was impending. Stevenson said he knew nothing. He expressed concern about Fritchey's concern. The Cubans had been pressing hard for a UN debate about sabotage and other "aggressions" which they charged had American backing. Stevenson needed to know the facts so that he could best defend the U.S.

"You're not pulling my leg, are you?" Fritchey persisted. "I understand that there are things you can't discuss with anybody."

Stevenson assured him again that he had no information and authorized him to "nose around."

Fritchey decided to question Schlesinger, because the historian was a long-time friend who used to write campaign speeches for ex-candidate Stevenson. By sheer luck, Schlesinger turned out to be one of the very select few in the White House who was knowledgeable about the invasion.

"What the hell is going on down there?" Fritchey asked. "Don't you think the Permanent Representative to the United Nations had better know a little about this?"

Schlesinger said he would see what he could do to get Stevenson briefed.

Turner Catledge knew more about the operation and was determined to run Tad Szulc's article about it. Long and detailed, it reached his desk at the *Times* on Thursday, April 6. A ruddy-faced Southerner—he was from New Prospect, Mississippi, and never lost his accent—Catledge was a popular raconteur who had started at the *Times* as an aggressive eighty-dollar-a-week Washington reporter during the Hoover administration. He relished the *Times*'s position of leadership and his own final responsibility for its contents. He had never forgotten what Adolph Ochs, the *Times*'s founder, once told him about the editor's role: "Don't ask me today what to print. I'll tell you tomorrow whether you should have printed it."

Still, elements in the Szulc story bothered him. He did not want to name the CIA. There were too many other intelligence agencies; any of them might be involved. He preferred such euphemisms as "U.S. experts." The story said the invasion was "imminent." Szulc had been reasonably sure it would come April 18, but had decided not to say so because he was not certain. Catledge did not want any predictions at all. They were too often wrong. In this case, the government could easily have proven the *Times* wrong by changing its plans.

Publisher Dryfoos was more deeply concerned. Would the *Times* be tampering with national security? Would it be responsible if hundreds or possibly thousands of Cubans died on the beaches and the invasion failed? Might the expedition be canceled and the *Times* be blamed for interfering with national policy?

Catledge consulted Reston by phone. Reston was negative. He didn't object to printing facts. But he was against the *Times* tipping off the world about the U.S. government's future plans. He also pointed out that an invasion could not be called "imminent" if it was ten or more days away.

Dryfoos was in touch with the President.* The President was upset. He told Dryfoos that he had not even given orders to release the necessary fuel for the operation. The publisher was gravely troubled.

Catledge decided to go ahead. He remembered his own motto, "When in doubt, print it." He was sure the *Times* was not telling Castro anything new. If the invasion failed, the paper might be blamed for it; but the public had a right to know what was happening. He did order the elimination of all specific references to the CIA and to any particular time when the invasion might take place. Then he ordered the biggest change of all. The news editors had dummied in the story to lead the paper's front page with a four-column headline. To *Times* readers, a headline of such size would spell something close to war. Catledge ordered a one-column head and moved the story near the middle of page one.

In the bullpen, the assistant managing editor on duty, Theodore Bernstein, a tight-strung perfectionist and the paper's expert on the meaning of words, and Lewis Jordan, the news editor, received word about the change in the play of the story with more than dismay. They were convinced a colossal mistake was about to be made. Both went to Catledge to protest. Jordan's face was dead white. His voice quivered with emotion. He and Bernstein said that never before had the front-page play been changed for policy reasons. They wanted the publisher himself to justify the change.

Catledge was enraged. The managing editor's final decisions were never questioned. Still, he turned around in his large swivel chair, phoned Dryfoos and asked him to come downstairs. By the time the publisher arrived, Bernstein had gone out to dinner. Dryfoos spent ten minutes explaining that he wanted the story played down because of national security and, especially, because he was concerned about the safety of the men who would have to face fire on the beaches.

With its watered-down text and relatively small, bland headline, the story became, as the *Times* executives had planned, less sensational. "Anti-Castro Units Trained to Fight at Florida Bases" was as far as the

*It can no longer be determined whether Dryfoos contacted the President or whether Kennedy was told about the story and took the initiative.

headline went. Szulc overestimated the Brigade to number five to six thousand men. His first reference to "United States experts" did not come until the tenth paragraph. Szulc was disgusted at the way his editors were pulling his punches. Nevertheless, alert readers could deduce what would happen—and soon—especially from the article's disclosure that training had been discontinued because the forces "have reached the stage of adequate preparation."

Ironically, a short shirttail item at the end of the story gave Bissell's show away. "Invasion Reported Near," said the tiny headline. According to this story from New York, CBS had reported "unmistakable signs" that invasion plans were "in their final stages."

Scanning these and other stories, the President was livid. "I can't believe what I'm reading!" he exploded at Press Secretary Pierre Salinger in the Oval Office. "Castro doesn't need agents over here. All he has to do is read our papers. It's all laid out for him."*

It was, in fact, more than the CIA laid out for Adlai Stevenson.

Stevenson was much more than the ambassador to the UN, and everybody recognized it. Twice candidate for President, he was far better known than anyone in the administration except Kennedy. Round, rumpled, urbane, easily recognized by the eggshaped bald head that made "egghead" synonymous with intellectualism, he was, to liberals, a symbol of integrity and thoughtfulness. To Kennedy, who had won the election by less than 200,000 votes, he was also a lingering political threat. Stevenson was eloquent. He stirred passionate loyalties. Many liberal Democrats were still, as the old campaign slogan had it, "madly for Adlai."

Relations between Stevenson and Kennedy were at best uncomfortable. They were old political rivals. Defeated, Stevenson had badly wanted to be Secretary of State. He was miffed when the job went to Rusk, whom he considered "wooden" and "just a good technician." The age gap between Stevenson, sixty-one, and Kennedy, forty-three, was a handicap. So were their differences of style. Stevenson could be discursive and agonize over decisions long after they were made. Kennedy liked his advisers to be concise and decisive. Stevenson

---

*Two weeks after the invasion, Kennedy felt differently. He told Catledge at the White House, "Maybe if you had printed more about the operation you would have saved us from a colossal mistake." More than a year later he told Dryfoos, "I wish you had run everything on Cuba . . . I am just sorry you didn't tell it at the time." Clifton Daniel speculated that "the Bay of Pigs operation might well have been canceled and the country would have been saved enormous embarrassment" if the *Times* and other newspapers had kept the public more fully informed. Scotty Reston felt "it is ridiculous to think that publishing the fact that the invasion was imminent would have avoided this disaster. I am quite sure the operation would have gone forward. The thing had been cranked up too far. The CIA would have had to disarm the anti-Castro forces physically. Jack Kennedy was in no mood to do anything like that."

thought Kennedy was too impulsive, too certain of himself. He might even blunder the country into atomic war.

For Stevenson, the UN job was not much of a consolation prize. He was never happy there. His famous wit rarely showed. He grumbled a lot. Kennedy detested his "whining." Stevenson told his principal Washington contact, Harlan Cleveland, the Assistant Secretary of State for International Organizations, "about once every week or ten days" that he would resign. Adlai acted as if Cleveland and the State Department worked for him. The UN job dictated otherwise: an ambassador takes instructions from Washington.

Stevenson had accepted the position only when Kennedy assured him he would have Cabinet rank, sit in the National Security Council and be consulted on major foreign-policy matters. The location and nature of the UN assignment often made this impossible. Stevenson had become the mouthpiece of his juniors. Still, Kennedy never underestimated the importance of Stevenson or of the UN. In the Cabinet Room, about a week before the invasion, he said he wanted Stevenson completely informed on Cuba; nothing spoken at the UN should be less than the truth, even if it couldn't be all of the truth.

On Friday, April 7, the President instructed Arthur Schlesinger to brief Stevenson in New York and told him, "The integrity and credibility of Adlai Stevenson constitute one of our great national assets. I don't want anything to be done which might jeopardize that."

On Saturday morning Schlesinger was running late. He was discussing his own misgivings about the operation with Rusk in the State Department. By the time his Eastern Airlines shuttle flight brought him to New York and he hurried into the headquarters of the 125-person U.S. Mission to the UN at Two Park Avenue, near Thirty-fourth Street, most of the briefing was over.

The briefer was Bissell's dapper go-between, Tracy Barnes. One of his CIA colleagues once described Barnes as "the soul of vagueness"; he never lived up to that reputation better than on that crisp, clear morning. The occasion made it easy. The men around the big oblong table in the mission's conference room were almost all his frends. He had socialized with the Stevenson family for years. Stevenson's deputy and law school classmate, the gentle Francis T. P. Plimpton, remembered how Barnes applied for a job at the Plimpton law firm when Tracy graduated from Harvard Law. Charles P. Noyes, the mission's minister counselor, was Barnes's Yale classmate. The two men had roomed together in London for two years during the war.

There was going to be a clandestine operation in Cuba, Barnes said. It was strictly a Cuban affair. It would have some American "cooperation," but only with the training and financing. The U.S. aid would not be visible. Barnes said nothing about an invasion or anything about the nature or size or timing or place of the operation, and nothing about air strikes or the training camps in Guatemala. He did mention that the agency had used an old American Army base to train guerrillas.

"For God's sakes, get that out right away," said Stevenson. Otherwise the reaction was mild. Almost all the men in the room had been in government, off and on, since New Deal days. They knew about intelligence operations. If too many people knew too many details, leaks were inevitable. Leaks were dangerous. There was no point in asking Barnes more than the men at the UN had to know to do their jobs.

Clayton Fritchey was mildly disgusted. He already knew more about the operation from Szulc's story in the *Times*.

Harlan Cleveland, sleek and towering over the others, had come to New York on the same plane with Barnes but had known nothing about the operation. The briefing made him uneasy. He could tell that Barnes had been sent to reassure Stevenson that the President knew what he was doing; that the United States was not going to invade another country but might help friendly invaders as long as it was their operation, not ours. Yet he felt Barnes was too "evasive." More seemed to be happening "than met the eye." Evidently it was policy that Stevenson was not to be told. It wasn't Cleveland's "task to question that policy."

The man most immediately concerned was Richard F. Pedersen, precise and dry, the mission's political officer. A career Foreign Service man, he had been a UN specialist in New York for five years. He would have to make sure Stevenson was prepared to argue the American case on the "Cuban item" that had been on the General Assembly's agenda since the previous fall. It concerned the Cuban complaint of "various plans of aggression and acts of intervention" by the U.S. It was now scheduled to be argued on Monday, April 17.*

Pedersen asked whether the "appearance" of the operation was going to be that whatever happened would happen from the "inside" or the "outside." Barnes said it would appear to be happening from the "inside" but would have "some outside participation." There would definitely not be "any American participation." Pedersen also wanted to know whether anything would happen during the current session of the

---

*Harlan Cleveland always thought it was "a stroke of genius" that the CIA had scheduled the invasion for the same day. This was sarcasm, of course. The timing of the two events was coincidental.

General Assembly, which was to last two more weeks. Barnes assured him that nothing would.

Pedersen was satisfied. Barnes's answers met his "political needs."

Stevenson said, "Look, I don't like this. If I were calling the shots, I wouldn't do it. But this is Kennedy's show. All I ask is three things: First, don't do anything till the Assembly adjourns. Second, nobody leaves from U.S. territory. Third, no American participation."

After the briefing, the discussion continued in even more careful terms over luncheon at the Century Club. Stevenson was there, along with Cleveland, Fritchey and Schlesinger. Later Schlesinger recorded in his journal: "AES made it clear that he wholly disapproves of the project, objects to the fact that he was given no opportunity to comment on it, and believes it will cause infinite trouble. However, he is substantially a good soldier about it and is prepared to try and make the best possible U.S. case."

It was to be a case nobody could make.

Final Doubts

By Saturday, April 8, Washington's celebrated cherry blossoms were in bloom. Around the Tidal Basin, in full view of the barred windows of Quarters Eye, there was a particularly lush concentration of them every year. This year was no exception. Tourist families and young couples were wandering about the grassy slopes and made a galling spectacle for the six men who had been called by Bissell to assemble in Jake Engler's ground-floor office at 1 P.M.

Bissell, the man who seemed to run their lives by stopwatch, as he did his own, did not appear. His secretary said he was detained at the White House. The men waited and reminded each other bitterly of more pleasurable ways to spend the weekend.

At noon, Bissell phoned his secretary, who passed the word that he would be further delayed. He suggested that the men go out for lunch and meet him at 2 P.M.

Jake and his crew went off to Napoleon's and started lunch with a couple of martinis each. Taking care not to refer in public to any recognizable places or people, they shared their pessimism over the constantly increasing restraints that were being placed on their operation. Lunch was followed by brandies.

Once the waiter left, Drain spoke up: "You gentlemen are masquerading as experts in overthrowing a government. Have any of you entertained the notion that this damned thing might not work?"

They all had, but they had never openly raised the possibility in a group. It was, quite literally, a sobering thought that made all of them edgy. Jake and Bender chewed on their cigars. Colonel Hawkins seemed insulted at the idea of his troops contemplating defeat. Jim Flannery wiped his bifocals with his napkin. Dave Phillips asked Drain what he thought the group could do.

"Not go back," said Drain. He realized he was proposing a quixotic gesture—a revolt of the inner circle—but for the moment he was serious. He suggested that they all go to play golf so that when Bissell showed up in Jake's office there would be no one to run the operation.

After a prolonged silence, Jake put down his brandy glass and said, "Come on, let's go back. Let's not stand him up."

Back they went, and nobody told Bissell about the palace revolution that failed to survive lunch.

Arthur Schlesinger saw the President in the afternoon and then wrote in his journal that Kennedy appeared to have made his decision to go ahead and was "not likely now to reverse it."

Kennedy had accepted the CIA assurances that the Brigade could "melt" into the mountains and told Schlesinger he felt he had pruned the operation from a full-scale assault to a large-scale infiltration. If the administration had to "get rid" of the Brigade, it was much better to "dump" them in Cuba, "especially if that is where they want to go."

The weight of what Lyman Kirkpatrick, the CIA's inspector general, later called "the double signature on the check"—the guarantees from Dulles and Bissell—had done its work in the President's mind. He was under the spell of Dulles' needling about the "disposal problem" that would be triggered by a cancellation. He remembered Eisenhower's urging to proceed. And, like Schlesinger, he was impressed by Bissell's "unsurpassed talent for lucid analysis" and "the workings of this superbly clear, organized and articulate intelligence."

Schlesinger too had been "transfixed" by Bissell and the assurance with which this persuasive teacher had lectured the meetings in the Cabinet Room, usually with a pointer in his hand, time and again. The New Frontiersmen wanted answers. Bissell seemed to have answers for everything.

While Barnes was holding his cautious preview for the group at the UN, Bissell had a call at his old but cozy, ugly stucco home at the corner of Q and Reno streets, near Wisconsin Avenue. Jake Engler wondered whether the boss was planning to come to the office. Bissell said he wasn't. Engler said that he and Colonel Hawkins would come to his home. It was urgent.

When they arrived, it was obvious that both visitors were extremely agitated. As soon as Bissell ushered them into the living room, they said they wanted to resign. They had discussed it in detail and considered this step with care. There was no choice. The project was out of control. Each day it was being pulled more out of workable shape. The B-26s were too slow and their range was too short. The change of landing site away from Trinidad was ridiculous. The expedition was too big to remain secret. The command control was inadequate; Hawkins should be on one of the ships offshore, as he and Jake had proposed. The politicians were wrong to reject this idea; by pruning away at the operation, they were making it technically impossible to win. The visitors' complaints kept coming.

Bissell could not get angry at the proposed desertions. He shared many of their views, but his feelings about success were not nearly so negative. Besides, he was not about to wash out more than a year of work. The operation had to go. If its two principal subcommanders left, the questions Bissell would face would have no end. So he was gentle. He appealed to Engler's and Hawkins' sense of loyalty to himself, if nobody else. Quitting wasn't going to produce more palatable alternatives. The project was too far along to be squelched. They might as well hang on and help to make the best of it.

Reluctantly, Engler and Hawkins decided to be good soldiers and left.

Since the President was evidently determined to go with the plan, Arthur Schlesinger also decided to make the best of reality. To help Kennedy think the impending events all the way through, he sent another memo to the Oval Office on April 10. It was nine single-spaced typewritten pages long. This time he praised the "skill and care" that had gone into "Cubanizing the operation and doing nothing which would be inconsistent with a spontaneous Cuban effort," and he proposed two ways to minimize possible backfires.

What if Stevenson could not convincingly deny that the CIA was behind the exiles, and Castro "flies a group of captured Cubans to New York to testify that they were organized and trained by the CIA?" Schlesinger thought "we will have to be prepared to show that the alleged CIA personnel were errant idealists or soldiers of fortune working on their own."*

Secondly, care should be taken to protect "one of our greatest

---

*Considering the prevailing atmosphere, this was not such a bizarre suggestion. It will be recalled that even in 1977 Bissell still contended that Gray Lynch and Rip Robertson, the first men ashore, joined the Brigade on their own initiative.

THE CIA PLOTTERS

Richard M. Bissell, Jr. (right, at Berlin Wall), directed all CIA covert operations. An expert sailor (top), he organized and ran the Bay of Pigs project. The "legendary" CIA Director, Allen W. Dulles (below), lent his prestige. Dulles' unpopular deputy, General Charles P. Cabell (bottom right), known as "Old Rice and Beans," was left in charge of the CIA during the fateful weekend of the Cuban invasion.

Richard Helms, CIA's most experienced spy boss (top), called the invasion "harebrained." Principal CIA operators included (counterclockwise): Tracy Barnes, "the soul of vagueness"; Howard Hunt, who plotted clumsily with Cuban politicians and, years later, bungled the famous Watergate break-in; Rolando Martínez, who captained 354 infiltration missions to Cuba and became one of the Watergate burglars; Robert K. Davis, who set up the Guatemala training bases; James E. Flannery, who mediated interoffice conflicts; David A. Phillips, who ran the propaganda shop. Robert Amory, Jr. (top right), was told nothing about the invasion although he was CIA's deputy director for intelligence.

The Cuban invasion was planned in barracks-like World War II "temporary" buildings near the Lincoln Memorial in Washington. Bissell's office was in Building K at top left, near the Potomac; "Quarters Eye," which housed the project's CIA operators, was in another area still farther to the left.

THE START-UP

José Pérez (Pepe) San Román (top left, in Castro prison after capture), was the U.S.-trained leader of the exiles' invasion brigade. Erneido Oliva (center), deputy commander, was the principal combat hero. José Basulto (right), sent to Cuba by the CIA in advance of the invasion to commit sabotage but then given nothing to do, was proud of his low brigade serial number, 2522, indicating he was among the first anti-Castro volunteers. The CIA's recruiting stations in Miami (below) were so busy that the operation became "as secret as Christmas Day."

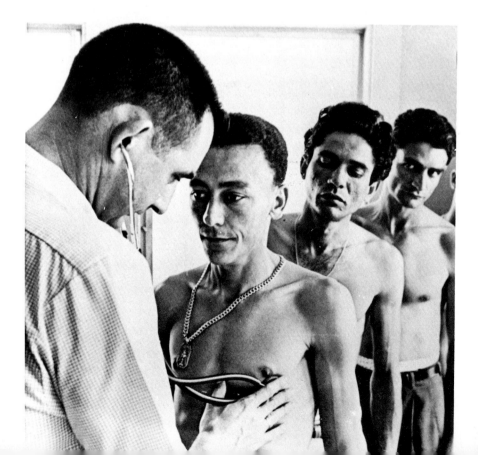

Throughout 1960, the invasion project kept escalating. At first, only 20–30 Cuban exile radio operators were to be trained at Helvetia, the Guatemala coffee plantation shown at top right. Eventually, a secluded mountain camp was built nearby to train more than 1,400 recruits. By comparison, the shacks that housed the pilots of the brigade's air force (center, right) were so comfortable that they became known as "The Hilton." Finally, the CIA had to construct a complete air base that cost $1.8 million (below).

Obsolete World War II B-26 bombers were picked by the CIA to support the invaders so that the operation could "look Cuban." As morale officer of the invasion pilots, the popular Eduardo Ferrer (left) had a tough job. Gustavo Ponzoa (bottom, left), leading the first pre-invasion air strike, found himself bombing aircraft that he used to fly in Cuba. The CIA assigned Mario Zuñiga (bottom, right) to fly to Miami and pose as a defector from Castro's air force, but nobody was fooled for long.

The brigade's air force was trained by American pilots whom the CIA recruited from the Alabama Air National Guard, including (clockwise) Joe Shannon, Billy Goodwin, Buck Persons and Riley W. Shamburger. In the final hours of the battle, six of the Americans flew combat missions without President Kennedy's knowledge. Shannon and Goodwin were the only ones who returned. Shamburger was the most popular (and most senior) of the four pilots who were shot down and killed.

In the early days of planning, President Dwight D. Eisenhower showed no great enthusiasm. Vice President Richard M. Nixon was the most militant of his advisers. Colonel (later Major General) Edward G. Lansdale (center, right), a specialist in insurgency, told the Pentagon that the CIA's planning was inadequate. Thomas C. Mann (bottom), the State Department's Latin American specialist, first thought the invasion was illegal but later decided it was justifiable self-defense against Communist aggression.

The CIA found the fiery Cuban exile politicians hard to handle, especially (top, left to right) Manuel Artime, Antonio de Varona and José Miró Cardona, who was president of the exile government which the CIA expected to establish once the brigade had gained a foothold on Cuban soil. Dr. José Almeida (above) was the brigade's chief physician, assisted by Dr. Juan Sordo, a surgeon (right).

The CIA's controversial military commander was Marine Colonel Jack Hawkins (top left). Air operations were run by Colonel Stanley W. Beerli (top right). A CIA agent from Texas, Grayston Lynch (bottom left), became *de facto* commander of the battle, along with "Rip" Robertson.

Rio Escondido (top), one of six tired freighters leased by the CIA to transport the invaders, was commanded by Gustavo Tirado (inset) and exploded early on D-Day under air attack. *Barbara J.* (bottom), commanded by Osvaldo Inguanzo (inset) was one of two LCI's (Landing Craft Infantry) used as command ships.

General Lyman Lemnitzer (top left), chairman of the Joint Chiefs of Staff, was shocked by the operation's disorganization. Clockwise: General David W. Gray chaired Pentagon advisory group; Marine Commandant David Shoup thought Cuban civilian uprisings were indispensable; Admiral Robert Dennison couldn't get his questions answered; Captain Sven Ryberg skippered command ship *Blagar*; Commodore Robert Crutchfield's destroyer was shelled off Cuba; Admiral John A. Clark commanded all Navy forces offshore; Admiral Arleigh R. Burke, Navy Chief of Staff, was the most active of the U.S. military leaders involved.

Opposite page: Carrier *Essex* (top), commanded by Captain S. S. (Pete) Searcy, Jr. (inset), was base for the jets that could have turned the battle's tide. Destroyer *Eaton* (center), skippered by Captain Peter Perkins (inset) and known as "The Five and Ten," led the invasion flotilla into the Bay of Pigs and was later shelled by Castro tanks. LSD (Landing Ship Dock) *San Marcos* (bottom) was key to the landings: it carried the small landing craft whose CIA crews handed them over to Cuban exile sailors off the beaches in total darkness just before H-Hour.

Jet fighter squadron VA-34, the "Blue Blasters," flew reconnaissance over the invasion but was forbidden to engage in combat. Their commanding officer, Cdr. Mike Griffin (top left), was ordered to have his pilots fly without personal identifications. Cdr. William J. (Jim) Forgy (top right) chased away Castro aircraft by simply flying next to them. Lt. Sam Sayers (bottom) was particularly upset when, toward battle's end, the jets were ordered to have all insignia painted out. The pilots' inability to help the brigade moved them to tears. When finally allowed to reconnoiter over Cuba, they had only an Esso road map as guide.

The brigade's frogmen, young, fit, and
first to hit the beaches, considered
themselves the elite of the invasion
force. At their U.S. bases, they trained
in swimming pools under the command of Andy Pruna (at extreme right
in photo at top) and José Alonso (photo
at top right). En route to Cuba aboard
the command ship *Blagar*, Alonso and
his team posed with CIA agent Grayston Lynch, whom they knew only as
"Gray." He is the balding man standing at extreme left in the second row of
photo at right. Gray commanded the
first group ashore and gave the OK for
the brigade to land. Photo at bottom
shows brigade soldier at weapons
practice en route to Cuba.

The best and the brightest at the Bay of Pigs: President John F. Kennedy tried to reduce the invasion's "noise level" during ultra-secret but strangely uninformed debates in the White House Cabinet Room. Robert F. Kennedy wanted opponents to keep silent. Secretary of State Dean Rusk opposed the expedition but never said so outright. Defense Secretary Robert S. McNamara was absorbed in logistical detail. National Security Adviser McGeorge Bundy (bottom row at left) cleared obstacles to facilitate the go-ahead decision. His assistant, Walt W. Rostow, thought it was "the most screwed-up operation there has ever been." Historian Arthur M. Schlesinger, Jr., then a low-ranking adviser, wrote Kennedy memos opposing the invasion but felt too intimidated by his seniors to speak up at meetings.

Opposite page: Advisers who thought the invasion a terrible idea (starting from top, left to right): J. William Fulbright, chairman of Senate Foreign Relations Committee; Under Secretary of State Chester Bowles; White House adviser Richard Goodwin; USIA Director Edward R. Murrow. All were ignored. Harvard professor John Plank (second row, center) rushed to Washington to warn the administration. *New York Times* reporter Tad Szulc broke the invasion story. Ambassador Adlai E. Stevenson assured the U.N. that Cuban planes landing in Miami were defectors—not knowing the statement was a lie.

THE
BATTLE

Blue Beach at Girón (top), at edge of the remote Zapata swamp, was "a land that time forgot." Larger landing craft (left) were cracked open by reefs which CIA intelligence failed to report. Untried new outboard motors of the plastic launches (below, left) looked fierce with death-heads on bow (inset), but many of the motors died. The mishaps slowed landings and left the invaders unexpectedly vulnerable to attack. Silvio Pérez (below), a Cuban navy veteran who later became a U.S. Navy officer, commanded the landing craft flotilla after training it (and heading off a near mutiny) in Puerto Rico. Fortunately, he was blessed with an indestructible disposition.

Residents awakened by first shots on the beaches included (clockwise): Rafael Moreira, whose water truck was punctured; Alejandrina and Narciso Mejias, whose bedstead was pierced by bullets; Félix Rivera, the cook at Blanco's bar, who pulled the covers over his head and stayed in bed; Victor Caballero, militiaman on guard at Red Beach; and Amparo Ortíz, whose husband, a *carbonero*, was ambushed during their evacuation.

Fidel Castro rushed to the invasion area. It was his favorite fishing spot, so he was familiar with every path. He set up headquarters in the Central Australia sugar mill (left) because he knew it had the region's only phone. In Moscow, Premier Nikita Khrushchev threatened the U.S. with retaliation. The CIA, expecting civilian uprisings, did not know how much Castro's revolution had done to help local swamp dwellers, most of whom worked as *carboneros* with their children (below, right), burning trees to make charcoal, their only fuel.

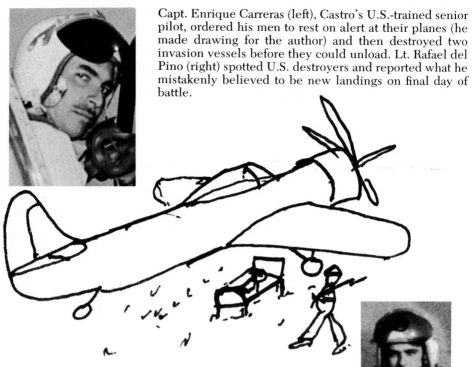

Capt. Enrique Carreras (left), Castro's U.S.-trained senior pilot, ordered his men to rest on alert at their planes (he made drawing for the author) and then destroyed two invasion vessels before they could unload. Lt. Rafael del Pino (right) spotted U.S. destroyers and reported what he mistakenly believed to be new landings on final day of battle.

The freighter *Houston* (below), hit by Carreras' rockets, was run aground near Red Beach by Capt. Luís Morse (inset), but its troops were slow to leave the ship and most of them never managed to join the battle.

THE BAY OF PIGS BEACHES:
Major Landmarks

1. Brigade's First Headquarters
2. Brigade's Last Headquarters
3. Blanco's Bar
4. Site of "Gray's" Landing
5. Coral Reefs
6. "Escondido" Sunk
7. Clubhouse: Location of the Wounded
8. Airport and Control Tower
9. "Castillito" Area
10. Frogmen Place Landing Lights
11. Principal Station of "Blagar"
12. Swimming Pool
13. Militia Radio Post
14. Huts of "Gironcito"
15. Resort Cottages
16. Militia Camp

AIR STRIP

8

TO RED BEACH

TO SAN BLAS

BYPASS ROAD

CITY STREET

TO GREEN BEACH

BLUE BEACH

16

14

13

2

7

15

12

3

10

9

5

11

6

Castro personally directed Cuban defenses at every step. His principal troop commander, José Ramón Fernández (at Castro's left, above) was greeted by impatient calls from his commander-in-chief whenever Fernández reached a phone. The other Castro commander, Félix Duque (left), a veteran guerrilla who fought with Fidel in the mountains before the revolution, raced to the beaches from his farm in his Buick, carrying an ancient bazooka. Without orders, Duque took charge of the eastern front and captured a key town before being captured himself. Henry Raymont (bottom), UPI's man in Havana, watched the invaders' first air raid from his apartment. He was among more than 100,000 political suspects who were arrested and he was almost executed.

Opposite page: Castro troops went to battle in buses. Their artillery and antiaircraft batteries had only recently arrived from the Soviet Union.

Opposite page: The invaders' bombers did considerable damage to Castro's troop movements. Bottom photo was taken after a raid on Palpite, a town near the invasion beaches where Castro forces set up a forward headquarters.

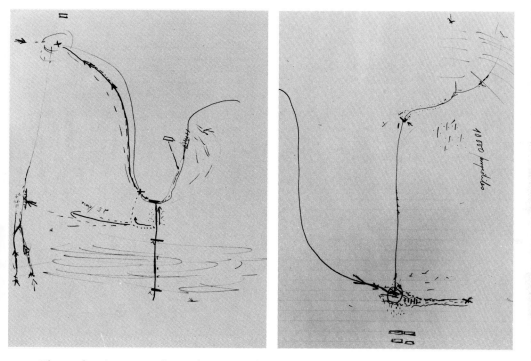

These sketches were drawn by Castro for the author of this book during a six-hour interview in the Cuban President's Havana office in June 1978, to aid Fidel in his recollections of his own movements during the battle for Red Beach (left) and later for Blue Beach at Girón (right). Castro had immediately realized that he had to squelch the invasion quickly to keep an exile government from settling in.

Exiles who fought a doomed fight with dwindling supplies included (top, left to right) Hugo Sueiro, Ramiro Sánchez and Juan Pou. Thomas Willard (Pete) Ray (right) and Leo Francis Baker (bottom, left) were the CIA's Alabama Air National Guard pilots who crash-landed after raid on Castro's headquarters. They survived the crash, but were then killed on the ground. Fernández Mell (bottom, right), a physician, was at the scene when the CIA fliers died.

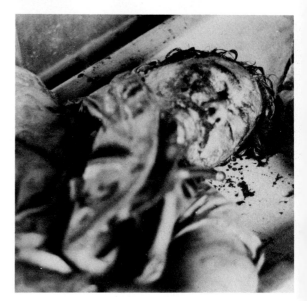

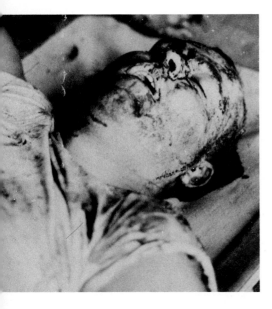

The invaders' planes could never be identified until they started attacking because they bore fake FAR insignia of Castro's air force (above). Nevertheless, many were shot down because they were slow and defenseless, and Castro's planes, which the CIA had expected to wipe out, commanded the air. When Castro's troops reached the sea, the *Houston* was still on fire (left). On the battle's third day, victory celebrations (bottom) broke out throughout Cuba.

THE AFTERMATH

Having suffered surprisingly light casualties, most of the invasion brigade wound up in Castro prisons to be placed on "trial." Even President Kennedy was stung when Cuban propagandists referred to brigade fighters as *mercenarios*. At the White House, he asked members of the aborted Cuban exile government for pictures of their soldier sons. Dr. Antonio Maceo produced a photo of Antonio Jr. (left, with Maceo Sr.). "Does this look like a mercenary?" JFK asked. After 20 months, brigade prisoners were released and greeted tearfully in Miami (bottom).

Nearly two years after the battle, brigade survivors lined up in Miami's Orange Bowl before President Kennedy. Forty thousand spectators wept and shouted, *"Guerra! Guerra!"* In fluent Spanish, Jacqueline Kennedy praised the soldiers' courage. When JFK was presented with the brigade flag, he promised it would fly again over "a free Havana." But in 1976, brigade veterans had to hire a lawyer to get the flag back from the U.S. government. It had been kept crated in a museum basement.

General Maxwell D. Taylor (left), later to become chairman of the Joint Chiefs of Staff, investigated the Bay of Pigs disaster for Kennedy. Lyman B. Kirkpatrick, Jr. (right), CIA inspector general, ran an internal investigation for the agency. His report made Director Dulles furious.

PHOTO ACKNOWLEDGMENTS

This photographic account of the Bay of Pigs project could not have been produced without the kind cooperation of the following individuals and organizations whose generosity is gratefully acknowledged:

Dr. José Almeida, José Alonso, The Associated Press, José Basulto, Stanley W. Beerli, Richard M. Bissell, Jr., Fidel Castro, Enrique Carreras, Council of State —Havana, Robert K. Davis, U.S. Defense Department, James E. Flannery, Eduardo Ferrer, William J. Forgy, Osvaldo Inguanzo, Dr. Antonio Maceo, *Miami Herald*, Museo de la Revolución—Havana, Rhoda Nathans, National Archives, *Operación Puma* by Eduardo Ferrer, Silvio Pérez, Albert C. Persons, David A. Phillips, Photo Facility Fort Monroe (Virginia), Rafael del Pino, Juan Pou, *Prensa Latina*, Art Rickerby for *Life* Magazine, Ramiro Sánchez, Joe Shannon, Dr. Juan Sordo, Gustavo Tirado, United Press International, University of Connecticut, U.S. Navy, U.S. Navy Military Sealift Command, Vanderbilt University Photographic Archives, Wide World, Yale University.

The two-page aerial photograph of the Bay of Pigs terrain (Girón and Blue Beach) was taken from a U-2 reconnaissance plane at an altitude exceeding 70,000 feet and was actually used for intelligence purposes in the invasion operation. Identifications of landmarks were added for this book by eyewitness sources.

The photograph on the front cover shows the Bay of Pigs at Red Beach near the end of the battle with the transport vessel *Houston* on fire in the background.

national resources," the character and repute of the President. Schlesinger wrote: "When lies must be told, they should be told by subordinate officials. At no point should the President be asked to lend himself to the cover operation. For this reason, there seems to be merit in Secretary Rusk's suggestion that someone other than the President make the final decision and do so in his absence—someone whose head can later be placed on the block if things go terribly wrong."

The memo no longer hinted that disaster was likely. "Above all," it said, "we must begin thinking very quickly of a man sufficiently astute, aggressive and influential to go to Habana [sic] as U.S. Ambassador and make sure that the new regime gets off on a socially progressive track."

The Cuban Revolutionary Council seemed a weak link to Schlesinger. To avoid step-by-step involvement of U.S. forces and prestige, the exile Cuban leaders had to be convinced that "in no foreseeable circumstances" would the U.S. send troops and that American prestige "will not be publicly committed to the success of the operation until we recognize a provisional government." He warned that the Council seemed to expect recognition as soon as the Brigade landed, and he suggested: "We must tell the Revolutionary Council that it cannot expect immediate U.S. recognition; that recognition will only come when they have a better than 50–50 chance of winning under their own steam; that this is a fight which Cubans will have in essence to win for themselves. These points must be made clearly and emphatically."

Two days later the President would make his press conference statement flatly ruling out intervention by U.S. forces. And in the Cabinet Room that afternoon he asked "sharply" whether the Council understood this ground rule. To avoid misinterpretation, he said he was sending Berle and Schlesinger to New York to make certain that Miró Cardona understood. There was no protest from the CIA or the military or Schlesinger.*

Dick Goodwin's doubts about the invasion were rising. D-Day was clearly imminent and he would be away at a conference in Rio de Janeiro. At breakfast, he decided to tackle Bundy, Rostow and Schlesinger and make a last, strong pitch for reconsideration. Even if the landings were successful, he argued, there would be "a massacre" in

---

*Hickory Hill, Robert Kennedy's countryside residence near McLean, Virginia, was overflowing with a birthday party for his wife, Ethel, on Tuesday, April 11. Mobs of children and dogs mingled with friends, relatives, dignitaries, colleagues of the New Frontier. The host took Arthur Schlesinger aside. "I hear you don't think much of this business," he said. He did not have to spell out what "business" he meant. He wanted to know why Schlesinger opposed the invasion and listened to the historian's reasons. "You may be right and you may be wrong," Kennedy said, "but the President has made up his mind. Don't push it any further. Now is the time for everyone to help him all they can."

Cuba. The Castro forces weren't the kind just to give up. There would be "house-to-house fighting in Havana." It would be "like Hungary." How would the United States defend this violence before the world?

The other men at the table said little. They suggested that Goodwin see Rusk. Rusk might still be able to change the President's mind.

Goodwin made an appointment with the Secretary at once. He took about twenty minutes to argue his case. Rusk listened and said nothing. Finally he leaned forward and mused softly, "Maybe we've been oversold on the fact that we can't say no to this thing."

Goodwin's "heart fell." If the Secretary of State felt that the debate was closed and nothing further could be said, then "the battle was hopeless." He responded nothing and left, only slightly consoled because he would be in Rio when the storm broke.

At the Joint Chiefs of Staff, General Gray received an "unfavorable report" from his Marine colonel, the logistics expert, who had gone to Nicaragua to check on the loading of the invasion ships. The colonel was appalled. Transportation for the troops was "totally inadequate." Gasoline was loaded next to explosives. Fuel was insufficient to support air operations. The gasoline drums weighed four hundred pounds each but were supposed to be handled by hand. Only hand tools were available for maintenance. The Pentagon emissary reported "a lack of planning" and "no control." It was his judgment that "logistically the operation would likely fall apart."

The colonel was explicit and prophetic. It was not so much that the Brigade lacked supplies. They carried twelve hundred tons. The big problem would be to bridge the gap between the ships and the beach in less than three days. This capability was "marginal without resistance, but impossible with it."

Except for adding a traveling crane, nothing could be done anymore. The CIA men in Happy Valley found the Marine "abrasive" and declined his advice. It was too late, anyway. Much of the volatile cargo had already been loaded. Luckily, there was to be no opposition. The intelligence had said so. The Castro air force would be wiped out and there were to be no people at the beaches.

General Gray was disturbed on other grounds as well. Too many loose ends were developing in the Cuba project to suit his organized mind. Nobody seemed to understand fully what would happen and why. There was never enough time. The invasion deadline of April 10 had not been met. The President advanced it to the seventeenth. Now it was Wednesday, the twelfth, and the general was en route to the White House for another meeting in the Cabinet Room. Secretary of Defense

McNamara and General Lemnitzer, the Chairman of the Joint Chiefs, were with him in the sedan. There had not been time to give them a paper, just drawn up by Gray's committee, stressing the "absolute necessity" of air supremacy. Gray read it to them in the car. He urged that the point be strongly made at the White House.

Just before the meeting, Gray took Tracy Barnes aside. "For Christ's sake, Tracy, this is the last chance," he said. He was still keeping after Barnes to set up a "full-scale military briefing" for the President. Again, Barnes assured him such a briefing would be held. It never was.

At this session, Bissell ran through a detailed timetable. The first troopships had already left Puerto Cabezas, Nicaragua, the previous day, six days before D-Day (D minus 6). The last ship would leave the staging area Thursday (D minus 4). For Saturday (D minus 2) three carefully interrelated events were scheduled: Nino Díaz would make a diversionary landing in Oriente; "limited air strikes" by three groups of Brigade B-26s would hit the Castro air force at its three bases; two fake "defector" Brigade pilots in B-26s would land in Florida to create the impression that the strikes were originating in Cuba. The main landings and air strikes would converge next Monday, D-Day.

Much of the discussion centered on the noise of the air strikes. Earlier, Bissell said he preferred an all-out strike on D-Day, rather than limited strikes on D minus 2 and on D-Day. It was felt that an all-out strike would involve so many planes that the fiction of their departure from Cuban bases would fall apart. The President wondered whether the strikes, even as modified, were still too noisy.

General Gray felt the compromises had created too much complexity. The solutions were fighting each other. The plan's fragility was reaching the breaking point. The main thread, the need for air supremacy, was lost. All-out surprise air attacks on D-Day were militarily desirable. They would deny advance warning to Castro. Now the surprise element was sacrificed for the politically desirable D-minus-2 strikes. They were needed to make the entire enterprise "look Cuban."

They would also make the enormously important Nino Díaz diversion more credible. The planners did not know there were very special morale problems on Díaz' ship and that one of its team leaders had had a critical training accident that aggravated those problems. The man was supposed to lead a group of ten to mark the beach. The day before the meeting in the Cabinet Room, he was teaching the group how to use hand grenades. One of the grenades went off, killed him and injured several others.

Seated behind Lemnitzer at the meeting, General Gray became extremely edgy. He was waiting for McNamara or Lemnitzer to speak up about the necessity of air control, as he had recommended in the car. Nobody did. Gray left the meeting feeling frustrated: too much time was being spent on political problems, not enough on military necessity. But now was not the time to spread more doubt and invite cancellation. Nobody seemed to want that—except perhaps Kennedy.

The President still withheld his approval. Bissell told him he could not delay much longer. The "no-go" time for the Díaz landing and the D-minus-2 air strikes was noon Friday. For the main landing it was noon Sunday. The President nodded.

Leonard Meeker thought it was not enough for him to oppose the invasion within the State Department. He ought to do something about it. What course was open to him that might help persuade the President to cancel?

Meeker, the square-faced, precise deputy legal adviser at State, had been thinking about the small meeting where Governor Bowles had disclosed the invasion plan without giving details. Bowles had been "very exercised"; he thought "President Kennedy should be persuaded not to go ahead."

Meeker agreed that the operation would be "a very large-sized mistake." He thought it was contrary to international law; secondly, armed intervention in a small country would hurt the United States around the world; thirdly, it was "entirely probable the operation would fail and we would have the worst of every world."

Failure seemed to Meeker implicit in Bowles's disclosure that Kennedy had decided to use no U.S. forces "no matter how the landings might fare." Meeker felt even worse when Bowles told the meeting that "President Kennedy really didn't want to talk about this anymore, but simply wanted to go ahead with it."

Meeker thought about his predicament for a day and then made an appointment to see Walt Rostow, the deputy assistant for national security, at 10:30 A.M. on Wednesday, the twelfth. He did not know Rostow. Calling on him was part of a careful strategy. If the President wanted to hear no more about calling off the operation, this placed it in the category of an unwanted pregnancy: either people weren't supposed to know or else they wouldn't talk about it. Surely, the White House National Security Council staff would be an exception: they would know about it, and they could reach the President. If the President had already heard all arguments against going ahead, the same arguments could still be persuasive if they came from his own NSC people too.

Meeker laid out his reasoning as "forcefully" as he could. Rostow said he had been working mostly on Vietnam and Southeast Asia. Cuba was part of Mac Bundy's domain. Rostow said he was in no position to pass judgment; he felt certain that Meeker's arguments had already been considered. Meeker concluded that the case was "pretty much closed." He left in less than fifteen minutes, feeling "very disheartened."

Rostow did see Bundy promptly and conveyed Meeker's anxieties. For the first time, Bundy confided "something" about the plan but said "the President was keeping his options open and, in Bundy's judgment, was inclined to be negative."

At about the same time another of the President's closest advisers received a very different impression. Theodore C. Sorensen, Kennedy's special counsel, had not been informed of the operation at all. Accidentally, he got wind of it at a meeting with Mac Bundy and David Bell, the budget director. Both were embarrassed when it turned out Sorensen was not informed. Sorensen went to Kennedy and asked about the invasion.

The President cut the conversation short. "I know everybody is grabbing their nuts on this," he said. Sorensen inferred that the President thought the project's opponents were chicken. The President was not going to be chicken. And he had heard enough from the doubters.

Phoning old friends in the new administration, Scotty Reston had picked up sounds of dissenting voices. He decided to make the most of them. On Tuesday, the *Times* ran an exclusive story by him on page one. It was one of his rare appearances away from his column on the editorial page. This time the editors moved Cuba to the lead position.

The story reported a "sharp policy dispute" in the administration "about how far to go in helping the Cuban refugees to overthrow the Castro government." Reston knew few details except that "the President has not yet decided how far to go." The story was colored by wishful thinking. "The conflicting concepts of policy and morality have raised a flurry," it said. The conflict was largely in the minds of Messrs. Fulbright and Reston. If the story was designed to stir public debate about Bissell's secret, it failed.

The White House was silent. President Kennedy motored to Griffith Stadium to toss out the first ball of the baseball season. The Washington Senators were playing the Chicago White Sox. The Senators lost as usual, 4 to 3.

The next day the *Times* emphasized the redefinition of Kennedy's intentions with a two-column headline at the top of page one: "President Bars Using U.S. Force to Oust Castro." The announcement could not have been more unequivocal or more prominently advertised.

Appeasing the Exile Leaders

At Harvard, Professor Plank, Schlesinger's former colleague, had a call from Berle. The new Cuban Revolutionary Council was becoming a monumental headache. The Council had been moved to the Lexington Hotel in New York to get it out of the frantic Miami atmosphere. Yet it had submitted a proposed manifesto hysterical in tone and lacking in substance. Tracy Barnes thought it was useless. Schlesinger said it made one wonder what kind of politicians America was thinking of sending back to Cuba. Could Plank go to the Lexington and persuade the Council to rewrite its declaration?

To deflate the Council's resistance, Berle, Schlesinger and the last American ambassador to Havana, Philip Bonsal, met at the State Department with Miró Cardona. Flushed and bald, the former Cuban Premier impressed Schlesinger as eager to please. The Americans pointed out that the manifesto was kind to foreign investors, property owners and bankers, all but ignoring farmers and workers. "It would be foolish," said Schlesinger, "if the Cuban Revolutionary Council turns out to be to the right of the New Frontier."

Miró agreed enthusiastically. He threw his hands into the air in a damned-if-I-do, damned-if-I-don't gesture. Whenever he gave a speech about social justice, half of his audience thought he was a Communist. He would do his best to cooperate with Plank.

At the Lexington, on April 11, Plank encountered little trouble in persuading the Council to accept more liberal economic and social platforms. Cubans were generous about words. Personalities were something else. Manolo Ray was planning to quit the Council. There were too many old-time right-wingers like Tony Varona. Plank talked to Ray quietly for a long time. If Ray dropped out, the Council would lose much popular appeal. Plank argued that the project was going forward regardless. Ray might as well go along and make the best of it. Ray finally agreed. Plank was pleased to be helping the Kennedy administration, right or wrong. Like Miró and Ray, he was damned whether he did or he didn't.

The next day, Berle, Schlesinger and Plank were walking down West Forty-third Street to have lunch with Miró Cardona at the Century Club. Berle and Schlesinger were to carry out the President's assignment to pinpoint for Miró just how much help the U.S. would give the Brigade. Plank was the interpreter.

As they walked, and then while they waited for Miró at a table in the club, Berle and Schlesinger rehearsed the one key point they had to make: the United States would take the Brigade to the beaches; beyond the beaches the Cubans would be on their own.

"That's what the President told us, 'To the Beaches,' " Berle said. "That's what the President said."

Schlesinger confirmed, "That's right, to the beaches."

Berle completed the exchange: "OK, that's what we'll tell Miró."

Plank thought it "very odd" to have this supremely sensitive business transacted in such a public place. Their table was apart from the others by almost twenty-five feet, but eavesdropping or bugging would have been easy. It seemed as "crazy" and "nutty" to Plank as watching Miró, on the way to dinner through the lobby of the Lexington the night before, greeting Brigade recruits as if they were all his sons and chatting volubly with them about the invasion. Plank consoled himself with the thought that Castro must know everything anyhow.

When Miró arrived at the Century, he was annoyed. He didn't like that the CIA was withholding details of the invasion's time and place from the Council. And what about U.S. military support? When Berle and Schlesinger told him that no American troops would be used, he was incredulous. Reminded of the President's press conference statement, he waved it away as propaganda warfare. Just how far would the administration really go?

"We'll take you to the beaches," said Berle.

According to the notes Schlesinger took at the time, Miró said that everyone knew the United States was behind the invasion. Nobody would object if it succeeded. Berle said it could not succeed without an internal uprising, in which event the United States would offer all aid short of troops to the provisional government on the beachhead. Miró predicted that ten thousand Cubans would join the invaders immediately. Berle told him there would be enough material help to go around if the Cubans would really revolt.

Miró said that if things went badly after the provisional government started functioning, he would call on all countries in the hemisphere for help. "This help must come," he said with utmost gravity. "You must understand what will happen to your own interests if we lose. You must commit yourselves to full support of our efforts."

As the luncheon broke up, Schlesinger and Berle walked out of the Century together. Plank was with Miró, who seemed "shattered." He told Plank, still unbelievingly, "No troops! I had an understanding they would send in the troops, if necessary, and give us what was required to make this thing succeed!"

In front of the club, Plank felt he simply had to console this amiable, agitated man with the owlish glasses. "To be frank about it," he said, "I can't believe they would let you people just die on the beach."

"No," said Miró, "I can't believe they would let us down, either."

At the time, it seemed to Plank he was using sensible judgment: the U.S. surely wasn't going to commit its prestige and logistical support and then let it all go down the drain. Later, he wondered if he had not mistakenly reinforced Miró's wishful thinking.*

Schlesinger was disturbed when he returned from New York. He told the President that Miró just did not believe he would get no American military support. He suggested mounting "a very tough effort" to persuade Miró to accept Kennedy's press conference statement about nonintervention. The President immediately phoned Bissell and told him Miró had to understand, else the project would be canceled. Bissell sent Barnes to New York the same day. Barnes reported getting "formal assent" from Miró, but he also doubted that the Cuban leader took him at his word.

Reducing the Air Strikes

With the President still undecided, Colonel Hawkins was dispatched to the Guatemala camps for a final appraisal of the Brigade's chances. Bissell awaited the old soldier's word impatiently. On April 13, Jake Engler sent Hawkins an "emergency precedence" cable: "Please advise emergency precedence if your experiences have in any way changed your evaluation of the Brigade in the last few days." It added critical new information: "For your information: the President has stated that under no conditions will the U.S. intervene with any U.S. forces."

The colonel's reply arrived at Quarters Eye the same day. Its meaning was unequivocal, its tone rousing. It began: "My observations have increased my confidence in the ability of this force to accomplish not only initial combat missions but also the ultimate objective, the overthrow of Castro."

*On May 25, 1961, Miró gave secret testimony before the Taylor Commission about his understanding regarding American support. The testimony does not clarify whether the following covers his memory of an April 3 meeting in the State Department or of another meeting subsequently, possibly the one in the Century Club: "I was asked to give a press conference in which I would essentially declare war against the Castro regime. I said I didn't feel I should declare war when there were so few people in the invasion force. However, Mr. Berle stated that 15,000 additional people would be available. I expressed surprise at this, stating that [Colonel] Frank had told me [at the Trax base] that they would have 30,000 additional men. While no statements were specifically made as to where these men would come from, I assumed they would come from the United States Army. After considerable discussion on this matter, Mr. Berle said that on his word of honor, we would have 15,000 additional men." Ernesto Aragón recalls that Miró returned from the meeting at the Century with assurances of additional manpower and that Berle had said, "Parole d'honneur"—word of honor.

It called the Brigade officers "enthusiastic," "intelligent and motivated with a fanatical urge to begin battle." It endorsed their prediction that the Cuban population would rise up ("They say it is a Cuban tradition to join a winner"). It lauded the training of the Brigade ("more firing experience than U.S. troops would normally receive"), the "remarkable smoothness" of the embarkation, and the Brigade's size ("a truly formidable force"). Its air force also won the colonel's strong approval. Finally he reported: "The brigade officers do not expect help from the U.S. armed forces."

Bissell could not have been more pleased. He had grown to like and respect Hawkins. The colonel had attended many of the meetings at the White House and had clearly impressed the President. Bissell made certain that Kennedy saw the cable right away. Its overwhelming optimism and timing were sure to give a big boost to a final "go" decision. They did. The President said so, then and later.* To him, it represented the final, unqualified word that the best military judgment found no flaws in the operation.

Meanwhile the CIA's intelligence had kept up its happy drumfire. Information Report No. CS-3/470,587 reported:

> The Castro regime is steadily losing popularity . . . The people have begun to lose their fear of the government, and subtle sabotage is common . . . Church attendance is at an all-time high as a demonstration of opposition . . . Travelers throughout the interior have reported that the disenchantment of the masses has spread through all the provinces . . . It is generally believed that the Cuban army has been successfully penetrated by opposition groups and that it will not fight in the event of a showdown . . . The morale of the militia is falling. . . .

The CIA's "Current Intelligence Weekly Summary" said: "Sabotage efforts against Cuban industrial and commercial installations are being stepped up. Insurgent bands are actively engaging Castro's forces in several provinces."

His sense of morality and history thoroughly aroused, Scotty Reston decided to make a final attempt to persuade the public and the administration to give deeper consideration to the implications of an invasion, if not to stop it. He felt "very conscious" of American efforts in the post–World War II years "to put some kind of ethical base under the new world order." The invasion struck him as "very wrong." It was in

---

*Robert Kennedy, who did not attend any of the meetings in the Cabinet Room, later said he believed that Hawkins' recommendation, more than any single factor, persuaded the President to go ahead.

"absolute violation" of U.S. principles. If Castro really posed a threat to American security, Kennedy "could go to the country and say this is what the situation is."

In his *Times* column of Friday, April 14, Reston hoisted his warning flag by again pressing the question of how far the administration would go to help the Cuban exiles. "If they get in trouble once they land," he asked prophetically, "will it continue to supply them?"

The column bristled with righteousness. It juxtaposed the proclaimed U.S. policy of nonaggression against the attitudes struck when America last intervened in Cuba, during the McKinley administration. Reston reminded his readers, who normally included President Kennedy, that McKinley claimed "divine guidance." Teddy Roosevelt thought the venture "good for the navy." Secretary of State Hay called it "a splendid little war." How far had the country come since McKinley?

In the White House, Kennedy picked up the phone and called Bissell. He said the Saturday air strikes could go forward. Then, "almost as an afterthought," he asked how many aircraft would participate.

"Sixteen," said Bissell.

"Well, I don't want it on that scale," said the President. "I want it minimal."

What was minimal? That was left to Bissell, who thought the informality of this decision-making was "rather odd," especially after all the "agonizing" weeks of haggling in the Cabinet Room. He did not question the President's decision. He was too pleased to hear that the strikes could go at all. That made it less likely than ever that the President might scrub the entire project. He passed word to Stan Beerli: only six planes were to fly.

A Crucial Landing Aborted

Early the next morning, Saturday, Ramón Corona's ship, the *La Playa*, ground to a slow, silent halt at the rocky mouth of the Mocambo River in Oriente province, thirty miles east of Guantánamo. All lights were out. Nobody spoke on deck. It was an emotional moment for Corona.

A very tall, extraordinarily handsome cattle rancher with an Erroll Flynn flair and a tiny, neatly clipped mustache, Corona was third in command of a force of 164 men. Oriente was his home. His father had been its governor. Until his escape in a tiny fishing boat a little more than a month earlier, Ramón had been director of all sports in the province. He had flown around in his own government plane, which made him invaluable to the resistance. He had been in charge of all the extensive guerrilla activities in Oriente and was happy to be back as its liberator.

Some seventy of his men were also from Oriente. So was their leader, the fiery Nino Díaz, who had once fought alongside Raúl Castro in the Sierra Maestra. For less than a month they had been trained in the same abandoned ammunitions depot near New Orleans where the frogmen had completed their conditioning. At the depot, much to their disgust, Díaz' men were joined by about a hundred other exiles, whom they didn't care for. The newcomers were not from Oriente. They didn't know their way around. They would be less than helpful with the mission that the force had been assigned by an American known as "Sark": to arm some five hundred guerrillas in the mountains and fight with them.

Not until after the Díaz group had left Key West were they informed that the liberation of Oriente was not uppermost in the minds of their CIA bosses. For the first time Díaz and Corona learned there would be other landings too. They had aboard a CIA agent, an American Marine sergeant of Portuguese extraction named "Curly," who told them about this. He did not say they would play an extremely important role. The CIA urgently needed to create a diversion. Díaz was a key to the success of the overall plan. Bissell wanted Castro to think that the Díaz group was the spearhead of the main invasion effort. Curly did not say so, because he had not been told. Security.

Díaz, Corona and the rest of the Cuban leaders aboard told Curly they would land. Caucusing among themselves, they agreed on a different strategy of their own: they would go ashore only if they could slip through the coastline quietly, join the guerrillas, and free their beloved Oriente.

Off the Mocambo River, they placed an inflatable rubber raft in the ocean. Nine men were to reconnoiter. Their leader was a dour old-timer, Renato Díaz, an operations officer with eighteen years' experience in the Cuban Navy. He had sour feelings about the invasion and had warned the CIA against using merchant crews; military personnel would do better.

Silently, the raft moved within five hundred feet of the coast. There were rocks everywhere. Through his prismatic glasses, Renato Díaz saw two trucks and a jeep stationary on shore. This was no place to slip inland. He "concluded the deception was not worth the sacrifice."

Back at the *La Playa*, the motorboats loaded with troops were in the water, but the old Cuban Navy man told Curly he could find no opening between the breakers. Curly was upset. They all agreed to make another try twenty-four hours later. That would still be twenty-four hours before other landings.

When a motorboat was sent the following morning, its crew reported that they got tangled in the breakers. Nino Díaz concluded that a landing was unwise and decided to head up the coast.*

Curly was furious but powerless. The Cubans considered him "our prisoner." They would not let the radio operator send any messages from him. He was confined to his cabin.

Four miles off the coast, Corona spotted four American destroyers in the distance.† As he moved closer to Guantánamo, he counted dozens of Navy ships. Would Oriente still be freed?

---

*The Taylor Commission's investigative report later said the landing failed "probably because of weak leadership on the part of the Cuban officer responsible."

† Neither the Díaz group nor Castro ever found out that these American ships were to be part of a ruse-within-a-ruse. At the request of the CIA, they were positioned so that Castro's radar men would assume they were part of an armada steaming in for a Normandy-style landing. Díaz and his men could not know of the destroyers' maneuvers because the CIA had deliberately failed to equip the *La Playa* with radar. The beauty of the CIA's great radar deception was lost on Castro and his defenders because they had no radar. Castro was merely informed that a ship was off Varacora; there were signs it might try to land a few hundred men. He was not concerned. There were enough forces on the spot to deal with them if they came ashore.

CHAPTER FIVE

The Attack Begins

First Strike

At Happy Valley, the Nicaraguan staging area's airstrip, B-26 pilot Gustavo Ponzoa was finally sure he would see action. The former Cubana Airlines pilot was intense, short, hawk-nosed, with the agility and the hungry good looks of a Spanish bullfighter. He had never flown in combat and never even had live bombs aboard except for two quick practice runs. But he was very excited and anxious to put his training to use. He was "completely convinced we were going to do it."

On the morning of Wednesday, April 13, a Constellation arrived from Washington with a group of American civilians who were clearly senior advisers. The B-26 squadron was isolated from the transport crews. The bomber crews started to live in a special tent surrounded by barbed wire and by Americans armed with automatic weapons. The Cubans could go to the mess hall and the showers only under guard and were "never left alone one second." Gus Ponzoa did not mind. He had learned about "security."

That morning the crews were briefed in the operations shack for almost four hours. They sat comfortably around a twenty-five-foot-long table watching a map of Cuba that almost covered an entire wall. A freezer was stocked with cold soda, and the ceiling was decorated by two unfolded orange-and-white parachutes. The Americans said that operations would begin with strikes at Castro's three military air bases: Campo Libertad on the outskirts of Havana; San Antonio de los Baños; and Antonio Maceo Airport at Santiago de Cuba in Oriente province. Each target was to be attacked by two planes. When Ponzoa was assigned to Santiago de Cuba, 450 miles southeast of Havana, he

173

laughed out loud with delight. He had flown there with an airline plane almost every week for twelve years and knew it "like the palm of my hand."

Then Luís Cosme, the Cuban chief of operations, asked for one volunteer to fly a "special mission." He gave no details. Ponzoa raised his hand at once. So did every other pilot in the room. "George," one of the civilians from Washington, picked Mario Zuñiga, the personnel officer, who had been a B-26 pilot in the Cuban Air Force and later ran his own crop-dusting business.

Ponzoa was disappointed not to be selected, but he was soon preoccupied with the personal briefings he received from an American known as "Joe"—Joe Shannon, one of the pilots from the Alabama Air National Guard—and General Reid Doster, whom Gus knew as "Mr. Reid." Over and over again, Gus took a magnifying glass and went inch by inch across the U-2 photos of the Santiago de Cuba airport. Two T-33 jets and three B-26 bombers were clearly visible. So were numerous small craft on the civilian ramp. He studied the machine gun emplacements in the trenches that surrounded the runways and the stacks of the antiaircraft guns. He paid particular attention to the hydrant that led to the underground fuel tanks. It was his priority target. Again he chuckled. How many times had he walked past that hydrant? A hundred times? No, maybe a thousand.

At one point, Gus and his briefers were joined by "George." Gus thought he was an American Air Force general; he talked like one and had the suitable air of command. Actually, he was an assistant to Colonel Beerli; an Air Force lieutenant colonel on detached duty with the CIA. George said that Gus was not to attack any targets except the planes on the ground and the fuel hydrant. Not "one single round of ammunition" was to be directed against buildings or anything else.

Gus thought of the nearby Texaco oil refinery—"a fantastic target, just a couple of rockets would have done it." He said to George, "I tell you what, when I get over there I'll do the shooting that I think has to be done."

"That's not the way we're planning it," George said. "You do as you're told. The people who do anything else will be court-martialed."

Zuñiga, meanwhile, was briefed by a former U.S. Navy pilot, a friendly, dark-haired Italian American known as "Chick." Under no circumstances was Zuñiga to discuss his mission with anyone for five years.* He was to fly to Miami and pose as a defector from the Cuban Air Force. It was part of an elaborate cover story to make it appear as if

---

*Zuñiga more than kept his word. He did not discuss his mission until he was interviewed for this book fifteen years later.

he, as well as the pilots who would attack the three airports, were coming from Cuba. Afterward he was supposed to "vanish" and not return to the operation, because the CIA was worried that he might talk about his mission.

Zuñiga, low-keyed, laconic and grimly serious, considered himself a professional military man who did not question superiors. He did not mind that the American officers had a bar where Cubans were not admitted. Rank was entitled to privileges. He did resent that his countrymen were only "pawns on a chess table," that even the top Cuban leaders were not allowed to participate in the planning of any operations. And he and his closest friends had privately agreed that the Bay of Pigs was "a bad spot" with its swamps and the long distance to possible hideouts in the mountains. They thought it would have been much better to land in Trinidad or Cienfuegos or another town "where thousands of people would be joining" from the local population.

Zuñiga had said nothing to his superiors about these reservations, but now he flatly refused to carry out one part of his orders. He considered himself anything but an actor and thought that the mission to Miami "was a little bit nutty," but he told Chick that he was willing to "go along with the game." However, he insisted on rejoining his fellow pilots in Nicaragua afterward. Otherwise he would not play in his assigned "movie actor show."

After some arguing, Chick relented and began coaching Zuñiga on the story he was to tell in Miami. He was supposed to say that he and three fellow pilots, all disenchanted with Castro, had been plotting their escape for months; that he had been flying a routine patrol from his base, San Antonio de los Baños, and decided to return there to make two strafing runs at the airfield; that he was hit by small-arms fire and had to head for Miami because he was low on gas. Chick had Zuñiga recite the story repeatedly until both were certain that Mario had it straight.

Wearing a baseball cap, green pants and white T-shirt—hardly the uniform of a military pilot on patrol duty—Zuñiga took off for the four-and-a-half-hour flight to Miami in a B-26 bearing the Cuban star, the number 933, and the initials FAR—Fuerza Aerea Revolucionaria. While he was still catching some last-minute rest in Puerto Cabezas, a CIA team had removed the cover from one of the engines, fired some bullets through the metal shielding, and replaced it on the plane to make it look battle-worn.

About thirty minutes from Miami International Airport, Zuñiga, flying at fifteen hundred feet, opened his cockpit and, in accordance with Chick's instructions, fired his pistol at one of his engines until it was feathered.

On landing, Zuñiga recited his story to reporters. Edward Ahrens, the district director of the United States Immigration and Naturalization Service, dutifully announced that the pilot's name was being withheld to prevent reprisals against the family he left behind in Cuba. Strangely enough, news photographers were allowed to take pictures. Zuñiga, again according to his orders, tried to cover his face with his hands, but didn't quite manage to bring off the act; half of his face appeared in some of the photos—enough to be happily recognized in the newspapers by his wife, Georgina, and their four children, whom he had left safely behind in their apartment on Southwest Twentieth Avenue (and presumably by anyone else who knew the relatively few Cubans qualified to fly B-26 bombers).

Mario did not, however, get to see his family. He was whisked off to Immigration headquarters on Biscayne Boulevard supposedly for "interrogation." Actually, he got some rest in a cell for deportees until he was picked up and taken to a motel by an American civilian whom he had met in Miami before he ever left for his training with the Brigade. They ordered a good meal from room service, and that night Mario was taken to Opa-Locka and flown back to Happy Valley in one of the regular C-46 cargo runs.

By that hour his cover story was already in shreds. Reporters had noted that his plane's machine guns had evidently not been fired and that its nose was of solid metal; Castro's B-26s had plastic noses. The press also wondered in print why the wayward pilot's name was withheld even though Castro would obviously know of any captain who happened to be missing from San Antonio de los Baños along with his B-26.

Gus Ponzoa's bombing mission against Santiago de Cuba was set for a 2:28 A.M. takeoff. He and Joe Shannon had spent hours beforehand checking his aircraft, No. 929, especially the armament: two 500-pound demolition bombs, ten 260-pound "frag" (fragmentation) bombs, eight machine guns in the nose along with 2,800 rounds, and eight rockets, four suspended under each wing. The plane was overloaded at 38,000 pounds. If it lost one engine, it could not fly with more than 35,000 pounds. Gus knew it. It was a small part of the risk.

Like all the Brigade planes, the aircraft carried Cuban markings. It also had the telltale solid-metal nose and a blue stripe along the fuselage. All Castro B-26s had plastic noses and no stripes. This was the

CIA's scheme for enabling American ships and planes to identify friendly aircraft while hopefully fooling Castro planes and ground defenders long enough to insure surprise and give the CIA craft an edge. Ponzoa thought this was shrewd thinking. He did not question why friendly forces would make quick identifications while unfriendly eyes would be presumed to be slow.

When the final weather briefing was over, General Doster rose and said gravely, "Gentlemen, you're going to make history today. Lots of luck to you." Then he personally drove Gus and his co-pilot, Rafael García Pujol, in his jeep to the aircraft.

Gus's wing man, Gonzalo Herrera in aircraft No. 933, was already on the runway. Gus put on his parachute. He was sweating profusely. He was the leader of "Gorilla" wing—the first man in the first group to take off in the first operation for the Bay of Pigs. Through his head went the unhistoric sort of thought that runs through men's minds on such occasions: "This is the real thing."

The beginning was leisurely. Ponzoa and Herrera arrived at the latitude of Kingston, Jamaica, under starry skies ten minutes ahead of schedule and circled slowly to use up time so that the attacks on all three airports could begin simultaneously. Daylight was less than an hour away when they lowered their altitude from eight thousand to five hundred feet. About 160 miles southwest of their target they dropped to fifty feet, barely skimming over the water to escape detection in case they would face radar. Ponzoa was becoming uncomfortable because daylight was approaching too fast. He had hoped to hit the target in the half-light of dawn, but the schedule was based on the time in Havana, where daybreak came fifteen minutes later.

Suddenly, twenty miles from the Santiago de Cuba airport and with the sun rising, Gus spotted a white Cuban patrol boat. His plane passed nearby, and he saw that the boat started signaling to shore. His flight plan called for him to circle out of sight of the airport and begin his attack from the mountains to the north. Now that he believed the boat had given the attack away, he decided to take the direct approach instead. Herrera was flying the defensive position just off his right wing. Gus gave him the signal to start moving in a hurry: he moved his right fist rapidly up and down. Side by side they lumbered over the cliffs off the airport, now flying at six thousand feet, and as Gus opened his bomb bays he saw a Cubana Airlines DC-3 with the number 172 taking fuel at the hydrant which was his first target.

He flushed with excitement. No. 172 was one of his old aircraft. He knew every bolt in it. Suddenly it was his target. It was "a fantastic experience. You're doing something *that* big and your life is at risk, and now it's going to be another man's life and your old aircraft."

He did not pause. Both of his 500-pound bombs were dropping before his thought was completed. He was at twelve hundred feet. As the bombs fell, he lost the normal amount of altitude and started recovering and veering left at eight hundred feet. He watched one wing of his old DC-3 flying through the air. Very heavy red-and-black smoke was billowing from the hydrant area. From the ground toward the left, red tracers of machine gun and antiaircraft fire started arching toward his aircraft. Followed closely by Herrera, he was almost over the ocean again when it occurred to him that he had felt only one shock wave after dropping both bombs. One of them never went off.

Over the cliffs they started their second run, with Herrera dropping a straight line of his fragmentation bombs at a hangar and the military ramp where two B-26s and other aircraft were parked from northeast to southwest. Ponzoa aimed his machine guns at the antiaircraft positions. By now the defenders were firing heavily from the north and the east. The pilots could not see the impact of Herrera's bombs; smoke from the burning fuel tanks cut visibility too much.

For the third run Gus decided to drop his six frag bombs at the military ramp, too. Again it was impossible to see what damage had been done. As he headed out to sea, he turned his head back and saw that at least one of the B-26s seemed to be untouched. For his fourth pass he decided to go after it with rockets and machine guns.

Everything was moving too quickly to take deliberate aim. "You're shooting by feeling, the angle, everything, you're not doing what you've read in the books." The first rocket was slightly short. The second went right into the side of the B-26. It blew up like an orange ball. Ponzoa's plane was no more than fifty feet above the runway as he turned left and up for his getaway. Herrera was two hundred yards in front of him and slightly to his right. Very slightly. Ponzoa noticed that his machine guns were still firing. They were stuck open. Herrera might fly into his line of fire any second. Ponzoa banked sharply farther to the left, and Herrera got away. Gus saw that the trigger of his guns had malfunctioned. Frantically, he wiggled it until the firing stopped.

On the fifth pass—they were supposed to fly no more than two— Herrera fired three rockets into a hangar that was still intact. The pilots could not know what was inside. Whatever it was, it blew up in red and blue flames. Ponzoa, flying as Herrera's wing man, was diving into a nest of machine guns off Runway 27 when he felt a click on the nose of his plane. He was hit, but his instruments indicated nothing wrong. He had no time to worry. He was too busy talking to Herrera, keeping in touch about who was going to do what.

All remnants of calm had left both men long ago. They did not bother using their respective code calls, "Gorilla One" and "Gorilla Two." They were shouting as loud as they could, addressing each other by their real first names.

"Gus, I've been hit several times," Herrera yelled when they had climbed to about four thousand feet. "I can see holes in both wings."

"OK, it's six-five, we've been over the airport twenty minutes," Gus replied. "Let's get out of here and go home." As Gus got closer, he could see hydraulic oil leaking from several places in the nose and fuselage of his partner's plane. Herrera was losing power. He slowed down. Gus slowed down. On the radio he could hear Raúl Castro, Fidel's brother, broadcasting from Santiago de Cuba. He was talking about "the beginning of the end," or so Gus understood him in the excitement.

Gus was "mad with joy," his morale "sky high." He made a "perfect" landing at Happy Valley, where General Doster was waiting in his jeep, smiling and giving him "a great salute." Although all of Herrera's tires blew out when he landed, he made it safely to the ground. Ponzoa was ecstatic. "You couldn't get a better bunch of guys," he thought. "We were strong as hell."

With Castro in Cuba

Castro was not relying on his intelligence reports. He lacked confidence in them. His agents were "not well organized." They did not have "a great penetration." He did carefully analyze news reports from Guatemala and Miami and, especially, statements of the Miró Cardona group and the U.S. government. The invasion was clearly imminent. He had plans to meet a "direct" attack by United States forces.* But when Kennedy firmly excluded use of U.S. forces against Cuba, Castro believed him. It fit his own scenario of what would most likely happen.

There would be an "indirect" invasion on the Guatemala model. He could not accept that the CIA expected an internal uprising "no matter

---

*On June 6, 1978, Castro told the author, "I would not like to reveal concrete ideas about that. Although twenty years have passed, we must always have plans in the face of an emergency, an invasion. But I can assure you, if an invasion by the U.S. had taken place, we would have mounted a tremendous resistance." He launched into a Churchillian statement of total defiance: "They would fight against hundreds of thousands of men in the mountains, in the fields, in the cities, and everywhere . . . [and] commit genocide. They would not have found anything intact. They would have had to destroy everything. They would have had to kill even the last revolutionary in the country . . . destroying the last stone of our capital city."

how stupid they could be." They had to know that the people largely supported the government and were armed. The invaders would select a place for a beachhead and establish a provisional government. "The danger would come afterward" when the U.S. would seek a "legal image" by asking the Organization of American States to intervene.

Castro's biggest problem was that fragments of Bissell's secrecy fig leaf were still in place, after all. Castro did not know the date of the invasion; the place; the strength; and most critically, he could not guess how the invaders would be deployed.

He did not think there might be as few as fourteen hundred men. His estimates ran from three thousand to ten thousand. If they were eager to set up a provisional government quickly, they would try for one major beachhead. Castro thought he could squash that quickly, although it would entail operational problems because he did not want to commit a large troop concentration in any one place in advance. If the invaders established small strongholds in many places, it would take much longer to wipe them out.

Castro ordered platoon-sized militia posts set up at every conceivable invasion point. They could at least spread the alert. Four days before D-Day he took special precautions about his favorite area, Girón and the Bay of Pigs. He ordered a battalion moved there. But without the motivation of obvious instant danger, his defense organization was too sluggish. The battalion never got there.

Castro was sleeping little, and mostly during the day. He was at "Point One," the national military headquarters in suburban Havana, at dawn Saturday when it was overflown at extremely low altitude by two B-26s.

"What are these planes?" he asked his staff. Nobody knew. As they watched, the planes started diving at Campo Libertad airport nearby. Castro and his men heard bombs falling and antiaircraft responding. Phone calls soon reported damage at Libertad, San Antonio and Santiago de Cuba.

Castro thought the attacks were "madness." Now he had "absolute certainty"—and plenty of warning—of an invasion. But where? When? How?

First Lieutenant Rafael del Pino had been half asleep in the barracks at San Antonio de los Baños air base at about 6 A.M. when he heard an airplane noise. He pulled on his pants and went outside to join his commanding officer, Enrique Carreras, who was already fully dressed. They looked up at a B-26, and del Pino said, "There is Lagas!" Lagas was a pilot from the Santiago de Cuba base. His arrival was expected. He was to reinforce San Antonio. It was the key base because it was closest to Havana.

Del Pino, twenty-two years old, wiry, short and high-strung—his fingernails were bitten down to the quick—was the youngest of seven pilots at San Antonio. They had eight planes—four T-33s and four Sea Furies—in various states of repair.

With less than a hundred hours on the T-33, del Pino would not have qualified for combat in most air forces, but he felt confident about himself and the base. Watching the B-26 making a left turn and heading for the principal runway, he did not think of Castro's visit the previous week. Angrily, Fidel had instructed the pilots at the flight line to disperse their aircraft so that a sneak attack would not catch them all on the ground. The planes had been parked together because that made them easier to refuel. Feeling challenged, one of the pilots told Fidel they would take off under "any conditions." Fidel laughed and said, "You want to bet?"

Now del Pino watched in disbelief when the B-26, nearing the runway, opened fire with rockets and machine guns. Without a word, del Pino and Carreras started to run toward the nearest jet, No. 715, parked more than five thousand yards away. With only two jeeps on the base, there was no transportation near the barracks. Del Pino was still without boots or shirt. When he was two hundred yards from jet No. 715, it was hit and exploded.

"Let's get over there!" shouted Carreras, pointing at del Pino's jet, No. 711, parked more than half a mile distant at the end of the center runway. They were getting close when they saw another pilot, Alberto Fernández, also barefoot, hurdle the three-foot fence of his home. He was one of the few married men with a house on the base. He headed for No. 711 and took off. Antiaircraft artillery had already chased away the attacker, who had also destroyed two DC-3 transports and an AT-6 trainer.

For Henry Raymont, United Press International's man in Havana, the Bay of Pigs started with what sounded like the roll of thunder. He was asleep in the apartment he shared with the local UPI man, Adolfo Mendino, when the grumbling noise awakened him shortly before 6 A.M. The apartment was in the suburb of Miramar, across the street from the Mexican Embassy and overlooking Campo Libertad.

Raymont, very nearsighted, grabbed his thick eyeglasses and sprinted to the bedroom window just in time to see two B-26s of the Brigade's Puma wing diving onto the airfield, bombing and strafing. He called the UPI, and for the next half hour, as the bombers made one pass after another, buildings blew up and Castro's Czech-made four-barrel antiaircraft guns coughed back in furious bursts, Raymont carefully dictated his blow-by-blow ringside account.

He was excited about his scoop, of course, but did not reflect on his incredible luck. All good reporters are born lucky, and Henry Raymont was an exceptionally good one. Short, quick, curly-haired and obviously myopic, he was irrepressibly cheerful and talkative. His thick lips rarely seemed to rest, and his interviews invariably turned into two-way sessions. Henry listened closely enough, squinting and smiling knowledgeably, but he also loved to gesticulate, interrupt, tell jokes, volunteer his own always fervently defended opinions in detail. News sources enjoyed talking to him, because he often passed along some fresh morsel of news or gossip.

He loved to play the man of culture and drop the names of his many well-placed friends, especially his intimate contacts in the worlds of diplomacy and classical music. He delighted in his role as a supranational figure, moving effortlessly from language to language, instantly at home on any telephone anywhere, pushing to be the first to know, eager not to do the conventional thing.

Raymont came to his role naturally. Born Jewish in Koenigsberg, East Prussia, in the days of Hitler, he fled with his parents, first to Riga, Latvia, then to Denmark, then on to Argentina in 1938. There he had most of his schooling and joined the UP at sixteen. The wire service sent him back to Scandinavia, then to London and, in 1948, to Washington, where he reported on Latin-American affairs from the State Department. Through the years he was openly critical of State's policies toward the proud Latinos. He thought they were being treated like unruly stepchildren. He became an American citizen, but always "identified more with Latin America."

In Havana, as usual, he was bucking the American mainstream. His UPI colleagues in Miami were reporting the CIA and the refugee view of Cuba and "creating an impression that the place was collapsing." Henry had reported otherwise, and he thought about that as he saw the bombers circle and thunder down for more runs on Campo Libertad, and watched how the young men of Castro's militia rushed to man the antiaircraft guns and kept firing and getting killed before his eyes. If morale had been as advertised by the CIA and the refugees, nobody would be operating those antiaircraft batteries.

He also thought about how sure he had been that there would be no invasion of Cuba. When the director of *El Mundo* had predicted the landings at their last weekly luncheon on Wednesday, Raymont had laughed at him and said, "You're beginning to believe your own propaganda!" He told the Cuban editor the old joke about Israel going bankrupt and a member of the Knesset announcing, "Gentlemen, I have a solution. Let's declare war on the United States. Then we will be occupied, we will have our reconstruction planned, and our economic problems will be over." And a member of the opposition objected, "Yes, my friends, but what if we win?"

Raymont told the editor that he knew Kennedy and "there now are very intelligent people in the White House. I know Arthur Schlesinger and Dick Goodwin and some others. Surely they're reasoning among themselves, 'What if there is an invasion and we do win, then where do we go?' I mean, American prestige in Latin America would be in shambles!"*

Henry had felt "smug" and thought he had "really scored."

Now he was no longer sure of his ground. He had not been able to spot any insignia on the attacking planes. Anyway, insignia wouldn't necessarily mean anything. Shortly after he arrived at the office around 7:30 A.M. he received a summons to present himself at 1 P.M. at the office of Cuban President Osvaldo Dorticos. Meanwhile, by phone, he joined the frantic speculation among his ambassador friends about the origin of the attackers.

When his UPI ticker chattered out the bulletin about Stevenson's speech at the UN, announcing that the planes had been Cuban defectors, he rushed, much relieved, to the Foreign Ministry and showed it to the ambassadors who had been assembled there by the Cubans. They watched angrily as Henry's bulletin was passed around. The ambassadors—and Raymont—naturally tended to believe Stevenson, even though they were just being shown American-made shrapnel collected after the raids. It meant little, because the Cubans were using U.S. ammunition, too.

When Henry saw Dorticos, he pointed out that shrapnel was hardly firm evidence. Dorticos said, "You've been very fair. I want you to go and see the auxiliary fuel tanks that we've just recovered and that were jettisoned by these planes."

Raymont decided not to bother inspecting the tanks. No plane flying from Cuba would have to jettison auxiliary fuel tanks soon after takeoff, but how was he to know that the tanks had actually been jettisoned by

---

*Raymont was not alone in his view that U.S. victory in Cuba would have produced even more problems than defeat. A year after the landings, when President Kennedy expressed his continuing disgust over the outcome to Clayton Fritchey of Ambassador Stevenson's staff, Fritchey said, "Mr. President, it could have been worse." Kennedy asked, "How?" Fritchey said, "It might have succeeded."

the attackers? It was a dramatic day, frustrating, and Henry felt increasingly ill at ease—"Stevenson or no Stevenson."

That evening, he called on another friend, the ambassador of the United Arab Republic, a former colonel in the Egyptian Air Force. It was sunset, and they were sipping martinis on the ambassador's terrace.

"Were these planes from outside or inside?" Raymont wondered.

"Look," said the ambassador, "you've been here long enough to know the Cubans. Do you think it's possible to arm those planes in Cuba over a number of hours without the entire island finding out about it?"

To Raymont, this judgment was all but conclusive. Depressed, he went to the Brazilian Embassy. The ambassador was out of town. Henry had lent him his record player and all his Mozart quintets. He started up the hi-fi and spent the evening listening to the quintets. "It was the only way to keep sane in those days," he said much later.*

At 10 A.M. on the day of the air strike, Fernández Mell reported to Castro at Point One, national military headquarters, the luxurious two-story villa on Forty-seventh Street in the Nuevo Vedado suburb of Havana, once property of a paper importer. Square-faced and well over six feet tall, Mell was another of the band who fought with Fidel in the Sierra Maestra. A physician, he was in charge of military medical services. He had just supervised the care of the grave burn cases after Bissell's air raid on Campo Libertad caused the explosion of several ammunition trucks.

Mell was ushered into the office of Sergio del Valle, still another Sierra Maestra veteran, black, seemingly easygoing, and now in charge of headquarters operations. There were several officers in the room, but only one desk. It was unoccupied. When Fidel was in thought, he usually paced or stood. When he stood, everybody did. He was smoking a cigar, but, as usual, nobody else smoked. It was their mark of respect for the Commander in Chief.

Fidel fired questions at Mell. How bad was the situation at Camp Libertad? How many dead? How many injured? The men fell into quiet, grave discussion. An invasion was obviously imminent. Where would the main attack come? Mell was certain they would face American troops. He knew history. The United States was always invading in Latin America. They would control the air. Then it would be difficult to move medical supplies. The supplies were low. It was going to be a difficult time. Castro kept pacing.

Later that day, on the ramp at San Antonio air base, Castro spoke to

---

*Raymont was subsequently among the more than 100,000 political suspects arrested. He was reported executed, and shortly freed.

the pilots, mechanics and antiaircraft-artillery men. He said he was certain the morning strike against the base was a prelude to more attacks. "Any attack they launch they will try to start by destroying our few planes," he said. Dispersing the planes was not enough. The pilots would have to spend the night sleeping under the wings.

This idea made sense to the senior pilot, Captain Carreras, but he decided to refine it. He had cots placed under the wings. One man rested there. Another pilot would stay awake in the cockpit, strapped in, parachute on, ready to roll. It was a tedious position to maintain, so the two men would switch positions every thirty to forty minutes. Nobody was going to catch Fidel's men napping.

At the graveside funeral of Saturday's bombing victims, Castro declared to a crowd of ten thousand, "The United States sponsored the attack because it cannot forgive us for achieving a Socialist revolution under their noses." It was his first public characterization of the revolution as "Socialist." No Cuban ever forgot the occasion. The crowd yelled, "War! War!"

"The United States delivered the planes, the bombs, and trained the mercenaries," Castro shouted hoarsely. "The Yankees are trying to deceive the world, but the whole world knows that attack was made with Yankee planes piloted by mercenaries paid by the United States Central Intelligence Agency." He read dispatches by American wire service agencies from Miami about Zuñiga's "defection" and commented, "Even Hollywood would not try to film such a story."

As Castro finished, he was handed a note reporting a United States warship moving toward the capital from the west. He shrugged, finished his address, and went to sleep in his Havana apartment around 11 P.M. for the first time in two days.

Furor at the UN

Following news of the air strike, members of the Fair Play for Cuba Committee marched up and down outside the United Nations Building, shouting, "Cuba, si, Yankee, no!" Inside, Frederick H. Boland of Ireland, president of the General Assembly, had just gaveled the Saturday session to order at 10:30 A.M., when Dr. Raúl Roa, the Cuban Foreign Minister, a short man with a little mustache, demanded the floor on a point of order:

"I should like to inform the Assembly, which is the supreme forum for the expression of the international conscience, that this morning, at 6:30 A.M., United States aircraft—"

Boland interrupted to rule that Roa's news was "not a point of order," but "one of substance." He called the Cuban out of order.

"Thank you, Mr. President," said Roa. "Which is of greater interest to the United Nations General Assembly, a purely procedural question or a breach of international peace?"

At once, Ambassador Valentin Zorin of the Soviet Union rose, also "on a point of order." He urged that the Assembly "discuss immediately the question of the aggression against Cuba." Eventually agreement was reached to air the Cuba issue at an emergency session of the UN Political Committee that afternoon.

In normally talkative Washington, news sources dried up. Presidential Press Secretary Pierre Salinger, not "witting" to the operation, told reporters at his regular press briefing, "Our only information comes from the wire service stories we have read." Newsmen at the Pentagon and the State Department did no better. Why wouldn't the immigration authorities in Miami release the names of the "defected" pilots? What about the auxiliary fuel tanks found jettisoned near Havana? The questions multiplied. The answer remained the same: "No comment."

President Kennedy plodded through an ostensibly placid Saturday schedule. At 10:27 A.M. he went to the White House conference room to shake hands with twenty foreign doctors and their wives who were visiting with his own physician, Dr. Janet Travell. He kept appointments with staff people. At 11:18 he walked into the eighth-floor reception lounge of the State Department and addressed a group assembled in honor of "African Freedom Day." At 12:40 P.M. he left by helicopter to join his wife, Jacqueline, and their children at their weekend home, Glen Ora, near Middleburg, Virginia.

One man who could not duck the issue was Ambassador Stevenson. He had to answer Roa's charges that afternoon. His entourage, unprepared, went scrambling for facts. Harlan Cleveland called the State Department's Bureau of Latin-American affairs. They said they'd check the CIA. The CIA sent back assurances that the bombings had been the work of authentic defectors from the Cuban Air Force. Cleveland's deputy, Joseph Sisco, drafted a statement denying United States involvement.

It was almost time for Stevenson to address the UN. He was waiting for his text in his UN office. It was in the U.S. delegation's suite of rooms on the ground floor of the UN's glass skyscraper—not an ideal place to work; it was hard to follow a conversation whenever a freighter or a tug chugged by on the East River and decided to toot.

The ambassador's political officer, Dick Pedersen, was next door, listening on an extension phone as Joe Sisco was dictating Washington's text for Stevenson to a secretary. First, it reemphasized the President's statement that "there will not be under any conditions—and I repeat, any conditions—any intervention in Cuba by the United States armed forces." Next, the U.S. would "do everything it possibly can" to make sure that "no Americans participate in any actions against Cuba." Third, the U.S. would "consider" the defecting pilots' request for political asylum.

Pedersen broke in. "Joe, that statement isn't denying—"

"Yes, we're denying it," Sisco said. "When I get through with the next paragraph, you'll see we're denying it."

Indeed, in the fourth paragraph Stevenson was to assure the UN that the pilots who had landed in Florida "apparently defected from Castro's tyranny" and that the planes "to the best of our knowledge were Castro's own."

Pedersen went over the statement with Stevenson. He told him that Sisco had phoned it in from Rusk's office; it had been gone over "very carefully." Nevertheless, Pedersen suggested that Stevenson call Rusk and "check it out personally." At that moment Sisco called. "Never mind," said Stevenson, "I'll talk to Joe about it." Sisco said yes, everything had been checked out carefully: the Cuban charges were denied. By now Sisco's own suspicions were aroused. He called Robert Sayre of the Bureau of Latin-American Affairs and asked if any of the statement's language could be changed. "No, you can't change one word," Sayre said.

For once, Bissell's security curtain was unflawed. None of the men involved—Sayre, Sisco, Cleveland, Pedersen, Stevenson, not even Rusk—knew that they were lying, that their story was a CIA cover job.* And only Rusk knew anything about an invasion of Cuba.

Stevenson was about to take his statement to the UN committee meeting when Charles Noyes, his minister counselor, was handed a wire service photograph of Mario Zuñiga's plane, No. 933, on the runway in Miami.

"Can we use this?" asked one of Stevenson's public-information officers.

"We can't use anything without approval of the State Department," said Noyes.

*"I thought I was giving Stevenson the truth," Rusk said in 1977. "If he was fooled, so was I."

He called an Assistant Secretary of State for Public Affairs in Washington and described the photo. "Is this clean?" he asked. The reply was "Yes."

Minutes later, Stevenson read his cleared text to the UN. Then he leaned forward and displayed the photo of Zuñiga's plane.

"It has the markings of Castro's air force on the tail," he said, "which everyone can see for himself. The Cuban star and the initials F.A.R., Fuerza Aerea Revolucionaria, are clearly visible."

Roa pointed out that markings could be painted on planes by anybody. Then he said that the "mercenaries bought by the United States have announced that tonight at ten o'clock they will again bomb Cuban citizens."

Among the TV audience was Dave Phillips, the CIA propaganda chief. He was watching from Quarters Eye. He had a special interest because he was an ardent Stevenson Democrat. As the ambassador went on to defend the "deceitful scheme" of Phillips' bosses, the old propaganda hand grew more and more surprised. He thought, "What a smooth, smooth phony this is!" Fascinated and repelled, he kept watching as Stevenson's eloquence mounted. Finally Phillips was all but certain: the ambassador had been taken in by the CIA hoax! He couldn't get over it. Was it possible, he asked Jim Flannery, that Stevenson hadn't been briefed?

"It's possible, I guess," Flannery said with a grimace. "Tracy Barnes and Arthur Schlesinger went to New York last week to fill him in. But you know Tracy. He can be charming and urbane and talk around a subject until you don't know what he means to say. Maybe he and Schlesinger gave Stevenson the flavor but not the facts."

Dick Pedersen, Stevenson's political man, felt much the same, but he had work to do. The UN debate was to continue Monday. The Stevenson delegation was ready with its strategy. It would present a statement so overwhelmingly complete with corroborative technical evidence about the "defector" planes that no doubt about the bombing raids would be left in anybody's mind.

Pedersen was in his apartment at One Lexington Avenue, overlooking exclusive, private Gramercy Park, when a colleague from the U.S. mission called with word from the department. The mission was to stop asking for more details about the planes. It "wouldn't be worthwhile to pursue that line of inquiry any longer."

This was how Pedersen learned that he, his chief and their associates had been lying to the world. Pedersen was "appalled." He knew that

Stevenson would also be appalled and would want to convey his feelings to the department. Pedersen took a cab to the office, thinking it would be best to draft a statement for the boss before breaking the news to him.

It was midafternoon Sunday before Dick Pedersen arrived in Suite 42A of the Waldorf Towers, the U.S. Embassy to the United Nations. Adlai Stevenson lived there, and most of his work was done in that spacious, elegant apartment with its spectacular view of the city and with Stevenson's own fine artwork, including original letters of Lafayette and Jefferson.

Pedersen's heart was heavy. Stevenson did not yet know that his skillful oratory the day before and even the photograph of the plane with which he was shown on front pages all over the world would damage his credibility for some time. Pedersen hated to break the news. When he did, Stevenson was "dismayed" but "very quiet." He was not the type who shouted, cursed or got red in the face. Besides, Pedersen was not an intimate. He was a career man; Stevenson had known him only a short time.

Almost gratefully, he took the telegram which Pedersen had drafted for the department, changed a word or two and told Pedersen to send it off. At 7:33 P.M. the "TOP SECRET—PRIORITY—EYES ONLY" Telex message arrived in the State Department, addressed to Rusk. Its full text was:

1. Greatly disturbed by clear indications received during day in process developing rebuttal material that bombing incidents in Cuba on Saturday were launched in part at least from outside Cuba.

2. I had definite impression from Barnes when he was here that no action would be taken which could give us political difficulty during current UN debate. This raid, if such it was, if exposed will gravely alter whole atmosphere in GA [General Assembly]. If Cuba now proves any of planes and pilots came from outside, we will face increasingly hostile atmosphere. No one will believe that bombing attacks on Cuba from outside could have been organized without our complicity.

3. I do not understand how we could let such attack take place two days before debate on Cuban issue in GA. Nor can I understand, if we could not prevent such outside attack from taking place at this time, why I could not have been warned and provided prepared material with which to defend U.S. Answers I made to Roa's statement about incident on Saturday were hastily concocted in Department, and revised by me at last minute on assumption this was clear case of attacks by defectors inside Cuba.

4. There is gravest risk of another U-2 disaster in such uncoordinated action.

STEVENSON

To intimates, the ambassador was much less diplomatic. He told Harlan Cleveland that he felt he had been "deliberately tricked" by his own government.

"I feel as betrayed as you do," Cleveland said.

The ambassador still did not know of the Cuban landings, now less than twelve hours away.

Further to support the notion that the "fig leaf" of secrecy was still in place, it had been decided that Allen Dulles would keep a speaking engagement made months before. He would leave for Puerto Rico to address a convention of the Young Presidents' Organization Sunday on doing business behind the Iron Curtain.

So eager was Dulles to maintain the aura of business-as-usual that he would not drop the masquerade even when he was alone with one of his closest CIA colleagues. Mindful that the frequently ridiculed General Cabell would be in charge of the agency over the weekend, Bob Amory, the deputy director for intelligence, decided to speak up when he caught Dulles in the boss's office just before his departure.

"You know I've got the duty tomorrow," Amory said, "and whether you know it or not, I know what's going on. Now what should I do if anything comes up?"

"You have nothing to do with that at all," Dulles replied abruptly. "General Cabell will take care of anything like that."

Amory followed orders. Sunday he came to the office at 7 A.M., "opened the cables from Uruguay and Nigeria and so on and so forth, and went home and played five sets of tennis." To himself he said, "Screw 'em!"

Reassuring the Cuban Brigade

Assurances of open American support for the Brigade fighters varied, but whenever the Cubans had raised the question, they had heard just enough to make them feel secure.

Gus Ponzoa brought up the issue indirectly when he was briefed by "Colonel George" from Washington about his strike against the Santiago de Cuba airfield. He asked the colonel why only six B-26s would fly; why not all sixteen? As General Doster and Joe Shannon listened, the colonel said six would be "enough." He should relax. What if it wasn't enough? Gus wanted to know. "Well," the colonel said, "we still have our cover over there."

That was enough for Gus. He did not examine the sentence closely. He did not ask where the "cover" would suddenly come from. The Americans, his friends, had assured him they would be on the spot if he needed them. He was "bright enough to figure out" that the U.S. jets would be "waiting somewhere." He thought about the forces at Guantánamo, and he had been told there would be "ships along the route watching." They were supposed to be weather ships, but he and his fellow pilots "knew" they were more than that. It all "sounded perfectly good."

At their briefing of the Brigade commanders and the ships' officers, Colonel Frank and the other CIA briefers used a similar word to calm Tony Varona of the Revolutionary Council. It was a word that later came to haunt every man in the Brigade. At the time it sounded exactly right. Its vagueness was questioned by no one. It was repeated by the senior officers whenever voices of doubts were heard among subordinates. Luís Morse, the skipper of the *Houston*, first heard it at the briefing shortly before he sailed. He would never forget it. The word was "umbrella." An umbrella above was going to guard the entire operation against Communist planes. The word made the rounds quickly among the Cubans. It was a comfort, perhaps the greatest comfort of all.

When José Alonso, the chief of the frogmen, first saw the García ships, he took Gray Lynch aside and told him he couldn't see how those "old tubs" could possibly be adequate to land an invasion force in Cuba. "Don't worry about that," Gray said. "This is not all there is." Then he said, "I want you to see the air force."

All the frogmen got into jeeps. Gray took them to Retalhuleu, where they were given a guided tour of the B-26s, C-54s and C-46s lined up along the runway. The frogmen watched the landings, the takeoffs of the practice and supply runs and the arming of the 500-pound bombs. It all looked encouraging. The water fighters felt much better. If their ships were feeble, at least their air power wasn't.

When Eddie Ferrer, the morale officer of the pilots, grew worried about the air strength, Wade C. Gray, one of the Alabama air "advisers," took him to the docks and showed him how the ships were being crammed with supplies. As an airman, Ferrer was relieved. If the air effort left something to be desired, at least the sea power looked good. Nevertheless, in the jeep riding back to the air base, he asked Gray why, if they weren't going to have tail gunners, they didn't have fighters?

"Who told you that we're not going to have fighters?" Gray said.

"There are no fighters; I don't see any."

"There will be a carrier with late-model jet fighters and blond Cuban pilots that have blue eyes and don't speak Spanish," Gray said. He smiled. Then he tapped Ferrer on the shoulder and said, "Don't worry, we can't miss!"

Ferrer relayed the conversation to the other pilots. They accepted what they heard, because they knew Ferrer; Eddie Ferrer didn't "talk any bullshit."

Rafael Villaverde, an eighteen-year-old assistant intelligence officer, also asked some of the CIA advisers why there were no tail guns on the B-26s. "You don't need them," they said. "You'll have escort fighters." Villaverde asked, "Where are they? I don't see them." The CIA men smiled reassuringly and said they would arrive in good time.

Juan Pou, who had volunteered to train for the hazardous job of forward observer in the heavy-weapons battalion, did not want to be considered less patriotic than his cousin Antonino, who was the second man to join the Brigade. (Antonino held serial number 2502; he was infiltrated into Cuba two weeks before the invasion, was caught and was executed by the Fidelistas.)

Juan made friends with his trainer, "Bob," a U.S. Army sergeant. All the Cubans looked up to Bob because he was "very straightforward," knew his mortars, and had fought in Korea. At thirty-three, Bob was a senior man. Bob told Juan that the Brigade was only a "spearhead." There would be "a tremendous umbrella" of air cover overhead, manned by U.S. personnel, as well as other landings by other forces—"many other people training for the same purpose in different places."

Bob and Juan agreed that it had to be that way, considering the size of the Brigade and the report that Castro was supposed to have 66,000 troops near the beaches. Bob talked about World War II landings at Tarawa and elsewhere in the Pacific, pointing out the mix of forces and material needed for such operations. Juan was convinced he was part of such a great experience.

On the *Río Escondido,* one of the five vessels of García's fleet, Andrés Manso, a rifleman in E Company of the Sixth Battalion, had felt very low. When he first saw the little dilapidated ship, his "heart was really shocked." Having to sleep on deck with 120 men and all those drums of aviation gasoline made it worse. He cleaned his BAR (Browning automatic rifle) and joined in the daily push-up sessions, and when he twice saw American destroyers in the distance his spirits perked up—but only briefly. "I don't know whether we'll make it or not," he told a friend.

Then the battalion commander explained about the pre-landing bombings, the air support and the situation ashore with "everybody ready and waiting to join." The men cheered. Manso slapped his friend on the shoulder and said, "We'll make it, we'll make it!" He visualized arriving at the home of his sister Candida in Luzero, a Havana suburb. He would shout, "Here I am!," and all his friends would "welcome the hero."

Eleventh-Hour Second Thoughts

At Happy Valley, Gar Teegan,* the CIA air operations director, was worried about the "terrible" morale of his Cuban pilots. His own was not so great, either. Fresh U-2 photos showed that only five aircraft had been destroyed Saturday. An indeterminable number of others had sustained at least some damage, but Castro had at least two T-33s and some Sea Furies operational. The strikes should never, never have been reduced. Now the element of surprise was gone.

Choosing every word painstakingly, he wrote a message to headquarters proposing an intermediate strike against Camp Libertad for sunset Sunday. He suggested using six planes, no more than before. They would not fly a direct route. They would attack from very low altitudes with the sun behind them, so there was a good chance they would not be spotted until they were over their target. The answer came clicking back soon: "Negative."

Colonel Beerli, Teegan's perfectionist boss in Washington, had his eye on the D-Day strike at dawn Monday. It was "crucial"—no less. He had spent the night in Quarters Eye, and by early Sunday morning he and his nine air operations officers had spread out large prints of U-2 photographs brought in by Art Lundahl's photo intelligence people and were selecting targets for D-Day. The aerial photos recorded the impact of Saturday's "minimal" mission against Castro's three military airfields; it was less than devastating, and there was no telling how many planes in the hangars had not been destroyed.

Beerli and his men were tense but not distressed. Pilots always brought back overenthusiastic reports. With the Castro air force's

*A pseudonym.

chronic problem of getting spare parts, the T-33s might not be in commission. Anyway, the photos showed no targets that couldn't be readily wiped out, as scheduled. Everything depended on Sunday, today.

Well before noon, Stan Beerli had Telexed the pilots' missions and targets to Nicaragua. In Puerto Cabezas, Gus Ponzoa and his colleagues were studying their maps, checking out their planes and watching the loading of the bombs. The men in Quarters Eye relaxed.

At Glen Ora that day, the President did the same, but only outwardly. He left Glen Ora for the Middleburg Community Center at 11:55, arrived at noon and attended mass at St. John's Parish. He motored back at 12:36 P.M. From 1:21 to 1:45 he hit golf balls on the west pasture of Glen Ora with Jacqueline and the Stephen Smiths. He gave signs of being under pressure. Yet his brother-in-law found him gloomy. Smith had been told about the invasion. Now the President told him again how worried he still was about the advisability of going ahead. He clearly was not looking for advice from Smith, and Smith offered none. The President had had the best advice there was, but he still did not act.

Time was running out. The noon deadline that Bissell had given Kennedy for a last-ditch recall of the Brigade's little fleet came and went. Bissell was in his office, waiting. The project did not have clearance to proceed until the President called. As yet, Bissell was not overly upset, because he had not told the President the truth about the ultimate deadline for scrapping the landings. The real point of no return was 4 P.M., not noon. Bissell waited, thinking. What was going on in the President's mind? Was he trying to gauge the effects of Stevenson's debate in the UN? Was he trying to buy more time? If so, for what? Might Rusk change the President's mind at the final decision point? Might Kennedy "turn chicken" on his own in the last moment, after all?

In Quarters Eye, Engler and Hawkins watched the minutes creep past 1 P.M. They began to think that there was a very real possibility the President might order the recall of the Brigade.

"What do you think is going to happen if we tell them to turn back?" Jake asked.

Both men were focusing on the same practical problem. The Cubans were so fantastically eager that they didn't care about the odds. Ordering them to turn back was one thing. Getting them to comply was another.

"The only thing we could do is strafe them," Hawkins said.

Dick Bissell did not think that JFK would turn chicken, but there was no way of knowing what he would do. It was Kennedy's first major presidential decision. Even if Bissell had known him more intimately, there was no way to predict how an inexperienced leader might react to pressure when the stakes were higher than he had ever dealt with. So Bissell waited, alone, nervous, mangling his paper clips as always, more and more tense as the time ticked past 1 P.M. But he was not frantic. He had operated past points of no return before.

There were almost no calls. Finally, shortly after 1:45, the President called. Bissell heard the familiar flat New England voice say, "Go ahead."

The President continued his determined show of business-as-usual. At 2:21 P.M., accompanied by his wife, the Stephen Smiths and a friend, Mrs. Charles Fout, he had motored to the Glenwood Park racecourse and watched two steeplechase races of the Middleburg Hunt Race Association. He stayed nearly half an hour. Then he left with Steve Smith, saying, "I've got to go back and do a little work." It was a splendid day in the Virginia hunt country. The sun was bright. The dogwood was in blossom. If the President was troubled by Stevenson's ordeal, he did not show it. Nor did he go back to work right away. From 3:30 to 4:05 P.M., Kennedy and Smith hit golf balls on the west pasture at Glen Ora.

Bissell's sense of relief, the knowledge that more than a year of buildup would not suddenly collapse, was profound—but it did not last long. Not much later that afternoon, the landings, though not even launched, were critically threatened.

It began on an almost jolly note. Hawkins, who had not been home for several days and had promised to take his wife to dinner, left Quarters Eye and said, "Don't let them do anything to the operation!" And then Cabell arrived, wearing a cap, sports shirt and slacks. He had been playing golf and was dropping by to bring himself up-to-date.

He asked Beerli what was happening. The colonel told him about the upcoming strike mission and the unfortunate news that several Castro planes had survived the Saturday bombings.

"Do we have approval for the mission?" asked the general.

Stan Beerli was stunned. There was no question in his mind that the mission had clearance.

"Yes, we do," he said emphatically.

Cabell was unimpressed. "Well," he drawled, "I better check this out." He said he was going to call Rusk.

Beerli reddened. He knew his way around Washington. If you asked enough questions, sooner or later you were sure to get the wrong answer. Especially if you called somebody like Rusk. Rusk would call in advisers. The advisers would call in more advisers. At best you could count on delays, and in this case, Beerli was convinced, extended delay would entail deadly consequences. D-Day was only a few hours off.

When it was all over, the CIA operators who watched events unfold in Quarters Eye that Sunday agreed the outcome would have been different if Cabell had not been in charge.

Taciturn and given to communicating by grunts whenever possible, Cabell had built an on-paper record that looked perfect for his job. A West Point graduate (class of '25), he was director of intelligence for the Air Force by 1948 and became Dulles' deputy at the CIA in 1953. Analyzing Cabell's success, his critics attributed it to political astuteness and a remarkable ability for keeping his mouth closed, especially during intra–Air Force controversies.

At the CIA he took few firm positions except when officers wanted to marry foreign nationals; Cabell felt they should resign as ipso-facto security risks. At meetings he often fell asleep, which worried his colleagues; they thought that with his ever-present cigar still clenched between his teeth, he might burn himself. Awake, he urged colleagues to be eager—he called it "forward-leaning" or "headsey."

Best of all, Cabell liked to go on inspection trips of CIA stations abroad—as many countries in as short a time as possible. Two retired colonels serving in the agency would have to squeeze themselves into their old uniforms to travel in attendance. Elaborate briefings were scheduled in every country. The material in the resulting reports, Bob Amory always said, "you could get out of Section Four of *The New York Times*."

During the Cuban affair, Cabell became known as "Old Rice and Beans." Having approved a weapons drop for some guerrillas, he learned that the supplies would take up only part of the plane. He ordered it filled with rice and beans. Dave Phillips pointed out that rice and beans, the national dishes of Cuba, were two items that were not scarce. "Son," said the general, "I don't want to have to explain to an appropriations committee why we're flying nearly empty planes over Cuba."

The guerrilla team leader radioed that the heavy bags almost killed his men and questioned headquarters' sanity. Phillips sent a copy of that message anonymously to Cabell, marked "Eyes only for DDCI" (deputy director Central Intelligence). Subsequently, he found out that Dulles had already sent Cabell a copy.

Cabell's insistence on contacting Rusk made Beerli particularly furious because he suspected that the general was grandstanding, that Cabell was delighted to step out of relative anonymity, to luck into a chance to call a man as highly placed as Rusk and let him know that old reliable Cabell was in charge and at full alert.

By now Beerli's assistants were gathering around. Vociferously, they supported the colonel's stand that the mission had been authorized, that questions would yield only confusion and, quite possibly, an answer that the CIA did not wish to hear. But Cabell could not be moved.

"Well, I'm going to check this out," he said and disappeared into a vacant office.

Less than five minutes later he emerged, looking grim. He did not say that the mission was being canceled, just that he had to see Rusk at the State Department.

Cabell had every reason to be disturbed. He had just had a call from Mac Bundy. Bundy said no air strikes could be launched until after the Brigade had secured the Girón airstrip, and strikes would ostensibly be launched from there. This was an order from the President.

Bundy couldn't discuss it further because he was leaving for New York "to hold the hands of Ambassador Stevenson." If the order caused Cabell problems, he should talk to Rusk. The Secretary held "the proxy of the President."*

As soon as Bundy hung up, he hurried to National Airport, still wearing his weekend sports clothes.

Cabell felt he had been hit by "a falling bomb." He considered himself an expert on air support. He had no experience with small, covert amphibious operations, but he had worked on plans for the Normandy invasion and succeeded in persuading the air staff to hit Nazi oil reserves rather than railroads. The Bay of Pigs was very different. However, it was clear to Cabell that protection of the Brigade from the air was vital.

Bissell had been called and hurried in, looking troubled.

"Dick, we better get over to the State Department," Cabell said. "Rusk is meeting us there so we can thrash this thing out."

*Materials on the late General Cabell's thoughts and actions are from his unpublished autobiography and were made available by his sons, Air Force Colonel Charles P. Cabell, Jr., and Benjamin Cabell IV.

As the two chiefs left, trailed by Tracy Barnes, the men of Quarters Eye let off steam. Howard Hunt was seething over the "agonizing uncertainty." Somebody said to him, "I bet Cabell's just doing this to give him a chance to puff himself up over a meeting with Rusk." Dave Phillips speculated that nobody would call the President "just to straighten out Cabell's addled brain." Several others cursed the bad luck that the general had to show up just then, of all times. Four-letter language was flowing without restraint.

Beerli tried hard to concentrate on the operations schedule. The Brigade was now definitely beyond recall. Its planes were few and thinly manned. The air strike was so finely timed that any tinkering could be "catastrophic." He thought it was like holding up dinner until you start wondering whether you're really waiting for breakfast. Meanwhile you're watching helplessly as your neatly orchestrated party turns to chaos.

Increasingly distressed, Beerli watched the clock, thinking of the five hours it would take for his B-26s merely to lumber their way to Cuba and back to Nicaragua for little more than a half hour over their targets. Soon the invasion flotilla would be highly vulnerable to the Castro aircraft whose destruction the men of the Brigade had been so often and so firmly promised. "This has got to go," he said. The alternative was death for the Brigade.

At the Pentagon, one of the few ranking civilian officials at work was Mac Bundy's brother, Bill. Late in the afternoon he was visited by two generals from the Joint Chiefs staff who were familiar with the plan for the second air strike. Bundy did not know that the mission might be canceled. He got the impression that his visitors wanted "to stiffen my back so there wouldn't be any chipping of the plan."

Eventually Bundy asked them, "What do you think are the chances of success?"

"About thirty-five percent," the generals said.

Bundy was "very surprised" and had "a sinking feeling" in his stomach. He had thought the chances were about seventy percent.

Rusk had understood that the second strike would coincide with the landings and would be made to appear as if it originated from the airstrip near the beach. The pilots could then be passed off as Castro defectors, like Captain Zuñiga. But with Zuñiga's cover story by now exposed before the United Nations, Rusk concluded, in view of Stevenson's difficulties, that a second strike from Nicaragua would raise the international noise level to an intolerable degree. There could be no more strikes until the aircraft could logically appear to be launched from the beachhead. He consulted Bundy, who agreed, and Rusk called Kennedy at Glen Ora.

When the Secretary pointed out that the second strike would surely look to all the world as if it came from Nicaragua, the President found it hard to follow the turn of events. "I'm not signed on to this," he said, Navy style. The two men then talked at length, and the President ordered the cancellation of the strike unless there were "overriding considerations." After putting down the phone, he sat quietly and shook his head. Clearly worried, he paced around the room. His guests, Stephen and Jean Smith and his old friend Lem Billings, had never seen him more gloomy.

Rusk, having sent Bundy off to New York to answer any further questions from the irate Adlai Stevenson, steeled himself to receive Cabell and Bissell.

When the two CIA chiefs arrived around 7 P.M. (Barnes had been asked to wait outside the Secretary's door), Rusk told them that he had been talking to the President on the phone, that he had strongly recommended that the Monday-morning strike be canceled, and that the President had agreed.

Cabell and Bissell protested "very strongly." They argued that the ships as well as the landings would be seriously endangered without the strike at dawn. Rusk argued that the ships were supposed to be unloaded before dawn; after that, the Brigade's B-26s could operate from the airstrip ashore. Bissell said that he felt that the success of the entire venture was being endangered and pointed out that "the landing was committed. It was too late to call it off." He was extremely agitated.

Finally Rusk relented. "Well, all right, I will call the President again." He had concluded that the strike would be "important, but not critical." No "overriding considerations" had come up.

As the tense CIA men listened raptly, Rusk told Kennedy that Bissell and Cabell were in his office; that they felt the impact of the strike's cancellation would be "very serious"; that they were pleading for its reinstatement.

Cabell felt Rusk had been "a good listener" and had given the President "an astonishingly complete and accurate account" of the effects of the cancellation order. He was all the more dismayed to hear Rusk telling the President, "But I am still recommending, in view of what's going on in New York, that we cancel."

Rusk listened for a moment. Then he took the phone away from his ear and said, "Well, the President agrees with me, but would you, General Cabell, like to speak to the President?"

"Well, you've put it to the President a second time," the general said. "I don't think he's going to override your recommendation."

Bissell said to Cabell, "Do you think he realizes that I agree with you?"

Cabell shrugged and said, "There's no point in my talking to the President."

Rusk rang off. He was under the impression that the CIA men thought the strike was important but not crucial. Bissell wondered whether he should have intervened more decisively. After all, Cabell was a thoroughly indoctrinated military officer. He was "absolutely determined that he wasn't going to take any risks exceeding what he had been properly and appropriately authorized." To be fair, what military man would argue with the Commander in Chief, especially when the Commander in Chief had already twice ruled against him?

Bissell, pacing, thought it didn't much matter. There was no point in losing his temper. Their cause was "hopeless" or at best "negligible." It wasn't just that an air strike might be "politically disastrous." Bissell recalled other influences that could have left the President with some doubt about the "absolute essentiality" of air supremacy.

Rusk, in particular, had referred in some of the earlier meetings to his World War II experience in irregular warfare in Burma and said "that operations of this sort did not depend nearly so heavily on air cover as did conventional amphibious operations by organized troops." Now, infuriatingly, ex-Colonel Rusk was the ranking member of the Cabinet.

And had the President perhaps heard rumors out of the Joint Chiefs that had come to Bissell's attention, rumors that said not all the chiefs were totally convinced that air cover was crucial, that General Curtis Le May, the Air Chief of Staff, had been reported less than fully convinced even though Le May was a strategic-bombing expert and not expert on tactical air support? JFK would have listened to Rusk and Le May. Their views "would have influenced him very significantly." It was maddening, but bureaucracy had its limits, even at the very top. It made no sense to talk further to the President now. Soreheads did not become CIA directors.

Cabell also thought it prudent to protest no further. He had no additional arguments to bring up and did not want to be redundant—unless he was going to block compliance by filibustering, which he considered but rejected. There was no time to lose. If the "stop" order reached the planes after takeoff, perhaps not all pilots would obey. Also, landings with full bomb and fuel loads would be very hazardous. No, it was best to quit arguing and make sure the President's order would still be carried out.

Later, Bissell and his men would have many second thoughts on the dramatic scene in Rusk's office that Sunday night. Not then. The might-have-beens did not come home to roost until much later. Catastrophe was not in the air. There was only the pressure of instant events. Planes waiting. Ships about to make shore. More than a year's machinations about to come to fruition. It was time for climax, for release, not more words, more delays, maybe cancellation after all. Now it was action without carping, risk-taking without looking back. Bissell knew about such things. He had done them all his life.

At Quarters Eye, Stan Beerli, the air operations boss, had felt the pressure building. With the five-hour flight time from the base to the targets, there was little more than one hour left before the B-26s would take off, and it often required more than an hour to get a message coded, transmitted and decoded in Happy Valley.

At 9:15 P.M., the men in Quarters Eye could tolerate the suspense no longer. Jake phoned the State Department. After some time he got Bissell out of Rusk's office. He was told that the strike was definitely off.

At 10:30 Beerli hurried across the street to the ancient structure at 1717 H Street which housed the special communications unit that maintained direct contact with the base. His heart pounding, he sent his "top air priority" cancellation message.

In the air operations tent at Puerto Cabezas, Gar Teegan thought there might soon be time for a short nap. The tent had turned silent. He was alone with the operations sergeant. It was nearly H-Hour and he was dead tired. The two days of short-circuited momentum had left him and his men anxious and emotionally drained. Now the first planes for the second strike were warming up. The others would leave before long. The slow little PBY sea rescue plane had already departed for Cuba. The planes carrying the paratroopers had taken off. The weather was favorable: no moon. Maybe the operation could still be pulled off.

His "commo" (communications) officer burst into the tent on the run and handed Gar the long message without saying a word. Gar skimmed it quickly: "Cancel . . . cancel . . . cancel . . . ," always followed by a number from the operations order. Gar knew the numbers by heart. Washington was canceling all the D-Day sorties except routine reconnaissance over the beaches.

He said to the commo man, "Hold it. Let's make doubly sure." He matched the Telex against the operations order. His memory had been correct. Washington was canceling all D-Day strikes.

"Get Reid!" he ordered the sergeant.

Quickly he drafted a protest to headquarters and handed it to his commo man. He could only point out the obvious: B-26s could never eliminate Castro's air power over the beaches; it had to be eliminated on the ground.

When Doster rushed in, Teegan showed him the message. The general cursed. Washington replied "Negative" to Gar's protest. Doster ran to his jeep and roared off to the flight line. Gar was left with his thoughts. What could possibly be going on in Washington that he didn't know about? He tried to read between the lines of recent messages from headquarters. One of them had asked whether any Castro naval vessels had been spotted. Could that have anything to do with the cancellation order? Hardly. Gar kept asking himself, "Why? Why? Why?" Why were they taking away from the operation step by step, as if it was destined to fail? He could come up with no reason. He knew only that it was "totally unbelievable," that "any hope for salvaging the operation was lost."

Doster stepped in front of the first group and gave the "cut engines" signal by making a slicing motion with one hand across his neck. Then he "threw a fit." He hurled his cap to the ground and yelled, "There goes the whole fuckin' war!"

Gus Ponzoa and some of his fellow pilots were still fueling their planes for later takeoffs when Doster, by now composed, drove up and told Gus, "This is straight from Washington. We can't make another flight. We've got to wait forty-eight hours.

Gus felt goose pimples. He was cold. "It was like a cold bucket of water poured over my head." Then he turned furious.

"Goddammit, they're crazy!" he yelled. "How can they do this?"

He got together with his wing man Herrera and another captain, René García, and together they wondered how the Cubans might take over the camp and fly missions on their own. Once the discussion got down to details, they agreed they would never be able to overcome the American guards and other security precautions. "It was one of those crazy things you see in John Wayne movies," Gus said later.

At about that time, Mario Zuñiga arrived back at the base from his cover-story mission to Miami, and his colleagues told him about the cancellation. He was as distressed as the others, because "it was going to be the biggest mistake in the whole thing. And everybody knew it."

Everybody didn't. At Fort Myer, near the Pentagon, General Lemnitzer was enjoying a quiet evening in his quarters, which actually was the house normally used by the Army Chief of Staff. He attended to personal correspondence and then watched TV for a while. Nobody bothered to inform the Chairman of the Joint Chiefs of any decisions concerning the "war."

Once he had sent his "stop" message, Colonel Beerli found he was calmer. The cancellation was "critical" to the Brigade, but "it would be no good assuming that it was doomed." You had to start "scrambling to salvage whatever you can." Besides, there were unknown factors. Perhaps the undestroyed Castro planes had been so damaged that they could not be launched. Perhaps they could be destroyed by infiltrators. Perhaps the latest report was true that Castro had panicked, gone into hiding, and his people were paralyzed into inaction.

Nor did he believe that Castro's T-33 jet fighters were "going to be a special factor." The T-33 was a training aircraft. It was affectionately known as "T-bird" and considered relatively tame for the jet age. Nobody was even certain Castro's T-birds were armed. In the U.S., they were mostly used to taxi important government personages around. Castro had only two or three T-birds; Beerli figured chances were small that they were all in good repair and flown by "somebody very proficient."

Jake Engler was much less sanguine. His first reaction to the scrubbing of the air mission had been disbelief. The entire operation had been constructed on the premise that no Castro plane would leave the ground. He thought, "We just *had* to have that air strike!" Then he started to reflect on all the gasoline stored on the decks of the ships. He feared they would all be sunk in flames. Mostly he thought about the men of the Brigade, the men he knew, whose wives and fathers and in-laws he knew, to whom promises had been made of protection by an air "umbrella"*—promises with the name of the United States government attached and with his own name too.

For well over an hour, Jake, Beerli, Phillips, Hunt and several other operators stood or paced around Cabell's desk in the control room of Quarters Eye arguing for reinstatement of the mission and berating the general in four-letter language. Why didn't he act like a man and go back to work on Rusk some more? Jake pounded on the general's desk and told him he was the lowest form of human being he'd ever seen. How could he let the men of the Brigade go to their death? All over the room, voices were raised to the bellowing level. Faces were crimson. Any form of rank-consciousness or civility was gone. These were emotion-driven men out of control.

---

*The assurances of air cover were so constant and persuasive that they sparked a bitter bit of gallows humor. When most of the Brigade's survivors were in Castro's prisons and they happened to hear a plane overhead, the cry invariably went up from the cells, "Don't shoot! It's one of ours!"

Throughout, the general "just sat and took it," puffing stoically on his cigar, saying nothing. Finally the men gave up.

Disgusted and exhausted from two days of pressure and no sleep, Jake went to the second floor to have a nap.

Dave Phillips' secretary, like everybody else in the operation, was spending the night in the office. During a brief lull in the early-morning hours, Phillips suggested that she take a nap in the little second-floor room for around-the-clock workers. It became known as "the dormitory." It was bare except for about ten folding army cots with dark-green canvas, some olive-drab blankets and a few pillows.

When she eventually returned, slightly rested, she reported that she had found a tall man sleeping on the cot next to her. She said she had never seen him in Quarters Eye before. Phillips checked the dark room. The man was Bissell. He had taken off only his tie and coat and was catching a fast forty winks before dawn broke in the Caribbean. He would have been embarrassed if he had known about Phillips' secretary. Bissell was courtly and shy with women on first encounter.

Cabell had not yet heard the last of the protests. When Colonel Hawkins came back from dinner and heard the news, he also lost control. He slammed his hand on the four-star general's desk and said, "This is criminally negligent!" Again, Cabell remained impassive.

At about midnight Hawkins, desperate and sobbing, phoned General Shoup at the Marine Commandant's Quarters on Eighth and I Streets. He said he was absolutely certain the operation would fail for lack of air support. Shoup "damn near choked." He agreed with Hawkins but said regretfully he could not help; "things had gone too far."

General Gray knew of no change in the plans when he left the Pentagon around 10 P.M. for his home on P Street in Georgetown. At midnight he was awakened by a call from Quarters Eye and was asked to come at once. When he arrived, he was informed by Jake and his assistants that the strike had been scrubbed.

"There goes your operation," the general said firmly but without emotion.

Gray then met with Cabell, who said, "I want you to think up things your people can do to help us." They decided to get the Navy to send some destroyers near the beach for early-warning "picket duty," which was eventually approved, and for air cover from the *Essex*, which was not. As General Gray left and turned down the hall, he told one of the CIA men, "Surely Cabell realizes that this means this operation is doomed to failure."

Nobody told the President what had happened to the venture before the first frogman set foot on the beach.

In Fort Myer, near the Pentagon, Generals Wheeler and Gray rang General Lemnitzer's doorbell about 2 A.M.

The Chairman of the Joint Chiefs, sleepy and in his bathrobe, inquired, "How did things go?"

"They canceled the air strike!"

Lemnitzer "couldn't believe it." It sounded so "unbelievable" that he called the JCS situation room to confirm it. "Pulling out the rug" like this was "absolutely reprehensible, almost criminal."

Wheeler and Gray said they had come to convey the CIA's urgent request for naval air cover over the beachhead later that morning. Lemnitzer was for it. He told the generals to instruct Admiral Dennison in Norfolk to order preparation of air cover. He also told the generals to consult the State Department before giving the final OK.

Then he "cooled off" and became philosophical. This was how "the whole damned thing was going from the beginning."

The cancellation of the air strike was the last straw for Jake Engler. At 2 A.M. he returned to his desk and wrote out his resignation from the agency in longhand. It said that he could no longer stand to be connected with this "shameful performance." He handed it to his secretary for typing. "You don't want me to type this," she said. He insisted. A few hours later he gave it to Colonel J. C. King, the almost-forgotten head of the Western Hemisphere Division. Engler never bothered to find out what happened to it. He was too busy thinking, talking, puzzling what might be done to avoid the sinking of the Brigade ships.

By 4 A.M., pressure from his staff and his own brooding about the near-certain fate of the Brigade ships triggered a visit from Cabell to Rusk's apartment in the Sheraton-Park Hotel. This time the general asked for jet cover from the *Essex* during the unloading and withdrawal of the vessels.

Rusk responded by awakening the President in Glen Ora. He did not transmit the general's request; he turned him over to the President directly. General Cabell offered Kennedy a series of air support options. All involved U.S. jets. There was no time left to fly in Brigade planes from Nicaragua, even if they had been up to the task of defending the ships against fighters, which they were not.

The President did not comment but asked to talk to Rusk. The conversation was very brief. Rusk hung up, turned to Cabell, and said that all the requests were disapproved. Indeed, the President now asked that the carrier move farther out to sea and stay at least thirty miles off the coast. He was still living up to his press conference promise that no U.S. forces would become involved.

In the "admiral's house" at the Naval Observatory on Massachusetts Avenue, Admiral Burke's alarm clock rang at 6 A.M., as usual. He glanced at the note pad near the telephone at his bedside. When he saw it was empty he became aware that "a very unusual thing" had happened. The telephone had not rung during the night. He called the Navy duty officer at the Pentagon and asked whether anything had happened. The officer said it had been "a very quiet night."

Puzzled, Burke called the Joint Chiefs duty officer. "Did anything happen last night?"

The officer said, "Things are now happening."

"Is it serious?"

"I think so."

Burke said, "I'll be right down."

He did not stop for breakfast. His driver took eighteen minutes to the Pentagon. When he walked into the Joint Chiefs situation room, Burke was told about the canceled air strike—about ten hours after the fact. He was "horrified" and "very mad." He had always considered this strike crucial. It was not only a matter of knocking out most of the enemy aircraft. The D-Day strike could have temporarily immobilized whatever flying capability Castro's men had left. After a strike against an airfield, damage to planes and runways had to be checked. There would be confusion, delays. How could the politicians "pull the strings out of an operation at the last minute"?

The Attack Begins

At midnight, the telephone awoke Lem Jones, the public-relations man, in his apartment at Thirty-ninth Street and Second Avenue in Manhattan. "This is it," said the familiar voice of Howard Hunt. Jones was startled. He had not been told this would be D-Day. On a pad, he took down "Bulletin No. 1," which he was to issue in the name of the Cuban Revolutionary Council.

Hunt dictated: "Before dawn, Cuban patriots in the cities and in the hills began the battle to liberate our homeland from the despotic rule of

Fidel Castro . . ." Jones typed the communiqué himself and took a taxi to the Hotel Statler on Seventh Avenue.

While Lem Jones was still typing, Ernesto Aragón, a lawyer who was Miró Cardona's interpreter and confidant, had been awakened by a call at the Lexington Hotel. A voice said in Spanish, "Do you know who is talking?"

Sleepily, Aragón said, "No, talk a little bit more."

"Well, you just saw me this morning," the voice said. Aragón recognized that it was Antonio Silio, a former member of the Cuban Supreme Court, now secretary of the Revolutionary Council.

"Get your things together and come to the Statler Hilton," Silio instructed. He was registered in Room 805 as "Antonio Hernández." Aragón was to go straight up.

Shortly after Aragón joined Silio, Lem Jones arrived with the CIA's communiqué. He said it had been composed by Miró. He was instructed to get it translated so that it could be released in Spanish as well as English. Both originals were to be initialed by Silio on behalf of the Council. The two Cubans were stunned. According to the scuttle-butt they had heard, the invasion was supposedly set for the twenty-seventh. And if the communiqué was from Miró, why was it unsigned and written in a language Miró did not master?

The moment was much too emotional for questions. Aragón did a quick translation. Silio affixed his initials. Jones hurried into a taxi to distribute the CIA's words to the wire services and the newspapers.

The communiqué was unsigned because Miró was no longer in New York. He and the rest of the Cuban Revolutionary Council had been hurried out of the Hotel Lexington at about 3:30 P.M. Escorted by Will Carr, they took the kitchen exit to avoid reporters in the lobby. Two black Cadillac limousines took them to Idlewild Airport. They were not told where they were headed.

After dinner in a private dining room at the airport, the cars took them to Philadelphia, where they boarded a small private aircraft. Visibility had been too poor for a takeoff in New York. Carr told them they would be part of "an important action." They were told nothing about the invasion. Among themselves, they agreed that they were undoubtedly going to join the troops to head for Cuba with them, as they had been promised.

They were surprised to land shortly after 2 A.M. at a deserted, blacked-out airfield. Tony Varona, the only one who had been there, identified it as Opa-Locka. They were taken by "Bender" to a barracks containing almost no furniture except cots, a wooden mess table and a few wooden chairs. There was no phone, but Dr. Antonio Maceo, a huge, handsome, barrel-chested former Havana surgeon, the only black man in the group, found a portable radio and turned it on. Like Miró and Varona, he had a very young son in the Brigade and was particularly anxious for news.

Over this radio, the men who were supposed to lead the fight for Cuban freedom heard Lem Jones's bulletin. They were incensed. Why hadn't they been allowed to be with their men? Varona, the most volatile of the group, accused Carr and Bender of "treason." The politicians became even angrier when they found out that they were not supposed to leave their barracks. Armed U.S. soldiers barred the doors. The official explanation was that the Cubans had to be prepared for a quick departure. Later, one of the Council leaders was warned that the area was infested by rattlesnakes.

At 3:44 A.M., Radio Swan called on the Cuban armed forces to revolt: "Take up strategic positions that control roads and railroads! Make prisoners or shoot those who refuse to obey your orders! . . . All planes must stay on the ground. See that no Fidelist plane takes off. Destroy its radios. Destroy its tail. Break its instruments. Puncture its fuel tanks. . . ." Dave Phillips' propaganda had worked in Guatemala. Nobody took it seriously now.

To the Cuban leaders in the barracks at Opa-Locka, the messages from Radio Swan and the communiqué issued by the CIA in their names sounded reassuring. But when Droller-Bender came into the barracks in tears to tell them in his heavy German accent that plans for the air strikes had been changed because of "political interference," their fury seemed to have no limit. They did not become calmer when they were issued khaki uniforms. If nothing else, they demanded to know what was really happening.

Droller called Dick Drain in Washington. "I've got to have help," he said. "They're getting the impression their sons are being slaughtered."

Bissell decided to send Drain to Opa-Locka, masquerading as "Colonel Baker of the Joint Chiefs of Staff." The flight in a two-engine CIA aircraft took six hours and triggered pain from a slipped disc in Drain's back that would last for months. In the Opa-Locka barracks, Drain, wearing civilian clothes, faced "a highly emotional situation." He could not answer most of the leaders' disgusted questions: Why were the air strikes canceled? Why did the Brigade have to land in swamps? What was being done to supply the men with ammunition? Above all:

Why did the leaders have to sit incommunicado in Florida instead of being allowed to join their sons in the fight?

The Council members were shouting and cursing. They threatened to break out of the barracks by noon the next day, even if they were going to be shot. Drain could only reply that he would faithfully report their grievances in Washington.

The CIA had no answers for anyone's problems that night. Its Radio Swan began broadcasting the first of many presumably coded messages: "Look well at the rainbow. The fish will rise very soon. The sky is blue. The fish is red. . . ." Listeners, friendly or unfriendly, were supposed to think that the Cuban underground was being alerted. To the underground the words meant nothing. They were gibberish composed in David Phillips' propaganda shop to build an ambiance of conspiracy.

Dick Pedersen was awakened in his New York apartment at about 6:30 A.M. One of his political officers at the U.S. Mission to the UN told him of the invasion.

Pedersen immediately called Stevenson in 42A at the Waldorf and broke the news.

"Yes, I know," the ambassador said.

He had not known for long. The news had just been broken to him over breakfast by McGeorge Bundy.

In Moscow, Khrushchev, as he wrote later, was "sure that the Americans would never reconcile themselves to the existence of Castro's Cuba." He heard about the invasion on the radio and "knew that no matter under whose banner the invasion was launched, it had to have the backing of the Americans." He fired off an angry note to Washington, charging that the United States had armed and trained the invaders and threatening to give Castro "all necessary assistance" unless Washington stopped the operation.

When his early morning class at Harvard University asked him what he thought about the invasion, the professor hadn't heard about it. The students told him what they had gleaned from the newspapers. The professor paced and pondered. Then he said, "Well, as long as we're there, I don't think it would do us any good to lose." The professor was Henry Kissinger.

CHAPTER SIX

Invasion

Rendezvous at Sea

The seven U.S. Navy destroyers had just formed a circle around the carrier *Essex* when a radio message sent them the order: "Skippers to the carrier."

The naval task force out of Norfolk had entered the Caribbean the previous week en route to a secret rendezvous off the Cuban coast with the seven vessels that made up the invasion fleet: the five merchant craft of García's fleet and the two converted CIA landing craft en route from Nicaragua.

On the bridge of the destroyer *Cony,* Captain Dunham, hoping finally to learn where he was headed and why, told his exec, Jack Wilson, "Your ship, old buddy!" He had barely pulled on his kapok jacket when the helo (helicopter) picked him up from his deck and whirred to the *Essex* with the other destroyer captains. They were taken to the cabin of Deacon Fickenscher, Admiral Clark's second in command. In the middle of it stood an easel covered with a white bedsheet.

"Well, I guess we're all here," Deacon said. "I'll go and get the admiral."

The little admiral walked in, and everybody rose.

"Sit down, gentlemen," he said pleasantly. "All right, Deacon, proceed." It might have been just another antisub patrol.

Fickenscher removed the sheet, and Dunham took a deep breath. Here was a map of Cuba with many zigzag tracks leading to the coast. Dunham was certain there was going to be an American invasion of the island.

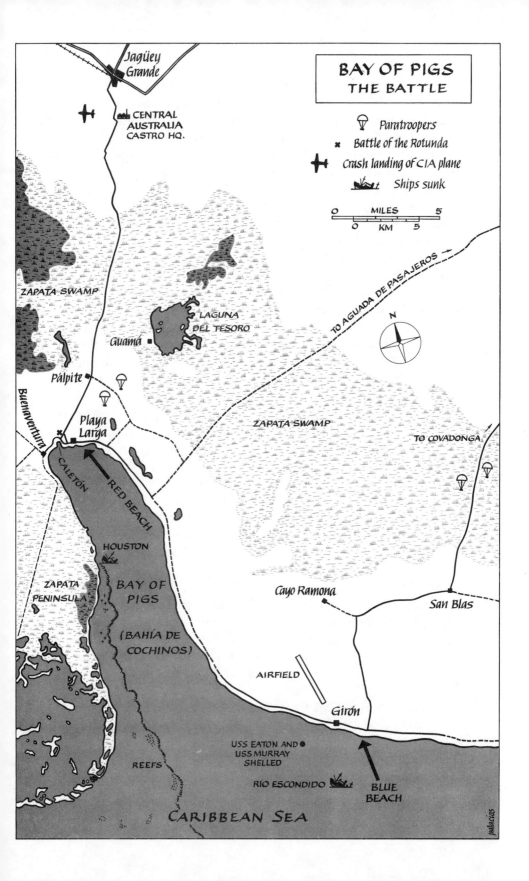

Fickenscher explained that the Navy task force was merely to escort "insurgent craft" to the coast. It was not supposed to look like a coordinated movement. Until they all hit a rendezvous point, each destroyer was to track one "skunk" (unidentified vessel) and help it navigate, if necessary. They were to stay out of visual range. Aboard the skunks, only each master knew of his invisible escort. Any directions were to be signaled only at night by twenty-four-inch lights whose beams were, if possible, to be bounced off clouds. Each destroyer captain was handed a slip of paper bearing the silhouette of his skunk. Captain Dunham drew Skunk G.

Back on the *Cony*, Dunham grew worried. He was supposed to confide in only one other man, his executive, Jack Wilson. "It was a big ocean." He knew the location of Skunk G—the *Caribe*—only very generally. It was a "pretty airy-fairy objective" when you "stopped to think of it." Dunham and Wilson didn't stop long. They kept walking all over their ship with their binoculars, peering everywhere, the sun in their backs. The crew obviously thought their behavior was mighty odd.

At dawn the next day, Wilson let out a whoop: "Captain, I think we got him."

Together they went into the pilot house and checked the drawing of the skunk's silhouette. Dunham said, "By God, that's it!"

The *Caribe* needed only a little coaching. That night, fortunately, there was a light, low cloud cover. Dunham and Wilson took the International Code of Signals, bounced corrective instructions off the clouds, and repeated them four times. This was not easy, because none of the signalmen could be told what he was doing. Yet when the skippers went down to the combat information center to watch the screen of their radar, the skunk was responding perfectly. Dunham thought it was "rather thrilling."

The technical triumph did not overcome a "sour taste" that began developing in Dunham's mouth when he was told at Fickenscher's briefing that all the destroyers would have to have their identifications obscured or altered. The *Cony*'s serial number was 508; only the "5" was to be obliterated. Dunham thought this was "ridiculous" cops-and-robbers nonsense: "Everyone knew who these ships belonged to."

The senior men aboard the García invasion ships were also feeling uneasy. Before he left for Cuba, Captain Tirado of the *Río Escondido* was handed about a hundred nautical charts in a sealed envelope by a CIA man who told him that all the charts for the invasion were included. The envelope was not to be opened until he was en route. About an hour and a half out at sea, Tirado found he would need five charts of which two were missing. He had to turn back to get them. That was not all that upset him. Although he left two days ahead of the other ships to make up for his faulty propellers, an American destroyer approached him later that night at sea and signaled him to speed up. Tirado felt this was one instruction he didn't need. He signaled back that he was doing his best. Still, the appearance of the destroyer was welcome additional evidence that the Americans were behind him.

Aboard the *Atlántico*, Dr. Sordo felt uncomfortable about the entire operation's prospects. He slept poorly because he could find space only underneath a lifeboat. The heating of food and smoking were prohibited; many men smoked anyway.

Shortly after nine o'clock one morning, Angel Maruri, Jr., the bulky second officer of the ship and son of the captain, decided to test the machine gun which had been mounted "real bad" by the Nicaraguan soldiers on the rudder housing aft. Some twenty men were resting on deck below. As Maruri began firing, the gun's welded deck plate broke. The barrel sagged to the roof. The gun kept firing (it was never remounted).

Dr. Sordo was only fifty feet away. When he rushed up, one man was dead; there was a hole in his skull where his brain had been, "a ghastly sight." A second man had been wounded in the Achilles tendon of the leg. A third man was the real problem. A large metal fragment had hit him in the abdomen, which soon turned hard. Peritonitis set in. Medical corpsmen brought morphine from their aid kits. The ship's crew produced two bottles of glucose, which Dr. Sordo gave intravenously. The ships were not equipped for a serious emergency; the wounded man urgently needed surgery; Dr. Sordo could only keep his pain down and his blood pressure up.

Breaking radio silence in violation of strict orders, the *Atlántico* radioed its base for help. It was quickly promised. More than twelve hours went by before the U.S.S. *Eaton* drew up in the dark and sent a launch with a doctor and a few sailors to evacuate both wounded. Dr. Sordo asked what had kept them so long. The Americans said they had had to wait for nightfall because of security. The destroyer's name had been painted out, but Dr. Sordo would never forget its number: 510.

Once the shock over the accident had worn off, the spirit on the *Atlántico* was better than before. They had all seen the destroyer. "Everybody felt confident we were not alone," said Second Officer Maruri, still feeling "real bad" about the shooting. Dr. Almeida felt warmly about the American help. "These people care," he said to himself. "It was beautiful." He made certain that there would be no emotional hangovers.* Many of the men thought the dead soldier should be buried in Cuba. Dr. Almeida opposed this for health and morale reasons. The man was buried at sea. "We don't want to go to Cuba with a dead man," he said.

Lieutenant Commander Edmund J. Maddock, air operations officer on the *Essex,* still did not know where he was headed. He had been considerably upset when the navigator would not tell him the whereabouts of his ship. He started tracking its course personally with a dead-reckoning tracer until he "suddenly discovered" that he was outside the Bay of Pigs. The secrecy smacked of the illegitimate. Maddock, who had flown calmly over Tokyo in World War II, had hated it when he was ordered to pilot messenger flights to Guatemala without a flight plan. He was instructed not to put these runs in his flight log. Once, when the tower operator in Guantánamo radioed him for his destination, he kept heading silently south, pretending that his radio had malfunctioned.

The fighter pilots of the "Blue Blasters" squadron, assigned to the *Essex,* became uneasy when their commanding officer, Commander Mike Griffin, summoned them to the ready room and told them they were to fly without dog tags or ID cards. They were even supposed to leave their wallets behind. The order was received with silent amazement. "To hell with that," Jim Forgy, the executive officer, said to himself. Immediately after the briefing he went to see Griffin in his stateroom. He was extremely agitated.

"We can't allow that to happen," he told Griffin. "If we go down we'd be classified as pirates or mercenaries! We'd be wide open to being shot on the spot!" (The pilots normally wore no insignia of any kind.)

"Those are the orders that came down," Griffin said unhappily.

"You go ahead with them," said Forgy. "Tell you what I'm going to do. Anybody who's going to fly with me is going to carry his dog tags and ID and credit cards and anything else they want to carry. I'm a naval officer."

Mike Griffin shrugged his shoulders helplessly. Forgy gathered that the CO was pleased that this order was not going to be followed. Jim talked to two or three of the officers and asked them to "pass the word around" to forget about flying without personal identification. Whenever Forgy flew a mission, he asked each of his pilots, "Got your ID?" He didn't want to be shot down with anybody that could be treated as a spy.

*Dr. Almeida later became a psychiatrist practicing north of Miami.

On the destroyer command ship U.S.S. *Eaton*, Captain Peter Perkins took down all his flags and ordered a crew over the side to paint out the ship's name on the stern. The lettering was raised, so anybody could still read it from close up. Even at a distance the configuration of the ship was unmistakably recognizable as an American naval vessel.

Commodore Crutchfield, commanding all the destroyers from the *Eaton*, was "taciturn." Perkins still had no idea where he was headed. When he took aboard two Brigade soldiers injured on the *Atlántico*, he gathered they were Cubans, so presumably the mission involved Cuba. Whatever it was, it was obviously important. Whenever his fuel ran low, a tanker would be nearby. The refueling was done at night with both ships blacked out. The tanker would "come zooming out of the dark." Every rendezvous worked perfectly. Perkins found it "just amazing, very magical." He was delighted the Navy worked so smoothly. He was also feeling "very, very goosy" knowing so little about an operation in which he clearly was a focal point.

Finally Commodore Crutchfield told Captain Perkins they would soon meet "some ships"; they were to escort them to a point about six miles off Playa Girón, Cuba. They would be in line formation. The García ships turned up in the right place at the right time. Perkins was "amazed how small they were" and "awfully ratty-looking."

It "wasn't any big deal" for Perkins. He had canvassed his ship at the last minute for sailors who spoke Spanish. Through them, he could talk to the García fleet over the little CB radios they had been given in Norfolk. Perkins just "went in front of them and led them on in." The U.S.S. *Murray* fell in line at the tail of the column. The ships were seven hundred to a thousand yards apart.

After seeing the flotilla off to the beach, Perkins was ordered to "hang around" in the area of the Cayo Largo lighthouse. Nobody told him why. He had by now figured out that the Cubans were staging landings; he guessed he might be called on "to render further assistance to someone up the line who made the decisions." He never lost his "goosy" feeling about the entire enterprise and for six days never slept except for naps in his chair on the bridge.

Hitting the Beaches

As the invasion fleet steamed late Sunday into the dark, silent Bay of Pigs in single file, Eduardo García stood on the bridge of the *Caribe*, glowing with pride. This was the place for an owner of ships to be. The scene reminded him of the movie strike force he had admired in *The Guns of Navarone*.

Aboard the five vessels of his merchantmen were most of the 1,543 members of the Brigade. Unlike the Navy men who had escorted them, they were well briefed on the plans—the pre-landing bombings, the promised air support, intelligence assurances that Brigade infiltrators awaited them ashore. Now Gray Lynch, the CIA agent with the main landing frogmen, was bent over the radar on the bridge of the CIA lead ship, the *Blagar*. It was just after 8 P.M. He had picked up the Cuban coast a short time ago. The radar had a range of thirty-two miles, and he estimated he was about twelve miles offshore. The little ships moved quietly. Everything was dark except for one light on each stern mast which could be seen only from the rear. Gray thought, "Oh, my God, here we are and where's that ship?"

Suddenly, to his relief, a "huge" blip appeared on the radar screen about a quarter mile off the starboard side of the *Atlántico*. It was the landing ship dock (LSD) *San Marcos* moving up the column of invasion ships rapidly, exactly on time. By the time the ships stopped, the LSD already had "ballast down": its crew had pumped in water to flood the well deck where all the three landing craft utility (LCU's) and the four landing craft vehicles and personnel (LCVP's) with their tanks, trucks and other equipment were waiting. As soon as the water was up to the level of the sea outside, the LSD opened its rear doors and the seven small vessels steamed out, manned by the CIA instructors who had trained its Cuban crews in Vieques.

An eighth craft appeared on Gray's radar, also according to plan. It was a landing craft mechanized (LCM) with an American Navy crew. It headed for the *Caribe*, picked up Silvio Pérez and his forty-three Brigade men and then moved along the next column of LCU's and LCVP's. At each landing craft, the CIA crew got off and the Cuban crew and vehicle drivers got on. Almost no words were exchanged. As Gray could tell on his radar, there were no slipups. Pérez got onto LCU No. 3, pleased to be in control of his own little fleet again. The invasion was fully operational for the first time. Soon it was moving in unison toward its targets: Blue Beach at Girón and Red Beach at Playa Larga.

Again the Cubans were impressed by the precision of American seamanship and the LSD's further visible demonstration of close Navy support. Most of the men had seen the *San Marcos* only as an enormous blacked-out shadow, but its size and distinctive sounds told them that it was an American mother ship. To Captain Juan Cosculuella, watching on radar, it loomed "like a tower." Captain Tirado of the *Río Escondido*, who had been in radio contact with the LSD, felt good when an American voice wished him good luck.

In less than one hour the *San Marcos* had disappeared. It had inserted the key in the lock to the invasion's naval power. Nobody at the scene knew that the key to the other lock—air power—had been tossed away in Washington.

Andy Pruna and three other frogmen on the CIA's *Barbara J.*, led by Rip, were determined to be the superelite of the frogmen elite. The others, aboard the other CIA ship, the *Blagar*, with Alonso and Gray, wore dark-green fatigues and were headed for the main landing at Blue Beach. The Pruna group wore bathing trunks, sweatshirts and sneakers, all of which they had dyed black. ("We looked so damned different, we almost got shot by our own people later.") Rip had looked at their M-3 submachine guns and snorted, "Throw those goddamn things away and get yourselves BAR's," and the Pruna group had followed the old commando's advice.

En route to their secondary landing at Red Beach, at the northern end of the bay, they fired their new weapons and practiced tossing hand grenades overboard. For entertainment, there was a spider monkey that liked to play tricks on the radio operator. Shortly before the men boarded their plastic black landing boat with its silent 200-horsepower engine, they painted their faces black with soot from the kitchen and raised the Cuban flag. "It was an emotional moment because we suddenly took on our identity," Pruna recalled. "I mean, we were going in as Cubans."

They were approaching shore shortly before midnight when the sky suddenly lit up above Blue Beach and Girón. Noise erupted that sounded like fireworks.

"What's going on?" Pruna shouted.

"The invasion has started," Rip said.

Pruna and the others cheered and yelled, "Now we're going to give it to 'em!" There seemed to be no further need for silence, so they kept on laughing and yelling; "it was like a carnival."

Pruna had assumed that Rip would lead his group to the beach, but Alonso on the *Blagar*, older and very proud, was startled when Gray joined him, carrying a BAR and wearing an ammunition belt, just as the frogmen who were headed for Blue Beach received a final blessing from one of the Brigade priests.

"What are you doing?" Alonso asked.

"I'm landing with you," Gray said.*

"No," Alonso countered quietly. "Here's where you stop. Don't misunderstand me. I'm grateful for all your teaching, but this part belongs to us now."

"I'm not staying," Gray said. "Believe me, you're going to be on your own. I'm coming right back."

This was, in fact Gray's plan. The main landing party was to start for shore in a fast eighteen-foot catamaran powered by two 70-horsepower outboards. The catamaran would tow a rubber raft with an 18-horsepower engine to which they would switch at about six hundred feet from the beach. Gray, thinking of himself as a "troubleshooter," intended to stay on the catamaran while the frogmen would scout and mark the beaches. They were to land at the extreme right, where a rock jetty with a small store would give them initial cover. The intelligence briefers had told them that most of the Cubans ashore were construction workers, building Playa Girón's new resort housing, and they would be asleep.

Alonso had developed deep liking and respect for Gray during the training period and did not argue long; and once the landing party could make out landmarks on the beach, he was glad to have experienced company. They could all hardly believe their eyes; their intelligence could not have been more wrong. The Cubans had installed tall, extremely bright arc-type vapor lights right on the beach. To Gray "it looked like Coney Island." Right next to what looked like a bodega, five locals were chatting. The area looked wide awake.

Gray and his men had decided to speak English throughout. Gray had picked up some Spanish during his adolescence in Texas, but he wanted to be sure to avoid misunderstandings, and he presumed that the Cubans ashore would not understand English. Most of the frogmen had attended college in the United States; all spoke English well.

All were, Gray thought, "very determined," but none had had even routine military experience. When Gray told them that the landing plans that they had memorized again and again had to be changed on the spot, they became understandably nervous. Yet a change was clearly needed. The bodega with its lights and its social life was a place to stay away from. The relative darkness in the center of the beach looked more opportune, but as Gray pondered the terrain and the inexperience of his men, he decided it was necessary for him to land and look around personally before signaling the *Blagar* to start landing the Brigade.

---

*When Gray Lynch testified before the Taylor Commission, General Taylor was amazed. "You landed?" he asked. Taylor smiled in the direction of Robert Kennedy, another commission member. "Did you have the Attorney General's permission?" Lynch said somberly, "No, sir, I simply followed orders."

His responsibility weighed heavily on him. A gravel road led right along the water on the beach. Behind it, thick, tall trees stood massed in total darkness. Any kind of trap could be lurking within. His intelligence people had finally conceded there were 108 Castro militiamen in Girón, but hadn't they missed the lights? Too much was at stake to take any more chances than were unavoidable.

"I want to know what's inside there," he said. "I'm going in with you." He jumped into the inflatable raft with the men and told Alonso, who was handling the stick on the outboard motor, to head for the center of the beach.

About a hundred yards offshore, one of their six red beach marker lights suddenly started blinking. Several of the men scrambled for it. Gray reached it first, covered it up and groped for the switch. It had been carefully taped on "off." The blinking, caused by a short, stopped. A minute later it started blinking again. Muttering his choicest epithets, Gray pulled out all the wires he could find.

Some eighty yards offshore Alonso felt his engine hit bottom sharply. The engine stopped. They had hit the coral reefs which the CIA photo interpreters had dismissed as "seaweed." Cursing, the men got out of the raft: first one on the left, the next on the right. Then they pushed it toward shore. They were waist-high in the water at first. Then it became deeper. Only Gray was still in the raft, prone, the barrel of his BAR pointing over the bow. He was about to hit the water.

Fifty yards offshore, he heard a jeep coming.* He told his men to squat in the water, turn their faces away and let it pass. But it stopped directly opposite the raiders. Gray never forgot the loud, long squeaking of the brakes. He raised his head for a look. At that moment the jeep swung around toward the sea, bathing the landing party in its headlights. At once, Gray started firing directly into them. They were the first shots at the Bay of Pigs.

Gray fired one complete magazine of twenty rounds and was starting on his second before the men in the water got the safety latches off their weapons and joined in. Two BAR's and four submachine guns poured hundreds of rounds into the jeep. Every third round was a tracer, so they could see the jeep being riddled. Finally the headlights died.

Gray jumped out of the raft, and the group, well spread out, waded toward shore, one man pulling the raft behind him. From the *Blagar*, Gray got a call on his walkie-talkie: on his left, the lights had gone out all over town, and he had been too busy to notice. He radioed back that he was on his way to place the landing lights.

---

*Gray later learned that the jeep had been alerted by the blinking red landing lights. The militiamen assumed that the CIA raft was a fishing boat and had come to warn it not to land at that spot because of the reefs.

Paying no attention to the silent jeep, the men ran up and down the beach, carrying the rubber raft along, placing the landing lights and getting the blinkers working. When they reached the bodega, they fired into it and all around it to immobilize the people within. They ran to the jeep. Two dead militiamen were sprawled in it. The windshield and all the tires were shot out. The front end was just about all bullet holes, but somehow the glass of the headlights had remained intact; the lights had gone out only because the battery and the wires had been hit.

Meanwhile, one of the frogmen ran to inspect the woods that had earlier aroused Gray's suspicions. Nothing. But a radio message came from the *Blagar*: "There's a truck coming toward your position!" Gray radioed back and instructed the ship to pull in broadside offshore at about three hundred yards and stand by to fire on the beach. Somebody had to make decisions, and he was the man on the spot. The surprise element was gone. It didn't matter. For once, the intelligence had been right: there was only a handful of militiamen in the town. Gray told the ship to rush the troops onto the LCVP's and was advised, "They're loading now, they're on their way."

Gray and his men ran to take cover behind the jetty. With the water up to their knees, they placed a white light on their raft to mark their position for the *Blagar*. Then they waited for the truck. It stopped on the other side of the woods and turned off its lights. Some twenty-five or thirty militiamen got out with flashlights. Some smoked cigars. When they reached the bodega, Gray and his party opened fire. The militiamen vanished into the woods. Gray instructed the *Blagar* to "blast them" with its machine guns and two .75 recoilless rifles. On the radio, the gunners had heard Gray mention his "white light." So they fired on it. Friendly bullets ricocheted all over Gray's party until two LCVP's radioed, "We're coming in!"

In the confusion, Gray had forgotten to warn them of the coral. They came "roaring in," having been trained for a landing on the sandy beaches in Trinidad, where they were supposed to hit the beach and ride up on it. The reefs punctured the double bottoms of both vessels. One sank shortly afterward. The men waded ashore wet but unharmed. Alonso could not restrain his annoyance about the reefs. "I told you about this," he said to Gray.

The CIA man decided that now was the time to bring the Brigade commanders ashore and sent his catamaran for them. They arrived at the jetty, led by Pepe San Román. Artime, the political head of the Brigade, picked up a handful of Cuban soil and made a speech. The troops took off for Playa Girón, where they fired furiously into the little pastel-colored bungalows of Castro's new recreation colony. There was almost no opposition. Pepe and Gray found an ancient Chevrolet behind the bodega. As the commander and his staff got in to drive off to secure the airstrip, Gray said, "OK, Pepe, I'm going back to the ship to take the Third Battalion to Green Beach."

It was the landing that never was. When Gray reached his frogmen on the beach, the radio operator said he was to call the ship.

"We have a very important message," the ship's captain, Sven Ryberg, told him. "Get back to the ship as fast as you can."

Aboard the *Blagar* again shortly before 1 A.M., Gray was handed a message on a yellow pad. It was from Washington, transmitted by the CIA station in Miami. "Castro still has operational aircraft. Expect you to be hit at dawn. Unload all troops and supplies and take ships to sea as soon as possible."

Gray was never told that the D-Day air strike had been canceled, so the message did not worry him unduly. He thought the Castro airfields would be hit as planned, that headquarters was being conservative and merely warning him that one or two enemy aircraft might emerge undamaged from the raids. He did not think it wise to take ships sixteen miles to Green Beach, where the troops might be hit before they could get ashore. The entire operation was running further and further behind schedule.

"We need to put that battalion ashore here right now," he told Ryberg, "because we're not going to lose them that way."

Over the ship-to-shore radio, Pepe agreed. He also wanted the LCU's with the tanks and other heavy equipment to land right away, not at daybreak as planned.

Gray demurred. "We don't want to lose anything on that reef," he said. "It's your decision, but I wouldn't do this."

Ashore, Alonso was questioning a fisherman about high tide. The old man pointed out a high-water mark and said it would be reached around 7 A.M. Alonso told Pepe, "If the LCU's land now you'll have a lot of people that may drown or break their legs." Pepe decided to delay landing the heavy equipment. It was brought ashore without incident just at daybreak. If the men on the scene had followed orders from CIA headquarters and moved "as soon as possible," another disaster would have been likely.

On the *Houston*, steaming toward Playa Larga and Red Beach, Hugo Sueiro, in command of the Second Battalion, had briefed his men. When he told them not to worry about early opposition because no communications existed within twenty miles of the beach, one of the men who had left the area only a few months earlier spoke up. "There's something wrong," he said. "When I left, there were microwave radio stations at Playa Larga *and* Girón."

Sueiro, a former lieutenant in the Cuban Army, was not too distressed. He had "unshaken confidence in the United States." He held a "firm belief if things go wrong we'd get helped out." He mentioned the radio stations to Erneido Oliva, the Brigade's second in command. Oliva shook his head. He was worrying about the Fiberglas boats that were supposed to serve as landing craft for the Second and Fifth battalions. They were so light and shallow that it was "ridiculous."

Rafael Villaverde was appalled by the screeching of the rusty old winches that swung the plastic boats over the side. He wondered whether the noise could be heard "maybe in Havana." Even Luís Morse, the relaxed skipper of the *Houston*, thought the boats were "good for nothing." Most of them promptly capsized. Soon only two of the nine were serviceable for the twenty-minute trip to the beach.

As Sueiro neared shore in the first boat shortly after 1 A.M., machine guns started firing at the *Houston*. It returned the fire. Oliva was not supposed to land until the Second Battalion was ashore. With everything going wrong, he decided it would be better for morale if he disembarked ahead of time. Barely on land, he was met by a man on the run who shouted, "There's a radio station only a hundred meters from the beach!"

Oliva went to take a look and couldn't suppress a laugh. His men were destroying the equipment as if they were acting in movies. One even threw a hand grenade. It was a farce. The equipment was still warm. The switches were on. So much for the CIA's intelligence that the beaches were without communications. The Castro forces had obviously been alerted.

At Blue Beach the alarm was triggered by Rafael Moreira. He was working the night shift, 6 P.M. to 6 A.M. He was driving his tractor, pulling a trailer with a light-blue tank holding two thousand gallons of water for the Girón recreation center swimming pool. The revolution was like that. Nobody in town had a toilet, much less running water. But they had a large kidney-shaped immaculately clean new public pool.

When he was some fifty yards from the pool and less than that from the waterline at the beach, he suddenly saw a large light at sea, not far away. Then tracer bullets were wooshing slightly over his head and to his right and left. Moreira stopped, stunned. The big light at sea started blinking. Moreira made himself fall to the ground and ran, crouching, to give the alarm at the militia post with its microwave radio station. He knew it must be an invasion. He was glad he had remembered to shut off the lights on his tractor. He wouldn't have wanted to show anybody the way.

Like almost all other civilians at the beaches, Narciso Mejias and his wife Alejandrina were asleep at home. Theirs was a one-room *vara en tierra* (poles in the earth) hut in Gironcito—Little Girón, a cluster of straw huts behind the resort cottages under construction by the ocean at Girón. They were awakened by loud noises shortly after midnight. It sounded like shots.

"What's that?" asked Alejandrina, frightened.

"Oh, that's nothing," said her husband. "Just those *orientales* again." Alejandrina was reassured.

The couple felt cozy in the iron-frame double bed under the tight-meshed, box-shaped mosquito netting that kept out the tiny, hungry mosquitoes for which the Zapata Swamp area was famous throughout Cuba. Some forty feet from the edge of the Caribbean, little more than shouting distance away from them, stood what Gray, the CIA man, had thought to be a bodega. It was Blanco's bar, the only business establishment in the settlement. Narciso and Alejandrina went there on weekends for a beer and maybe a little dancing to the juke box. On Saturdays the bar stayed open late, until 1 A.M. Often drinkers visited from out of town, *orientales* from Oriente province to the east. When the out-of-towners felt happy, they trooped outside and shot their pistols at the sky. It was unusual for them to do this now—Monday morning, with a new work week about to begin—but Narciso and his wife did not think about that. They were sleepy and had to be up early. Narciso was a mason's helper working on the Girón cottages. He was very soft-spoken and looked like an Indian. Their son, Gregorio, stirring in his own bed a few feet away, was seven, but there were no schools nearby, so he was footloose around home all day and his mother had to keep an eye on him.

Then a shot ripped into one of the nine-foot raw poles that held up the straw walls of their teepee-shaped hut. Now they knew they were not hearing revelers from Blanco's bar. Bullets hit their *fogón*, the little stove that burned the local charcoal. Another two bullets tore with deafening noise into the iron headrest of their bed, inches over their heads. The couple hit the ground and crawled under the bed—the hut had neither floor nor electricity—with Alejandrina seizing Gregorio in one sweep of her arm. She was shaking and sobbing.

When the shooting briefly stopped, they all rushed into the dark unpaved street. Neighbors were shouting, "Ships are shooting at the houses on the beaches!"

Narciso remembered Saturday's air raids. The United States was behind them. Fidel had said so. The ships that were shooting had to be United States vessels. The troops had to be Americans. He told his wife he would ask the sergeant at the militia post in the new pink cottage near the recreation center what to do. The sergeant told him they would all have to evacuate later, if possible. There were no weapons to distribute.

Narciso ran home and found his wife out in the back of their hut. Tearfully she showed him the little iron tub she had used the previous afternoon to boil the family wash. She had left the wash soaking in water. Now the tub was empty of water. Bullets had riddled it and the laundry within. When she hung the laundry later, she found it was full of holes. She had to use the clothes as rags.

Félix Rivera met the invaders at Enrico Blanco's bar.

Félix liked his job there. The boss was a Spaniard and generous. Once when Félix had been broke, Enrico had loaned him ten pesos to go into town and had not asked for the money back. Enrico served beer and rum to the customers at his eight tables—there was no real bar—and he sold them cigarettes. Félix' job was strictly cooking. He fried lobster and other local fish and fixed sardine snacks for the drinkers. Often he had little to do, because many customers came only for one beer and then played dominoes. Félix enjoyed one big fringe benefit: Blanco let him sleep in the one room above the bar. It was windowless but free.

Félix, black, handsome and wavy-haired, had cleaned up his kitchen when the bar closed at midnight. He was not yet asleep under his mosquito netting at about 12:30 A.M. when shooting started. It seemed to come from the *castillito,* the ruins of the small castle-like stone structure at the end of the rock jetty jutting into the Caribbean about fifty yards away.

The firing was scattered. Félix didn't worry. He thought it was the local militia, maybe practicing, maybe just firing by accident. It happened all the time. Then he heard voices. "Come on, *compañeros!*" said one. "We're on Cuban soil!" Another said, "Get on the ground and you won't get hurt!"

Félix thought about getting hurt. He decided to remain flat in his bed. In the war movies he had seen, people always got hurt when they moved around. Nobody ever got hurt staying in bed. He was going to stay put.

Outside there was a shout: "OK, everybody inside come out!"

Félix sighed, put on his short-sleeved white cook's uniform and opened the door. Suddenly there were soldiers in spotted green uniforms "all over the place." They said they had come from the United States. They sounded like Cubans, but at least one looked like a *norteamericano*.*

The men set up a radio in the bar. They started calling for reinforcements but seemed to get no answer. They asked Félix if he would join them and fight on their side. He said he had never handled a gun (which was true) and had only recently arrived from Oriente and did not know his way around the area (not true). He was determined not to join any fighting. People got hurt fighting. He had seen it in the movies.

At Red Beach, one of the first to resist the Brigade was Víctor Caballero, on guard duty in the fishing hamlet of Caletón. The duty was boring but not inconvenient. His *bohío* was ten yards from the little inlet at the innermost point of the Bay of Pigs. His militia post was a Coast Guard motor launch moored thirty yards away, with a lieutenant and five men sleeping aboard. Víctor, a black-haired, wiry carpenter whose teeth were in poor repair, had his rifle and wore a red armband. At night the militia did not bother putting on uniforms. One of the men had knocked on his door at midnight to alert him that his tour of duty was coming. They stood guard in twosomes. Nothing ever happened.

Víctor was chatting with his buddy near their launch when the other man said, "What's that noise out there? It's something hitting."

It sounded like the hard thumping of lumber being unloaded. They never could figure out what it was, because tracer bullets from automatic weapons began whizzing overhead. The men in the Coast Guard boat were up when Víctor reached them. They all tried to head the boat out of the inlet. The tide was too low. They reversed the engine, returned to shore and started to dig a little trench about ten feet from the waterline for their .50-caliber machine gun. A big ship had become visible in the bay. Sometimes there were lights. The firing kept coming.

Víctor and his men found empty sacks at the nearby construction site. They also found piles of sand. Shoveling furiously, they made their own sandbags and built a protective embankment for the machine gun. It was semicircular, nearly two feet high and two bags thick. They opened fire with the gun before their impromptu fortification was ready.

The lieutenant tried the radio on the launch without success. He tried again. He called Víctor and the others into the cabin in the front of the boat. He said he wanted them to hear what was being broadcast. It was an appeal for them to surrender. The voice said they were being liberated from Communism and that Castro was a prisoner. The

*This could only have been Gray Lynch.

militiamen shook their heads and agreed they were being attacked by the CIA or U.S. forces. It could be no one else. Nobody took the surrender demand seriously.

Tracer bullets kept hitting around the machine gun. The men fired whenever something visible moved in the bay. Two of Víctor's *compañeros* were wounded, one in the foot, the other in the head. Víctor helped the man with the foot wound to safety. Then he returned to his home to look in on his wife, Florentina, his seven-year-old daughter, five-year-old son, and five-month-old baby daughter. They were stretched out, fully dressed, on the floor. All were crying.

Víctor told them they had to leave. The house was too close to shore. By now his *fogón* was shot to pieces. Bullet holes had riddled the walls and Florentina's pots. He told his family to lie flat under a big construction crane. It was cool, so he covered them with a bedsheet and ran back to his machine gun. A man had to defend his home and family.

Thirty yards from the water, also at Caletón, Amparo Ortíz, a *carbonero's* wife, was crying, though not because of the invasion. It was about 2 A.M., but the tiny round woman could not sleep. She was lying on her bed, dressed in black skirt and white blouse. Her mosquito netting was not up. Her sister María sat next to the bed, consoling her. Amparo's eighteen-year-old son, Ramón, had died of a heart attack eight days before. He had been a healthy young man. His death was unfathomable. She could not stop crying. She did not want to stop crying.

In addition to her husband, sobbing quietly in another bedroom, five relatives were staying in their *bohío*. All had come to comfort the couple. Suddenly their four-room thatched-roof hut—it had real walls of raw palm tree planks—was engulfed by shots. One of them loudly pierced the strip of zinc on the roof. Amparo's nephew said, "I'm going to the cooperative to see what's happening."

The fishery cooperative was the center of the settlement and of its life. The *rotunda* (traffic circle) where the road forked to Girón was a short way to the east.

As the shooting continued, everybody except Amparo hit the floor. She was too nervous to keep still. She paced and peered out the window. Many little lights were bobbing in the bay. It was a brightly moonlit night. Not far away, she saw a large ship.* The local militia's motor launch was anchored a few feet away. Over its radio, Amparo heard a voice: "We've come to free Cuba from Communism!" She could not stop crying.

*The *Houston*.

By sunup she was in the dirt by the side of the highway *rotunda*, surrounded by her husband and a dozen relatives and villagers from Playa Larga and Caletón, including two children. The militiamen had said a truck would pick them up and take them inland. They had fled their homes without taking any of their belongings. The shooting continued.

Two planes with the familiar Cuban FAR markings flew overhead. They came from the sea and were headed in the direction of Havana, yet everyone was certain they were friendly. "There come our planes now!" one woman shouted. Almost in unison, all the women shouted Castro's revolutionary slogan, *"Patria o muerte!"*—"Fatherland or death!"—to urge their pilots on. Then they heard many shots from the air very close down the road. The planes were strafing. They were enemies.

Finally the truck from the Buenaventura cooperative arrived. Everybody but Amparo clambered quickly on its flat bed. With her tiny legs, she could barely make it into the cab next to the driver. He started north. Fire of submachine guns from the side of the road opened, almost immediately. Amparo, petrified, crouched down. The driver kept going. He was shot in the leg and one eye. He kept his foot on the gas until the truck lumbered to a halt, the gasoline tank in thick flames.

A relative helped Amparo out of the truck. The shooting had stopped. Looking back, she saw that her sister was still on the burning truck. She was dead. So was her fifteen-year-old grandniece. Several wounded were groaning on the road. She did not see her husband. A young woman had a badly bleeding chest wound. The bullet had gone out her back. Her husband tried to carry her away, but the shooting began again.

In the bushes, the survivors found Castro's 339th Militia Battalion. Twelve of their men were dead. Some were lying on the road. Amparo was frantic about her husband. As the firing continued, she dashed from body to body until a militiaman yelled, "Lady, you're going to get killed!" He pulled her down by her skirt. Then he was hit in the chest and began to bleed furiously. His submachine gun fell from his hands. Amparo got him up, placed his arms around her back and tried to walk him to safety. Her right side hugged him closely. Blood soaked her clothes and her right leg. She looked down in horror. She could stand no more of it and bolted through the bushes looking for her husband.

She found him in a culvert by the road, dead, with bullet holes throughout his midriff. He had to have been hit early on the moving truck and rolled off its platform. A truck from the Playa Larga resort construction lot stopped. It was driven by a *miliciano*.

"Come on," he shouted, looking at Amparo's blood-soaked right side. "We're picking up all the wounded."

"No," she said, "I won't get on unless you pick up all the dead too."

The soldier picked up her husband's body and then, one by one, the other dead and wounded. Amparo sat with her husband until his body was unloaded with the other dead. She cried for him and for her son.

The invaders knew little about their own situation. At about 10 A.M., when Erneido Oliva, the second in command, was finally able to establish faint radio contact from Red Beach at Playa Larga, on the western front, with his chief, Pepe San Román, at Blue Beach in Girón, he reported that the Second Battalion had routed a machine gun emplacement of *milicianos* on the beach and was pushing inland. But there was no word from the paratroopers who were supposed to set up roadblocks ahead (they were lost or retreating). He did not know the whereabouts of the Fifth Battalion, which was supposed to land with him (it lingered permanently outside the battle zone). He asked Pepe for support—a tank and a squad of infantry. Pepe told him that he had no communications with any other units and that the ships had left. He would send the tank and the men.

Now Oliva's luck turned. His forward company spotted a truck of militiamen rumbling unsuspectingly out of the brush. A white-phosphorus grenade from the Brigade scored a direct hit. The truck blew up. Those who were not killed ran off. It was not until two-thirty on Monday afternoon that Oliva's men faced an enemy battalion of nine hundred men approaching in more than sixty vehicles. By luck, San Román's tank arrived—Oliva's men kissed it—and two Brigade B-26s appeared overhead. Oliva radioed the planes to attack the column. They dropped bombs and rockets. Caps flew into the air. Men screamed and ran. Gasoline tanks blew up. Fire billowed all along the road. Oliva estimated that less than half the enemy battalion survived its retreat.

Over the radio, Oliva heard the Brigade bomber pilots talking. They were under attack by a T-33 and a Sea Fury. Both B-26s were shot down. Over the battlefield, masses of vultures appeared. They kept circling, swooping down, and circling.

Two of the five García ships meanwhile had been knocked out. At 6:30 A.M., with the Second Battalion ashore but the Fifth still aboard, the *Houston* was hit amidships near the waterline by a rocket fired from a Sea Fury. Miraculously, there was no explosion. Luís Morse, the captain, had been pouring a cup of coffee for his quartermaster when water came rushing into a huge hole in the ship's side. A fire broke out below. The ship's fire hose was useless; it had been riddled by machine gun bullets. Two men were dead, five wounded.

The engineer called the bridge. "Water is coming up," he reported.

"Stay there, stay there," Morse ordered. "Give me all you got." He had lost control of the rudder, but he was determined to beach the ship so that the troops could get off. He launched one of his two lifeboats. The other was useless; it was full of holes caused not by bullets but, long ago, by rot. Morse limped within seven hundred yards of land, but many of the men jumped overboard. Quite a few drowned. Others—the Fifth Battalion was the last to be organized, so many of its men had little training—seemed paralyzed.

Rip and his frogmen arrived in a rubber raft to help. "Get off, you bastards," Rip yelled, "it's your fucking war!" Still, many of the 130 soldiers did not move until after the *Houston's* stern sank with almost all cargo still aboard. On shore, Dr. René de La Mar, his right arm bleeding badly from a machine gun bullet in the elbow—he was never able to work ashore, yet he refused pain killers because he did not want to be drowsy—watched his entire field hospital go down. Erneido Oliva, the Brigade's deputy commander, watching with the doctor, said, "This is it. If we can't stop one Sea Fury, shit! Now I have nothing to fight with."

The *Río Escondido* followed less than three hours later. The first air attacks had left it undamaged, and one of the LVCP's had taken its troops to the beach by 9 A.M. when many voices started shouting, "Sea Fury! Sea Fury!" Captain Tirado had no time to curse the fact that his volatile cargo and the Brigade communications van, all scheduled for offloading hours before, were still aboard. From no more than three hundred feet, a Sea Fury headed directly for his port side and fired eight rockets. One hit the deck near the bridge. The two hundred barrels of aviation gasoline caught fire at once. The fire started moving forward rapidly. There were fire extinguishers aboard, but they were totally inadequate for a gasoline fire.

One close look told Tirado that his ship was lost. He went to the radio room on the bridge and called the "American task force commander" whom he had never met, whose name he did not know, and who had never commanded a unit larger than a company of U.S. Army tanks. The "commander" who replied was Gray on the *Blagar*.

Gray was furious. He had been firing his .50-caliber machine gun so steadily during the earlier attacks that the barrel had overheated and turned white. Gray had ordered the gun replaced when he heard the "Sea Fury!" shouts. Now he insisted on using the original gun, unaware that one of his men had already pulled a latch from the gun's underpinning. Seeing the *Río Escondido* under attack, he fired almost straight up at the Sea Fury. Suddenly the entire gun bounced off its mount. He never let go until he fell on his back, the gun barrel across his shoulder. His men dragged him away just before he could be severely burned.

He never got a further shot at the *Río Escondido's* attacker. Cursing, he watched the fire lash out. When Tirado said over the radio, "I'm going to give instructions to abandon ship," Gray only said, "OK," and issued orders for the invasion ships to send all available small boats to pick up the crew.

As Tirado left the radio room, two of his men had already jumped overboard. He urged the rest to jump, too, and then hit the water himself. All the men were picked up; only one sustained wounds in the entire incident.* Their escape was close. The flames were shooting a hundred feet high, and the crewmen in their orange life vests were huddled in their boats perhaps 250 yards away when the first of three explosions sent up a fireball and then a mushroom cloud. Captain Tirado permanently lost half his hearing in both ears.

At Blue Beach, Rip shouted into his radio, "God Almighty, what was that? Fidel got the A-bomb?"

"Naw," Gray said, "that was the damned *Río Escondido* that blew."

He was watching the fireball lift off the water to reveal the ship's stern upside down, its two workable props sticking up into the air. They kept working to the end, turning slowly as the ship gurgled downward. The sinking of the communication van could not have been more serious. Air and ground forces were completely cut off from each other. Other "commo" was either very difficult or else impossible, especially since the soldiers' hand radios got wet during landing.

By afternoon, Gray was getting pounded by messages from headquarters. "Go to sea," they instructed again and again. He ignored them. He was busy firing from the *Blagar* at attacking planes. He knew the Brigade's ammunition would not last beyond the first day. The ammunition was critical. The men had to have the ammunition from the *Atlántico* and the *Caribe*. He also kept thinking about Pepe San Román. He couldn't "run off and leave him there."

Headquarters became more specific. He was to take the ships outside the twelve-mile limit, unload the supplies onto the LCU's and return after dark. The Navy would be asked to provide "safe haven." That made sense to Gray. García's ship crews were so busy fending off one air attack after another that they could get no unloading done. He would

---

*The German shepherd supplied to Tirado by the CIA was missing and presumably drowned.

have trouble explaining the situation to Pepe because there could be no talk of Navy cover on an open channel.

"Pepe, we're going to have to go," he radioed to shore.

"OK, but don't desert us!" Pepe replied.

"We're not going to desert you," promised Gray.

To Commodore Crutchfield on the *Eaton* he radioed, "We're coming out." The slowest vessels, the three empty LCU's, went first. The *Atlántico* and the *Caribe* followed. The *Barbara J.* and the *Blagar* brought up the rear. Five miles offshore, a B-26 came heading toward the port side of the *Blagar* only about a hundred feet above the water, pointed directly amidships. Gray radioed all ships to hold their fire: "This guy means business. We either get him or he's going to get us!"

With the attacker about three thousand feet away, Gray started firing a few rounds to check the distance by watching where his tracer bullets burned out. At two thousand feet, with the B-26 in range, he shouted, "Open fire!" Every weapon on every ship opened up. Almost at once, the plane started bobbing up and down like a porpoise. Gray thought it was evasive maneuvering. He kept firing, running through two boxes of ammunition before the B-26 was a thousand yards away. Then he saw white mist trailing out of the plane's wings. The pilot was firing his .50-caliber machine guns in short bursts. They hit either just high or just low. The pilot was not in control of the aircraft. Gray's tracers were tearing right into his nose. The ships' fire was "chewing him apart."

At about three hundred yards, the Castro pilot fired his rockets. At that moment, Gray realized that the white mist had been gasoline. The rockets landed just short of the ship. The bomber exploded into a ball of fire, pancaked into the sea, and bounced across the deck of the ship, lifting its stern clear of the water. On the bridge, Gray watched one wing cartwheeling eight or ten feet below him. Part of the tail dropped on the deck. It was on fire, which Gray's crew put out. The rest of the burning wreck landed in the sea, so close to the ship that Captain Ryberg had to order a sharp turn to avoid it.

The captain showed the strain. "What are we going to do? What are we going to do?" he asked Gray. All they could do was keep going and hope for Navy cover. They had just survived a rocket attack from a Sea Fury when they passed the twelve-mile zone and spotted the *Eaton* and the *Murray* on the horizon. They radioed Crutchfield for protection. An astounding reply came back: "My heart is with you, but I have orders not to become engaged."

For a moment, Gray felt like asking "the bastards" whether they would "stand by to pick up survivors." Without help, he was certain that all the ships, which had gradually come under his command without anyone saying so, would be sunk. Then he felt defiant. They had fought off air attacks before, they'd do it again. He was much more concerned about the *Atlántico* and the *Caribe* with all their ammunition. When the last air attacks began, both had left the scene at full speed. Repeatedly, the *Blagar* called them. They did not answer. On the radar, Gray watched them move farther and farther out of reach.

Death in the Air

Shortly before sunup on D-Day, Captain Eddie Ferrer, the morale officer of the Brigade pilots, neared Cuba at the controls of his C-46, the first of six aircraft from Puerto Cabezas that were to drop 177 paratroopers northeast of the beachhead. In the twilight about seventy-five miles offshore, he spotted strange shapes in the sea. "What the hell is this?" he asked Raúl Solís, his co-pilot, who had flown for the Cuban Navy. Solís shrugged.

Approaching, they saw an aircraft carrier and two destroyers also heading in the direction of the beaches. Ferrer and Solís grinned at each other. Solis started whistling "Anchors Aweigh." They were certain that the ships were en route to join the battle. "Hell, we can't lose," Ferrer said. As he passed over the carrier at eight hundred feet, he dipped his wings and saw American sailors waving. It was "a beautiful sight."

Ferrer went into the cabin and shook hands with all the men. They had also seen the *Essex* and the destroyers and were in great spirits. They were going to "kick those Communist asses." Alejandro del Valle, the paratroop commander, embraced Eddie and said, "Don't drop me badly, I don't want to finish the war too soon!" They agreed they would meet soon again and have a beer.

Passing over the Brigade ships and Girón shortly after 6 A.M., Ferrer pushed a red button. His thirty paratroopers watched their red warning light flash. They got up and adjusted their gear. Ten miles farther, over the San Blas road at eight hundred feet, Ferrer overflew a jeep with three men who fired at them with rifles and pistols. He felt his plane being hit but decided that the damage amounted to nothing. He also decided to take his paratroopers a short distance farther than planned and drop them precisely over the road junction in San Blas so that the men in the jeep would not pick them off as they made their slow descent.

He pressed a green button. The green light went on in the cabin. All paratroopers jumped out the rear exit in less than fifteen seconds. All hit the San Blas road safely.

Ferrer's orders were to inspect the Girón airstrip on his way back to make sure it was usable. He had completed his second circle over the field at about five hundred feet and was heading seaward when he saw a B-26 approaching up ahead and slightly toward the left. He was not alarmed. Hadn't the American advisers said that the sky would be theirs? "Hey," he said to Solís, "there are some of our people!"

Solís looked terrified. "No," he shouted, "goddammit, this is a Castro B-26! This one has a plastic nose!"

By now they could see smoke of machine gun bursts puffing out of the B-26's wings. Ferrer, unarmed in a plane that had a maximum speed a hundred miles less than his enemy, was petrified. Without thinking, he headed directly toward the B-26. It saved his life. The bomber pulled his nose down to avoid a collision. Ferrer applied full power. He headed toward the invasion fleet, figuring, correctly, that the ships would fire at his pursuer.

He was racing for a cloud to hide in when he saw another of his C-46 paratrooper planes followed by a Sea Fury. Since the C-46 could not outrun his attacker, he cut his power and put down his flaps and landing gear to fly at eighty miles per hour. It didn't work. Ferrer never could determine whether his comrade stalled out or was shot down by one of his own ships.

Pulling out of his cloud at full power, Ferrer looked at Solís. The co-pilot's face was pure white. Eddie tried to light a cigarette. For a while he couldn't make it, he was trembling so much. He glanced down and found he had wet his pants. He was never ashamed to admit it. It was much worse to be a sitting target in the sky where you "can't even throw a rock at the other guy."

They made it back to Happy Valley by 10 A.M. and had a beer. Dr. Marrs gave them pills, and they hit their bunks for the first time in forty-eight hours. Ferrer was much too tired to think of everything that had gone wrong.

Two hours later, Dr. Marrs shook Eddie awake.

"What's going on?" the pilot asked.

"Gar wants to see you," said the doctor. "Let's wake up your crew."

Gar Teegan, the CIA air operations officer at Puerto Cabezas, told Ferrer and his men that the Brigade badly needed ammunition. He said nothing about the sinking of the *Río Escondido* and the *Houston*. He told Ferrer that his C-46 was being loaded. Ferrer was to land at the Girón airstrip, keep his engine running during the unloading and "get out." A B-26 would escort him. It was clear that Gar wasn't sure Ferrer could make it. "If you see any fighters, go back, because you won't have a chance," he said.

Takeoff was scheduled for 2 P.M. Ferrer wanted to get to the beach by twilight. As his plane was being "superheavily" loaded and he was warming up the engine, the Cuban air contingent's chaplain, Father Cipriano Cavero, edged his five feet three inches into the cockpit and said, "I know you're going to Girón for a mission. I want to go."

"Father, you're crazy," Ferrer said. "You can't go. They've got priests in the Brigade."

The little priest kept arguing. He absolutely had to be on the beaches. The pilot said he would be violating orders if he took anyone except his crew. He was walking around the bulky plane—the men called it "the watermelon"—and told the PDO's (parachute drop officers) to keep the doors and windows open, install two machine guns and tie them in place with ropes. He was tired of being a sitting duck in a defenseless aircraft. The priest kept following him, begging to be taken to the front.

Exasperated and certain that this would be the way to shake off the good father, Ferrer seized his own submachine gun, thrust it into the priest's hands and said, "The only way you can go in this airplane is if you're willing to fight with this."

"I will," the priest said and grabbed the gun. His eyes popped out.

Ferrer said, "Climb in."

Badly overloaded with twenty thousand pounds of ammunition, Ferrer cleared the trees at the end of the 5,600-foot runway "by one inch" and lumbered along at 120 knots. This was too slow for his B-26 escort to stay nearby. Then the bomber pilot reported that his machine guns were stuck and his center tank was not working. After some argument, Ferrer persuaded the pilot to turn back. He couldn't have helped against fighters anyway.

Fifty miles south of the beachhead, the radio came alive with a cry: "May Day! May Day! This is Puma One!" It was one of Ferrer's friends, José Crespo, trying to bring back his B-26 from a bomb run at the beaches. He radioed Ferrer not to proceed; two T-33 jets and one Sea Fury were patrolling the area. They had already shot down another Brigade B-26. Crespo said he was saved when two American jets from the *Essex* flew between his plane and the Sea Fury that was attacking him. When the Castro pilot saw the jets, he turned and left.

At that moment, Ferrer heard the machine guns firing from the cabin of his own plane. Two planes were heading for him on his right. Even the priest was on his knees emptying Ferrer's M3 out of a window. As the planes came closer, Ferrer was horrified; they were American jets.

"Cease fire!" he shouted. "They're our friends!"

The firing continued. His men couldn't hear him. Only when the navigator rushed back did the firing cease. Apparently all the shooting had gone wild.

Ferrer identified himself to Crespo by his code name, Falcon One, and asked for Crespo's situation. The stricken plane's left engine was destroyed. Most of the navigation equipment wasn't working. Crespo couldn't tell what else was wrong; something was, because he was losing air speed steadily. He wanted Ferrer to fly back to base within sight of him "so if I fall in the water you know where I am and they can pick me up tomorrow." Ferrer agreed. It was getting dark. He did not want to abandon his comrade. Besides, there was little chance that he could land his ammunition, no matter how urgently it was needed—not with two T-33s nearby.

Two hours out of Cuba, Eddie Ferrer asked Crespo how he was doing. "I'm losing air speed and altitude," Crespo radioed. "I'm going to have to ditch pretty soon."

Father Cavero asked to use the radiophone to call Crespo and his co-pilot. Would they like him to hear confession? They did. Ferrer and his men removed their earphones. The priest stepped behind a bulkhead and took the confessions in private.

Another hour later, Crespo said, "Eddie, the situation is bad. I'm three or four hundred feet from the water. I'm going to have to ditch in about two or three minutes."

Ferrer responded, "God bless you. I hope you make it all right. You have been very brave, and your co-pilot too. I will try to look for you tomorrow. Give me a last holler just before you get into the water."

About ten more minutes passed before Crespo's shout came over the radio: "Hitting the water!"

The next day Ferrer returned to search the area. He found no trace of the plane or its men.

By Tuesday the Cuban pilots at Puerto Cabezas had become an intractable problem. All were exhausted. Many were disgusted. Some had turned chicken. They were no longer making extra turns over the targets Teegan found that only about one third were "ready to go." With the others, the Americans "had to beg them to go." By now, "it took several hours to get some of their crews in the aircraft, and then they aborted the mission." They constantly "found excuses not to do the job." You "could count the number of 'tigers' on one hand." The experienced, relatively rested American pilots had become desperately needed.

For the first time, Bissell authorized American pilots to fly combat missions. They were volunteers known as "Peters" and "Seig"—CIA contract men, not from the Alabama National Guard. Joined by the most courageous Cubans, including Gus Ponzoa, they headed for Cuba at 2 P.M. Barely over land, they spotted a long column of trucks and tanks approaching Girón and Blue Beach. The Castro troops mistook them for friendlies, an accident that happened consistently to both sides. Instead of dispersing, they began to cheer. It was a deadly mistake. The six Brigade planes swooped down, dropping napalm and regular bombs, firing rockets, inflicting an estimated eighteen hundred casualties and destroying seven tanks.

Gar thought the mission had been remarkably fortunate. He had asked Washington for jet air cover from the *Essex* for the first time. Headquarters messaged back that it would try to get authority. No word had come. Gar briefed his bomber crews on a "scissors" maneuver which sometimes, with enormous luck, made it possible to trap a T-33 between two well-coordinated B-26s. What had really turned the mission into a shining success, as Gar knew, was the circumstance that Castro's pilot's happened not to have been in the air.

Later that day, Gar called the two senior American pilots, Riley Shamburger and Joe Shannon, to the operations tent within its special bamboo security fence. Reid Doster was there. None had slept for three days. All were kept alert by Dr. Marrs's pills.

As a squadron operations officer back in Birmingham, the boisterous Major Shamburger had been one of four Alabama pilots who had been briefed on the operation in Washington. Lieutenant Colonel Shannon, his squadron commander, had also been in that select group. The other Americans had been told they were back-up pilots, to fly in combat in the event of dire need. Shamburger and Shannon had been warned they could not fly at all. They had too much intelligence information in their heads.

Shannon had been happy to hear that. He was a shy man, pink-cheeked, open-eyed, cherubic. He had flown fighters all over Africa and Italy in World War II and B-25s in China and India. He had been a full-time instructor pilot with the Air Guard ever since. He was almost forty, had three children and had not been eager to fight anymore.

Now he felt differently. He had a stake in the success of the mission. He had been "terribly disappointed" when the "no-go" message had arrived canceling the second air strike while he had been on duty in the operations tent Monday morning. He couldn't understand what Washington was waiting for. Now they had changed their minds again. Teegan told him and Shamburger that headquarters had given clearance for five B-26 missions to be flown that night. Four crews were to be American. All the others had already been briefed. Shannon felt "no reluctance." He was "excited." The sheer fact that he and Shamburger were permitted to fly was "sign of a desperation effort." It also made him think that Washington had not yet given up.

Gar's instructions were brief. They were to penetrate the beachhead area and destroy whatever they could, especially trucks and tanks. Shannon and Shamburger knew the roads well; they had briefed the Cuban pilots about them repeatedly. Both pilots carried maps and photos. Both planes would have two extra tanks with spare fuel. Shannon would also carry a napalm bomb. Washington had only very lately authorized the use of napalm.

The two pilots got about two hours of fitful sleep. Takeoff for the nine-hundred-mile trip was 3 A.M. Shannon went first, then they flew side by side. Shannon's napalm bomb, suspended under one wing, created a drag and slowed them down by five to ten knots per hour. Joe felt no trace of fatigue. The sun was still low when they hit land about twenty miles east of the Bay of Pigs. They corrected their course and quickly spotted a cloud of dust. It was a column of trucks.

"You go in first and get rid of your napalm," Shamburger radioed Shannon.

"OK." They had earlier agreed on this tactic because flying with napalm created an extra hazard.

Shannon started to turn toward the dust. Then he heard a hoarse, high-pitched yell from his comrade:

"I'm hit and on fire!"

"What'd you hit?"

There was no answer. At that instant, Shannon saw Shamburger's plane at one hundred feet over the beach, headed for the water at three hundred miles an hour. He watched him hit the sea hard at a shallow angle. There was no chance of survival for the happy-go-lucky pilot or for his co-pilot, Wade C. Gray, who had been a radio and electronics technician at Hayes Aircraft and lived in Pinson, a Birmingham suburb.

It was not Shannon's first experience watching death in combat. He had lost several of his tent mates on two of his missions during the war in Africa. Anyway, there was no time for reflection. Directly over the beach at two hundred feet he spotted the Castro T-33 that had hit Shamburger. Shannon pulled right toward the T-bird as hard as he could. Instinctively, he knew that if he turned away from the jet it would hit his lumbering old plane too. As it was, the Cuban pilot had no choice. He had to evade. And he did, pulling up abruptly. Shannon slid by directly under him. Less than two hundred feet separated the planes. Briefly, they headed in opposite directions. By the time Shannon turned to train his guns on the jet, it had turned steeply up into the sun to be less visible.

Shannon never saw it again. He stayed at full throttle, heading toward base. The clouds were small and widely scattered. He stayed "inches off the water"—his only protection against attack. He was becoming angry thinking of Riley Shamburger and the beer-and-barbecue parties which he and his wife had attended at Shamburger's big house in suburban East Lake, with Riley munching his favorite addiction, "parched" peanuts. Joe Shannon "wanted revenge." When he landed at Happy Valley, the first to get back from that morning's missions, he said he wanted to fly another mission right away. Gar and Doster shook their heads. There would be no more flights.

Billy Goodwin, another of the Alabama B-26 pilots who was substituting for Cubans that morning, also learned of Shamburger's death at close range. He had left base at 1:30 A.M. with four rockets, two napalm bombs, and five hundred gallons of extra fuel instead of bombs in the bomb bay. For the past three days, he too had been too worried about "the war" to sleep, but his yellow "Bennies" kept him going. The sky was turning gray when he hit Cuba at 5:30 A.M., missing the beach at first by fifteen miles—"not bad for a nine-hundred-mile flight." Off the beachhead just before sunup he spotted an enemy convoy. Goodwin had not flown in combat before, and he never forgot his first target: two jeeps, one three-quarter-ton carryall and four two-and-a-half-ton trucks.

He had the enemy vehicles lined up in the sights of his machine guns and pulled the correct switch. The guns would not fire. He was over the convoy now. He pulled the switch to release his napalm. The napalm would not release. Frantically he kept hitting the switches. Nothing happened. Then he spotted three tanks. He fired his rockets, but the ammunition was not armor-piercing. He hit one tank, but the rocket ricocheted right off. One rocket did hit a truck.

It was 6:03 A.M., time to turn back, especially since the Cubans in the target convoy had shot one cylinder off his right engine. It slowed him to 190 knots from his normal cruising speed of 230. He was starting to fly just over the water when he heard Shamburger and Shannon talking to each other over the radio. It was a shock to hear and recognize their familiar voices after so many hours of silence. Billy made his presence known.

"Have you seen any of our little friends?" asked Riley. Billy knew this was Shamburger's way to refer to the enemy.

"Yeah," he said, "but my guns won't fire."

"Don't feel like the Lone Ranger," Shamburger said. "Mine won't work, either."

Billy heard Shannon say, "Riley, where are you?"

"Behind you and to your right."

Then Billy heard Shamburger's shout, "I'm hit and on fire!" He listened helplessly as Shannon repeatedly called Riley without getting a reply. Then Shannon said quietly, "T-birds got Riley."

Moments later Goodwin encountered two unmarked jets that turned out to be American. A third one was about a thousand feet higher and to the left. Goodwin was amazed. Nobody had told him there were friendly aircraft in the area.* At first he thought the jets might be unfriendly. In fact, if he "hadn't been strapped in, I'd have jumped so bad I'd been off to the moon." His own plane carried Cuban markings, but the Americans somehow knew he was friendly. He could see the freckles in the area of the pilots' eyes between the oxygen masks and the tops of the helmets.

He gave them a thumbs-up signal and tried to motion them toward Joe Shannon, who presumably needed help. It irked him not to be able to talk to the Americans. There was no way. Their radios operated on a VHF frequency, Billy was on UHF. It was another unanticipated flaw in the planning.

Goodwin was almost over the Cayman Islands when he heard Shannon call for assistance. Goodwin told him he could not help. He said he was running low on gas, his right engine was missing, and his guns would not fire. He encountered two more B-26s and told them what had happened over the beaches. They turned back.

The only Cuban pilot to make it to the beaches that morning, Gonzalo Herrera, the most daring man in the Cuban crews, was still in the air. He had been assigned to strafe and bomb artillery positions in the San Blas area. He had managed to drop his entire bomb load on his targets, but he could tell that his B-26 had been hit. One propeller was vibrating, and the right engine was losing oil pressure.

He was skimming across the swamp behind the beachhead just above treetop level when he heard an American pilot call in distress, "Mad Dog Four! Mad Dog Four! May Day! May Day! T-33 attacking us." He then heard the voice begging for help from the *Essex*: "We are Americans! Help us!" An American voice replied, "I am a naval officer and I must obey my orders."

*The message that the President okayed a 6:30-to-7:30 A.M. air cover from the *Essex* did not reach Puerto Cabezas until all but the last plane had left the base. Gar Teegan tore it out of the Teletype, jumped into his jeep, and made a dash to the flight line. The right engine of the B-26 was already turning. Gar jumped on the left wing, ran to the cockpit, waving the yellow slip of paper, shouting, "We've got the air cover!"

Herrera turned when he reached the water, climbed to a thousand feet to check his engines, and spotted enemy trucks rolling down a highway. As he dived at them, his machine gun firing, he heard another May Day call from the American B-26 in distress. This time the call was broken off by an explosion. Herrera turned and saw a ball of fire approximately one mile to his right.

Herrera had witnessed disaster for two more Americans: Thomas Willard (Pete) Ray and Leo Francis Baker. Ray had been a technical inspector at Hayes in Birmingham. He lived in Center Point and had maintained his pilot's proficiency rating by flying B-26s and F-84s in General Doster's Alabama guard unit. Baker, born in Boston, had been a flight engineer for Hayes and also worked hard at running two pizza parlors in Birmingham.*

Navy in Handcuffs

The Navy airmen on the carrier *Essex* had been confined to a maddening spectator role. On Tuesday Commander Mike Griffin landed his "Blue Blasters" A4D jet on the flight deck and came up to the bridge to report to Captain Searcy. Griffin had just overflown the beach area and helplessly watched the Brigade being driven back to the sea. Searcy was shocked by the pilot's appearance. Griffin's face was blue. Tears were running down it without restraint. He was so angry and upset that it took a couple of minutes before he could utter a word. "I hate to see a grown man cry, but I didn't blame him," Searcy said later. The captain was "surprised" that some of the pilots didn't take the battle into their own hands and drop bombs against orders. He "wouldn't have blamed them."

Earlier, Jim Forgy, the executive officer of the jets aboard the *Essex*,

*Dr. Férnandez Mell of Castro's inner circle of commanders found the remnants of the plane smoking heavily when he got there a few minutes later. Mell remembered his instructions to capture as many invaders as possible alive, especially any pilots. Leading some twenty militiamen, he came upon one of the pilots (Ray) holding a hand grenade. The American removed the firing pin and was ready to throw the grenade when a submachine gun blast killed him from two yards away. Mell and his group ran into a small swampy wooded area. He heard shouts: "Surrender! Surrender!" He yelled, "Don't shoot! Don't shoot!" He heard a shot followed by a burst of submachine gun fire. He was at the scene within seconds. A militiaman was standing over another body: a blond fair-skinned man wearing gray pants, white T-shirt and tennis shoes. He was still breathing. The doctor bent down. The man was clinically dead of multiple wounds up and down his body. Mell was furious. "Why did you shoot him?" he yelled at the militiaman. "He shot first!" Mell searched the body. He found a buffalo nickel; a U.S. pilot's license, number 0832321-M; and a Social Security card, number 014-07-6921, in the name of Leo Francis Bell, 148 Beacon Street, Boston, Massachusetts. (This was the identification given to Baker, one of four Alabama Air National Guard pilots killed that morning. On June 8, 1978, a spokesman for MINREX, the Cuban Foreign Ministry, told the author that Baker's body was still in a Havana morgue. Why was it never reported or released? "We're waiting for the U.S. government to claim it," he said.)

had flown reconnaissance with his wing man Tim Lanahan, still under orders only to report back the "unusual." He reported much that troubled him: he saw fires on the beach; bombers bombing just beyond the beach. He was mad. He was sure his Cuban "friends" were getting beaten, and he assumed he was free to act against unfriendly planes. No one had instructed him otherwise.

He was cruising at 25,000 feet when he spotted a Castro T-33. He "tallyhoed the guy." Within seconds, he "vectored in and got ready" with his 2.75 rocket pod. Both planes were diving for the ocean now. Forgy was "right on the guy's tail, right up his pipe." He had a radar gun lock on the T-33. Then he heard the air controller's voice from the *Essex*. Forgy had not been communicating with him for some time, but the controller was obviously following the action on radar, and his voice was frantic.

"Don't fire, don't fire!" he shouted. "Rules of engagement have been changed."

Forgy cursed, chased the T-33 to something like fifty feet above the sea with his weapons silent—and then let the enemy jet slip away.

Patrolling the coast on a later mission, Forgy called the air controller for permission to examine a trail of black smoke more than twenty miles away. The smoke was not difficult to spot; in the brilliant sunlight visibility often was as much as forty miles. Moving closer, he found a Castro Sea Fury "sitting right on the tail" of a B-26 of the Cuban Brigade. The bomber's starboard engine was on fire. The Sea Fury was closing in for the kill.

"I've got a Sea Fury shooting this B-26 down," Forgy radioed his controller. "Request permission to take positive action."

"Stand by."

The silence seemed to last for minutes while Forgy followed the Sea Fury, slightly to one side, hoping to distract the enemy.

"Negative," came the response from the *Essex*.

Cursing again vividly, Forgy took up a position just a few feet off the much slower Sea Fury's left wing and started "flying formation on him." If he couldn't shoot at the enemy, he would try to scare him away. The wing-to-wing escort lasted perhaps two minutes. Then the Sea Fury backed away and headed toward Cuba. Forgy joined up with the bomber and gave him the thumbs-up signal for "Are you OK?" The bomber pilot's thumb shot up cheerfully. The fire in his engine seemed to be going out. A plane loss had been prevented without a shot.

On the bridge of the carrier, Deacon Fickenscher, the admiral's man, was plagued by other troubles. The ultrasecret communications entailed special codes and equipment that introduced special problems. A system he had privately arranged with Commodore Crutchfield on the *Eaton* was working. The *Eaton* was the only ship constantly moving into Cuban waters. It was vital to know when it was operating there, subject to attack at any time. Whenever he entered Cuban territory, Crutchfield would say, "Red light" over the voice radio. When he left, he said, "Green light." On Wednesday at 6:30 A.M. Deacon received a message of about 250 words from Washington. It was a just-decoded order to launch four Skyhawks, which were supposed to protect B-26s headed for the beach. Deacon didn't know it, but these jets had just been specially released for limited combat by President Kennedy. The launch was scheduled for six-thirty, clearly no longer possible. The planes were airborne shortly before seven-thirty. Deacon knew they would almost certainly miss their rendezvous. He had done his best. Nobody could execute orders before they were received.* Obviously, communications with Washington were not working right.

Later that morning, Deacon began getting urgent messages from Admiral Burke. They came in the clear—uncoded. "What kind of attack?" they demanded to know. "Any damage?"

Fickenscher was mystified. It sounded as if the CNO thought an American vessel was under attack. Deacon knew of nothing like this. It took half an hour to clear up the confusion. Burke had insisted on setting up a special emergency voice code to let him know once every hour whether the fleet was OK or facing enemy action. The signal was two sets of two letters each. The letters changed every twelve hours. A junior officer had failed to change the code at the appointed time.

The same morning, Admiral Burke's demands for more information on the overall combat situation grew more insistent. The admiral had displayed irritation right along about lack of data. Frequently he asked questions that the *Essex* had already answered. Each time, Deacon retrieved a copy of his answer and asked the communications officer, "Did that message go out?" Each time the same conversation ensued: "Yes, it went out." "Was it received for?" "Yes, it was received for."

When this happened again Wednesday, Deacon thought to ask, "Who received for it?" The response was: "Londonderry, Ireland."

The problem was the single side band high-frequency radio which the carrier had just taken aboard in Norfolk. It was brand-new, and, because time was short, it was bolted to the deck by a makeshift jury rig that could cause trouble. So could the special air blowers needed to keep the

---

*After taking extensive testimony on this incident, the Taylor Commission attributed it to "an undetermined reason."

unit working. So could the sunspot activity and other atmospheric abnormalities prevalent in the Caribbean at that time of year. Fickenscher cursed. It was the old story: once something starts to go wrong, everything goes wrong.

In Norfolk, Admiral Dennison, the Atlantic Fleet commander, had read a copy of the complicated message authorizing temporary air cover from the *Essex*. He shook his head and reddened. "Do not seek air combat," it said. And: "Do not attack ground targets." What was the point? How can you protect somebody if you can't shoot? It was "ridiculous." "Bumpy Road," the Navy's code for the operation, should have been called "Quagmire."

The jet pilots aboard the *Essex* were not told that President Kennedy had personally authorized them to protect the Brigade bombers or, in fact, that there was anything unusual about this latest sortie at all. Mike Griffin, the commanding officer of the "Blue Blasters," led the flight: two sections, a total of four unmarked Skyhawks.

"We're going to rendezvous with some B-26s and escort them to the beach and wait for them to come out, and if anybody is following them, we'll take action," he said.

At the appointed time and place the four jets started circling very slowly—"dogging it at maximum endurance speed," as Jim Forgy, the executive officer, remembered. Circling in a holding pattern at twenty thousand feet, they slowed down so that their fuel lasted for almost one hour and forty-five minutes of circling and more circling. Sam Sayers found it "boring." He was his normally relaxed self. He had no reason to attach special importance to this mission. Forgy, increasingly resentful ever since he was first asked to fly without identification, found the circling frustrating in the extreme: "It was a complete comedy of errors bordering on lunacy."

When their gas was almost exhausted, Griffin radioed the *Essex* air controller, "This is Flying Tiger 301. . . . No joy or playmates"—no rendezvous, no B-26s—and all four planes headed home. It was one more mission that accomplished nothing.

Wednesday, April 19, was Ed Maddock's birthday. The air operations officer of the *Essex* spent most of it swearing and, like most of the pilots and air officers aboard, "goddamn near in tears." His air operations room was right next to the ship's CIC (Combat Information Center), so he could hear most of the radio traffic. What he heard was heartbreaking. The Brigade ashore kept pleading for help. The jets off the *Essex* kept pleading for authority to intervene in the battle. "What the hell are we here for, anyway?" Maddock asked himself. "We're just sitting with those planes designed for close air support."

More than once, he watched Mike Griffin and his pilots returning from their fruitless patrols, tears in their eyes, swearing, banging their helmets against the ship's bulkheads out of sheer frustration, constantly tempted to ignore orders and wipe out those few, slow Castro planes that were causing so much havoc. Maddock watched the pilots and thought, "I wish they weren't that careful."

Even the unexcitable Sam Sayers found that he "became very emotional about the whole thing." He could see gunfire on the beaches, "the guys being pushed back into the ocean," and all he could do was "fly up and down and watch them get massacred." This was hardly fulfilling his job as he saw it: "We were supposed to protect them, and yet they wouldn't let us do it." On one flight his section leader called the *Essex* air controller and put it bluntly: "Hey, these guys are getting the hell shot out of them! Let us go down and attack." The answer came quickly: "Negative."

Then Sayers' "Blue Blasters" squadron received an order that "staggered" him: they were to paint out the numbers and insignia of all their aircraft. Sayers found it difficult to believe that this "would ever happen." Ed Maddock thought it was preposterous: the AD4 was a plane with a "very distinctive" silhouette, and the U.S. was "the only country in the world" flying it. Harry Swinbourne, the assistant air officer of the *Essex,* also asked himself, "Who're we kidding?" and wondered whether the order was "really legal."

From the primary flight control station, which overlooked the flight deck like a control tower at a civilian airfield, Swinbourne watched a most unlikely sight. The order was to neutralize the silver-gray planes as rapidly as possible, but only dull-gray paint was aboard, and few paint brushes and no spray cans were found. The men went to work on the planes with moplike swabs. Swinbourne thought, "God, they look terrible!" More than his sense of the aesthetic was offended: American fighter planes were not supposed to deny their nationality.

Mess cooks and bakers were recruited to help on the swabs, and sometimes as many as two hundred of the ship's company were watching—muttering, swearing, shaking their heads. In less than two hours the amateur paint job was done and the squadron received orders, first, to fly reconnaissance over and behind the beaches, and, later, to help spot survivors of the Brigade who might be picked up by Navy vessels.

The new assignments made the pilots feel even worse. Sayers "didn't like flying around up there in an unmarked airplane at all." It was "silly" that he felt "sort of like going into battle without your flag waving," but that's exactly the way he did feel. It occurred to him that any pilot who was shot down might not be protected by the Geneva Convention and would "probably be shot as a spy or something."

And now the chances of being shot down had markedly increased. No American plane was attacked from the air at any time during the entire operation, but when Jim Forgy, the executive officer of the squadron, led flights over the beaches, he and his men repeatedly drew fire from the ground. The first time he was attacked, Forgy asked for permission to strike back and received the usual "Negative." After that, he just ignored the shooting. Overflying Cuba, the *Essex* pilots had almost no idea where they were going. Security about going to Cuba had been so superior that they were reduced to taking directions from one tattered Esso roadmap which someone happened to find aboard the carrier.

Infiltrators Abandoned

In Santiago de Cuba, José Basulto, the CIA's man in Oriente province, had worked at a leisurely pace. He had rented a room at a boardinghouse for students, taken physics and math courses at the university, and told everybody how much he hated the priests who had taught him in Boston. Following his instructions, he had called on a local doctor who had José's radio and code books buried separately under flower beds in his garden. The radio was in a waterproof black box measuring two by two feet. The doctor dug it out one night, along with the codes, when José identified himself by bringing him a bag of golf balls as a prearranged "present."

Whenever Basulto needed his radio, he kept it in a red suitcase which he stowed in the ancient gray Peugeot he had purchased and kept "so dirty nobody could look in." He had been regularly in touch with the CIA, whose operators sent him dates when he was to transmit. Each time, he was allowed ten minutes to establish communication and another ten for his messages, but there was little traffic. Once the CIA inquired about an iron smelter that had been out of commission for years. He was asked for—and supplied—details about gun emplacements at the entrance to the harbor and the fuel supply and types of planes at the airport.

Underground fighters in the nearby hills had asked him to arrange an aerial arms drop, but all they got was instructions on how to prepare for such a delivery, an art in which the resisters had long been trained.

Eventually, José received confirmation that a "pre-pack" with ten tons of weapons would be dropped April 18, so Saturday, April 15, he was in the town of Manzanillo, some thirty-seven miles west of Santiago de Cuba, to help the underground receive the arms.

By midmorning he was returning home in his Peugeot. He carried his fake CIA driver's license in the name of Ernesto Martínez and was ready to pose as a drug salesman with a bag of samples he had borrowed from another infiltrator. He did not have his radio along. There were signs of excitement on the road, but José did not stop until he was flagged down by militiamen, who frisked him and searched his car and all others on the road. There had been an air raid on Santiago de Cuba, he was told. It was the only word he ever had about Gus Ponzoa's bombing, before or after the event. He was never asked by the CIA for an assessment of the damage or any other impact of the raid.

No radio contact was scheduled for him until the seventeenth, but he was sure there must be instructions for him now. He rushed to pick up his radio and raced with it to the nearest place he could think of, the home of his relatives. They had not known that he was working for the underground and were understandably frightened. José gave them no choice. He set up the radio in a bedroom and hid the antenna as best he could between trees in the yard. Then he sent his "Q" signal, meaning "Is there any message for me?" No answer came.

At 11 A.M. Monday Basulto received a signal marked "QSP"—most urgent. José decoded it instantly: "A large well-armed force has landed in southern Las Villas Province," it began. It instructed him to "interrupt communications," "blow bridges" and arrange for an uprising.

Basulto had heard more news than that over the Castro radio many hours earlier, and now "half the town" was being arrested. He was totally disgusted, yet his caustic sense of humor still did not abandon him. He wired back: "Impossible to rise. Most patriots in jail. Thanks for your damned invitation. Closing transmission." He had three pounds of TNT hidden away, but it was clearly ridiculous to use them. He collected two friends from the local underground and said, "Let's go to the beach." They drove forty-five minutes out of town and went swimming. On the road they were stopped by troops, but their identification papers were not questioned. They spent the day at the beach, "had a ball," and told each other that they deserved "a break."

In Havana, infiltrator Edgar Sopo had moved into a young couple's apartment on the north side of town, where he kept five submachine guns, a case of hand grenades, and the script of the speech he would make after he seized the radio station. He had had trouble falling asleep and had finally dozed off when his hosts banged on his door around 5:30 on April 17. They shouted, "Wake up, wake up!"

"What happened?"

"Well, listen to the radio! These people say the landing has started!"

"No, no," Sopo shot back, "this is crazy! They're mistaken." His voice, normally very loud and penetrating, had risen to a roar. Then he relaxed.

He told himself that the Americans would never fail to let him know before starting the invasion. He thought that the combat he heard described on the radio was a premature uprising of a resistance group that had been plotting in Cienfuegos, the town closest to Girón on the invasion beach. When it became apparent that the real invasion had begun, Sopo still refused to become upset. He told his hosts, "The invasion is going to be so powerful, they don't need us."

His colleague Jorge Recarey quickly found out otherwise. He was hidden in a safe house in Varadero, a resort which is the point closest to the U.S., still waiting for orders to go ahead with the "something big" that he and his Havana friends had originally scheduled for the tenth. He was asleep on the morning of the seventeenth, when an old man who lived in the house awakened him at 3 A.M. and said, "Listen, young man, there's something on the radio that I want you to hear."

He could tell that the invasion was really on, and he was delighted. "Now we're going to get them," he thought. He did not stop to wonder why he had not been notified. When he was unable to reach anyone in Matanzas by phone, he quickly got a friend to drive him there in a 1959 Buick. He was going to join his newly trained guerrillas, blow up the railroad bridge, open the prison doors and put all their other careful plans into action.

It was a one-and-a-half-hour trip. The night was clear and gentle, the road deserted. Jorge listened to the news on the car radio—it sounded as if the invasion was making some headway—and held on to the book he always had with him. It was a technical volume on sugar-growing. Jorge had cut enough out of the pages to make room for the .22-caliber pistol he had bought for forty dollars in a shop on Twenty-second Street and Second Avenue Southwest before leaving Miami. It was not much of a weapon, but it felt comfortable to cradle it on his lap.

It was almost six o'clock and dawning when the Buick hit an intersection where one branch of the road from Matanzas forked off to Girón and the Bay of Pigs. Headed for the beaches, an enormous military convoy came rumbling down the road. The Castro forces were moving at top speed. There were trucks with troops, trucks with trailers, antiaircraft batteries, and more and more trucks with troops. The troops were singing and shouting, *"Viva la revolución!"* and "We're going to kill them all!" For more than three miles, right into Matanzas, bumper to bumper, without letup, the convoy raced, and Jorge Recarey could do nothing but watch from the Buick as the enemy rolled to crush his friends on the beaches.

"We're really going to get it," he said sadly to his young driver, who had developed a severe case of the shakes.

And when Jorge saw the convoy rolling across the very bridge he had been all set to blow up, he put his face into his hands and "cried like hell." It was hours before he could start to think about ways to get out of the predicament where Colonel Hawkins and the CIA had abandoned all the infiltrators.*

Castro Strikes Back

The phone in Castro's apartment had rung at 1:15 A.M. on Monday. Point One reported landings at Girón. Fidel had understood the implication at once. The isolated area with its very few roads was topographically "perfect" for setting up a government. The beachhead had to be wiped out at once, "in a few hours." He had to call Ramón Fernández.

Ramón José Fernández was asleep in his second-floor room at the militia cadet school in Managua, outside Havana, when a guard knocked and shouted, "The Commander in Chief is calling you!"

Six feet three and built like a basketball guard, Fernández was in charge of all militia training. The training was one of Fidel's many personal projects. Fidel called him frequently, though not usually so late at night.

There was no phone in Fernández' room. He pulled on pants and boots, went to his first-floor office and heard Fidel say, "They've already come!"

"They've already come? What?" Fernández was sleepy and confused.

---

*Jorge got a message to his mother in Arizona, and she arranged to have him picked up by a car sent from the Italian Embassy in Havana; he stayed there for eight months and was then able to leave for the U.S. Edgar Sopo smuggled himself into the Venezuelan Consulate by posing as a grocery delivery boy. José Basulto drove to Guantánamo and climbed over a ten-foot fence to safety in the U.S. naval base. Five of their fellow infiltrators were executed. Seven were still in prisons seventeen years later.

"The *mercenarios* have already come! They've landed at different points at the Zapata swamps!"

Fernández was silent. Fidel told him to go to the cadet school at Matanzas, sixty-five miles east of Havana, take its student battalion to the beaches, and confront the enemy without delay.

Fernández called for his new light-gray Toyota jeep, his driver and several of his staff. He had not yet finished dressing when Fidel was on the phone again. He told Fernández not to bother calling the school. He himself would phone and place the cadets on combat alert. Fernández should leave at once.

"Take a car and go to Matanzas at full speed," Castro said.

Fernández could not have been more eager to go. He realized there was no other unit near the invasion site. He would be the first commander at the front. All his life he had been preparing for such a role. Now thirty-seven, he had been first in his class at the Army Cadet School. Then he trained at the U.S. Army Field Artillery School, Fort Sill, Oklahoma. As a captain and principal of the cadet school, he had conspired against Batista and served two years as a political prisoner on the Isle of Pines. Only one deficiency in his record rankled. He had not been with Fidel in the Sierra Maestra. Here was his chance to make up for that.

But first he needed maps, and the storage room was locked. The man with the key could not be found. It took a while to break down the door. Fernández was putting on his pistol when Fidel called again.

"Are you still there? Are you still there?" Fidel shouted. "You haven't left yet?"

"No, Commander, I'm still getting dressed."

Shortly before 3 A.M. Fernández left with five other men jammed into his jeep. He told the driver to move at maximum speed, but he thought the Zapata landings were a secondary attack. The area was just too remote. He had been there for the first time on a trip with Fidel only weeks ago. They had had lunch at *la boca,* the mouth of the canal to Guama. He remembered Fidel's love for the area. He also remembered the mosquitoes. No, the main attack would surely hit around Havana, where there were still remnants of the bourgeoisie that might be in sympathy with an invasion.

When Fernández arrived at the Matanzas cadet school, he was told Fidel had phoned and was awaiting his call. Fernández immediately phoned Point One and told Castro that instructors from the school were seizing every truck in the area so that the cadets could have transportation.

Fidel said it was essential that they leave immediately. Fernández told him he still had to appoint heads of companies. The school was not organized as a combat unit. Fidel told him what road to take and rang off. His impatience could not have been plainer.

Angel Jimínez, twenty-two and movie-star handsome, was very sleepy. He was a cadet at the militia officers' school in Matanzas. During the previous night the cadets had been roused from bed by several alarms. Nothing ever happened. Now it was just past 3 A.M. and the recording of the bugle call for a general-combat alarm croaked over the school loudspeaker system.

Jimínez lined up, yawning, outside his barracks in his underwear. It was foggy. He could think of nothing except going back to sleep. Recently he had begun to learn about 82-millimeter mortars. He had never fired one. So far the instructor had only explained the parts. Now an officer called his name and appointed him mortar platoon chief. They all got dressed and climbed onto a diesel truck just commandeered from a nearby construction lot. The driver was a very frightened civilian.

Jimínez did not know where his convoy was headed or why. The only thing that was clear was that his truck was running out of gas. When they pulled into Coliseo, they filled up at a gas station. The man there seemed to know that something unusual was happening. He let Jimínez sign a receipt for the gas. Jimínez was pleasantly amazed. Whatever was going on must be not only unusual but serious.

Before nightfall his outfit counted twenty-two dead.

Captain Enrique Carreras sat alert and strapped up in Sea Fury No. 541 on the runway at San Antonio base twenty miles west of Havana at about 4 A.M. The operations officer drove up in a jeep and told the captain about the invasion. Carreras was surprised. He had been thinking of air attacks, not landings. They had started discussing priorities—which planes should attack troops and ships, and which should defend the base—when word came that Castro wanted to speak to Carreras personally.

The pilot unstrapped himself and ran 150 yards to the control tower building. An ordinary civilian phone was suspended from the wall. He was tense but not surprised that the Commander in Chief was calling. Everyone knew that Fidel liked to keep in touch. Hadn't he come around only a week ago to tell them to disperse the planes?

"Commander, give me my orders," Carreras said.

The response left no doubt about Fidel's decisiveness and priorities.

"At this moment a landing is taking place at Playa Girón," he said. "But I want you to sink those ships! Don't let those ships go!"

"I'll fulfill your orders," said the pilot.

"We shall win," said Fidel.

"We shall win," repeated Carreras.

Castro was preoccupied by two interlocking objectives. He wanted the supply ships sunk before they could unload. Then the beachhead had to collapse and the provisional government wouldn't settle in. He also wanted his few planes in the air. Then they couldn't be destroyed on the ground. If they were eliminated, the enemy would control the skies. Then more ships would come. They would be unmolested. Then it would only be a question of time for the feared provisional government to dig in after all. He had to control the air. Only Carreras could do that.

Carreras had no combat experience, but he was thirty-eight, had four children,* and was by far the most seasoned of Castro's pilots. Professorial in manner, he had been trained at Kelly Field, Texas, in 1945. In 1953 he had studied at the Air University, Maxwell Field, Montgomery, Alabama. In 1954 and 1955 he had trained at Craig Air Force Base, Lackland Air Force Base and Nellis Air Force Base, and had become the first Latin American to fly at supersonic speed. His U.S. experience had soured him on Americans. His trainers acted like "supermen" and made Latinos feel like "Indians in jackets."

Carreras thought about Castro's order to sink the invasion ships and leave the landing craft and the troops alone for the time being. He would fly his Sea Fury, not a jet. The Sea Fury was slow, but it carried bombs. It was their best weapon against ships. His wing man would also fly a Sea Fury. He designated a third pilot to fly a B-26. He told them of Fidel's order. They waited in their planes until six-thirty, about twenty minutes prior to daylight. They would fight at dawn.

Rafael del Pino, the youngest T-33 pilot, was very nervous. He had never even fired from his plane in target practice. Here he was flying against experienced pilots from the United States, an aggressor he had previously respected. After he had been arrested in an anti-Batista demonstration in 1954 while still in high school, his father had sent him to a boarding school, Harrison Chilhowee Baptist Academy in Seymour, Tennessee, near the Great Smokies outside Knoxville. The people there had been humble Baptists, like himself, and he liked them.

He was also uneasy about his outfit's planes. The automatic starters on the old British Sea Furies didn't work. The mechanics had to start their

*Eventually he would have ten.

single engine each time with a boot, a socket and a rope, like an old outboard motor. The burners on the T-33s were so worn that the engines developed excessive temperatures. Sometimes there was a flame-out and crash on takeoff. Del Pino had barely walked away from such a crash of T-33 No. 701. When trouble later developed on No. 713, the mechanics went to the wreck of No. 701 and found enough parts to patch up No. 713. Then No. 713 had a flame-out. Now del Pino was rooting for the plane he was flying, No. 711.

When he spotted an enemy B-26, he tensed. His teacher, Carreras, had told him to shoot only from "real close," when he could see the other pilot's helmet. He opened fire from less than two hundred yards and kept firing when a fragment of the enemy plane hit the nose of his jet. He thought that the B-26 had a tail gun (the Brigade planes had none, to keep weight down and flying time up), and that the gun was firing at him.

In a moment, the enemy plane hit the bay, and del Pino realized that he had made still a second mistake. He should have jettisoned his rockets before attacking. The fragment that hit him could have blown them up.

Point One headquarters called Fernández Mell at the doctor's Havana apartment shortly after 5 A.M. "The invasion is on!" Paratroopers had landed near Girón. Fidel thought it was the main attack. Mell took his pistol, rifle, backpack, a sweater, a canteen of water, and drove his 1960 Buick to Point One. Fidel was pacing in the office of Sergio del Valle, the director of headquarters operations. He needed someone to lead 120-millimeter artillery batteries to the beach area. Mell volunteered and set off to Palpite in the swamps. When he arrived, Fidel, like the ubiquitous Scarlet Pimpernel of fiction, was already there by the side of the road, pacing.

In San Pedro de Mayabón, fifty miles north of Girón and the Bay of Pigs, there was a knock on Félix Duque's door at 6 A.M. "*Commandante!* There's been a landing at the swamps!"

Duque, whom Castro had appointed troubleshooter for finishing the Girón resort cottages, was no longer in agrarian reform. He was running a 112,000-acre vegetable enterprise. He liked wearing his fatigues, his major's insignia and his pistol. The appearance was misleading. It was for old times' sake. Duque did not think of himself as a military man. He no longer held any rank, not even in the militia. The Army was "interesting" when there was action. In peacetime he hated it: "Too many rules." But action! Action he loved.

Pulling on his clothes and pistol, Duque ran to his bedroom closet and grabbed the bazooka and six shells he had kept there since the Sierra Maestra. He could never hit anything with a bazooka. He had proven that again one Sunday recently when he and his wife, Elida, fired it in back of their house the way nonsocialists practice tennis. She didn't hit anything, either. Nevertheless, a bazooka was handy for a fight against *bandidos*.

It sounded to him as if the landing was another infiltration attempt. There had been so many of them. The great noise of a bazooka would scare those *bandidos*. As soon as he maneuvered the bazooka into the front seat and turned on the car radio—as an important manager he drove a 1959 Buick—he knew this was something bigger. He picked up four buddies of his vegetable farm, all militiamen with rifles, and headed for the swamps at a hundred miles an hour.

When they reached Colón there was "an atmosphere of mobilization." In Aguada de Pasajeros they heard shelling. The entire population seemed to be milling around the streets. Duque was trying to pinpoint where the action was centered. He still could not be certain. It did not occur to him to call anyone for orders. There was talk about fighting at San Blas. Who needed orders? There was no time to lose. The road through Yaguaramas was the good one. The road through Covadonga was shorter. He roared off to Covadonga.

When Ramón Fernández' jeep, running well ahead of his militia battalion from the Matanzas cadet school in its borrowed trucks, stopped at the militia post in Jovellanos, where Highway 3-20 turns south toward the swamp area, the local captain handed him the phone. Fidel was on the line. He wanted to be reassured that the battalion was following quickly. "Establish your command post at the Central Australia sugar mill," he said. "There's a phone in the manager's office. Pick up the phone there, and I'll be at the other end."

Heading with his two other planes through darkness toward the beaches—they had their lights on because he did not want to collide with his inexperienced fellow pilots—Captain Carreras did not worry about the size of the force he would face. Overflying the Bay of Pigs at dawn, he was stunned. Many shadows were darting about at sea; they were landing craft. Several large ships became visible in the dim morning light, one of them deep in the bay. From four thousand feet he made out two small "warships." Immediately he heard the coughing of the machine guns that the CIA had not wanted to install. Carreras thought it was antiaircraft artillery.

It was "a Normandy invasion"! He had seen many documentaries of those landings. Although he normally evaluated experiences in a literal, even pedantic style, no other comparison came to mind. Understandably, his perspective was vastly different from that of President Kennedy or Bissell. He thought of his creaky planes, his green pilots, and, as he radioed his other men to fly guard overhead and started diving at what later turned out to be the *Houston*, he thought of his defective gyroscope.

He needed speed to dodge the enemy fire. The weight of his bombs was increasing his wind resistance. He had to drop them first. To do this efficiently, he had to get "very close" because of the defective bomb sight. He dropped both bombs and climbed. Both were near-misses. He began diving again. When he saw the stern of the ship, he released all his eight rockets. Gaining altitude, he saw oil pouring out of the ship. It started moving. He zeroed in for a strafing run with his machine guns. This time he saw the water all around the ship changing color. The accompanying warship—it was the *Barbara J.*—started out of the bay.

Carreras' fuel was dwindling fast. He headed toward San Antonio. Overflying the base, there was enough gas for two belly rolls, the sign of victory.

Castro had not yet committed the bulk of his forces. He was still wondering: were the Girón and Playa Larga landings really the main ones? The microwave radio stations there had fallen silent. Were these perhaps diversionary attacks designed to fool and trap him into a commitment in a side show? It was still too dark for effective reconnaissance. Were there more ships requiring more air attacks for which he might have to redeploy his tiny air force?

Then came word of paratroop landings in the neighborhood. That was his signal. He decided the swamp landings had to be the real enemy effort. He ordered massive troop and artillery movements to reinforce the Matanzas cadets. The battle was truly on. Everything now depended on Fernández and his cadets getting into action, and fast.

Fernández' jeep pulled up at the dirty pastel-green administration building of the Central Australia sugar mill outside Jagüey Grande shortly after 8 A.M. The manager said a lot of local men wanted to fight, but there were only eight rifles. Many paratroopers were reported in the area. The town was supposed to be surrounded.

Fernández hid his jeep, sent out patrols and called Castro, who said he was not to leave the phone under any circumstances. Speed was essential. The enemy had been spotted seven hours ago and as yet only the air force was fighting.

Back over the Bay of Pigs in his Sea Fury shortly after 8 A.M. for the second mission of the morning, Captain Carreras forgot the most important lesson he taught his student pilots about combat. "Use your necks!" he told them. He wanted them not just to look down at targets but to look all around, especially overhead.

That morning Carreras had eyes only for the *Houston*. When he made sure it had stopped with the stern sinking, it was almost too late. Overhead and from the right rear, a B-26 opened fire. The tracers passed just over Carreras' cabin. From below and to the left, another B-26 attacked. Carreras could see both pilots' helmets all too clearly. The first plane passed close under him. Carreras opened fire. The left engine of the B-26 started smoking. The other plane sought refuge behind the friendly fire of the ships.

Carreras remembered Castro's order to go after the ships and went diving at what turned out to be the *Río Escondido,* carrying the Brigade communication van. He hit it with all eight rockets. It exploded, but as he climbed his engine started failing. It trailed little flames. He throttled down and limped to base, where the mechanics found cylinder No. 1 perforated. This time he took no chance on belly rolls. When he jumped to the ground, his legs were shaking badly.

In his Buick, Duque, his four vegetable farmers and his bazooka braked to a halt in a cloud of dust on the main street of Covadonga shortly before 9 A.M. There seemed to be a war on. Families were evacuating. Planes had been bombing up ahead. People talked of paratroopers landing near San Blas. Paratroopers? *Bandidos* had no paratroopers. Duque began to think he might be facing the United States Army and Air Force.

A dozen militiamen gathered around him. They said *mercenarios* were nearby, advancing. The militiamen wanted to defend the local sugar mill. They couldn't agree how. There were no weapons to arm more people. What could fewer than twenty men do?

Leaving his Buick parked on the main street, Duque shouldered his bazooka and started marching down the San Blas road at the head of his force. He thought about the Sierra. He would set up an ambush, just as he had with Fidel in the mountains. When he found a windmill at the entrance to a curve, he told his men to take cover behind a drinking trough for animals. He instructed them not to shoot until he shot first; to save their ammunition ("don't shoot for the hell of it"); and that he hoped for prisoners so he could disarm them and distribute the weapons back in Covadonga.

Almost immediately, two enemy trucks advanced slowly into the curve. Duque let them come closer. Then he fired his bazooka. The grenade landed about eight feet short, but it ricocheted into the lead truck. After a twenty-minute firefight the enemy withdrew, leaving behind the trucks, two submachine guns, several pistols, a lot of ammunition, backpacks, canteens, concentrated American food and hastily bundled-up parachutes. There was blood on the trucks and on the ground.

Back in Covadonga, Duque thought to call Army headquarters in Santa Clara up north. He knew the man who answered. They had fought together in the Sierra. Duque said he had made contact with the enemy. He was told to stay put and organize the defense of the area.

"How many are you?" asked headquarters.

"Twenty."

"Hold at all costs!"

"OK." Duque did not ask about the general situation. He felt it was none of his business; he "wasn't an active member of the armed forces." And he had work to do. All Cubans did, and they were doing it in a way that would have given pause to Bissell, Colonel Hawkins and others with low regard for Cubans.

At 10 A.M. Fidel was on the phone again to Fernández at Central Australia. He had been calling almost every ten minutes. Fernández was finally able to tell him that the Matanzas cadet battalion had arrived, as well as the 225th Militia Battalion—country people armed only with M-52 Czech rifles and only twenty bullets for each weapon.

Fidel ordered Fernández to send the cadet battalion south at once to take "Parite." Fernández checked his map. He found no such town. Fidel repeated the order. Fernández still could not find the town. Fidel told him they had both driven through it recently when they had lunch at Guama. Fernández still could not find it. Finally both men went down their maps town by town and found "Palpite." "That's the town," said Fidel. "The map is wrong!" It was.

The 117th Militia Battalion arrived in Covadonga on trucks from Havana at noon. Duque, impatient to get moving, was told to take two companies and advance to Girón. He felt like a field marshal. With the infantry came 122-millimeter howitzers, 185-millimeter cannons and 137-millimeter antiaircraft artillery, all recently arrived from the Soviet

Union. Duque had never seen such weapons, much less used them. The gun crews didn't appear experienced, either. The antiaircraft men looked as if they were not yet out of high school.

Barely on the road, they were overflown at very low altitude by a B-26 with Cuban markings. It circled. Duque felt protected. The plane started strafing. One truck caught fire. Three men died. Duque hit the ground, cursing lengthily. He was not as upset at the duplicity as he was at the lack of a radio to pass a warning up the line.

Taking along his mortars, he advanced two miles toward San Blas and hit another enemy stronghold. His mortars fired until they ran out of ammunition. Duque sent a jeep back for more. When the jeep returned, it was blown up by shells from a 57-millimeter recoilless gun. Five men were killed in this engagement.

Duque reached the outskirts of San Blas at sundown. He had underestimated the defenders. They were well dug in and had tanks. He was on a straight stretch of road with swamps on both sides. It was time for his men to get some sleep in the bushes. Duque thought about how to use his arsenal in the morning. Most of his artillery was too far in the rear. His bazooka was useless. So was the flamethrower that had joined him—the first that Duque had ever seen. It wasn't going to be easy to advance to Girón. San Blas was in the way.

Fernández phoned Fidel shortly after noon and reported that Palpite had been taken. Castro was exuberant. "We've already won the war!," he shouted. He told Fernández about the ships sunk and of planes shot down at the beaches. "Let's go take Playa Larga right now," he said. Then he said Fernández should wait right there. Fernández inferred that the Commander in Chief would come to take charge personally. This was indirectly confirmed when he called Point One in Havana a few minutes later and asked for Fidel again. "He's not here now," said a cautious voice over the open phone line.

Fernández soon learned that Fidel's exultation about the winning of the war had been premature. The attack toward Playa Larga was stalled. *Mercenario* planes were doing considerable damage. Castro arrived at Central Australia about 3:15 P.M. Antiaircraft artillery rolled in shortly afterward. Finally Fidel authorized Fernández to leave the phone and proceed to Palpite. He was taking over himself at headquarters. Fernández had pinned up some maps on the wall and wanted to take them along. "No, no," said Fidel. "What do you think? Leave them here. *You* go!" Fernández hurried off without maps.

At sundown he received a handwritten order from Castro in the

Palpite *bohío* he had taken over as headquarters. The message said that Castro was sending another twelve howitzers so that the attack on Playa Larga could be preceded by *"un barraje infernal,"* a hellish barrage. Almost immediately, Castro appeared personally to arrange his barrage and to dispatch the 111th Battalion toward San Blas. Fernández and his staff were upset. They were eager for Castro to leave at once. The town was being shelled. Constantly there were more dead and wounded. This was no place for a commander in chief.

Shortly after midnight, Castro traveled by jeep to the junction of two dirt roads through the swamps, a little more than a mile west of Playa Larga. At 1:30 A.M. he was pacing, waiting for a force of about twenty tanks. The attack on Playa Larga was going too slowly to suit him. He had other plans. He "knew every single road there" because of his frequent vacation and inspection trips to the area. He took pride in his "good memory for roads." The tanks could use the side roads to bypass Playa Larga, take it from the rear, and plunge on toward Girón. The tanks were late. He kept pacing.

When they finally arrived, they brought a message from field headquarters in the Central Australia mill. Havana reported another landing at Bahia Honda on the north coast of Pinar del Río province west of Havana. Fidel was surprised.

"Is it verified?" he asked. He was told that it was.

"How strange," he said. Everything indicated he was facing the main enemy force right where he was. He pondered. Had the enemy sent a reserve force from Miami? The message from Havana said contact had been made with the enemy at the new site.

"Well," Fidel said, "it seems like the main battle is going to take place near Havana." He left instructions for tank attacks over the side roads he knew so well and rushed back to Point One. Arriving there at dawn, he was told no enemy force had been found in Pinar del Río, after all—and that the tank attack he had ordered over his side roads was not taking place. The local commander simply did not know those useful little roads.

Castro had fallen for a CIA trick. The agency men called it a "dog and pony show." Eight boats, thirty-five to forty feet long, each towing several smaller craft, all manned by agency personnel, had left Miami loaded with secret electronic gear. Beginning about five miles offshore, the boats dispersed. Some went to the edge of the shore, but none touched land and no men left their craft.

From this network of floating electronic stations the operators set off a sequence of lights, sound effects and electronic signals that was supposed to look to the Cubans ashore—and to any possible radar—as if a large invasion force were moving in. Later, the equipment simulated fighting ashore. The deception was flawless. By daybreak the "invasion" had evaporated.

In his Palpite *bohío*, Fernández learned that Castro was leaving the front but that his interest in the operation remained as intensive as that of a company commander. "I am solving the problems of the ammunition for the cannons," his latest message from Central Australia said. "The other tanks will reach Australia in the morning. [Major] Augusto [Martínez Sánchez, whose civilian job was Minister of Labor] will remain at Australia. I will have to leave for Havana in a little while. I shall be in constant contact with you. Send me news constantly about the development of operations. Forward! Fidel."

Shortly before dawn, an eight-point order from Fidel, dispatched at 4:40 A.M., reached Fernández through Martínez. It gave step-by-step instructions for deploying the tanks. Point eight was: "Fidel says Playa Larga has to be taken *sin excusa"*—without excuse.

Stuck along the road three hundred yards from San Blas, Duque, still shouldering his bazooka, decided not to wait for his main artillery force. He wanted to get on to Girón. He lined up two cannons and some antiartillery guns in the soggy ground by the road and ordered them to fire straight into the twenty or so houses of the settlement. They kept firing until shell casings were piled up four feet high and the guns had sunk deep into swamp soil. He entered San Blas at 8 A.M. and found mostly rubble, dust—and booby traps that killed two of his men.

He gave his bazooka to a man in a heavy weapons platoon. It was too heavy, and he really was no good with it.

He was sitting in his jeep, writing a report to his rear command post to let them know he was about to start on the last four miles to Girón, when a jeep arrived with a message from the commanding officer of a nearby tank unit. It said he should stay where he was and not try to take San Blas.

"That's crazy!" he yelled. "I've already taken San Blas!" War had been less complicated in the Sierra. At the Bay of Pigs, everybody was uninformed and confused. At least Duque was beginning to tell that perhaps his side was winning.

With Playa Larga in his hands, Fernández, still pursued by Castro's orders, was busy reorganizing his troops. Two new messages arrived from Central Australia headquarters. Both started: *"Dice Fidel"*—"Fidel says." The first, at 10:10 A.M., told him to advance to Girón. The second, at 12:15 P.M., was marked "Urgent" and admonished him "not to waste time or the opportunity to finish with these people." He was to seize Girón by 6 P.M. that day, Tuesday. The grip around the beachhead was tightening.

Fernández had dispatched two battalions toward Girón when an "urgent" five-point message arrived at 6:15 P.M. from Central Australia, again beginning "Fidel says . . ." Fidel was saying that this was "the psychological moment" to pursue the enemy forces "ferociously." Second, they were "totally surrounded." Third, another commander was advancing toward Girón from the east, and Fernández had better "hurry up or he is going to get there before you." Fourth, "Now or never is the moment." Fifth, "Send information." The message was signed *"Muerte al invasor"*—"Death to the invader."

Fernández shook his head. His troops had another twenty miles to go. The enemy might be surrounded, but you'd never know it from the resistance his men were meeting all along the road to Girón. It looked like a long twenty miles.

In San Blas, Duque decided he'd better find his tanks and tell them not to fire at him and his men in the town he was not supposed to have taken. Driving his jeep along a side road shortly before midnight, accompanied by one of his captains, he turned a curve, heard tanks, signaled with his headlights and braked right in front of them. He had never seen tanks so close up. Men in spotted camouflage suits moved up on both sides of the road. They had to be *mercenarios*, but they were too surprised to point their guns at him.

"Who are you?" asked one.

"Duque."

"What are you doing here?"

"I think I made a mistake."

He was disarmed and taken in a 1958 Oldsmobile convertible to Girón—where he found "hell." Artillery fire and air raids never seemed to stop. His interrogators refused to believe that he worked in an agricultural enterprise and had taken San Blas without tanks. Pepe San Román and Artime came to question him. They also refused to believe his story. Sitting on a pile of sand and concrete blocks outside a beachfront cottage marked "G-2" with a crudely hand-lettered sign, Duque listened while San Román and Artime shouted at some officers to get back to the front. A radio man was shouting in English into a hand microphone.

Suddenly Duque saw jets overhead. The atmosphere on the beach changed abruptly. Everybody cheered and waved. Duque was told that the planes were promised "reinforcements." He was not upset, because he "didn't know what was going on." Toward midafternoon the atmosphere changed again. The invaders became depressed. One changed into civilian clothes near the G-2 building. Others got into boats to escape and were strafed by planes. Duque became uneasy. The confusion was dangerous. As a prisoner, he might yet get killed by "friendly" fire. He was determined to get away.

Shortly abandoned by his fleeing captors, he walked away. Later that day he met up with Fidel, who introduced him to some Cuban journalists. "That man has more lives than a cat," Castro said. Duque was pleased. He was also anxious to get home. He took a jeep to Covadonga and got into his Buick. It had waited for him, dusty but undamaged, just where he had left it on the main street three days earlier.

On Wednesday, Rafael del Pino took off at 1 P.M. for another attack against Girón. This time he faced an entirely novel situation at the beach. It amazed him. He saw a destroyer offshore. It had to be an American ship. He had instructions not to attack U.S. ships or planes unless he was attacked first. But between the destroyer and shore he spotted a number of small craft and a lot of floating wreckage. He concluded that he was seeing another landing—reinforcements for the invaders ashore.

Diving to an altitude of little over a hundred yards, he strafed the little boats. He did not want to miss any opportunity to destroy them. He saw his tracers hitting the boats. He thought the destroyer would fire at him. Instead, it was moving away.

Five minutes later, climbing and heading for base, he radioed: "San Antonio, this is seven-eleven. Reporting new landing."

The base replied, "Roger."

Del Pino had spotted the *Eaton* and had no way of knowing that a new landing could not have been farther from the mind of Commodore Crutchfield on the bridge. Crutchfield had been thoroughly impressed by his orders not to linger in enemy waters any longer than absolutely necessary. In response to the mounting pressure from Washington for better information on the combat situation, he had been reconnoitering and had taken the *Eaton* almost all the way into the Bay of Pigs. He had passed the *Houston* and reported its desperate condition. Now he was hurrying away from shore.

Del Pino's news of a second landing reached Sergio del Valle, Castro's director of headquarters operations, at Point One while Castro was driving back to the beaches to resume charge at the front. He was out of contact with headquarters; there was no radio in his car.

Del Valle was torn. The message spoke of no U.S. warships. It said only that ships offshore were lowering boats.* "A spirit of decision, of fighting" pervaded headquarters. Still, with the Commander in Chief out of reach, he and his men discussed using planes and artillery against the reported landing but postponed action. It was clearly a crisis moment.

About an hour later, Castro reached a major town, Jovellanos, ducked into a store and phoned del Valle.

"What is the news?" he asked.

Del Valle described the "second landing."

"No," said Castro. "It's an evacuation. We must stop it." He was acting on instinct. He was sure the invaders had already been defeated. In such a situation it would be "very difficult" to organize another attack. He was aware that he might "create a global conflict" at that moment. He did not want to do so. He wanted only to destroy the evacuation craft and told del Valle to give the necessary orders. World War III had been avoided.

Major Fernández felt disgusted. He had been eager to take Girón by 6 P.M. Tuesday, as Fidel ordered. Now it was Wednesday afternoon, and he was stalled about two and a half miles away from final victory over the invaders. The new road along the water was excellent, but the thorny brush was impenetrable on the left; the shoreline less than twenty yards on the right was so rocky that it was difficult to find secure footing for his artillery. He was at the head of almost two thousand men, but the terrain kept them bottled up. Enemy fire was heavy. There were a lot of casualties. His men were thirsty and exhausted.

They were marching again during a lull in the shelling at 2:10 P.M. Suddenly a staff captain pointed out two warships at sea. The two men ran to a grassy knoll under a tree off the left side of the road. Fernández peered through his Zeiss field glasses. The ships were definitely destroyers.† Nobody in the area had destroyers except the United States Navy. They were less than two miles away, definitely in Cuban waters, and advancing rapidly. Their guns were uncovered. Many small

---

*No boats were leaving the *Eaton*. Del Pino's radio message may have become embroidered as it passed down the line. Possibly del Valle, reconstructing the incident with Castro's help in 1978, confused it in part with the scene of the following day when destroyers lowered launches for rescue operations.

†The *Eaton* and the *Murray*.

boats were moving between shore and the ships. Some seemed to be coming, others going. Fernández thought there must be forty of them, perhaps fifty.

He scribbled a note to Central Australia headquarters reporting that reinforcements were landing for the invaders and asking for another battalion of infantry and a battalion of tanks. Digging furiously through his pockets for pen and paper, he lost the keys for his car in Havana. His note went off by motorcycle messenger. By now, his troops had stopped along the water, pointing and talking excitedly about the ships. "Everyone wanted to fire."

Fernández "could have hit them without any doubt." He had no instructions on how to deal with American ships. Earlier, he had spotted American jets. He had ordered them fired upon, unsuccessfully, but that was different. The planes were "violating our air space and taking part in the intervention." If he had hit destroyers some distance away and they had claimed they were merely patrolling in international waters, there could have been "transcendent consequences."

Fernández was very conscious that he had to be "a responsible officer." He held no grudge against the United States. He had been treated with kindness during his training at Fort Sill and even had fun, including a mad three-day seven-hundred-mile round trip to the Mardi Gras in New Orleans. But he was not about to give the commanders of those destroyers a convenient excuse to initiate reprisals and escalate the war. Also, "it was not logical to think that two destroyers would attack by themselves." They would have gone in with air support, and the U.S. jets had not attacked.

He did not reach this conclusion at once. At first, keeping his field glasses trained on the guns of the onrushing ships, he thought the destroyers might possibly attack. When they slowed and "almost stopped," he began to think they would not fire. It was "the most dramatic moment" of the war. It was very lonely. He keenly missed having some other responsible person to exchange opinions with.

The pressure around him mounted. His men kept demanding to fire. They resented the casualties they had suffered. Fernández had three 85-millimeter howitzers and six mortars. He ordered them lined up on his right, almost directly at the water. On his left he lined up his three armored Soviet half-tracks with their self-propelled guns. Girón was forgotten for the moment. He ordered his guns to fire individually— only at the small boats; he thought they might be bringing "another brigade." No one was to fire at the destroyers. Fernández kept watching through his glasses to be sure they were not being hit. At that moment, about twenty more 85-millimeter howitzers arrived. Their commanding officer also begged to shoot at the destroyers. Fernández ordered the guns to join his lineup and to follow his previous orders. His new front now stretched for some 150 yards.

The discussion about firing on the destroyers did not last long. A teacher of military cadets all his professional life, Fernández had the lecturer's voice, the commander's manner and the uninterruptibility that kept students and subordinates moving his way without much question.

Then Fernández saw planes of his air force also attacking the small boats. He was delighted. It was the first time during the entire battle when he had seen friendly planes.

The destroyers turned away after about thirty minutes, Fernández estimated later. It did not seem so at the time: "It never seemed to end."

Confusion in Washington

When first word of the invasion had reached Washington, even James Reston of *The New York Times* was sold on the line put out by the CIA in the name of the uninformed Cuban Revolutionary Council. Attributing his reporting to "reliable information reaching here," Reston wrote from Washington that no "invasion" had taken place. The action was on a much smaller scale, involving only two hundred to three hundred men and mostly to land supplies for the underground. The U.S. authorities were not sure of the fate of the landing parties, he reported, because Cubans "have assumed control" over the operations.

To the President, the situation looked terrible but not irretrievable on the evening of D-Day. The beachhead's survival seemed to depend on ammunition resupplies. The ammo ships had gone fifteen miles out to sea, he was told, but would come back that night. U.S. Navy ships might have to be used, after all. Kennedy still didn't want to be chicken. "I'd rather be an aggressor than a bum," he told his brother Robert.

The Attorney General thought the President "was prepared to go as far as necessary to assure success." The immediate problem was that the White House was consistently five to seven hours behind in its battle information. When it arrived, it was fragmentary. Who could make intelligent decisions? It seemed as if this was not yet time for drastic moves.

Toward 9 P.M. on Monday, as even the fragmentary news began to spell out total disaster on the beaches, Bissell remembered that Dulles was due back in the United States momentarily from his weekend with the Young Presidents' Organization.

"You'd better get out to the airport and brief AWD," he told Dick Drain.

Driving a four-year-old CIA-owned Chevrolet, Drain arrived at Friendship Airport in Baltimore shortly before Dulles' small agency plane taxied to a stop on the ramp. He drove to planeside as the director got out, smiling, wearing a dinner jacket, followed by his wife and a young aide.

Drain stepped forward to shake hands. "I'm Dick Drain. I was sent to brief you, sir."

"Oh, yes, Dick, how are you?"

Dulles was relaxed and affable. Drain drew him aside.

"Well, how is it going?" asked the director.

"Not very well, sir."

"Oh, is that so?" He put on what Drain always called Dulles' "Jean Hersholt look"—the jolly but quizzical expression made famous by the old character actor.

Mrs. Dulles and the aide were sent off in Drain's Chevy so that Drain could brief the director privately in Dulles' Cadillac.

"Well, what's your news?" inquired the director.

"It's a fast-breaking situation, sir," Drain began. "Things could have changed since I left, but we're hanging on by our fingernails."

The director's eyebrows rose. He puffed on his pipe.

"Today's air strike was killed," Drain reported.

"Why did they do that?" the director inquired softly.

"Stevenson was raising hell with the President," Drain said. "If you're asking my guess, my guess is this thing is all going to hell."

The rest of the twenty-five-minute ride to Dulles' Georgetown home passed largely in silence. Dulles continued to seem unperturbed. Drain was astounded at the director's lack of reaction.

Finally Drain ventured, "If it isn't presumptuous of me, sir, I wish your brother were still alive." For eight months prior to John Foster Dulles' death, Drain had served as special assistant to President Eisenhower's Secretary of State. He had been in charge of liaison with the CIA. The Secretary had been cantankerous to work for, but he was never subdued and indecisive like Rusk.

The CIA director nodded, but his thoughts seemed to have strayed elsewhere. Drain was becoming increasingly uncomfortable.

When the Cadillac drove up at Dulles' home, the director asked

Drain to come in and have a drink. Drain declined politely, but the boss clearly wanted company.

"Do come in," he said. "Have a drink. We need a drink."

Settled with a scotch in the director's library, Drain felt certain that the boss would finally quiz him about details of the CIA's worst debacle and then rush off to the phone. Instead, a scene ensued that Drain found so unreal he could never forget a minute of it.

"Dick, you served in Greece, didn't you?" Dulles asked. "I have to go to the White House tomorrow to a reception for [Greek Prime Minister Constantine] Caramanlis. Can you refresh my memory about him?"

Drain's jaw almost dropped, but he sipped on his drink and managed to say, "Well, sir, let me remind you he's deaf as hell . . ."

(In Moscow, at approximately the same hour, *Pravda* reported that Allen W. Dulles, the notorious American master spy, had absented himself from Washington and gone to Puerto Rico to direct the Bay of Pigs operation from a secret command post.)

Walt Whitman Rostow, Mac Bundy's assistant and old chum from Yale, attended his first meeting on Cuba at 7 A.M. Tuesday in the Cabinet Room of the White House. At the far end of the table sat three other friends, all "evidently shaken": Allen Dulles, whom Rostow had known since OSS days in World War II; General Cabell, with whom he had worked on air plans during the war; and Bissell, his revered former professor. Near Rostow sat Bundy and Major General Chester V. (Ted) Clifton, the President's military aide. On the other side of the table, at the center, sat Kennedy, looking isolated, very alone.

Dulles reported that the operation was failing. The Brigade was trapped on the beaches. Castro was moving strong forces to encircle and overwhelm them. Bissell filled in details. The President asked a few questions but offered no comment. He looked steeled for a disaster—with the New Frontier less than ninety days old.

Afterward Rostow said to Bundy, "Mac, if you and the President want me to help you mop up this mess, I'll be glad to do so."

Later Bundy told him, "Maybe you ought to go over to CIA headquarters and monitor what's going on."

Rostow left immediately for Quarters Eye.

When Harlan Cleveland reported from the State Department to the White House later that morning, the Cabinet Room had been turned into an emergency command post. Notes and newspapers littered the table. Maps were displayed on easels; each Navy vessel was represented by a tiny magnetic ship model. Military and civilian assistants rushed in and out through three doors with urgent messages and bits of bad news freshly torn from wire service news tickers. Ranking officials ducked out periodically in search of telephones or coffee.

Off and on, the President and Robert Kennedy were there all day. Hour by hour, the news worsened. Six to ten men sat around the table at various times. They seemed stunned. Cleveland guessed they were asking themselves how such bright, powerful personages could have ended up in such a difficult, embarrassing spot.

Pressure was constant. Stevenson needed instructions for what to tell the UN, and Cleveland drafted language for the President's approval before phoning it to New York. Pierre Salinger had to know how to respond to impatient reporters milling around the West Wing entrance hall. Feeling detached but sympathetic, Cleveland watched his former Marshall Plan boss, Bissell, rush in and out, looking increasingly wan, with instructions for Gray Lynch and the men on the beach.

Burke, commanding the American military power at the scene, was the most consistently active participant. Cleveland did not find him militant, yet he was "pressing for every yard of ground he could get in the direction of more American participation by American forces in at least limiting the damage."

The President kept resisting. He demanded minimum visibility of Americans, even in a rescue operation. Navy vessels should stay over the horizon, out of sight of the Cuban coast. Fascinated, Cleveland watched a "stricken look" cross Admiral Burke's face when the President picked up one of the little magnetic destroyer models and moved it over the horizon. It clearly pained the admiral to see the President bypass all channels of command—and all tradition. As a student of managers coping with crisis, Cleveland was chagrined to see how obvious it was that the President's only executive experience had been as commander of a PT boat.

The situation would have stymied anybody. The White House command group knew that the ammunition ships had not reached the beaches. They could not understand why. Ammunition was critical. There was no assurance the beachhead could be maintained even if the Navy were ordered in to help hold it. "It wasn't just the question of committing U.S. forces and saving the war—it wasn't that simple," General Lemnitzer said later. "It was a question of whether or not the Navy could save it if you sent them in."

At 1:37 P.M., Admiral Burke called the Joint Chiefs from the White House and issued instructions that Admiral Dennison at CINCLANT in Norfolk was to order photo and visual reconnaissance, using unmarked jets from the *Essex*, to determine the situation on the beach. The aircraft were to be authorized to protect themselves against attack but were to take "all precautions to avoid being identified as U.S."

At 2:49 P.M. Admiral Burke called the Joint Chiefs to have CINC-LANT order the preparation of "unmarked naval planes," this time "for possible combat use." The number of planes was left to CINCLANT's discretion. Burke said to pass along word that this did not signify an intention of U.S. intervention.

What was happening on the beaches? The lack of timely "commo" was maddening. The confusion caused by secrecy and the consequent multiplicity of codes and systems made it worse. It took Admiral Burke "a couple of days to find out that two ships were one and the same, that different names were being used for the same ship."

At 7:57 P.M. the Joint Chiefs advised CINCLANT that unmarked C-130 Air Force transports were being readied to drop ammunition on the beachhead that night. The aircraft were being moved to Kelly Air Force Base. Packing crews were on their way there. Flight crews were ready. Eight B-26s and four T-33s were also set to reinforce the Brigade air force.

All was useless. There weren't enough pilots to fly the bombers and fighters out of Nicaragua. The C-130s could not have reached the beachhead before dawn, which would have been essential to keep the risk reasonable. The reconnaissance jets from the *Essex* reported they could spot no fighting. The White House group decided there "wasn't any point in going in" anymore except perhaps to rescue the Brigade off the beaches.

Throughout the day in the Cabinet Room, Kennedy did not ask enough questions, Harlan Cleveland thought. And the President failed to ask about situations in context; he would ask a "very specific question about some little piece of the jigsaw puzzle and you had to sort of guess what the rest of the jigsaw puzzle was in his mind."

But Cleveland was "terribly impressed by how much faster the President recovered psychologically than anybody else in the room." His manner with the others was reassuring. They would get through this crisis somehow.

At lunch with Scotty Reston of the *Times* and Arthur Schlesinger, the President had been candid and calm. Schlesinger had rarely seen him more controlled and effective. He was looking ahead, especially to replacing Dulles at the CIA. Retaining the aging operator had probably been "a mistake," he said. "Dulles is a legendary figure, and it's hard to operate with legendary figures." He found it hard to assess what Dulles meant when he spoke. "Bobby" should have the job. He was "wasted" in the Justice Department as Attorney General. It was "a hell of a way to learn things," but CIA would have to be dealt with.

Defeat at the Bay of Pigs would be "an incident, not a disaster." He wasn't going to be pushed into committing U.S. forces. Wouldn't American prestige suffer? The President was philosophical. "What is prestige?" he inquired. "Is it the shadow of power or the substance of power?" He was going to work on the latter. The administration would be "kicked in the can for the next couple of weeks," but it wouldn't be deflected from its purpose.

His main concern was the brave men on the beaches. He had sent them there. He had to save as many as he could.

Kenneth O'Donnell, the President's appointments secretary and confidant, hated formal White House functions. Whenever he spotted his name on the guest list, he crossed it off. He had done so again for the annual Congressional Reception, scheduled for 10 P.M. Tuesday, but this time the President told him, "I want you there." Grumbling to himself, O'Donnell, scrawny and laconic, a charter member of Kennedy's "Irish Mafia" from Boston, went to Stein's near the White House and rented white tie and tails that didn't fit.

The President lingered in the West Wing as long as possible, hoping for better news. Gloomily, he went to the Mansion to change to white tie and tails. At 10:15, with Jacqueline on his arm and his head high, he entered the East Room. The Marine band, dazzling in red dress uniforms, played "Mr. Wonderful." Smiling, the President and the First Lady started the dancing.

Soon Kennedy's military aide, Ted Clifton, tapped O'Donnell on the shoulder. Urgent messages were accumulating in the Oval Office. The President wanted O'Donnell to take over the phones.

As the President, seemingly unconcerned, mingled and chatted with the guests, Mrs. Kennedy danced with their old friend Senator Smathers of Florida. They were stopped by Robert Kennedy, who took the Senator aside and said, "The shit has hit the fan. The thing has turned sour in a way you wouldn't believe!"

Sitting in the President's chair, O'Donnell received a call from Walt Rostow. Instantly he realized the operation "was going in the shit house." Rostow had just returned to Quarters Eye in his Volkswagen after a brief stop at home to take a bath and change into a sports jacket and gray flannels. He found Bissell, unshaven and haggard, surrounded by his associates. The state of their emotions was obvious. Several were shouting. Their composure had disintegrated. Their morale was going fast. Rostow shared fragmentary reports of "more and more gory details" from the battle. Somebody said, "We've got to persuade the President! The President must send the Air Force in."

It occurred to Rostow that these men had never seriously contemplated that the President would hold to his policy of noninterference in the operation: "It was inconceivable to them that the President would let it openly fail when he had all this American power."

Bissell and Rostow decided the President ought to have a fresh report. Rostow called O'Donnell to set up a meeting for midnight, when the reception would break up, and drove Bissell to the White House in his Volkswagen.

It was a most extraordinary session. Nobody present would ever forget it. It began at 11:58 and lasted until 2:46 A.M. Like the President, Vice President Johnson, Rusk and McNamara were in white tie. General Lemnitzer and Admiral Burke were in dress uniform, medals gleaming. As Bissell began laying out options, Rostow was struck by the contrast of the scene with the reports of the Cubans dying on the beaches and the Revolutionary Council threatening suicide in Miami. Later he would write: "The limits and dilemmas of power—the relationship of power to the fate of human beings—was never more clear or poignant."

Bissell felt "it was a moment of desperation"; Rostow thought his old professor was "most extraordinarily disciplined." With admiration, he listened as the CIA chief argued that the operation could still be saved, but only if the President authorized using jets from the *Essex*.

Burke agreed. "Let me take two jets and shoot down the enemy aircraft," he pleaded.

The President said, "No." He reminded Bissell and Burke that he had warned them "over and over again" he would not commit U.S. forces to combat.

Burke suggested that unmarked jets be permitted to fly over the beaches as a show of strength with orders not to fire.

The President didn't like the idea. He pointed out that there always was the possibility that the jets would be attacked and fired at after all.

The admiral next suggested bringing in a destroyer. It could arrive in less than two hours. "One destroyer opening fire could have knocked the hell out of Castro's tanks," he said later. "It might have changed the whole course of battle."

The President got angry. "Burke, I don't want the United States involved in this," he said sharply.

Burke, feeling he had "never been so distressed," raised his voice. He wanted to be "as forceful as I could be in talking to the President." He said, "Hell, Mr. President, but we *are* involved!"

As the discussion progressed, it became clear that the participants were arguing from two entirely different perspectives. Bissell and Burke still hoped to make the operation succeed. The President, seconded by Rusk, hoped only to minimize the damage. He concentrated on what Mac Bundy later called the "forlorn business" of "extrication." Rostow was struck by Kennedy's deep personal concern about the fate of the men on the beaches. The President had "a small unit commander's attitude toward these people."

Up to that moment, Rostow had been under the impression that the men could always escape "into the hills." Rusk asked about "the hills." General Lemnitzer told the President it was "time for this outfit to go guerrilla." The Chairman of the Joint Chiefs was amazed when Bissell said "they were not prepared to go guerrilla." Nobody realized that the Brigade was a captive of the swamps. Rostow was chagrined that the President "really didn't have a very good visual picture of the whole thing."

Shortly after 1 A.M. Schlesinger joined the group. Bundy, calling from the Oval Office, had reached him at home in Georgetown just as he was getting into bed, "dead tired." As he entered the President's office, Schlesinger found the men gloomily reading dispatches from the beaches. Bundy told him there was "no real news." The President wanted Berle to calm down the Revolutionary Council in Miami; if Berle couldn't be found, Kennedy wanted Schlesinger to go.

Schlesinger found himself in the middle of a "desultory" renewal of the debate about a jet strike from the *Essex*. The President finally authorized a flight of six unmarked jets to fly cover for a B-26 attack from Nicaragua. They were not to attack planes or ground targets. They could defend the Brigade bombers if these were attacked. Schlesinger thought it was "a somewhat tricky instruction." Rusk interjected that the mission meant a deeper commitment. The President raised his hand just below his nose.

"We're already in it up to here," he said.

Bissell hurried out of the room to issue instructions for getting the Brigade bombers moving out of Puerto Cabezas.

"Keep your chin up," the President told him.

When Berle arrived, Kennedy told him about his problem with the Revolutionary Council. "One is threatening suicide," he said. "Others want to be put on the beachhead. All are furious with CIA. They do not know how dismal things are. You must go down and talk to them."

Berle agreed and said, "I can think of happier missions."

As the meeting broke up, the President told Schlesinger, "You ought to go with Berle."

Schlesinger noted that even under the pressure of the emergency, false assumptions aggravated the difficulties of making decisions. The military *assumed* the President would order American intervention. The President *assumed* they knew he would refuse to escalate the miniature war.

Rostow found himself unable to go home. He sat in O'Donnell's office until almost 4 A.M., not doing "a damn thing" yet unwilling to leave the command post. O'Donnell and Pierre Salinger were talking quietly to the President in his office. O'Donnell had "never seen him so distraught." He came "as close to crying" as Kenny O'Donnell had ever seen him. Suddenly the President broke off the conversation and went outside, coatless. There was a touch of spring in the air. Silently, his old friends O'Donnell and Salinger watched as the President walked slowly around the south grounds for forty-five minutes. He told his brother Robert later that he would have done more if only he had known "what was going on."

Collapse

By midnight Monday the Cuban invaders were desperate. In Girón, Pepe San Román was waiting for the ammunition vessels to return so that the Brigade could keep on fighting. He was never told that the ships were in headlong flight, pursued by the U.S.S. *Eaton*. Furious, he, along with Artime, Raúl Granda and two other men, took a small boat to sea to search for them. The men took turns yelling into their tiny radio. Eventually they were screaming at the top of their lungs, "Goddammit, where the hell are you?" They saw artillery fire on Red Beach. They saw no ships. When they returned to the beach, exhausted, they tried not to show their rage. They told the men ashore they were certain the ships would return in good time.

At the traffic circle on the northern outskirts of Playa Larga, Oliva had dug in for the major engagement of the Bay of Pigs, "the battle of the *rotunda*." Reinforcements had arrived from Girón: most of the Fourth (heavy-weapons) Battalion, ammunition and two more tanks. Six mortars and two bazookas were set up in strategic positions. At 7:45 P.M., four batteries of Soviet-made 122-millimeter howitzers had opened fire on his positions. They kept pounding, more than two thousand shells in four hours. The concussions were terrible. Many men went into shock. They were too dazed to hear orders. But they did not break.

The first three Stalin tanks rumbled into the *rotunda* about midnight. They were the vanguard of twenty tanks, but Oliva had set a superb trap. With the roads bordered by swamps, the Castro troops were forced to try breaking through the *rotunda*. Oliva was ready for them.

Tank was pitted against tank. They were firing point blank, twenty yards apart. The first two Stalin tanks were knocked out, one of them by a tiny fighter who used to cut the men's hair in the Guatemala camps and was known as "Barberito." He ran around the tank and peppered it with shells from his recoilless rifle. They made no dent in the tank, but their sound scared its crew into surrendering. The commander later wanted to meet the man who accomplished this feat. By then Barberito had been killed by a machine gun burst.

One Brigade tank ran out of ammunition quickly. The driver, Jorge Alvarez, known as "Little Egg," blew up an enemy tank with his last shell. Another tank roared up. Álvarez hurled his tank at it. They kept crashing into each other. The Stalin tank tried to position his gun against Little Egg. Álvarez kept bumping the enemy so furiously that the Stalin's gun barrel split. Oliva and his men watched in awe. It reminded them of a struggle between two "prehistoric monsters."

The fighting was so confused and confined that the treads of Castro's tanks ran over their own wounded.

Then Oliva was hit by infantry attacks. He directed the fire of his men and held the enemy off. He had instructed his mortars not to fire until he gave the order. At 1 A.M. he did, first with regular ammunition, later with white phosphorus. Screams went up from the Castro side that sounded to Oliva "just like hell."

Hour after hour, men fought and fell and died. More Castro tanks rumbled into the *rotunda*. One was hit by a sixteen-year-old soldier from ten yards away; the explosion knocked him out and the tank ran over him. A handful of Oliva's men, out of food and water and almost out of ammunition, started to run. Oliva seized a cannon and a shell and faced an oncoming tank from the center of the road. The fleeing men saw him and stopped. So, amazingly, did the tank. The driver got out and surrendered. He told Oliva that the Castro force had numbered 2,100 men. Those who were not dead or wounded* were retreating on the run. Of Oliva's 370 men, twenty had died, about fifty were wounded. His men started to call him "Maceo."†

---

*A Castro defector later estimated that Oliva's men had inflicted some five hundred deaths and more than a thousand wounded.

†Antonio Maceo was the great hero of Cuba's wars of independence and the grandfather of the physician with the same name who was in Opa-Locka as a member of Miró Cardona's Revolutionary Council.

Oliva's victory at the *rotunda* was bound to be short-lived, and he knew it. He was out of ammunition. His men were hungry and exhausted. *Milicianos* were starting to infiltrate into his positions. Sniper fire was on the increase. Another major attack at dawn was inevitable. Oliva had dispatched a messenger to San Román at Girón: the situation at Playa Larga was critical. Pepe sent a man back with a jeep. Oliva was ordered to resist until "the moment of death."

Oliva thought this was a useless gesture. He ordered his force to board its five trucks, and they retreated to Girón. Arriving at 8:45 A.M. Tuesday, he went into conference with Pepe and Artime in the concrete bungalow under the palm trees at the coastal three-road intersection where San Román had set up headquarters. They studied their maps. With Playa Larga undefended, fighting continued only in the San Blas area. There, supported by infantry and mortars, the paratroopers had stabbed ahead almost to Covadonga before encountering long columns of Castro troops and tanks.

Inflicting heavy casualties, the Brigade units fell back, resisted, fell back more. Roberto San Román was rationing mortar shells carefully. When he was asked for six, he sent two. Other ammunition was low everywhere, nearly gone at some outposts. Castro artillery fire had started at 4 A.M. and never stopped. Brigade casualties were light—the troops were well dug in along the San Blas road—but enemy pressure was becoming irresistible.

Oliva proposed that they consolidate all units and strike eastward toward Cienfuegos and the Escambrays. He felt certain that Castro's heaviest attacks would come from the west, the direction of Havana, and that the Brigade would be driven into the sea. The battle was at its most critical point. Escape to the mountains should at least be attempted. "It's better than to be killed," Oliva said.

Pepe had a lot of reasons for rejecting the idea. He said the mountains were too far away. He thought there had to be enemy troops around Cienfuegos. The Brigade lacked ammunition to fight its way through and there weren't enough vehicles to transport everybody. With communications lacking, the men on the ammunition ships would never find them, and—this was the commander's underlying conviction—the ships would surely come today, because the Americans would not let them down.

On the bridge of the *Eaton*, Commodore Crutchfield felt pressure building. He could talk to Pepe San Román via a small CB radio, and the Brigade commander's requests for ammunition and air cover were growing more insistent. Lieutenant Jim Rowsey, an air controller who had been loaned to the *Eaton* by the *Cony*, kept rushing up to report that the pilots from the carrier *Essex* were flying wing on Castro planes, "begging to shoot them down." The atmosphere was "very emotional."

Crutchfield felt "rage that we couldn't help those people" ashore. After all, the United States had "brought them in there and put 'em ashore." Indeed, he had placed the Brigade there personally. He "never thought we'd let them down." He was sure he would "get orders to bail them out. It didn't make sense not to." It was also a matter of "professional pride; we don't start something and let it go sour."

Aloud, he could only say, "No!" to Rowsey. To Pepe he radioed that he fully realized the seriousness of the Brigade's situation and was passing along the Cubans' pleas to the people who could do something about them.

Gray Lynch had just started on his first sleep in more than thirty-six hours when a *Blagar* crewman shook him and said, "Hey, we're having some trouble in the engine room."

Gray collected Andy Pruna and his frogmen. Three men wearing life preservers had stopped the engines and were waving pistols. The frogmen disarmed them.

The mutineers were crewmen from the sunken *Río Escondido*. All day they had been huddling terrified in the mess hall. Some were praying. Others kept shouting, "They're going to kill us, they're going to kill us!" The *Blagar* crewmen who were doing the fighting defiantly refused to wear life preservers. The men who were fished from the sea when the *Río Escondido* exploded refused to take theirs off. They were beginning to make the *Blagar* crew nervous, especially after Gray decided to head his ship to the beach to unload the ammunition aboard. There was very little, but that was better than nothing.

When he and Ryberg calculated that they would not be able to finish unloading before daylight, they realized they would be hit by new air attacks. "We're going to have this mob on here while we're trying to fight off planes," Gray said. "Let's get rid of them." They decided to head back, transfer the mutinous men to the *Barbara J.*, and make back for shore. En route to the *Barbara J.* they got a new order from headquarters: forget the unloading mission. Everything depended on the return of the *Atlántico* and the *Caribe*.

Sleepless on the bridge of the *Eaton*, Commodore Crutchfield and Captain Perkins were beginning to feel like firemen. Jets from the *Essex* had spotted the fleeing *Atlántico* and *Caribe*, whose stocks of ammunition were so critically needed ashore. The *Eaton* was supposed to intercept the freighters and persuade them to return. They stopped by the *Essex* to pick up a Marine colonel with a briefcase—rumors had it that the case contained cash in the event the Cubans required that kind of persuasion. Then they raced south at thirty-two knots, thirty-six knots, "full speed, four boilers on the line."

Soon their tanker appeared out of the darkness as if by magic, as usual. They refueled at top speed and raced on. About a hundred miles south of the Cuban coast they caught up with the *Atlántico*. Crutchfield told his Filipino mess steward to tell the skipper over voice radio in Spanish that the situation on the beach was desperate and that the ship's cargo was absolutely essential. The *Atlántico* turned around.

The *Caribe*, with Eduardo García, the owner of the García line, aboard, was 218 miles off Cuba when the *Eaton* caught up. It would not reply to radio messages. The *Eaton* cut in front of the freighter and signaled with its blinking lights: "Stop your engine." The Marine colonel went aboard.

García was apologetic. His radios were out of commission. His captain had the microphone shot right out of his hand. He did not mention that he was furious at having been "double-crossed" by the Americans. They had told him, hadn't they, that his ships needed no guns because all Castro planes were going to be destroyed beforehand. When the enemy aircraft were not destroyed, nobody bothered to tell the shipowner about it: "When you have a partner you don't change the rules without telling him." He was responsible for his ships and the crews who had served him so many years. When he heard the colonel's account of what was happening on the beaches, he did agree to go back.

At about 2 A.M. Wednesday, Gray Lynch received a puzzling message from headquarters: "The Navy has been authorized to remove the Brigade from the beaches." The evacuation would come Wednesday night. All the Brigade ships could be used. The principal work would be done by Navy landing craft manned by American personnel in T-shirts.

Gray knew that the landing craft were handy. While visiting the *Essex* he had seen two LST's (landing ship tanks) crammed with artillery and tanks and two AKA assault transports with landing craft on their decks and hanging over the side. They were the backbone of a reinforced amphibious task force which also included some 1,200 Marines.

But why talk about evacuation now? The Brigade was still reasonably intact and fighting. The ammunition run of the *Atlántico* and the *Caribe* would presumably resume soon. Gray had also had word that the wounded were about to be airlifted from the Girón airstrip and, mistakenly, that F-51 fighters were coming from Nicaragua. It looked as though they were "going to pull this thing out." He asked himself, how could he tell Pepe to hold on because "we're coming with everything" and at the same time instruct him to get ready for evacuation?

It made no sense to Gray. It would make no sense to the Brigade. Headquarters knew it was all over. The men at the scene did not. Gray decided he would transmit the essence of the Washington message to the beach but he would "camouflage it."

"I want you to listen carefully," he radioed Pepe. "I want you to know that if things get very, very bad we are prepared to come in and take all of you off."

Pepe's voice was tired but firm. "No, Gray, we will not evacuate. We came here to fight. If it has to end, let it end and right here." At no time was there further talk of evacuation.

At about 6 A.M. the San Blas front came to life for a final time. Gonzalo Herrera of the Brigade air force, hearing "May Day!" distress calls from two American colleagues but unable to help them in his lonely, cumbersome bomber, dived at the Castro forces massing for an attack north of the town. He strafed them, came back for a second pass, and placed two napalm bombs with precision.

Alejandro del Valle, the handsome twenty-two-year-old commander of the paratroopers, some of whom had made their way to the front, climbed on top of a tank and seized this opportunity for an attack of his own. Ignoring heavy artillery fire, his men moved forward. It was a quixotic effort, yet enemy ranks gave way. Soon del Valle's men ran out of ammunition again. Men of the Third Battalion started running back. Some paratroopers joined them. Aided by Pepe San Román's brother, Roberto, del Valle turned a threatened rout into a slow retreat. The outcome was inevitable. By early afternoon Castro tanks were firing into the Brigade's positions from a straight line. The last forty defenders jumped into a captured Soviet truck. It was knocked out by a Brigade tank which mistook it for an enemy vehicle. The driver was killed. Roberto was wounded. Slowly the last remnant of the San Blas front began the fifteen-mile hike back to the flames and smoke that were Girón.

In the meantime, Radio Havana had broadcast official government communiqué No. 3: "The participation of the United States in the aggression against Cuba was dramatically proved this morning when our antiaircraft batteries brought down a U.S. military plane piloted by a U.S. airman who was bombing the civilian population and our infantry forces in the area of Australia Central."

The radio said that papers found on the American pilot's body identified him as Leo Francis Bell from Boston. It said his height was five feet six inches.* This was Leo Baker's height.

By that time Gonzalo Herrera had made it back to Happy Valley. He had been lucky. He had grown groggy and flew so low he almost hit a wave. He took his last "Benny" pill. It hardly helped. He tried to radio the *Essex*. It did not respond. When he landed, his friends inspected his plane and shook their heads. They had counted thirty-seven holes.

At about 5:15 A.M. one of the *Blagar* radio operators placed a message on top of the pile of other decoded messages to the right of Gray's ship-to-shore microphone. Gray glanced at it and let out a whoop of joy. The message said that four unmarked jets would arrive over the beachhead. The scheduled time was only about forty-five minutes away. He was to tell the Brigade to mark their front line with panels. Word spread instantly around the ship. Everybody cheered. There was no reason to believe anything else: the planes must be coming to furnish the requested air cover. The *Eaton* relayed another message from the *Essex:* Pepe was to let them know, via Gray, the instant they saw the jets.

Gray passed the word to Pepe: "Jets are coming!"

For the first time, the Brigade commander became emotional. "I want you to know these pilots are the answer to our prayers," he said.

At precisely the scheduled time, Pepe came back on the air: "Gray, they just passed over us."

"Are you sure?"

"It has to be," Pepe said. "They're of a shape we're not familiar with and they wiggled their wings at us."

*The American pilots who participated in the combat were released on Bissell's authority, without knowledge of the President. Kennedy did not find out about the Americans' participation until nearly two years later. On February 25, 1963, Senator Everett Dirksen of Illinois, the Republican minority leader of the Senate, announced he had discovered that four U.S. fliers died at the Bay of Pigs. At midnight Kennedy called his Air Force aide, Brigadier General Godfrey T. McHugh, at home and woke him up. He had found out that McHugh, on instruction from the CIA, had written Riley Shamburger's mother that "neither the CIA nor any other government agency possesses the slightest pertinent information on your son's disappearance." Kennedy was furious. "Godfrey, how could you do this to me?" he demanded. "The whole Senate is after me! And how could you lie to that poor woman?" McHugh said he knew no more about the pilots than the President did, but he'd find out about them. When the general went to his office at 5 A.M. he found an angry handwritten note from the President and went to work. At 8 A.M. he walked into the President's bedroom and said, "Mr. President, I have the answers." The President growled, "You'd better have some answers!" When McHugh told Kennedy the facts, the President said, "My God, why are you standing there? You've got a lot of asses to chew!"

"Where did they go?"

"They disappeared inland."

A few minutes later, Pepe was back, sounding anxious: "We're under attack by Sea Furies. Where in the hell did those planes go? They were too high! Tell them they've got to come down very low next time."

Gray passed the word to the carrier and asked, "What about that?"

The carrier said those had been reconnaissance planes. Gray was to ask the Brigade for the coordinates of all ground targets they wanted hit. Gray got the information from Pepe and passed it on.

"We have a launch leaving now for the beach," the voice from the carrier said.

"Will this launch strike targets?" asked Gray.

"Wait!" After a moment the carrier came back: "This launch is flight cover. The next launch will be armed to strike."

He heard nothing further about air strikes. Eventually he radioed the *Essex* that the promised jets had not arrived: "If you have future schedule for them, please advise." There was no response. He felt that his world had shrunk. Nobody seemed to be there but Pepe and he.

Whenever the *Blagar* was far from shore, the voice link with Pepe grew so weak that Gray had to shout his messages as loudly as he could, usually several times. He gulped grapefruit juice constantly but could not avoid hoarseness. At some point after seventy-two hours in the little radio room, he lost his sense of time. He did not know or care when he last had had food. Fatigue became a problem. At times Gray fell asleep in the middle of reading a message from Washington. His head simply hit the table. He tried to take brief naps, but his was the only voice that Pepe knew and trusted. The Brigade commander would talk to nobody else. The Cubans drank their own kind of thick, strong coffee out of the usual little espresso cups. Gray and Rip poured it into themselves from big Navy mugs. It helped.

The Brigade's confidence in the Americans would have been even lower if they could have seen the ten-by-twelve-foot radio room under the bridge of the *Blagar*. The air was stifling. The portholes were closed to maintain blackout. The walls were too warm to touch. Two small fans made the place bearable. They also kept blowing havoc into the papers piled all over the table that took up a whole wall. Another wall was covered by five loudspeakers blaring voice messages from action spots: the beach; the *Eaton;* the Nicaragua air base; the invasion ships; the landing craft. Detachable microphones for two-way contact hung under all speakers but one—the one connecting the *Blagar* with the beach. That mike was mounted on a stand and stood before Gray Lynch.

Bare-chested and unshaven, Lynch sat hunched over the center of the table. He was sweating profusely. Remnants of the soot that had blacked him out for landing still covered his neck, ears and wrists. He was talking to Pepe and at the same time writing radio messages in longhand on legal-sized yellow pads. Five radio operators worked nearby. Rip, Captain Ryberg and other men moved in and out.

This was the command post of Bissell's war. Gray, the retired tank captain whose very presence violated presidential policy, was the unappointed commander in charge. Nobody else was in touch with the men on the beach. Nobody had as much control over the entire operation.

If his superiors in Washington were frustrated by poor communications, they would have been vastly more upset if they had seen Gray at work. He had borrowed every available radio operator, including Cubans from the *Río Escondido*. One operator transmitted. One received. Three decoded. Still, the incoming messages piled up so quickly that soon nobody was available for encoding. Most outgoing traffic to Washington was sent in the clear with requests for "immediate answer in the clear."

But headquarters would not send in the clear. It just piled on more and more work by sending coded messages through its automatic encoders, not realizing that the *Blagar* lacked such equipment. Gray was so hard pressed that he never told headquarters his men were running up to two and a half hours behind in the tedious task of rendering Washington's signals into English.

Gray had not given up hope. Shepherded by the Navy, the *Atlántico* had been retrieved to Point Zulu, about thirty-five miles south of the coast, by 6 P.M. Tuesday, the *Caribe* by about 9 P.M. Immediately, ammunition from both vessels was loaded into the LCU's. Gray told the crews to load up the little craft to the hilt. There was no telling when there might come another chance to bring the Brigade what it most needed in order to survive.

Orders from CIA headquarters were to unload ashore and be back at Point Zulu by daybreak Wednesday. Since the heavy loads would slow the boats down, Gray, Rip and Captain Ryberg re-computed their travel time. It would be impossible to finish unloading before dawn. Air attacks were inevitable. Safe delivery of the ammunition was vital. They wired Washington that air cover was essential unless all ships were to be lost. By this time, the LCU's, the *Blagar* and the *Barbara J.* were headed for the beach. About thirty miles off the coast, headquarters wired: "Hold where you are."

Gray was not alarmed. The air cover would probably arrive later in the day. At worst the boats would unload Wednesday night. As he waited, he tried to keep up Pepe's morale. It was difficult because the news on the beaches grew steadily, sickeningly worse.

On the western outskirts of Girón, along the road to Playa Larga, Oliva, the last Brigade fighter to give up, organized what the Brigade came to call "the last stand of Girón." Having learned at Playa Larga what bazookas could do against tanks, he massed seven of the tubular weapons along a curve, together with the men of the Sixth Battalion. The Second Battalion arrived from the beach. Oliva placed it in reserve. Then came three Brigade tanks. He stationed them pointing at the curve.

Shortly before 10 A.M. one of Fernández' tanks lumbered around the curve. A bazooka stopped it. Then came an armored truck. Another bazooka hit took it. A second tank advanced and was blown up. A third met the same fate. Infantry assaults rolled against Oliva's men, one after another. One Brigade 81-millimeter mortar squad fired so fast that its weapons started to melt. Pounded by Oliva's tanks, by the Sixth Battalion's riflemen and by white-phosphorus shells, Fernández' column retreated. Oliva brought the Second Battalion into the line. He could no longer raise Pepe on the radio in Girón. He did not know that the battle of the Bay of Pigs was all but over.

By midday Wednesday, Gray and Rip were sick of their inaction. After noon they decided they had had all they could take listening to the pleas from the beach. Pepe was beginning to sound "pretty bad." The two CIA men looked at each other. More or less simultaneously, they said, "Let's go!" They no longer thought the Brigade could last until nightfall. Air support or not, they were going to take the LCU's to the beach and unload the ammunition. They were going to "ram them right up on the beach." This time they did not beg for air support. They radioed headquarters that they were leaving for the beach and suggested "some kind of air support" if Washington didn't want the ships sunk.

"We're on our way in," Gray radioed Pepe.

Just then a great cheer went up on the *Blagar* and the *Barbara J*. They were steaming shoreward side by side. The LCU's led the way. Quite by accident, the *Eaton* and the *Murray* passed them, headed for a reconnaissance mission of the beachhead. For a while, the ships were aligned. It looked like the happy ending of a movie.

Of course, the landing craft could not keep up with the destroyers. Gray calculated they would hit the beach about 5:30 P.M. He did not tell Pepe. The pressure on the beach began to grow critical about 2 P.M.

"Hold on, Pepe!" Gray shouted into the radio. "We're going to be there!" A few minutes later, he decided he just had to give the Brigade commander an estimated time of arrival. He fudged by one hour: "Hold until four-thirty," he said. "We'll be there with everything!"

Around 2 P.M. one of Castro's tanks, firing from behind the three tanks that the Brigade had immobilized, knocked out the middle tank of the three that Oliva had stationed along the road. It was afire, threatening to blow up its two ammunition-heavy neighbors. Oliva shouted for someone to take the burning vehicle away. Little Egg Álvarez, wounded in the right ear and bleeding badly, got out of his tank, jumped into the burning one, and drove it up the road in a cloud of smoke and flames.

He happened to park it next to the Brigade mortar squad. Its men yelled to take it away before there was an explosion. Álvarez managed to put out the flames with the tank's fire extinguisher. When he jumped out of the tank, singed by fire and with blood staining his camouflage shirt, the mortar men thought he was sure to die. But Little Egg ran back to his tank. Before he could get into it, Oliva came up and promoted him to captain. Oliva felt it was an "illogical" act, but what else could he do to reward such courage?

In hand-to-hand combat and all but overrun, Oliva ordered G Company of the Second Battalion to counterattack. The company ran into murderous fire. Enemy soldiers cried, "Fatherland or death!" Each side shot at everything that moved in the tangled vegetation. G Company was cut off and had to be extricated by a tank. But it stopped the advance.

A strange silence settled over the front.

To Commodore Crutchfield on the *Eaton* the battle did not seem to end, either. Rejoined by his faithful shadow, the *Murray*, he had been reconnoitering slowly alongshore. Washington was still pressuring for information. He could see some small boats bobbing between the *Eaton* and the shore. Suddenly he spotted tanks rumbling toward the beach from the left. They were only some two thousand yards away. They opened fire.

One shell wooshed over the bridge. It landed about fifty yards too long to hit. Another was fifty yards short.

Captain Perkins, also on the bridge, thought they had been bracketed. The ship's gunners were ready. They asked for permission to return the fire.

Crutchfield refused. He did seriously consider returning the fire. If the shells had landed "any closer," he would have.* However, the desirability of extreme caution had been so thoroughly planted in his head that he felt he should wait. Washington clearly did not want the destroyers or the carrier or its jets involved in warlike acts. Now was the time to stay cool. Yes, he had orders to defend himself. But was this a serious attack? He judged it was not, that the shells were strays. They came from tanks, not from artillery, which would have been far more serious. Fernandez' artillery fire was not landing close to him. Crutchfield thought the shelling was erratic and didn't really threaten the *Eaton* or the *Murray*.

He told Pete Perkins to get under way. Followed by the *Murray*, they moved east, away from the beach and enemy fire. They hated to leave the little boats behind. There might have been Brigade men aboard who were trying to escape. It could not be helped. Next time some shells might hit a destroyer and they would have to fire back. Nobody wanted to start World War III.

Armando López-Estrada, the dark-haired, intense communications officer of the paratroop battalion, was in the last group to retreat to the beach. He had wanted to "hold until we die." Only when they ran out of ammunition for the second time and it was clear that no more was coming did López-Estrada, who was twenty, let himself be convinced by his comrades that there was no point in waiting to be captured.

On the entire Girón beach, he counted twenty-seven men. T-33s were machine-gunning them. Castro artillery pounded in from overhead. In the distance, two destroyers were moving away. About a mile offshore López-Estrada saw an empty sailboat. He swam toward it. Twenty-two men reached the twenty-two-foot craft, followed by the jets and their bullets. Not wanting to be a better target, they did not raise the sail. Frantically they tried to move the boat by paddling with their hands. It would not move. After a few minutes they realized that the boat was at anchor. They cut it loose and got away.†

A heated argument had broken out on the flag bridge of the *Essex*. Admiral Clark, Captain Fickenscher, Captain Searcy and their staffs had

---

*Fernández conceded in 1978 that two stray shells might well have bracketed a destroyer, but he said he did not see such shells. Crutchfield, as an admiral in retirement, said in 1977, "I have many times wondered, what if I had made a different decision at that point? And sometimes I say, perhaps I should have. I could have justified returning that fire very easily." According to its records, the Taylor Commission's seventeenth meeting on May 1, 1961, heard about none of this when it investigated the Navy's role near the beaches. Crutchfield had been asked to attend along with Admiral Clark, but was not asked one question.

†After fifteen days at sea, twelve survivors were rescued by an American oiler. Alejandro del Valle, the twenty-two-year-old commander of the paratroopers, was among those who died of thirst and starvation.

been greatly affected by the messages from Commodore Crutchfield aboard the *Eaton,* relaying Pepe San Román's desperate pleas and recommending American help with an evacuation. The senior command on the *Essex* also had transcripts of Gray's conversations with the beach. The operation was unmistakably about to collapse. The men on the flag bridge had the power to change history. Captain Searcy was particularly distressed. He said their honor was being impugned. They all felt stung.

The little admiral could not have been more sympathetic. Three times he had queried Washington, "Is there any change in the rules of combat?" Three times he had been turned down. "It was agonizing, just like ignoring a man dying of thirst begging for a drink of water." He always assumed that "sooner or later they would change the rules of combat or pull us out entirely." And he couldn't imagine withdrawal: "It's just too cold-blooded and brutal to say, 'OK, fellows, this isn't working, goodbye now!' "

He asked Deacon Fickenscher what he thought. Deacon had been mulling over the possibilities. He ticked them off. They could soften up the enemy with air strikes. They could move the destroyers near the beach to try to pick up the Brigade. They could do pickups with their S-4 helicopters, which would be more dangerous because the helos made better targets.

None of the men had slept in four days. As the heat of the debate grew, Admiral Clark said, "Deacon, I think we ought to hold this conversation in my cabin." In the cabin he explained, "You and I cannot afford to be arguing in front of the rest of the staff. We will argue in here and then decide what we're going to do, and then we'll stop arguing."

Deacon said, "Fine!"

Quickly they agreed it really came down to their instructions. They had no authority to take any of the steps Deacon had suggested on the bridge. The decision had, in effect, been made by Crutchfield: to "stay as close to the beaches as he could without acting like he was about to start a little private war with the destroyers."

Back on the bridge, Fickenscher sent Crutchfield a heartbreaking message: "You can't help them, but you can't tell them."

It was the only way to get his meaning across on an open-voice channel which was almost certainly being monitored by the enemy: the Navy was not going to invade Cuba; it was also not "just going to turn around and sail away." The command on the *Essex* still "kept hoping all the time" that Washington would change its mind.

Shaking his head sadly, Crutchfield barely had time to say a few words to Pepe: he could not help. Pepe could see why. It was the moment when Crutchfield had to move the *Eaton* in a hurry to dodge Fernández' shells.

At Brigade headquarters ashore, Manuel Artime, the flamboyant psychiatrist whom the CIA had appointed political head of the Brigade, felt hope for the first time since the landings. The appearance of the destroyers could only be a sign of American intervention. The *Essex*, distant but clearly visible, was an impressive presence. Jet support finally seemed imminent. It could turn the tide of the battle in no time. He heard Gray shout, "Don't pull out, Pepe, don't pull out!" This was not the time to concede defeat, and Artime told Pepe so. Looking more than ever like a ferocious Ernest Borgnine in a scene of high movie drama, Artime made his usual fervent pitch.

Pepe had had enough of Artime's emotionality and unkept American promises. In the final hours, his voice had turned more and more resigned. His situation spoke for itself. His troops were dispersing. Messengers brought word that tanks were close. The ammunition was depleted, the supply ships were not in sight. The artillery barrages were so loud and homed in from so close that Pepe evacuated the headquarters bungalow. He was crouching on the sand, some twenty feet from the water, alternately shouting into the radio through the noise and pressing it against his ear to hear Gray's pleas to hold on. Even if the Americans were really coming, they could not make shore on time.

At 2:32 P.M. he told Gray he thought tanks were breaking into the town. Pepe's last message was: "Am destroying all equipment and communications. I have nothing left to fight with. Am taking to the woods. I can't wait for you."

He motioned the radio operators to do away with all headquarters equipment. They went to work with their rifle butts. Whatever could not be destroyed that way was riddled by bursts from their Thompson submachine guns. With forty-six men and their staff, San Román and Artime pushed into the swamps.

One of the Brigade's forward artillery observers, Juan Pou, had hiked back to Playa Girón from his post outside San Blas. He had heard no order to retreat. He just saw men straggling by, all headed for the beach. He "went with the crowd."

The scene at the beach astounded him. Tanks were standing around idly, out of ammunition. The machine guns mounted on vehicles were out of ammunition. Men were running about in every direction, shouting, debating what to do. An American destroyer was steaming away from the beach; the white foam of its wake seemed to mock Juan.

How to get out? Pou was a poor swimmer, and there were no boats within reach anyway. Some of the men said they would wander along the shoreline hoping to be picked up eventually if the destroyer returned. This sounded too uncertain to Pou. "I'd rather go into the swamps," he said.

When Oliva entered Girón he suspected the worst. It was ominously silent along the beach road. A radio operator stopped his jeep and reported that the headquarters staff had escaped. Oliva would not believe it. Then he saw the headquarters post with its destroyed equipment. When he asked for Pepe San Román, somebody told him that Pepe had left on the sailboat that was still in view (it was in fact Pepe's brother Roberto on the boat). Oliva believed he had been deserted by his chief. He shook his fist at the ocean and promised the troops who encircled him that he would never leave them.

When the men saw the destroyers leave, some tried to shoot at the American ships in their anger. Others fired at the boats and rafts that bobbed offshore. Then they fired into the tires of their trucks and destroyed their tanks. Little Egg Álvarez booby-trapped his tank and made sure to pump plenty of bullets into its telescopic sight.

Then Oliva led the men eastward in a column. Finally they were off toward Cienfuegos, just as he had wanted the Brigade to escape one long, very long, day ago. Now it was much too late. A few hundred yards after they began marching, two T-33s and a Sea Fury dived and strafed them. They ran into the swamps. It was the end for the last of the Brigade.

Ramiro Sánchez—short, round-faced, a photographer by trade—had watched the *Eaton* from the unfinished Girón resort clubhouse with the other wounded. He had staggered in water up to his neck and almost drowned under the weight of his ammunition boxes and grenades when he had to wade ashore after his landing craft slammed against a reef. He spent a whole night combing the jungle for air-dropped supplies that could never be found. He cheered with his friends when he saw three low-flying American jets overhead in close formation, and mourned when they did nothing. Then his jeep was strafed. The man next to him was hit in the head. Sánchez jumped out. The driver, dazed, started the jeep and drove over Sánchez' left leg. The Castro artillery and aerial bombardment never stopped. Now, with the wounded, he found a little radio and heard Americans talking on ships offshore. Sánchez yelled into it, "Help us! Help us! Help us!" in English and in Spanish. The *Eaton* turned away. "Whsst! There he went!"

Whatever was left of the Brigade was fleeing eastward past the clubhouse. Sánchez' father, a Brigade supply officer who had survived the explosion of the *Río Escondido*, found him and said it was time to go. The father, the former head of the Presidential Palace guard in Havana, was in his fifties and rotund. He carried a BAR rifle and had two ammunition belts slung over his shoulders like old Pancho Villa. Ramiro had only one boot. It did not matter. His other foot and leg were heavily bandaged. He could move only by hopping on his good leg. They decided to take along Ramiro's pal from the jeep, the man with the head wound. As the three started into the swamps, supporting each other, bandages stained with blood, Ramiro thought of the famous picture he had in a book back in Miami. It showed battered soldiers of the American Revolution hobbling, heads up, down a road, the Spirit of '76. That's what he and his father and his wounded friend looked like now.

They hobbled through the swamps for days. On the third day, the second day after their only canteen of water went dry, they ate chunks of the cortex from amasico trees. In the mornings they tried to lick moisture off the leaves of trees, but everything was dry. They had no destination. They only wanted to get away from the beach. Suddenly, miraculously, they found a dry well in the woods. It was about ten feet deep. The man with the head wound was in no shape to make the climb down. Ramiro's father was too big. Ramiro climbed down and started digging with his hands. One foot down he found water. They took the bandage off his leg, used it to lower the canteen, drank, and moved on. One morning they were sleeping, exhausted. Sánchez felt he was being kicked. *Milicianos* were swarming all around him. Sánchez could not stand by himself. He "didn't care if they kill me." The Castro men took them back to Girón by jeep and gave them oranges. The jeep needed just ten minutes to make the trip that had taken them five days.

Even though the radio link with Pepe had fallen silent, Gray and Rip on the *Blagar* did not give up. Doggedly trailing their LCU's full of ammunition, they kept sailing toward shore, calling for Pepe to "come in." But when the *Eaton* radioed it was receiving fire from the beach, it seemed pointless to go on.

As they turned around, they spotted a plane coming from shore. Every man reached for his weapon. They were furious. This was one Castro pilot who wasn't going to get away. Soon they recognized they were tracking a little ninety-mile-per-hour American PBY air-sea rescue craft from Happy Valley looking for survivors from a plane that had ditched. It plowed a zigzag search pattern, a slow and lonely symbol of all that had gone wrong.

Rip returned to his ship. He went into his cabin and did not come out for a long time.

Gray stayed in his radio room, periodically calling for Pepe as darkness fell. Hardly anyone said a word. Gray thought that for once the old saying "The buck stops here" worked in reverse. The buck wasn't stopping with the chiefs in Quarters Eye. It was stopping here with "us Indians because we're the ones at the end of the line." It was the first time he felt ashamed of his country.

CHAPTER SEVEN

Aftermath

Wake of Defeat

As the planners in Washington tried to come to terms with defeat on Wednesday, Walt Rostow was concerned about Robert Kennedy, whom he hardly knew. The Attorney General, who had not attended any of the preinvasion planning meetings, showed much more than the President how distraught he was. He refused to accept the debacle and was needlessly upsetting the other advisers. On Tuesday, RFK had warned the presidential circle harshly in the Cabinet Room that they were to make no statements that didn't back up the President's judgments all the way. In midafternoon Wednesday, with the President absent from the room for a few minutes, Robert spoke, Rostow thought, "in anguish." He called on the advisers "to act or be judged paper tigers in Moscow." They were not just to "sit and take it." With all the famous talent around the table, somebody ought to find something to do.

Everybody stared. They were "absolutely numb." Only Rusk, who almost never showed emotion, pounded the arm of the President's empty chair.

Rostow asked Kennedy to step out of the room for a moment. On the portico near the Rose Garden, he pointed out that "if you're in a fight and get knocked off your feet, the most dangerous thing was to come out swinging." That was the way to get badly hurt. "Now was a time to dance around until our heads cleared." There would be plenty of times and places to show the Soviets that Kennedy and his men were not paper tigers. This was "a time to pause and think."

The Attorney General looked up expressionlessly. "That's constructive," he said.

Tempers softened after that. Waiting later for the arrival of Miró Cardona and the rest of the Revolutionary Council, Rostow watched the President in the rocking chair of the Oval Office, looking at the headlines of the tabloid Washington *News* trumpeting the final collapse of the Brigade.

The President "let the paper crumple onto the floor without a word."

At seven that morning, Schlesinger and Berle, President Kennedy's emissaries to the Revolutionary Council, still incommunicado at Opa-Locka, had arrived on a military plane at Miami International Airport. Greeting them were Jim Noble, "Bender" and Bob Reynolds, the CIA Miami station chief. They were all driven to a hamburger stand, where they transferred to another car. Schlesinger began to feel "like a character out of a Hitchcock film." They stopped at the old hangar which the CIA used as headquarters and called Washington for news. There was none. When they entered the Revolutionary Council's heavily guarded shabby barracks at eight-fifteen, a radio was on, but the men were asleep. Awakened, they were a "pitiful sight" in their khakis, especially to Jim Noble, who had known them all in Cuba.

Miró Cardona and several others broke into tears. Miró, relieved to see an old friend, gave Jim an *abrazo* and kept pleading, "Jim, don't leave me! Don't leave me, please!" The CIA man "had never felt worse" in his life. Trying to reassure the Cubans as best he could, he could offer little. These men wanted news from the beaches, news from their sons. The visitors were in the dark, too.

Assembled around a plain wooden table, the Cuban leaders poured out their frustrations and demands. Miró, sad and dignified, spoke first. Schlesinger was shocked at how much he had aged. He looked a decade older than at lunch in the Century a week before. Given more pilots, Miró argued, the battle might still be won. If not, the men of the Revolutionary Council should be permitted to die with their troops on the beaches: "It is this which I request, this which I beg."

The fiery Tony Varona was bursting with anger. Sputtering, he listed his grievances. The CIA had bypassed the Council. It had ignored all the resistance groups. He had been deceived during his visit to the training camps. Now the Brigade had run out of pilots, yet thirty experienced Cuban fliers were in Miami, eager for action. American planes and Marines should be sent in. Why not? Castro had Soviet tanks and technicians. If the Americans evaded their responsibility, who would trust them again in Latin America or anywhere else?

Manuel Ray impressed Schlesinger with his calm and directness. Citing details, Ray documented how the CIA ignored sabotage plans readied by the resistance ("For over a month we have had a tunnel under the Havana electric-power installation"). Promises of military support were broken ("We were told that ten to fifteen thousand men would be available"). The Council was impotent ("Action is taken in our name . . . without our knowledge"). Ray still had faith in President Kennedy, but he insisted that "those who really run things begin to assume the responsibility" and that the Council "abandon the pretense of command, go to Cuba and fight as soldiers."

Carlos Helvía, an Annapolis graduate and former Provisional President of Cuba (he was going to be the new Foreign Minister), also protested the Council's "accountability without authority." He thought "massive air attacks" could still turn the tide, but "if these boys are going to be wiped out on the beachhead, our place is to die there with them."

After Varona summarized the principal demands—reinforcements, air strikes and transportation of the Council to the beaches—he warned that his group would no longer tolerate being kept incommunicado. "We don't know whether we are your allies or your prisoners," he told Berle and Schlesinger. At noon he planned to leave for Miami and summon a press conference. "Let them shoot me down if they dare."

Berle and Schlesinger talked privately, "much moved by the power and bitterness of the protests." They considered sending the Council to the Nicaragua base. It was too late. A call to Washington brought the final verdict: the operation was all but over. Even evacuation seemed no longer possible. Pacing in the sunshine, they wondered how they could tell Varona and his friends the appalling news without risking a public denunciation of the United States, particularly the CIA. The only way was to take the leaders to Washington to see the President. "Only Kennedy could save this situation."

Jim Noble, shaken, hovered nearby as Schlesinger picked up a wall telephone in the headquarters hangar and called the President. Jim did not like or trust the young historian. But Schlesinger made an eloquent plea into the wall phone. "This is a Pearl Harbor!" he told Kennedy. "They're really upset! They've been kept in the dark on this goddamn thing!" The President said he wanted to see the Cubans at the White House as soon as they got back to Washington.

The Council members took the news silently and changed into civilian suits for takeoff.

John Plank, the Harvard professor, was summoned later that morning from his class in international relations by a call from Berle. The aged New Dealer said he was phoning from Opa-Locka and was about to take the Revolutionary Council to Washington to see the President. The

Council needed a reliable translator. "They want you," he said. "You get down to the White House as fast as you can."

Plank canceled his class and made the next shuttle flight, taking no suitcase or topcoat; he reached the White House just in time.

While the Council waited in the Cabinet Room, Berle and Schlesinger told the President how the Cubans had been detained under something like house arrest. Kennedy, "exceptionally drawn and tired," said he was shocked; the CIA had left him uninformed about that. Plank and the Cubans were ushered in and seated on two facing couches in front of the Oval Office fireplace. Kennedy, cordial and self-possessed, rocked in his rocking chair while his naval aide, Commander Tazwell Shepard, gave a brief battlefield report with the help of a map.

With Plank translating—and the President urging him to move along faster—Kennedy expressed his regret over the failure of the operation. He read Colonel Hawkins' last-minute cable from Nicaragua with its glowing appraisal of the Brigade to help explain why he had thought the troops could succeed without American help. He reaffirmed he would not use American troops because the struggle against Communism had many fronts; the U.S., as the leader, had to balance all its responsibilities.

Plank, quickly reflecting how hard a moment this must be for a new President, admired Kennedy's performance ("You suddenly know why these guys are born to command").

No matter how tragically the invasion had ended, Kennedy continued, the American commitment to Cuban freedom stood firm. He assured the Council members that he shared their grief and reminded them that he too had seen combat. "I lost a brother and a brother-in-law in the war," he said. "I know something of how you feel." He seemed especially stung that Castro had called the Brigade "mercenaries." Acting again like a PT-boat commander, he asked whether any of the Cuban leaders had pictures of their soldier sons.

Dr. Maceo, the surgeon, was startled. He wondered how the President knew about the three Council members' sons in the Brigade. Greatly touched, he took out his billfold and showed the President a passport-sized photo of Antonio Junior, a grave, pale teenager.* The President held up young Antonio's picture and asked, "Does this look like a mercenary?"

The Cubans said little. As they were about to leave, the President assured them they were "free men" who could go anywhere and say

*Although Antonio knew no more about medicine than what he had picked up hanging around in his father's surgery in Havana, he was serving as a medic. While his father had no word about his safety until four days later, the young man was aboard the *Lake Charles*, the one ship that failed to arrive at the beaches in time for the battle.

anything. Schlesinger thought he "had never seen the President more impressive" and noted that "in spite of themselves, his visitors were deeply moved." Soon Kennedy joined them for sandwiches and tea on the second floor of the Mansion to discuss the rescue operations. Schlesinger was struck by the thought that "Kennedy was prepared to run more risks to take the men off the beaches than to put them there."

The President invited the men of the Council to use the Cabinet Room to write down their suggestions for future action. "John," he said to Plank, "you'll stay with them, won't you?"

Plank, not certain that he liked being called by first name quite so quickly, was taken aback and started to say something about having to get back to his classes. Then he realized how inappropriate this would have been. ("My Commander in Chief was giving me a direct order.") He said, "Of course I will."

Just before two black limousines picked up Plank and the Council to go to New York, the professor found Schlesinger and said, "Arthur, I don't have a shirt and I don't have any money." Schlesinger told him not to worry and came back in a few minutes with an envelope containing two hundred dollars. Plank was more impressed than relieved.

At Quarters Eye, David Phillips, the propaganda chief, had finished composing more "cryptic nonsense" messages for Radio Swan to broadcast. Fighting nausea, he went downstairs to the war room. Jake Engler was "white with remorse and fatigue." Colonel Hawkins "held one hand across his face, as if hiding." Another man scratched his wrists so fiercely that blood stained his cuffs. Still another left the room and later said he had vomited into a wastebasket.

Flannery arrived around 6 P.M. to get a paper signed. Bissell was trying to persuade Jake Engler and Colonel Hawkins to go home and get some rest. They had finished talking about the latest progress in picking men of the Brigade out of the water. The Navy was doing as much as Kennedy's rules permitted.

"We've done all we can," Bissell said. "Why don't we all get some sleep?"

Somebody asked, "Whom do we get to watch the store?"

Bissell turned to Flannery and said, "You!"

Toward 11 P.M., Flannery had to phone Bissell at home. To his amazement, the boss was up, relaxed, enjoying a pleasant old-fashioned family evening. Mrs. Bissell was playing the piano. There was no hint of depression or defeat.

At 6 P.M. on Wednesday Allen Dulles had an appointment with his old friend Dick Nixon at the former Vice President's home, which he still maintained although he was now practicing law in California. Nixon had flown in to be briefed on foreign-policy developments for a speech he was to make in Chicago the next week. A message was waiting for him: Dulles would be at least an hour late.

When the CIA director arrived after seven-thirty, Nixon saw at once that "he was under great emotional stress." He asked Dulles if he would care for a drink. "I certainly would," said Dulles. "I really need one. This is the worst day of my life!"

"What's wrong?"

"Everything is lost," the CIA director said. "The Cuban invasion is a total failure."

Nixon registered amazement. He had been following the news of the invasion but had "never" thought "it would be allowed to fail."

As Dulles related it, a "sharp difference of opinion" had developed about the invasion plans among "soft-line" and "activist" advisers in the Kennedy administration.

"It took great courage," Dulles said, "for the President to go forward with the plan." It was a tragedy that the soft-liners "doomed the operation to failure" by last-minute "compromises."

The next day, President Kennedy invited Nixon to the Oval Office to tell him of his meeting with the Frente leaders.

"Talking to them and seeing the tragic expressions on their faces was the worst experience of my life," he said. "Last night they were really mad at us. But today they have calmed down a lot and, believe it or not, they're ready to go out and fight again, if we will give them the word and the support."

JFK started to pace. With generous use of four-letter words, he told his number-one political enemy that all military experts and the CIA had assured him the invasion would work. He did not mention the cancellation of the air strikes, which Nixon considered "fatal." Nixon said nothing until the President asked, "What would you do now in Cuba?"

"I would find proper legal cover, and I would go in," said Nixon. The former Vice President cited what he considered legal justification for "armed intervention by U.S. forces."

Kennedy replied that his Russian experts as well as Walter Lippmann, the columnist, who had recently interviewed Khrushchev, had told him that the ill-tempered Soviet Premier was feeling "very cocky." He told Nixon, "There is a good chance that, if we move on Cuba, Khrushchev will move on Berlin. I just don't think we can take the risk."

As the conversation turned to Laos, Nixon thought Kennedy had been chicken when he canceled the air strikes and had turned chicken again when the operation had failed.

Victors and Vanquished

On Thursday, equipped with captured documents, maps and a pointer, Fidel Castro spoke on television for nearly four hours. Alternately he radiated fire, irony, contempt. He retraced some of his movements during the battle. He gloated over how the planes that the *mercenarios* had bombed at Campo Libertad had been useless dummy targets; all had been previously grounded. Scoffing at the CIA for underestimating the loyalty of the Zapata *cienagueros* for whom the revolution had done so much, he drew a comparison between the mechanistic mentality of the Yale planner-intellectuals versus the assertedly humanistic outlook of his Sierra Maestra club.

"Imperialism examines geography, analyzes the number of cannons, of planes, of tanks, the positions," he shouted. "The revolutionary examines the social composition of the population. The imperialists don't give a damn about how the population there thinks or feels."

He laughed at the poor CIA intelligence and read from captured documents that had judged his planes to be "in flying condition but not in combat condition." He referred to erroneous enemy reports of MIG-17s in action. "We have no MIG's," he chortled. "I wish we had had some MIG's here during those days!" Implied was a hint to his Soviet allies. He was grateful for all the help he could get. But when help was unavailable, he was able to help himself.

It was a masterful propaganda performance. It could not have been more dramatic or explicit. For four hours, streets throughout the country were deserted. The population listened, laughed, cheered. In militia camps, hundreds of men stood up hour after hour around one TV set. In the end Cubans were, for once, more fully and accurately informed about recent history than the people of the United States.

Outside the Bay of Pigs that day, Gray radioed Rip aboard the *Barbara J.* A message had come from headquarters: Would the two agents and the frogmen volunteer for a rescue mission? Reconnaissance planes had spotted a large group of survivors from the *Houston* on the west side of the bay. The Navy was authorized to take the rescuers to the beach.

Rip came to the *Blagar* to discuss the mission.

"Well, let's go," Gray said.

"Okay," said Rip, "but let's send a message back up there first. There's just been too much crap in the last two or three days. There's been too many promises made. We don't know whether they've thought this out."

Gray agreed that they should no longer blindly follow every suggestion just because it came from Washington. This time they would go to the top to be sure they weren't going on another wild-goose chase, especially since nobody could predict how Castro was going to interpret a Navy rescue effort.

They messaged headquarters that everybody was volunteering, but they wanted all information verified by the director personally. Only when they received a message from Dulles, saying that he personally vouched for the information, did they agree to transfer to the *Eaton*. Their rubber boats barely made it through twelve-foot waves, the aftermath of a tropical depression that had tossed all the ships around at force-four winds during the preceding night.

Aboard the *Barbara J.*, Rip told Pruna, his lead frogman, "Get your gear, Andy. Get your boys together. We're going to an American ship."

On the *Essex*, Andy met two officers, a colonel and a captain; neither was wearing insignia. They asked the frogmen about the operation but seemed to know more about it than the men who had been ashore.

"Would you guys be ready to go back in if we went with you?" asked the colonel.

"You're goddamn right we would," Andy said.

"Well, we're waiting for word to go in with you."

They waited a day. No word came. The frogmen were transferred to the *Eaton*, where their reception was even better. Several crewmen were "almost in tears." They griped about being fired on and not being allowed to fire back. They cleaned the frogmen's weapons and, dirty as the Cubans were, made them eat at the captain's table. Then they gave the men clean khakis. Pruna thought it was "incredible" to watch just how upset the Americans were. They kept saying, "Forgive us." One officer told Pruna, "Christ, I don't know what the hell is going on in Washington." Andy thought there wasn't one man who "wouldn't have gone in there and kicked 'em on their ass."

At daybreak next morning, the *Eaton* moved slowly past the grounded *Houston*, searching the coast through binoculars. Since it bore no identifying name, the ubiquitous destroyer was flying its "holiday flag"—its largest—because the searchers wanted to be sure they would be recognized as Americans. Shortly after 9:30 A.M., west of Cayo Miguel, they spotted their first four survivors. The men jumped up and down and waved "madly." The destroyer signaled them to show that they had been seen but kept going to cover the rest of the area before launching boats to make pickups. The men ashore grew frantic. They thought they were being left behind and started running along the beach trying to keep up with the destroyer.

Two teams of frogmen, one of them led by Gray, went ashore. One survivor had been drinking salt water and could not talk at all. Eventually they found twelve men. Some wore shorts. Most were naked. All looked like skeletons and bore deep cuts over their bodies. Gray could not understand the wounds until he went ashore and searched the woods. The thorns on the dry bush were so long and sharp that two complete sets of khakis were shredded off his body in three days and he too was covered with scratches.

The searchers picked up one group of five survivors, who, amazingly, had all their clothing and weapons and needed neither water nor food. Organized by the chief engineer of the *Houston*, they remained calm and thoughtful. They had covered forty miles. They walked only in the cool of night, slowly, easily, always on the hard sand right next to the water's edge. During the day they rested in trenches they dug into the moist sand under low-hanging branches of heavy, shady trees at the edge of the swamps. There they found tree stumps filled with rainwater. In the surf they grappled for mussels and other shellfish. They could have survived indefinitely.

The next day, four U.S. destroyers were lined up about a thousand yards apart, their sterns pointing toward the reefs. Rip Robertson's twenty-six-foot whaleboat, its long U.S. flag trailing in the water, was cruising through the lagoons. The Navy crew was shouting through a megaphone for survivors to come out of the bushes. Suddenly a few did. They were crawling on hands and knees.

A Castro helicopter had been roving up and down the beaches. Still nobody wanted to fire a first shot in any war between the United States and Cuba, so it never fired at the ships. When it saw the Brigade survivors, it swooped to near treetop level and opened fire at the Cubans. As Commodore Crutchfield watched from the *Eaton*, a little Navy AD rescue plane, obviously under orders not to shoot, slowed down to about a hundred knots per hour and started a "contact run." It was literally going to knock the helicopter out of the air. But the helicopter was more maneuverable. Just before a collision, it would flip itself aside. Crutchfield thought "it was the darnedest thing to watch."

The AD made several runs. It never caught the helicopter. It did create some badly needed time for the whaleboat, which belonged to Captain Dunham's *Cony*. The captain was very agitated. His crew was at the railings hollering "like a cheering section." The whaleboat had run aground on the beach. The men, heavily armed with Browning automatic rifles and all wearing helmets, had loaded the survivors and were trying to get moving. The men on the *Cony* were mostly shouting at the lieutenant junior grade in charge. He was very young. It was his first command. The men were trying to energize him, not that he needed it. "Get off the beach!" they yelled. While the helicopter was busy ducking, he did.

Crutchfield went to talk to the survivors in the *Eaton* mess. There were twenty-six of them by now, fed and cleaned up, still limp and scared. Crutchfield felt compelled to cheer them up. "You've lost a battle, but I don't think you've lost the war," he told them. He felt foolish saying it, "because they *had* lost the war." He did not think he was lying, because he "couldn't believe, even at that stage, that we would let the whole thing go sour."

Eight days after his last full night's sleep on the starboard wing of the *Eaton's* bridge, Crutchfield sank back into the black reclining chair where he had worked and occasionally napped. He called for the ship's physician. "Doctor," he told him, "I'm exhausted. Can you prescribe anything?"

The doctor said, "Commodore, what you need is a good drink." He went below and brought up a tiny individual-drink bottle of Old Crow bourbon. "Here," he said, "I prescribe this for you."

On the *Cony*, Lieutenant Jim Rowsey, the air controller, reported back to his skipper, Captain Dunham. The captain asked how Crutchfield was doing. Rowsey said the commodore had been "at the brink of tears for days."*

The chief radio operator who had been brought to the *Essex* by the CIA to run communications between the fleet and Washington and had been installed in Captain Searcy's in-port cabin asked permission to join the captain on the bridge.

"Sure, make yourself at home," Searcy said.

The radio man obviously had something on his mind but could not say it. He put his elbows on the railing and held his head in his hands.

"What's the matter?" asked the captain.

The man turned around slowly: "Captain, this is the first time in my life I have ever been ashamed of being an American."

Pete Searcy said, "Chief, I feel pretty much like you do."

Both men turned toward the sea and stared at the glistening water.

---

*In 1977 Crutchfield recalled, "I was so worn out and so disgusted that I was tempted to turn in my ship and just quit. Really, I was that emotional. I think if somebody had asked me what did I want to do at that moment, I would have said, 'I want to resign from the Navy!' "

Of all the orders Searcy had received that week, the last jarred him the most. He was to assemble all orders and logs covering the time of the operation—the operation order, the deck log, the navigation log, the combat information center log, the engineering log, everything— and personally burn them. Sighing, he called for the Marine who served as his messenger. Together they gathered up the files and the bulky ledgers and took them below, next to the engine room, to the incinerator. The Marine opened the chute. The captain threw the books and papers into the fire and watched them disappear. Not a word was spoken. Pete Searcy was "disgusted, upset and plain mad." To himself he said, "This is a big damn cover-up."

While the sea rescue effort was in progress, the air base at Happy Valley was "like a graveyard," thought Eddie Ferrer. He was sitting on his bunk when two Americans appeared and silently handed each Cuban airman a Toshiba transistor radio. Ferrer was taken aback. He had expected no farewell present, yet this was what the radios were obviously meant to be. He looked at the little radio in his large hairy hand, momentarily nonplussed. Then he asked for a second one. He would give one to each of his sons back in Miami. The boys might as well get a souvenir out of his nine-month absence from home.

Although he thought all his missions done, Gus Ponzoa, the pilot who began the war with the initial air raid on Cuba, was asked to perform one more. In the sparkling afternoon stillness he went to the tent where he had gone so many times for spells of exhausted sleep with his friends of the B-26 squadron. He opened the wooden foot lockers at the foot of twelve beds. They were the beds of the men who had been killed. They had not left much behind. He took out their spare fatigues and underwear and left them on the floor. He sorted out all maps and charts and official papers and took them to the trash burners and set them on fire. Alone, tears in his eyes, he sorted out each man's personal belongings. He placed the articles in green duffel bags and labeled each bag with the man's name. No photos had been allowed in the camps, and there were none. There were just letters, books, Bibles, little Cuban flags, and rosaries. When it was time to fly home, Gus insisted on loading the bags himself onto the DC-4.

On the twenty-third, the first fifty Cuban airmen, pilots and ground personnel were flown back to Miami. Eddie Ferrer was in charge. He sat silently next to Gus Ponzoa, smoking. Every ten or fifteen minutes, Gus said, "Thank God, thank God it's over." At the arrival hangar in Opa-Locka, only customs and immigration officers greeted the airmen. The officials seemed "disrespectful." They had a hard time getting across to the milling, impatient Cubans that each man had to exchange his khaki shirt for a civilian sports shirt. "Security" made it important that they not look military. Each arrival also had to be issued a temporary "parole paper" to admit him into the country.

Eddie Ferrer had his men line up in formation and called them to attention. He told the head of the immigration men, "If there is anything you want from these people, let me know. And don't give me any bullshit. I'm tired of seeing you people treating us like dirt."

The immigration men apologized. Everybody changed shirts and got his admission paper. There were no farewell ceremonies. The men were driven to a house in southwest Miami in a yellow school bus. This time there was no zigzag route for "security." Cars with Cuban drivers were waiting to drive them home. Three days later Ferrer was told to report to the Frente office in Coconut Grove, where a Cuban handed him three hundred dollars in cash. A month after that he received a mimeographed letter advising him that he was entitled to no further "compensation." There was no letterhead and no signature. The envelope carried no return address.

In Guatemala City, Bob Davis, the CIA station chief, was frantic not only about the project's outcome but about the state of the Americans who had trained the Brigade. Davis felt he couldn't drink. His stomach was so fluttery he would have thrown up. Colonel Frank and several others "had been on a drunk for about three days." They locked themselves in their rooms in a CIA safe house and refused to come out. Davis thought one or more might kill themselves, they were in such despair. Some disappeared and couldn't be found for days. Their fury at the politicians in Washington was limitless. Davis thought they were unsettled enough to kill people: "If someone had gotten close to Kennedy, he'd have killed him. Oh, they hated him!"

President Ydigoras was philosophical. "These things happen," he told Davis. "I've been in politics all my life."

Davis grieved. In less than two months his auburn hair had turned totally gray. He was forty-three years old.*

It was cold and windy at Anacostia Air Force Base in suburban Washington when Gray Lynch and Rip Robertson arrived on April 27 to

*Jim Flannery's family was away from Washington, as was Jake Engler's, so Jim had the CIA project director at his home for supper. Jake looked terrible. Jim asked: "When are you going to take some leave?" Jake said he was about to take two weeks off. "Going fishing?" "No," said Jake, "I'm going down to Miami to see the fathers and mothers of the boys in the Brigade and apologize to them." And he did. Jay Gleichauff saw him circulating among the Cubans "in complete shock. He walked around in a daze like a zombie." Wherever Jake went "men were crying."

testify before the General Taylor inquiry. The three men from the agency who met them were wearing topcoats. Gray and Rip shivered in the khakis and short sleeves they had been given on the *Essex*. They had flown on Navy planes directly from the carrier via Guantánamo and Jacksonville, still looking like very unconventional troops.

Both were burned all but black from the sun. Gray's paratrooper boots had turned white from salt water, and he carried all his belongings in a cardboard Hershey bar box. Rip wore badly torn moccasins. His gear was in a filthy sea bag stenciled "U.S.S. ESSEX." The hands of both men were covered with cuts from coral and tree thorns. The agents who welcomed them said they would have to stay out of sight until security men could measure them for decent clothes in the morning.

They were taken to the Shoreham Hotel, where the CIA maintained a suite under the name of a legitimate company, and all five men went up the back elevator from the parking lot. On the lobby floor two middle-aged couples got on, wearing tuxedoes, furs and much jewelry. They looked at Gray and Rip, and their noses went up in the air. Rip poked Gray and grinned. Gray broke through the silence and said, "What floor did you say the plumbing was out on?" Everybody relaxed.

The two men from the Bay of Pigs stayed up until almost 6 A.M., finishing most of a bottle of Jack Daniel's and refighting the battle. This time they won. On the fifth floor of the Shoreham, the enemy was nothing. The two troopers "just wiped them out" and went to bed.

Rip didn't like being measured by the security men when they came by to see what size clothes he needed. After they left he said, "I'm old enough to dress myself." He had more than two hundred dollars in expense money and took off for downtown Washington. He was walking down the street in his khakis and moccasins, unshaven, when a friend, an American businessman he had known in Nicaragua, called, "Hey, Rip, what are you doing here?" Rip couldn't think of anything to say.

"You've fallen on hard times," the businessman said. "Here"—he pulled out his card, wrote his hotel and room number on it and handed it to Rip—"call me and I'll get something going for you."

Rip looked at the card; it had a twenty-dollar bill wrapped around it.

When Rip got back to the hotel, there was a new security man on duty. The man said to Gray, "Who is this guy?"

Gray decided to cheer up their homecoming. "I don't know," he said.

Rip started a line of double-talk and finally mumbled something about "freedom of the press." The security man turned white. A reporter! He rushed to the phone in the bedroom. Gray shouted after him, "Wait, wait! Don't get excited. That's just Rip."

Gray phoned Colonel Hawkins, who seemed surprised to hear from him. "My God," he said, "where are you?" Gray told him, and the guerrilla chief said, "Well, can I come up there to see you?"

"Sure, come on up."

When Hawkins arrived with several other men from paramilitary operations, he told Gray and Rip, "You know, when this thing was going on I thought: I'll never see those two guys alive again. I never thought you'd make it out of there. Also, the reason I didn't call you this morning, I thought probably you didn't ever want to talk to us again."

Gray was amazed. "We're not blaming you people; we know darn well you didn't do this. We'd like to know who did."

"Well, it was out of our hands," said Hawkins. "The President shot this thing down."

Gray had been an admirer of the President and had voted for him with enthusiasm. Now he was "absolutely shocked." It was like "finding out that Superman is a fairy."

After he got back from Nicaragua, General Doster of the Alabama Air National Guard went to Washington to complain about the operation. He was furious and "wanted somebody's ass." By the time he reached the capital his desires were in closer focus. He wanted "a fifth of Scotch and then I want to see that son of a bitch Bobby Kennedy."

Instead, he saw a Navy captain who was supposed to debrief him. Not much information was developed at that session. Doster was too angry.

"This is the most fucked-up, asinine operation I ever saw," he said.

"You are the maddest man I ever saw," said the captain.

Doster never got to complain to anyone else.

Some months later, back in Birmingham and still trying to get over his resentment, Doster received a call from his friend General Winston P. Wilson, chief of the Army and Air National Guard and known as "Wimpy." Wilson ordered him to come to Washington right away. When Doster got there, Wilson took him to see a top CIA executive in the modern new glass-and-chrome agency headquarters in Langley, Virginia. The CIA man handed Doster a letter that turned out to be a commendation for the general's effectiveness in the Cuban project. Grudgingly pleased, Doster was about to put this souvenir in his pocket when the CIA man said he couldn't have it. It was "secret" and had to go back into the agency files. Doster felt "like a dumb ass."

The Brigade survivors in Cuba were taken to Havana. As the bus filled with Brigade prisoners turned left onto the east–west Central Highway of Cuba, Pepe San Román put out his left hand, just as Colonel

Frank had instructed the Brigade leaders during their briefing in Nicaragua to dramatize how easy their victory would be. "I put my hand out and we went straight into Havana," Pepe said later. He felt misled and very bitter.

For nine men, the ensuing twenty months of captivity never began. They did not survive an eight-hour trip in a sealed truck (others emerged alive because they scratched holes into the truck's aluminum walls with their belt buckles).* For twenty days the survivors were questioned in Havana's Sports Palace under a sign, "Fatherland or Death. We Won." Most of the prisoners were decently treated most of the time. Artime was twice threatened with death by shooting; once a pistol was placed in his mouth and the trigger pulled, the hammer falling on a chamber that was empty.

Castro demanded a $62 million ransom. After an elaborate mass trial, the negotiations dragged on and on. Attorney General Robert Kennedy made personal pleas to the officers of the Pharmaceutical Manufacturers Association and to baby-food manufacturers. Eventually, Castro settled for $53 million worth of food and drugs. At 6:06 P.M. on Sunday, December 23, 1962, the plane with the first returning prisoners landed at Homestead Air Force Base. "My God, they're really here!" a Cuban woman screamed, and fainted.

The following Saturday, the Brigade lined up in the Orange Bowl before forty thousand people, many of them weeping. Erneido Oliva handed President Kennedy the Brigade flag that had flown for three days over the headquarters at Girón. "I can assure you that this flag will be returned to this Brigade in a free Havana," shouted the President, visibly moved.† The cheers that greeted him were tremendous. "*Guerra! Guerra!*" went the shouts. And "*Libertad! Libertad! Libertad!*"

---

*All told, 114 men of the Brigade died. Castro captured 1,189. Approximately 150 were unable to land; or were never shipped out; or made their way back.

†By 1975, the flag, measuring 70 by 49 inches and showing a rifleman with fixed bayonet lunging forward, was kept in a wooden crate in the John F. Kennedy Library in Waltham, Massachusetts. The veterans were restless about its fate. Many were disgusted because even the Republicans Nixon and Ford learned to live with Castro. Each year chances seemed to decrease that the Brigade flag would fly over a free Havana. The men wanted their emblem back. Juan Pérez Franco, the president of their Veterans Association, wrote the Kennedy Library and demanded its return. Dave Powers, a close Kennedy friend who had become curator of memorabilia, was sympathetic. He had no room to display the flag, to do it justice. It had become property of the government's housekeeping branch, the General Services Administration. Did they have the legal right to restore property even to its original owners? GSA attorneys had to study the document under which the Kennedy family had deeded the President's belongings. It would take time.

The men of the Brigade, resenting the bureaucratic delay, hired a Miami attorney. Finally, on April 14, 1976, Powers drove to Boston's Logan Airport to meet the attorney, Ellis Reuben, and there, in the Eastern Airlines lounge, Reuben signed a government receipt for the flag. He did not have much time. His return flight to Miami was due shortly. The crate with the flag had already been shipped as cargo.

If anything, the cheers mounted when Jacqueline Kennedy stepped before the microphones and said in Spanish, "I feel proud that my son has met the officers. He is still too young to realize what has happened here, but I will make it my business to tell him the story of your courage as he grows up."

By the time of the Orange Bowl, Eddie Ferrer was feeling somewhat better about his experience as morale officer and pilot for the CIA. For many months he had been waking up frequently at night, upset over dreams of dead fellow pilots. He was very nervous. He smoked more than ever, often more than two packs a day. He hated the United States government—"not the people," he always said, "just the government."

In Miami, the Cuban misadventure actually improved the feelings of local people toward Cuban refugees. Eddie Ferrer found that when he mentioned he had fought in the operation, most people thawed. "We feel sorry for you," they said. "We're ashamed of the government. Is there anything we can do?" People just became "a lot nicer."

Now the young President made his way down on the field in the Orange Bowl, his hair getting blown in the breeze. He was shaking hands with each leader, exchanging a few words here and there.

"You didn't get any help from us," he remarked to Ferrer.

"No, Mr. President, but I expect it the next time," said the pilot.

"You better believe that there's going to be a next time," the President told him.

Eddie Ferrer stiffened and beamed. It was good to have such a President, after all. He "believed in him again."

Juan Pou, the forward observer, was lined up with the heavy-weapons battalion. He felt personally honored that the President would come to see them. When the President promised that the Brigade flag would fly over a free Havana, Pou cheered and clapped. It was a dramatic moment, and Pou, a cordial man with sunny disposition, soon to become an officer in the U.S. Army, was essentially an optimist. The euphoria was brief. What had the President really said? He had not offered military help to liberate Cuba. He certainly had not announced another invasion. Pou had all but expected some such gesture. He felt let down. Again.

Kennedy at Bay

Before his 10 A.M. press conference on Friday following the invasion, the President had breakfast with Rusk, Bundy, Sorensen, Schlesinger, Goodwin and Salinger in the little second-floor dining room of the

Mansion. He said he had been reading in the morning papers some purported inside stories about who was to blame for the Bay of Pigs decision. He noted "acidly" that the Joint Chiefs were largely unmentioned, which meant that the stories had probably leaked out of the Pentagon.

"There is only one person in the clear," he said emphatically. "That's Bill Fulbright. And he probably would have been converted if he had attended more of the meetings. If he had received the same treatment we received—discontent in Cuba, morale of the free Cubans, rainy season, Russian MIG's and destroyers, impregnable beachhead, easy escape into the Escambray, what else to do with these people—it might have moved him down the road, too." Schlesinger never forgot how Kennedy emphasized each point with the presidential hand stab that was becoming familiar to TV viewers.

When Bundy recalled that Schlesinger had opposed the venture, Kennedy said caustically, "Oh, sure, Arthur wrote me a memorandum that will look pretty good when he gets around to writing his book on my administration. Only he better not publish that memorandum while I'm still alive!" In no mood for wit except gallows humor directed against himself, he added, "I have a title for his book—*Kennedy: The Only Years*."

Before he left for the press conference in the State Department auditorium, Kennedy told the group there was only one way to cut off speculation about the Bay of Pigs decision—to tell the truth: while all senior officials who were consulted backed the expedition, the final responsibility was his alone.

Facing the reporters, Kennedy brushed aside the stories about who was to blame: "There's an old saying that victory has a hundred fathers and defeat is an orphan."* What mattered was only one fact: "I am the responsible officer of the government."

That afternoon, Schlesinger stuck his head through the open door of the President's office. He wanted to say goodbye before leaving for a meeting in Italy. Vice President Lyndon Johnson was talking to the President, but Kennedy waved Schlesinger inside. Their subject was the CIA. The President was saying again he could not comprehend how seasoned, bright officials like Dulles and Bissell could have been so grossly in error.

Schlesinger thought the President "looked exceedingly tired, but his mood was philosophical." He realized that vulnerable spots in his

---

*When Schlesinger later asked him about the source of this apt quotation, Kennedy said: "Oh, I don't know; it's just an old saying." In fact it is attributed to *The Ciano Diaries, 1939–1943,* of Count Galeazzo Ciano, Mussolini's foreign minister, who used it in a journal entry of September 9, 1942.

administration had been uncovered, especially in the CIA and the Joint Chiefs. "We can't win them all," he said, "and I have been close enough to disaster to realize that these things which seem world-shaking at one moment you can barely remember the next. We got a big kick in the leg—and we deserved it. But maybe we'll learn something from it."

Later that day, Maxwell D. Taylor was in the middle of a business luncheon in New York when he was given word that the White House switchboard was trying to reach him. The retired Army Chief of Staff and one-time paratroop division commander had published an influential book the year before, *The Uncertain Trumpet*. Now, as president of Lincoln Center for the Performing Arts, still under construction, he was only dimly aware of what had happened in Cuba. He hardly knew the new President. He remembered that numerous officials communicate through the White House switchboard and couldn't imagine that Kennedy might be calling him. He finished luncheon leisurely before returning the call.

The White House operator immediately switched him to the President. Kennedy said he was in "deep trouble" because of the Bay of Pigs. Could Taylor come to Washington the next morning at ten o'clock to discuss this?

In the Oval Office Saturday, Kennedy gave Taylor the assignment to investigate the affair. Vice President Johnson and Mac Bundy were there. Others drifted in and out. A reaction to the first reaction of the decision-makers had set in. Fascinated, Taylor watched from alongside Kennedy in his rocking chair. "I sensed an air which I had known in my military past," Taylor wrote later, "that of a command post that had been overrun by the enemy. There were the same glazed eyes, subdued voices, and slow speech that I remembered observing in commanders routed at the Battle of the Bulge or recovering from the shock of their first action. The latter was a more accurate analogy because this new administration had, indeed, engaged in its first bloody action and was learning the sting of defeat."

Elspeth Rostow was listening to her husband Walt as he returned from the White House, exhausted and exhilarated by the post-Bay of Pigs crisis. "You know what you all are?" she asked. "You are junior officers of the Second World War come to responsibility." Rostow thought he had not heard a better characterization of those bitter days.

David F. Powers, the President's aide and confidant, was an excellent listener, and after the Bay of Pigs collapsed the President needed to talk. Each day at 1 P.M. the two men swam together in the White House pool. Officially, the swim break was therapy for the President's back. In truth, it enabled the President to talk.

Kennedy was angry. Powers had never seen him in a darker mood. Dave understood: "It was the first thing he ever really lost." The President was especially wistful about his own branch of the service, the Navy, and its chief.

"Arleigh Burke sat right across from me," he told Powers as they swam. "I've been reading about 'Thirty-Knot Burke.' He was terrific! I was a lieutenant on a PT boat! You should have seen how impressive it was to see the Joint Chiefs of Staff show up with all that fruit salad [decorations on their uniforms]! And they'd have colonels carrying pointers and maps."

The President told Powers he had asked Burke, "Will this plan work?" and Burke had said, "As far as we've been able to check it out, the plan is good."

Memories of the operation's planning meetings kept paining the President. He returned to recite them to Powers again and again. How could he, with less than three months in the White House, discount what he had heard and read about men with the reputations of Burke and Allen Dulles? And why was the need for air *cover* not brought out much more forcefully beforehand? The planners had talked only about air *strikes*. The President was only beginning to understand that air cover had become necessary after the operation was under way because the air strikes had failed to wipe out Castro's planes as Colonel Beerli, Bissell and their men had planned.

With his dead-serious, brilliantly analytical special counsel and thinker, Ted Sorensen, the President talked with less emotion and in greater detail in his office, in the Mansion, and while they walked on the White House south lawn. These conversations* became the operation's only full presidential postmortem.

Kennedy told Sorensen that he had held "grave doubts" about the Cuba operation ever since he heard about it as President-elect in Palm Beach. He was "astonished at its magnitude and daring." While he had inherited it from his predecessor, it couldn't be scrapped like an Eisenhower policy. After all, there were physical inheritances: the planners, the Brigade, and the exile leaders too.

The President soon found himself caught up in the operation's "now or never" feeling, and with good reason. He was told the Brigade was difficult to hold off. Guatemala was pressuring to close the camps, so the

*Their summary here is drawn from Sorensen's memoir, *Kennedy* (New York: Harper & Row, 1965).

choice was either to send the exiles to Cuba, where they wanted to go, or to disband them and have them broadcast their resentment. Russian arms were constantly building up Cuban strength. To the President, the plan seemed to entail no actual aggression by the U.S., no evident risk of U.S. involvement, little risk of failure.

Kennedy told Sorensen that Dulles said to him in the Oval Office, "I stood right here at Ike's desk and told him I was certain our Guatemalan operation would succeed, and, Mr. President, the prospects for this plan are even better than they were for that one."* Kennedy did not feel that his campaign pledge on behalf of the "fighters for freedom" was forcing his hand. He did think that cancellation of the operation at a late date would be a show of weakness inconsistent with his worldwide stance against the Communists and an admission that Castro ruled with popular support. It would guarantee that Castro would long be around to harass all of Latin America.

When he did give the "go" order, "I really thought they had a good chance," he told Sorensen. Besides, it looked like a no-lose solution. If a group of Castro's own countrymen could, without overt U.S. help, establish a new government, rally the people and oust Castro, all Latin America would be safer. If the exiles were forced into the mountains as guerrillas, the operation was still a net gain.

Air cover was always out of the question, Kennedy said. "Obviously, if you are going to have United States air cover you might as well have a complete United States commitment," he said to Sorensen, "which would have meant a full-fledged invasion by the United States." In that event, Kennedy would not have permitted the exiles to be defeated. But he would never have approved an operation in the first place. American forces were below strength. If they had been tied up in the Cuban mountains, the Soviets would surely have moved in Berlin or elsewhere.

The decision to go ahead without U.S. combat forces was based on representations by the CIA and the military that it would succeed on its own, Kennedy argued. He felt assured on that score by the Joint Chiefs and Colonel Hawkins. He was also assured that the Cuban exiles fully realized there would be no U.S. intervention. It was after he collected these assurances that Kennedy told his April 12 press conference, "There will not be, under any conditions, any intervention in Cuba by United States armed forces."

When the President made the last-minute decision to cancel the

---

*This may have been a conversation different from the one in which Dulles predicted a twenty percent chance of success for the Guatemala operation if aircraft were supplied. Or possibly, either the Dulles or the Kennedy memory was in error.

second air strike, he told Sorensen, he should have canceled the entire operation instead.* By then it was clear that the first—and key—objective of the attackers, the destruction of Castro's Air Force, had not been realized. The Tuesday-night plea from Gray Lynch for air cover to protect an ammunition run to shore was not passed on to the President; nor was he specifically aware of the desperate need for ammunition. He did realize that the entire operation he had authorized bore "little resemblance" to what he *thought* he had approved.

Sorensen found that the President had approved a quiet reinfiltration, plausibly Cuban in its essentials, not an "invasion" of a magnitude exaggerated by headline writers, by the Cuban Revolutionary Council, and by public-relations releases dictated by the CIA.

In case of failure, the President was sure the guerrilla option was open to the exiles. He had not been told that the terrain was unsuitable, that most of the exiles were not trained for guerrilla warfare, or that the eighty-mile route to the Escambrays would be too long, swampy, and covered by Castro troops. The CIA had never told him that the guerrilla option was out. Nor had it told the Brigade that this was the President's fail-safe plan.

The President thought he was permitting the exiles to decide whether to risk their lives for Cuba without overt U.S. support. Instead, many assumed that U.S. forces would eventually come to their assistance, if necessary, presumably neutralizing Castro's air strength with jets. Many also assumed that larger Cuban forces would land and that the Brigade would be joined by the underground or guerrillas. These assumptions of the exiles were not made known to Kennedy, just as his assumptions were not transmitted to them. It did not help that the Revolutionary Council was kept out of contact with the Brigade and that its head, Miró, did not pass along to his own followers the repeated statements by Kennedy and his emissaries that no U.S. military help would come.

The President further thought he was approving a plan that could succeed with help from Cuban underground fighters and military deserters, as well as an eventual uprising of a rebellious population. He was not informed of Castro's relative popularity or the effectiveness of his police-state measures, reinforced by mass arrests. Kennedy's approval was based on two possible outcomes—national revolt or flight to the hills. In reality, neither was "remotely possible."

Kennedy thought he was rushed into his approval because Castro would soon be strong enough to defeat the invasion—when in fact

*Kennedy did not discuss with Sorensen how the Brigade could have been persuaded to turn back just short of H-Hour on D-Day.

Castro already was. The President understood that the Cubans had only obsolete, ineffective air strength; that they had no communications to the Bay of Pigs area; and that they had no effective forces close enough. All these understandings derived from his White House briefings. All proved wrong.

Assured that the plan he was approving would be secret and successful, he discovered too late that it was too large to remain secret and too small to succeed. Kennedy blamed excessively close control of the operation by the CIA for the fact that he and the exiles were "largely uninformed of each other's thinking"; and he blamed the agency's overenthusiasm for its rejection of evidence on Castro's political and military strength—which would have been available from State Department and British intelligence, if not from the agency's own intelligence sources.

Though Kennedy was outwardly calm and hopeful, rallying the morale of his men and planning ahead, Sorensen found him "beneath it all angry and sick at heart." He seemed "a depressed and lonely man." He felt personally responsible for the men who had lost their lives and for the 1,189 whom "his government had helped send to their imprisonment" and possible execution. As he walked with Sorensen on the south lawn that Thursday after the battle, one day after the collapse, ninety days after he came to office, the President sensed that the Bay of Pigs "had been—and would be—the worst defeat of his career." He revolted against the outcome because it was "the kind of outright failure to which he was not accustomed." Later, Arthur Schlesinger would write of that day: "The gay expectations of the Hundred Days were irrevocably over, the hour of euphoria past."

Kennedy knew he had "handed his critics a stick with which they would forever beat him." He assured Sorensen he did not mind assuming full responsibility. He could see the outlines of what had gone wrong. Yet he still could not grasp how he could have allowed himself to be trapped into accepting so many false assumptions. "How could I have been so far off base?" he inquired aloud. "All my life I've known better than to depend on the experts. How could I have been so stupid to let them go ahead?"

Mac Bundy gave his old professor the word in May: the President wanted Bissell to go.

Bissell, content that he had done his best to make the Bay of Pigs succeed and knowing that Allen Dulles' successor would want to name his own DDP anyway, was resigned to leaving the bureaucratic struggles after twenty years. He called Ken O'Donnell and made an appointment to see the President.

Kennedy received him warmly. Bissell said he understood he was to leave the agency. When would be the best time to quit?

Kennedy again acknowledged his responsibility for the Bay of Pigs. He said, "If this were the British government, I would resign, and you, being a senior civil servant, would remain. But it isn't. In our government, you and Allen have to go, and I have to remain." He told Bissell there was no rush.

Relations between the two men remained friendly. They frequently met in the White House about continuing CIA operations. When Bissell was awarded the Medal of Freedom, Kennedy turned it into a cheerful public occasion. He did not categorize Bissell with General Cabell, whom he disliked, and the Joint Chiefs and other military men who, he felt, had given him poor counsel. Bissell was, after all, one of the "brightest guys" in the administration.

When John McCone, the tough old West Coast shipbuilder, was named to replace Dulles, Bissell and he agreed that the DDP should quit in December. Then McCone's wife died. He asked Bissell to stay on. Bissell declined. "I've talked to Bobby Kennedy about this, and he talked to the President," said McCone. "They have changed their minds. They will be delighted to have you stay on, but not in the DDP position." They wanted Bissell to become deputy director, an administrative post. Bissell thought it over for a few days and declined.

"The agency's loss will be great," said McCone, "but from your point of view, I think you're wise."

Girón Today

Cubans do not call it the Battle of the Bay of Pigs. It is undignified. They call it the Battle of Girón. It is a big word in Cuba, "Girón." The maps on the happy colored travel folders identify it as the site of "the first defeat of imperialism in America." All the new red-and-cream-colored buses are trademarked "Girón"—and they were the first buses to be manufactured in Cuba. Veterans of the battle are regarded as Americans might respect survivors of Valley Forge.

Girón 1978. Crabs still own the fine, hard roads to the beaches. The mosquitoes are still so aggressive that the Guama resort village on Treasure Lake is often near-empty, even on weekends. There is electricity, but there are still no phones. Girón never became a tourist center. It housed students of a new fishery school. There was talk again of turning the bungalows into a resort at last, twenty years after Castro started Félix Duque working on his dream. The airport, once so vital in CIA strategy, stands deserted, its control tower gutted, another grandiose dream. Who would fly to Girón?

The *carboneros*, still sooty, still watch their pungent ovens around the clock, though their charcoal goes to town on trucks. In Gironcito, Narciso and Alejandrina Mejias still sleep under mosquito netting, but their *vara en tierra* hut has been torn down. They have moved up into a *bohío* with a floor, and Alejandrina owns an electric iron. In Playa Larga, Amparo Ortíz lives in a comfortable stone bungalow with large framed photographs of the son who died inexplicably at eighteen and her husband, the *carbonero*, who was ambushed with her sister on a truck long ago.

Alejandrina and Amparo still cry softly when they speak of the night when they awoke to hear shots in the Bay of Pigs and strange men came to the swampland that enchanted such a curious trio of fallible explorers—Christopher Columbus, Richard Bissell, and the bearded trout fisherman in the green fatigues whom they all call "Fidel."

CONCLUSION   # It Could Happen Again

Irving L. Janis was a professor of psychology at Yale University with a special interest in decision-making. In 1965, like so many other Americans fascinated by John F. Kennedy, Janis was reading *A Thousand Days*, Arthur M. Schlesinger, Jr.'s, masterful account of the assassinated President's brief administration. Its chapters on the Bay of Pigs puzzled him, especially the historian-author's eyewitness observation that the decision-making meetings in the White House proceeded in an atmosphere of "assumed consensus."

Janis asked himself: How could shrewd men like Kennedy and his advisers "be taken in by the CIA's stupid patchwork plan"? At a Yale seminar on group psychology he suggested that their lack of "mental alertness" might have been "akin to the lapses in judgment of ordinary citizens who become more concerned with retaining the approval of fellow members of their work group than with coming up with good solutions to the tasks at hand."

Shortly afterward, the professor's sixteen-year-old daughter, Charlotte, mentioned at the dinner table that she needed a topic for a modern-history paper she was supposed to write for her history class at Amity High School in the Janis family's home town, Woodbridge, Connecticut. Her father remarked that there seemed to be a lot of interesting material on the decision-making that went into the Bay of Pigs. He told her what had aroused his own interest.

Charlotte immersed herself in the library and composed a paper, "The Groupthink Hypothesis and the Bay of Pigs." Her father was impressed with the new supporting data she found. The paper won an A

313

from Charlotte's instructor and frequent mention by her father in his talks on group behavior to university audiences. Social scientists began writing to him asking for *his* paper on the Bay of Pigs. He wrote back explaining that he had none and enclosing his daughter's. When a Stanford professor wrote him that he had discussed the groupthink theory with Schlesinger and that Schlesinger said there might be something to it, Professor Janis embarked on his book *Victims of Groupthink.**

Using only published material, it examined four fiascos: Pearl Harbor, the escalation of the Korean War, the escalation of the Vietnam War, and the Bay of Pigs ("A Perfect Failure"). By way of counterpoint, it reviewed the making of the Marshall Plan and the management of the Cuban Missile Crisis, both foreign-policy developments where groupthink decision-making was not in evidence.

I happened to come across Dr. Janis' book in 1975 and was provoked by it. My recollections of the Bay of Pigs episode were dim, but I have long been wary of the herd instinct that can develop in groups. Some of the most fruitful executive decisions I have witnessed were the result of a leader's courage (or independence) in ignoring the choruses advocating caution (or "hard-nosed" incaution) that had prevailed in group meetings. Decades of reporting for newspapers, magazines and books—and editing the reporting of other writers—have also left me profoundly suspicious of library research. Too often I have seen it perpetuate errors of earlier writers.

Eyewitness participants—matched against other eyewitnesses and, wherever possible, against documents—know best. This applies particularly to an undertaking with the Rube Goldberg complexity (and lack of cohesion, to put it gently) constructed by the CIA to put Castro out of business. There *had* to be more to the making of the Bay of Pigs disaster—so colossal, yet so deliberate—than groupthink.

There was, yet the seeming mindlessness of the Kennedy group and the consequent impotence of the individual intelligence of its members demand explanation. The genesis of "assumed consensus" became clear to me when I talked in 1977 with Roswell L. Gilpatric, who attended a number of their meetings in the Pentagon and in the Cabinet Room as Deputy Secretary of Defense.

An almost theatrically handsome corporation lawyer, four times married and given to sartorial splendor that makes his pink shirts (with white collars) not seem foppish, Gilpatric, Yale '28, had been with the prestige-encrusted Wall Street law firm of Cravath, Swaine and Moore since 1931. As a former Under Secretary of the Air Force (1951–53), this

*Boston: Houghton Mifflin, 1972.

stately personage knew his way around among long knives, the standard weapons in the corridors of the Pentagon. Not an easy man to impress or to hoodwink.

Gilpatric spoke very softly, almost in wonderment still. Dulles, he said. Dulles lent the ambiance. Ambiance was important. Bissell, yes. "A remarkable person, a very effective advocate." Gilpatric knew about advocates, and he had known Bissell—as had so many in the Bay of Pigs in-group—since Yale. Bissell had "great prestige." He "could take on Bob McNamara intellectually." (I remembered how Lyman Kirkpatrick had pointed to Dulles and Bissell as "the double signature on the check" that underwrote the operation.)

Gilpatric said, "I kind of got religion." An interesting locution, considering how much at the Bay of Pigs was done, by all concerned, on sheer faith.

McNamara? Well, McNamara was "brand-new." Gilpatric found him preoccupied with organization; organizing the Pentagon with its grand duchies and rotten boroughs would tax any man. For the Bay of Pigs, McNamara's role was "review only." So was Gilpatric's own role. The Deputy Secretary remembered "shifting around in the seat" of his chair at the meetings. "There was a paucity of questions." This awakened his attorney's sense of caution and made him feel uncomfortable. He wondered about the assumptions of Castro's weakness. But he remained silent. He did not "chide himself" until afterward. Why?

Well, they were all so very new. They didn't know the President. They "didn't know how far we could speak up." They felt "inhibited" about "second-guessing judgments that Eisenhower made." Gilpatric paused and shook his head. The late President Ike would have marveled at his power in absentia, particularly over a decision for which he had such small enthusiasm until he dumped it into Kennedy's lap.

So even the departed President became part of the assumed consensus; even Kennedy felt strongly pushed by the Eisenhower sponsorship. In my talks with General Taylor, the general reconstructed Kennedy's thinking like this: "The greatest military man in America, the President of the United States, got this thing going and gave it to the CIA. Why should I, a young President who doesn't even know the telephone numbers in the White House, rush in and try to challenge the basic assumptions?"

If the men in the Kennedy group felt the affinity of old school ties strongly, why did they also feel handcuffed by a sense of unfamiliarity, newness? The answer comes easy with hindsight. Nothing permeates the Cabinet Room more strongly than the smell of hierarchy, especially in the honeymoon days of a new administration. And the three men at the top of the heap, the President, the Secretary of State and the Secretary of Defense, *were* new not only to each other (they had barely met) but to the Executive Branch of the government. Kennedy was plucked from the infighting of the Senate. Rusk from the isolation of the Rockefeller Foundation. McNamara from the commercial strategies of Ford in Detroit. The team was not yet a team.

But too much can be made of group dynamics. The five key decisions of the Bay of Pigs were not made in a group, nor even, for the most part, in a group setting: (1) The decision to escalate the adventure from a plausibly deniable infiltration effort into an invasion was made in Bissell's head; (2) the decision to weaken the first air strike and make it "minimal" was made unilaterally by Kennedy; (3) the decision to cancel the second strike was made by Kennedy late on a Sunday night by phone in consultation with Rusk and Bundy; (4) the decision to give the "go" order was made by Kennedy after extensive lonely soul-searching; (5) the decision not to escalate the invasion in the face of great temptation posed by incipient disaster—to become a "bum," not an aggressor—was made by the President, sparring fiercely with Admiral Burke; other advisers were practically silent.

Inevitably, the President's personality and power shaped events more than they shaped him. The initiative and responsibility were his. He relished both. Action. That's what he had become President for. That's what the country wanted. "Vigah," as he said it, especially after the sleepiness of the Eisenhower years. It was "the hour of euphoria," Arthur Schlesinger later wrote. The flowering of Camelot. His youth, wealth or Catholicism could not defeat Kennedy. His confidence in his own luck was unbounded. "Everyone around him thought he had the Midas touch and could not lose," Schlesinger wrote. No man ever wore bigger seven-league boots.

It is doubtful that the President realized how powerfully the other side of that coin worked against him. If he felt he could not pin down Dulles because one doesn't trifle with "a legend," the charismatic, freshly anointed Kennedy was also sacrosanct to his advisers. Even the crusty Admiral Burke told me he hesitated to speak up to this charmed young man until it was far too late. Kennedy also filtered the information that went into his decision-making by stifling protest and potential resistance. Schlesinger and Goodwin were mere junior spear-carriers and feared they might become branded as nuisances. Schlesinger was finally told by Bob Kennedy outright to shut up. Other nay-sayers—Bowles, Murrow, Hilsman, Meeker—were silenced by nonadmission into the inner circle. Influential potential nay-sayers— Ted Sorensen, Clark Clifford, Adlai Stevenson—were left ignorant because they were generalists or too intellectual and therefore presumably not action-minded. Rusk had a quasi-orthopedic problem. He could not put his foot down.

General Taylor told me, "There is a time when you can't advise by innuendoes and suggestions. You have to look him in the eye and say, 'I think it's a lousy idea, Mr. President. The chances of our succeeding are about one in ten.' And nobody said that."

Charisma and ego do not account for all of Kennedy's power. Nor does his strong wish not to be called "chicken," especially compared to old Ike. JFK's early executive style helps to explain much, and not only his technique of inspiring what Harlan Cleveland called "cooperation by reticence." Kennedy had not administered anything more complex than a PT boat. He had, as Bob Amory said later, no Dean Acheson to cross-examine the CIA men or the military. His own questions were too narrow to expose systemic weaknesses. He was too easily cowed, too, not by specialists in fields where he had worked himself, but in worlds new to him.

"If someone comes in and tells me this or that about the Minimum Wage Bill," the President told Schlesinger after the battle, "I have no hesitation in overruling them. But you always assume that the military and intelligence people have some secret skill not available to ordinary mortals." And so the rosy promises of success from Dulles, coupled with veiled threats about the Brigade's "disposal problem"; the soft, superbly marshaled sell of Bissell; and the final "Banzai!" message by the battle-hardened Colonel Hawkins from the scene in Nicaragua, all sank in deep.

It is too easy to dismiss Rusk and Burke's carpings about Kennedy's "informal sense of administration" as the nitpicking of paper-shufflers. As I traced the growth, graftings and transplants of the Cuba project, it became evident that it suffered not so much from disorder as from lack of much order at all. Even the gentle Taylor Commission Report, which Kennedy himself commissioned, clucked over the absence of coordination at the top, not to speak of chaos below: "Top level direction was given through ad hoc meetings of senior officials without consideration of operational plans in writing and with no arrangement for recording conclusions and decisions reached." The report might have singled out the rapid succession of changes in the plan, the countermanding of basic decisions by presidential phone calls without consultation with others and the consequent lack of feed-around so that on D-Day no one except Bissell had a clear grasp of what was approved and what was not, much less why or what for.

There was more to this than the traditional awkwardness of a new administration finding its way around Washington or Kennedy's executive inexperience. The venerable committeemen of the Eisenhower administration had spared themselves the making of many tough decisions by playing ping-pong with them in a beehive of committees, subcommittees and concurrences. Douglas Dillon's memory of Ike's Cabinet puttering with the placement of a door in the plan for an airport is a case in point. The New Frontiersmen were determined to gas this bureaucracy. If their filial fear of father Ike kept them from throwing out the Bay of Pigs because it was Eisenhower's baby, they could at least stage a filial revolt against his fuss-pot ways by throwing out his bathwater.

The famous Kennedy pragmatism was rooted not only in a certain arrogance. It went with a quality brought up in my conversations by an admirer like Goodwin, himself a man with a reputation for wielding a wicked hatchet. He spoke of Kennedy's coldness, detachment. Nothing less would have sent a handful of Cuban tools where they wanted to go, given the high risk. The Cubans, of course, played into this cynicism by consciously ignoring the many danger signs they saw so clearly. When Erneido Oliva told me he would have gone on this mission with fifty men, even if they had had to swim, he was not mouthing a phrase. The Cubans, in their guileless fervor, required protection from themselves. They did not get it from Kennedy and his men. Tools were meant to be used as tools. If the tools were human, too bad. Shedding tears for them after they were caught in a trap not of their making—that was another part of a tough job, the job of leadership.

To lead. To marshal the diversity of prejudices, styles and ancient feuds of competing bureaucracies. It is a presidential millstone. Perhaps nothing is more difficult to reconcile than the military and the civilian mind-set. To the Bay of Pigs the military brought understandable resentment from the start. This was a military venture for many reasons: the selection and orchestration of so much equipment, the complexity of interlocking land-air-naval strategies, the sheer size of the effort.* If the CIA could tame the Guatemala ant, this said nothing about the Cuba elephant.

To relegate the military to advisory back seats for a war because of misguided hopes that the core of the war could remain secret was to invite less than the best attention from the Pentagon chiefs. "By about November 1960, the impossibility of running Zapata as a covert operation under CIA should have been recognized and the situation reviewed," concluded the Taylor Commission. In their heart of hearts,

---

*The internal CIA estimate of the operation's cost, $50 million, is all but certain to be vastly less than all-inclusive.

some of the military thought the project was mildly mad. But warriors are not in business to shun wars, and whatever happened was not happening on their turf. Not giving them full and timely information made them feel unwanted, untrustworthy. Not to trouble telling them of two key decisions that materially altered air strategy was bizarre. But, like the Cubans, the military allowed themselves to become chessmen.

"By acquiescing in the Zapata plan, they gave the impression to others of approving it," said the Taylor Commission. It softened the charge by adding, "They reviewed the successive changes of the plan piecemeal and only within a limited context, a procedure which was inadequate for a proper examination of all the military ramifications."

Sixteen years after the event, Admiral Burke, pacing and fuming over his memories, said, "What the chiefs could have done is pound the desk and insist. We stated our case and then shut up. We should have been tough, but we weren't." Why not? Well, Burke said, they had never operated that way before, "building on sand," not "staffing" an operation. They relied on CIA assurances of uprisings in Cuba. And, as Burke did not point out, they could hardly be expected to turn themselves into recalcitrant troublemakers in the eyes of a new leader, a war hero at that.

To Kennedy, the chiefs' amenable attitude meant consent, and he told Burke so after the battle. To the chiefs, going along meant they were being good soldiers, not arguing with the Commander in Chief beyond a discreet point. No one worked more diligently than General David W. Gray to tighten up the bolts of the creaky Bay of Pigs vehicle. He blames himself for not having done still more. Of the meeting in the Cabinet Room where he had urged his chiefs to insist absolutely on air control and they did not, Gray said, "I guess I should have whispered something to Lemnitzer." Why hadn't he? As a one-star staff man, Gray knew his place as his chiefs knew theirs.

Kennedy was forgivably disposed to try leaving the dirty work of removing Castro to the CIA, the government's department of dirty tricks. Unlike the military and the State Department, the CIA got things done without so many committees, concurrences and pyramiding delays. It did not shirk tricky, nasty jobs. It didn't bellyache and constantly say that something was too audacious or couldn't be done. Bissell's impatience, energy and intellect were compatible with Kennedy's own. Bissell promised swift cancer surgery by enthusiastic ghost surgeons. And he wasn't stiff-necked. When Kennedy wanted the operation scaled down and its World War II invasion overtones muted, Bissell could be depended upon to re-engineer his tattered operating room promptly and without complaint. The President was too inexperienced and too isolated to determine the fatal balance which the Taylor Commission encapsuled in a single sentence: "Operational restrictions designed to protect its covert character should have been accepted only if they did not impair the chance of success."

Failing the President, it was Bissell's job to define that balance, but by the time the operation was hammered into its final form Bissell was wearing four hats. He had been allowed to become defendant, prosecutor, jury and judge (subject only to Kennedy's veto from the appeals bench). Such talent is not given to any man. Bissell's assistant, Jim Flannery, said it best: "Sheer brilliance could not overcome the fact that the clandestine service is essentially people." Even Bissell was not exempt from this constraint.

The culpabilities of the CIA are too painfully numerous to recite in their entirety. They range from manageable flaws—the unsuspected reefs and microwave-radio stations, the untested new outboard motors on the impractical landing craft, the ineptitude of Howard Hunt, Gerry Droller and their ilk—to such misjudgments of arrogance as the reluctance to place guns on the invasion ships, the underrating of the destructive power of Castro's T-33s, and the eagerness to "Cubanize" the expedition to the point where it was in fact almost as sloppy as it looked. These are the mistakes of a man who, like Bissell, thinks that technicians and their details are too unimportant to be left to generals.

The threatened resignations of Jake Engler and Colonel Hawkins, in protest against the operation's cutbacks, could be dismissed by a confident boss like Bissell as a passing outburst of frustration from underlings who saw themselves prevented from putting forth their best efforts and couldn't be expected to appreciate the constraints of keeping their baby alive at all in the climate of the Cabinet Room.

At another level stands Bissell's stifling of potential protest within the CIA by creating an isolation-within-isolation, refusing to use his own internal capabilities—Richard Helms, Sherman Kent of the Board of Estimates, Robert Amory of the intelligence service—to investigate Castro's true strength in depth. The failure to place Americans on the *Caribe* or the *Atlántico* with their vital stores of ammunition and to post a CIA command ship with a senior commander offshore are further acts of an operator determined not to brook interference with his personal will and to exercise control—direct personal control from the top—at almost any cost.*

---

*Control officers aboard the *Caribe* and the *Atlántico* might have made no difference, as the experience of "Curly's" attempt at CIA control over the Nino Díaz diversionary group showed. The much-abused Cubans had their points of defiance.

Two more serious errors were described in the Taylor Report as "the failure to make the air strike plan entirely clear in advance to the President and the Secretary of State" and the fact that "the President and senior officials had been greatly influenced by the understanding that the landing force could pass to guerrilla status if unable to hold the beachhead." An imprecise planner or briefer might have left such an impression inadvertently. Bissell was not noted for imprecision, and the wishful thought that the Brigade could melt into the mountains was grotesque and inexplicably negligent.

I mentioned this concept to a guerrilla fighter of that countryside, Félix Duque. He thought he wasn't hearing right. I asked him how long it would take for troops to march from the beaches to the Escambrays. He could not make a guess. The terrain was terrible. It was not a reasonable question.

Most puzzling, at least at first glance, was what the Taylor Report called "the failure to carry the issue of the air strikes to the President when the opportunity was presented and explain to him with proper force the probable military consequences of a last-minute cancellation."

This charge needs a close look. Consider the scene. Rusk, never more than lukewarm toward the project, has seen it boomerang in the United Nations. The United States stands defenseless before the UN as an aggressor, a sneak and a liar. The President, having scaled down the project and agonized over unleashing it at all, issues his cancellation order. General Cabell is not the man to argue with higher headquarters.* Dulles has placed himself neatly out of reach. It's late Sunday night. There is no time for still more meetings. The planes are on the runway. Soon the Brigade's frogmen will start placing the landing lights for the Brigade. Who would use "proper force" to argue against the Commander in Chief about the presidential decision just before midnight? Who could conjure up the "probable military consequences" of the cancellation? Rusk, the former headquarters lieutenant colonel in Burma? Cabell, the political general who drops rice and beans on Cuba? Bissell, whose military experience is limited to photo planes prowling at over seventy thousand feet?

Consider, especially, Bissell's bind. General Taylor told me, "An operator, very intent, has been on this thing for a year, has been living it and breathing it, and is dying to go ahead. He isn't going to tell the President, 'Mr. President, we can't really make this thing go on this

---

*In my talks with General Taylor, he offered this scenario of Cabell's thinking: "What am I going to say to the President? Am I going to say this is going to fail if we don't get those planes in? He immediately could ask me, 'Suppose I put them back on, what can you guarantee?' "

scale, because it's too small and too fragile,' not if he's just been lectured about the noise level and the secrecy. So the thing kind of suffocated of itself."

Surely, Bissell could be pardoned for not seizing the telephone to Glen Ora because he felt the CIA cause was "hopeless." And yet. With hindsight, consider other motives for keeping still. Fatigue? Pride of a star salesman countermanded one time too often? Lack of faith in the capability of one air strike to make a critical difference? Fear that the extreme fragility of the entire operation might finally be unmasked and lead to terrible questions—was it really possible to win with Brigade bombers flying five hours to gain thirty or forty-five minutes over Cuba without fighter protection?—questions that could trigger, just possibly, a scratching of the landings at the ultimate deadline?

The most sweeping critique of the operation was the one conducted in the late spring and summer of 1961 by the CIA's inspector general, Lyman B. Kirkpatrick, Jr. A tall, lean, handsome man, ruddy-cheeked and with piercing light-blue eyes, Kirkpatrick had been a leading candidate to succeed Dulles. He was sidetracked to the IG post after he contracted polio in 1952 following a trip abroad for the agency, and was confined to a wheelchair.* General Cabell and other agency brass felt that his physical handicap precluded his advancement.

Kirkpatrick and his inspectors interviewed some three hundred CIA men who worked on the Cuba project. His report, never declassified and probably buried forever, was devastating. Its findings were reflected in an article Kirkpatrick published in 1972 in the *Naval War College Review*. It noted that "no one seriously studied" whether it was even possible to overthrow Castro in the first place. Strong indications existed that it wasn't. "If there was a resistance to Fidel Castro," Kirkpatrick wrote, "it was mostly in Miami." And: "All intelligence reports coming from allied sources indicated quite clearly that he was thoroughly in command of Cuba and was supported by most of the people who remained on the island."

The President, Kirkpatrick concluded, did a terrible job of informing himself. Kennedy "seemed to think this was going to be some sort of mass infiltration that would perhaps, through some mystique, become quickly invisible." And: "It is not known whether the President examined in any depth the concept of the air raids or the attention they would attract." (It can be argued that it was Bissell's job to brief the President on such weaknesses. It was, in theory. In real life, this is like

---

*In 1978, Kirkpatrick, still ruddy-cheeked and cheerful, and still in a wheelchair, presided at Brown University as a professor of political science and was considered by President Jimmy Carter for the job of CIA deputy director.

expecting a salesman to assure his customer that his company's refrigerator does not cool well when the weather turns warm. Superior salesmen need not be liars. Their thinking does tend to become colored by inordinate faith in their product.)

The operation's cover appalled Kirkpatrick. Miami was a "goldfish bowl." So were Guatemala and Nicaragua, small, gossipy communities where "nearly everybody knows what is going on." The IG suggested the Brigade "could have been isolated somewhere in the vast reaches of a Fort Bragg or a Fort Benning" (which ignored the State Department's phobia against training foreigners on U.S. soil).

The Guatemala operation was a preposterous precedent, according to this insider. It "only succeeded by the narrowest of margins," and President Arbenz "had but a very limited force to support him as opposed to Castro, whose 200,000-man army and militia were rapidly increasing in both quality and strength."

Kirkpatrick pooh-poohed Bissell's notion that the operation could have been kept secret. "It lost all of its veils, all five, before it was ever mounted," he concluded. "It was well known that it was totally supported by the United States. And at some point along the line somebody, somewhere around the President should have said, "Mr. President, this is going to create one hell of a lot of noise!" No senior adviser (except Fulbright) said this because, as Kirkpatrick remarked, the operation "was handled as though it was so sensitive that people who were trusted with the highest secrets of the government could not be trusted with it." (General Taylor also told me it was "incredible" how the President could have gone along with the commitment to covertness "without ever challenging it.")

In my conversations with him, Kirkpatrick continued this barrage with still further criticism. Was it really impossible to turn back the invasion flotilla at the last moment? "Nonsense," he said; "a couple of destroyers would have stopped them." Why was nothing known about the reefs offshore? Because no leader was sufficiently qualified in amphibious operations. Why were below-par agency men recruited for the operation and so few who could speak Spanish? Because the operators failed to go through the personnel rosters systematically and didn't take advantage of Dulles' order to assign top priority to the venture. Why was so much ammunition and all the communications equipment packed into one hull? "Because they failed to look at the manifest like they failed to look at the rosters."

Why was the job handed to the CIA at all? Because, said Kirkpatrick, the success in overturning governments in places like Guatemala ("heady wine," as Jake Engler told me) insinuated the notion into the heads of policy-makers, even the genial Ike, that the CIA could secretly perform "with baling wire" what generals could no longer be allowed to do openly with armies, not if a nation wanted to maintain international respect.

In my view, Castro's fate was placed in the hands of the CIA and kept there past November 1960, when the project became too ambitious for a clandestine service, past Kennedy's efforts to scale it down, and past the fatal midnight crisis of the canceled air strike, principally because of the CIA's independent, arrogantly elitist ways and Bissell's ambition to accomplish his superman task, his refusal to share its control and his inability to give up on it even when it was almost certainly doomed.

Why would a brilliant man behave that way? When I traded notes with one of his former colleagues about Bissell's fidgety habits—the twisting of the paper clips, the tossing of the rubber ball—this CIA colleague, smiling speculatively, brought up the psychotic clicking of metal balls, the trademark of Captain Queeg in *The Caine Mutiny*.

I have not formed a sinister picture of the architect behind the Bay of Pigs. He could lose his temper over trifles. So do many highly intelligent people. Moments of the most intense crisis found him composed and functioning rationally. When others collapsed into despair, Bissell could enjoy his wife's piano-playing. When even the serene Allen Dulles went through the roof over Kirkpatrick's sizzling IG report and informed everybody that he considered it a self-serving hatchet job, Bissell, Kirkpatrick's principal target, remained calm and polite. "A thoroughly decent man," everyone said. "Civilized." Such a man is not sinister and not psychotic. A Dr. Strangelove would not be admired, even in disaster, by sharp-eyed intellects like the Bundys, Schlesinger, the Rostows and the rest of Bissell's many well-placed fans.

What, then, moved Bissell so irresistibly in the wrong direction? Consider objective.

In the world of the late 1970s, it can be argued that the urge to depose Castro was at best an overreaction to the man and his dictatorial regime, at worst irrational. The world of 1961 was a very different place. The "Iron Curtain" was an impenetrable reality. East and West seemed to be camps rigidly incapable of even limited compatibility. Wars, cold and hot, were part of the climate. Even nuclear war was entirely thinkable, as the placement of Soviet missiles in Cuba a year following the Bay of Pigs demonstrated all too dramatically. The West's refusal to curb the malignancy of dictatorship at an early stage had lately presented to the world Hitler and World War II. Nikita Khrushchev, now almost fondly remembered as an uncle-like character actor who stomped around Iowa pig farms, was an appalling monster when he rattled his missiles and displayed his uncontrollable temper by pounding his shoe on his desk and screaming he would "bury" the West.

Such traumatic, even searing memories were fresh and real in the minds of the men behind the Bay of Pigs. Their urge to eliminate Castro, while ethically indefensible, is easy to understand. One wonders how many American voters would, in those days, have endorsed even the CIA's grotesque assassination plots if the question had somehow appeared on a ballot.

If the objective was well within the mainstream of national thought, it certainly fit Bissell's vision of his ascent from anonymous second-echelon bureaucrat to the summit of the policy-makers. Kennedy had promised him Dulles' job upon the old man's retirement. Which placed Bissell on probation. Another personality might have cooled it. Not Bissell. He was the thunderer of *The Harkness Hoot*. He didn't need job security for his family. He relished risks—in his mountain climbing, as skipper of his boat, as commander in chief of the Richard Bissell Air Force with its fleet of U-2s thumbing noses at the whole earth. To control the never-before-controlled, to systematize messes, in economics as in spying—his life was made of such challenges.

His colleagues also thought he felt an urge to prove himself as tough as the CIA's alumni from OSS who fought behind enemy lines in World War II. Bissell sensed that Kennedy would not, as the President put it to Sorensen, "grab his nuts" in fear of the Cuban caper. Bissell would not grab his, either.

And yet. Why would a careful planner bull ahead with a scheme which, in retrospect, was so absurdly vulnerable? After all, "it was," as Walt W. Rostow said to me, "the most screwed-up operation there has ever been." Bissell first spoke up in his defense in an interview with *The Washington Evening Star* in 1965. He conceded he could be "criticized for allowing this chipping away to go on, without insisting on the whole plan or cancellation" and that he was too "involved in seeing it go ahead." He insisted that the venture failed "because of lack of control of the air" and said, "If we had been able to dump five times the tonnage of bombs on Castro's airfields, we would have had a damned good chance." In a letter to Schlesinger in 1965, he floated much the same thesis and pronounced himself "on balance, unregenerate."

In my conversations with Bissell, he maintained that the smallness of the expedition's air force was the plan's "worst mistake" (which ignores the reality that Kennedy refused to use even its few planes fully). He said that the impossibility of the guerrilla option had simply not been "thought through," and that the lack of contingency planning was "sloppy." An early large-scale internal uprising had never been in the cards, he insisted. But a firm beachhead might have become its catalyst in a week or two.

Bissell's former student, Mac Bundy, agreed in 1977 that the air strength was not only too small; it was much too small, but he pointed out that the planners said nothing about it. "They didn't say, 'Look, you've got to double your bet,'" he observed. He felt that the canceled strike was only "a marginal adjustment." One theme ran through all the meetings, as Bundy saw it: "JFK was playing for table stakes. He wasn't going to the bank." Bundy blamed himself in one respect: "I had a very wrong estimate of the consequences of failure, the mess."

It must still be asked: Could the venture have succeeded as it was mounted at H-Hour? Conceivably, just possibly, yes. I believe that if the supply ships had been able to withdraw safely before sunup and return at night to unload all their ammunition, the beachhead might have lasted for an unpredictable length of additional time. If a second air strike had knocked out the remaining T-33s and Sea Furies, it would have taken still longer for Castro to apply full pressure against the Brigade, and the exiles' planes could have begun to fly from the Girón airstrip. With or without Castro's planes, a reasonably secure beachhead could have become a base for a Miró Cardona government. How far the United States and other Latin-American countries might have supported such a government is anybody's guess.

The Bay of Pigs was a wild gamble. It was not mad. It failed because Kennedy and Bissell failed. They failed for altogether human reasons. The drive for gutsy action. The reluctance to cut losses except at the risk of a world war. The lure of a tar baby, whether called Cuba or Vietnam. Egos so tall that the eyes and ears can shut out whatever one prefers not to see or hear.

The final arrogance, the failure to inform themselves about Castro's strength and his people's spirit or even to inform their own infiltration teams, I attribute to the gook syndrome. American policy-makers suffer from it chronically. They tend to underestimate grossly the capabilities and determination of people who committed the sin of not having been born Americans, especially "gooks" whose skins are less than white. It was nearly fatal in Vietnam. It could have been fatal off the Bay of Pigs when the destroyer *Eaton* was bracketed by two stray shells. World War III quite possibly was short-circuited only because three intelligent men—an American commodore, a Cuban jet pilot and a Cuban troop commander trained at Fort Sill, Oklahoma—happened to keep their cool. An accident of luck.

Two types of leadership were working against each other: the Yale brand versus the Sierra Maestra brand. These were not necessarily predatory cliques. Leaders, as all people, surround themselves with helpers they feel comfortable with, who proved effective in the past—birds of a feather. The Yale intellectual mind-set did sell the Sierra Maestra guerrilla mind-set short. Yale lacked respect, if it thought about it at all, for human assets: the verve of a Félix Duque setting off to do battle with his bazooka and without orders; the skill and pride of the Cuban Air Force pilots and their mechanics' ingenuity in patching up worn-out planes; the doggedness of a Víctor Caballero improvising his own sandbags to protect his machine gun; the pride, the compulsion, the childlike bounce of the odd-looking, bearded guerrilla fighter in the fatigue suit whom everybody called by his first name, who knew how to maneuver and judge a battle from phones in shops and offices.

"They underestimated the fanaticism and combative spirit of those who supported Castro unconditionally," wrote Philip W. Bonsal, the last American ambassador to Havana. "The notion that this support would melt away and that tens of thousands of Cubans would defect or refuse to fight if the hundreds of Castro's opponents, whom the United States had armed and trained, obtained an initial success, was simply wishful thinking."

Arrogance. Wishful thinking. Human. They were human. All leaders are human. It could happen again.

The People Behind
This Book

It was a large, peaceful room in a Birmingham, Alabama, motel, a link in one of those enormous, faceless chain enterprises that mass-produce identical units of comfort. I was interviewing an American pilot who had flown in the Bay of Pigs operation. He was in his forties, bright, calm. He had been talking about his experiences "down south"—the word "Cuba" was still stamped "secret" in his mind. The airport with its Alabama Air National Guard headquarters, his base seventeen years ago and still his headquarters now that he was a civilian pilot, was a few blocks away.

The spools in my tape recorder had been absorbing his memories for more than two hours. I had been following him intently, interrupting often, asking for detail, still more detail, asking him to go again and again over his memories of flight plans, radio messages sent and received, turns over the target, enemy aircraft eluded, how he felt at each point of each mission.

Only when we stopped for coffee did I notice how upright this seemingly calm, certainly articulate man sat in the soft fake-leather easy chair. His spine was an inch or two from the chair's back. The palms of his hands were cupping the armrests tightly. They looked as if they had never moved.

In the homes of the Cuban exiles in Florida the scene rarely varied. The low new suburban houses, overfurnished and overdecorated in bright colors, often much gold, were almost painfully neat, spotless. Appointments with these men were cumbersome to arrange. If I called at 8 A.M., they were off to work. If I called at 8 P.M., they were probably

328

not home yet. Cubans work hard. Dinner was late, Latin style. The best time to talk was after 10 P.M. The interview, always in the untouched-looking living room, would start slowly. I would make sure to mention names of other men with whom I had talked. Not Bay of Pigs veterans at random, certainly not planners or trainers of the CIA whom the Cubans had never met or knew only by first names or fake names. Defeat needs the company of friends. I mentioned other Cubans who had served in the same unit or traveled to the beaches on the same ship and could therefore be trusted.

After a while, the man's wife would come in, hesitantly, sometimes to be introduced, often seemingly ignored. She would sit down, listen, look at her man, never say a word. If there were children at home, they would edge in next, perch on the periphery of the room, perhaps with young wives or husbands, listening to memories flow.

Most of these men had never been interviewed. In most homes the wives and in-laws obviously had never heard these memories before, at least not in detail. Defeat is not easy to share.

Seventeen, eighteen years later, for the men who were there, the Bay of Pigs remained a peak experience of their lives, for some *the* peak experience. Feelings ran high, as they do about high experience. Among Castro's veterans in Cuba, the feelings were unambiguous: indignation over the homeland violated, the families threatened, the revolution challenged, insulted; these men talked easily, searched their memories energetically. Among the retired CIA and the American military men, emotions were mixed. But not about why the operation failed, who was to blame. It was the goddamned politicians. They turned chicken. They whittled at it, interfered, weakened it, doomed it. It was inexcusable, near-treason.

Why open it up now? Secrecy is more than an obligation. It is a habit. When I talked to Richard Drain, the CIA director of operations for the Bay of Pigs project, he was working on fund raising in the office of Bishop Francis Sayre of the National Cathedral in Washington; before Drain went home at night, he still turned his "in" and "out" baskets upside down to show nonexistent security officers that he had not left any nonexistent classified papers lying about.

The CIA men searched their consciences, called one another up before they would be interviewed, to check whether this book project was legitimate, whether they owed it to history to talk out of school.

I also believe they talked because their boss talked, and I believe Richard Bissell talked because he is a gentleman, a teacher, a man who knows *noblesse oblige*, especially obligation to history.

For the exile Cubans, talking triggered even more and deeper problems. Their long-ago agreement not to discuss the operation had been voided when the Brigade commanders told their stories in a book back in 1964 (*The Bay of Pigs*, by Haynes Johnson). This did not solve the personal problem of how to talk about what almost all viewed as betrayal, betrayal by the assassinated President, more especially by his cursed advisers, Rusk, whom they saw as gutless, Stevenson, whom they saw as the world's most despicable coward. Finally, these men had to deal with the problem of their betrayal by America, the country that welcomed them from tyranny, that they loved, that had since made them reasonably happy and prosperous. Many Cuban exiles had still not worked that problem out: what America owed them (another try at unseating Castro?) and what they owed America (silence?). It was not a matter of their talking only about failure. It was talking about a dear relative who had sold them down the river long ago but more than made up for it later.

The Americans and the exile Cubans talked, I believe, and they almost all did talk, because time had eased internal conflicts. "The statute of limitations had run out," as one of them said, on the secrecy agreements. Conscience likes repressed memories to come out. And, years later, it is no longer so painful to talk about ancient surgery. Sometimes it is even interesting. Especially when you have never been told what really went on in the operating room and, suddenly, here comes a perfect stranger, a writer, who knows, and who is willing to tell you right in your own living room what you have wondered about for years. I always told.

I owe special debts to some.

Barbara Lang Stern had the idea.

Richard M. Bissell, Jr.'s, early confidence in the project made it possible.

Theodore C. Sorensen, my friend from the days when President Kennedy still misspelled his name, opened crucial doors in the Kennedy circle.

Arthur M. Schlesinger, Jr., interrupted his own work to rummage through memories and files.

David A. Phillips, James E. Flannery, Richard Drain, Lyman B. Kirkpatrick, Jr., Robert K. Davis, Robert Amory, Jr., and Jake Engler, all formerly of the CIA, opened many once secret doors.

Dr. James E. O'Neill, Deputy Archivist of the United States, assisted by Judith Koucky, helped cope with the classified bureaucracy.

Eduardo Ferrer opened doors of the Cuban community in Miami.

General Reid Doster opened the doors of the Alabama air contingent.

Fred Sherman of the *Miami Herald* and his wife, Eleanor, provided logistical support in Florida.

Bienvenido Asbierno of the Cuban Foreign Ministry directed the search for the "impossible" eyewitnesses and ran interference through the Cuban bureaucracy.

Admiral Arleigh Burke lent personal prestige that opened Navy doors.

Anna C. Urband of the Department of the Navy located the all-but-vanished American skippers and pilots.

Grayston Lynch answered questions that no one else could answer, because he was there with his photographic memory.

Juan Ortega Gatell and Carmen Quintana translated the flood tide of words in Cuba.

General Maxwell D. Taylor allowed himself to be annoyed and interrupted by too many questions.

Senators Abraham Ribicoff and Lowell Weicker wrote helpful letters to officials with whom their influence counted.

William W. Moss made the John F. Kennedy Library accessible.

Too many people to be named opened up personal memories filled with pain: the men of the Brigade, the Alabama pilots, the civilians in Playa Girón and Playa Larga.

Juan Pou, Juan Pérez Franco, Silvio Pérez, Andy Pruna, José Alonso, Ramiro Sánchez, Raúl Masvidal, Juan Cosculuella, Osvaldo Inguanzo, among many others, helped locate crucial eyewitnesses.

Erneido Oliva, second-in-command of the Brigade, was helpful despite great apprehension.

Hugo Yedra opened doors at the Permanent Mission of Cuba to the United Nations, and in Havana.

Michael Korda, editor in chief of Simon and Schuster, thought it would work when nobody else thought so.

Some who could have helped chose not to do so. They had their reasons.

Colonel Jack Hawkins refused to discuss any aspects of his role as the military commander and then carefully informed the CIA that he had done so.

José Pérez (Pepe) San Román, the Brigade commander, was unwell and begged off being interviewed because, as he said with agitation on the telephone, the events "ruined my life."

The CIA bureaucracy of the present stonewalled and confirmed suspicion about itself by refusing to admit the time off the clock on the wall.

Bibliographical
Notes

The literature on the Bay of Pigs is fairly sizable but fragmentary. Most of the persons on whose eyewitness accounts this book is largely based had never consented to be interviewed before. Many were still reluctant. Some would be interviewed only after they learned that associates had discussed their own (and their associates') roles. Several asked that their real names still not be revealed.

Many key men—the Kennedys, Allen Dulles, Adlai Stevenson, General Cabell, Tracy Barnes, Miró Cardona—are deceased. Many United States government documents were ordered destroyed in 1961, particularly those generated in the Pentagon and by the U.S. Navy ships. Documents used in this book—principally the available sections of the Taylor Commission Report—were only lately declassified as a result of persistent efforts over two and a half years by the author which were stubbornly resisted, especially by the National Security Council staff.

The bureaucratic resourcefulness in covering up and stalling on the disclosure of long-ago bad news must be witnessed to be believed, despite presidential protestations and "Freedom of Information" laws. At this writing, interagency committee meetings are still in progress to debate whether to declassify "desanitized" versions of certain records of meetings of the Taylor Commission seventeen years ago. As to source material available earlier:

A Thousand Days, by Arthur M. Schlesinger, Jr. (Boston: Houghton Mifflin, 1965), contains the best overall account of events so far. It is especially valuable because of the author's day-by-day contacts with President Kennedy prior to the invasion and his familiarity with the nuances of Cuban exile politics.

Kennedy, by Theodore C. Sorensen (New York: Harper & Row, 1965), devotes a mere eighteen pages to the Bay of Pigs. They are the best available defense brief for Kennedy, superbly marshalled, and also singularly valuable

332

for their account of the President's private and unsparing postmortem thoughts.

The Bay of Pigs, by Haynes Johnson (New York: Norton, 1964), was written in collaboration with the leaders of the invasion Brigade and is a masterful, encyclopedic reconstruction of the exile Cubans' involvement. However, very few nonexile sources were available to the author at the time of publication. This work, incidentally, is not in the Cuban National Library, and the Cuban leaders seem not to have read it.

"Give Us This Day," by E. Howard Hunt (New Rochelle, N.Y.: Arlington House, 1973), is a belated grab bag of Bay of Pigs memories, admittedly written off the cuff, without benefit of notes or interviewing, by the former CIA agent, Watergate burglar, and pulp novelist. It contains useful insights into the preinvasion politicking among Cuban exiles in Miami but very little else, reflecting the author's limited involvement in the project. It is not distinguished for accuracy of detail.

Operación Puma, by Eduardo Ferrer, is a painstaking compilation of the air war conducted by the Cuban exiles, based on extensive interviews and records, by a participant pilot. It was published in 1975 by the author, but only in Spanish and distributed largely in the Miami area.

The Invisible Government, by David Wise and Thomas B. Ross (New York: Random House, 1964), contains careful research on the Bay of Pigs to buttress the book's overall indictment of CIA duplicity and incompetence. It reveals some of the then unknown operations of the Alabama Air National Guard and of Radio Swan. But its value on this event is restricted by the authors' lack of access to primary sources.

The Cuban Invasion, by Karl E. Meyer and Tad Szulc (New York: Praeger, 1962), is a fascinating little (160 pages) book, the first on the subject, detailed and shrewd in its interpretation of Cuban politics, indigenous and exile, astonishingly short on facts considering the reportorial skills of the authors.

The John F. Kennedy Library in Waltham, Massachusetts, contains valuable if highly selective and often self-serving oral histories of such knowledgeable men as Richard M. Bissell, Jr., Lyman B. Kirkpatrick, Jr., and Admiral Arleigh Burke. The most enlightening and effective of these recollections is from Robert Amory, Jr.

The memoirs of General Maxwell D. Taylor, Kenneth O'Donnell and David F. Powers, Pierre Salinger, Richard M. Nixon, Adolf A. Berle, Walt W. Rostow, Roger Hilsman, Nikita Khrushchev, Mario Lazo, Chester Bowles, and David A. Phillips contain vignettes about the Bay of Pigs that shed flashes of color but little light, and tend to raise more questions than they answer. General Taylor's literate autobiography, *Swords and Plowshares* (New York: W. W. Norton, 1972), is, at least on this subject, a monument to excessive circumspection or sketchy memory.

"A Perfect Failure: The Bay of Pigs," the second chapter of the intriguing book by Professor Irving L. Janis of the Yale University psychology department, *Victims of Groupthink* (Boston: Houghton Mifflin, 1972), is discussed in detail in the Conclusion following Chapter Seven.

Of the many articles in magazines, the less said, the more mercifully history is served. They reflect mostly the CIA's zeal to hush up the whole affair and blame other government agencies as artfully as manageable. An article by Charles J. V. Murphy, "Cuba: The Record Set Straight," in the September 1961 *Fortune,* is an obvious major CIA leak, but is so fragmentary and askew (Murphy was a close personal friend of Allen Dulles) as to make a caricature of its title.

Two works in the periodical literature are valuable:

"We Who Tried," by John Dille and a team of reporters from *Life* (May 10, 1963), based on interviews with members of the Cuban exile Brigade conducted shortly after their release from prison, represents the Time, Inc., method of vacuum-cleaner reporting at its most impressive: dramatic, thorough and emotionally affecting. Despite the magazine's skill in picture research, the article is illustrated by drawings, a reflection of how stubbornly the many available photographs were suppressed.

"Paramilitary Case Study—The Bay of Pigs," by Lyman B. Kirkpatrick, Jr., in the November–December 1972 issue of *Naval War College Review,* is an opinionated yet extraordinarily revealing glimpse into the thinking of the man who, as inspector general of the CIA at the time of the Bay of Pigs, conducted the agency's internal investigation of its failure and was denounced for his honest efforts.

The literature from Cuba also reflects an absence of systematic study, which the authorities are now eager to remedy. A four-volume potpourri of memories, *Playa Girón: Derrota del Imperialismo (Defeat of Imperialism),* is in the Library of Congress in Washington. Castro's television speech of April 23, 1961, *Playa Girón, A Victory of the People,* is also available there, even in English translation. It does not come close to doing justice to his detailed "adventures" as discussed with this author for the first time in a six-hour interview on June 6, 1978, in the Commander in Chief's third-floor office at the Council of State building on the Plaza of the Revolution in Havana.

Amanecer en Girón (Dawn at Girón), by Rafael del Pino (Havana: Instituto Cubano del Libro, Editorial de Arte y Literatura, 1969), is this T-33 jet pilot's slim (102 pages) but vivid recollection of the tiny band of Cuban airmen who made all the difference in the battle.

The most detailed and valuable—if again fragmentary—documentation on the Cuban side of the fighting is a two-page account by Magali García More in the April 21, 1976, issue of *Granma,* the daily newspaper of the Communist Party of Cuba. It is based on interviews with Ramón José Fernandez, then a principal Army commander and now Minister of Education, as well as his meticulous files of battle orders from Castro and his other records.

Chapter Notes

CHAPTER ONE: PLOT AT THE CIA

Interviews

Almeida, José, M.D.; Alsop, Joseph; Amory, Robert, Jr.; Basulto, José; Bissell, Richard M., Jr.; Bundy, McGeorge; Bundy, William P.; Castro, Fidel; Catledge, Turner; Cheever, Francis Sargent, M.D.; Cushman, Robert E., Jr.; Davis, Robert K.; Doster, George R.; Drain, Richard; Engler, Jake; Ferrer, Eduardo; Flannery, James E.; Goodwin, Richard; Gray, David W.; Gray, Gordon; Helms, Richard M.; King, J. C.; Klein, Herbert G.; Kirkpatrick, Lyman B., Jr.; Liebert, Herman W.; Nodal, Rodolfo; Parrott, Thomas; Persons, Albert C.; Phillips, David A.; Rostow, Eugene; Rostow, Walt W.; Spinks, John O.; Varona, Antonio de.

Documents

Church, Frank, chairman, Select Committee to Study Governmental Operations with Respect to Intelligence Activities, *Alleged Assassination Plots Involving Foreign Leaders*, Senate Report No. 94-465, Nov. 20, 1975 (Washington: U.S. Government Printing Office, 1975).

Taylor, Maxwell D., chairman, Cuban Study Group, "Narrative of the Anti-Castro Cuban Operation Zapata," June 13, 1961, sanitized version declassified May 8, 1977 (Part I of Taylor Commission Report).

Ibid., "Memorandums for Record of Paramilitary Study Group Meetings," April 22 through May 25, 1961, sanitized version declassified June 23, 1978 (Part II of Taylor Commission Report).

Books

Catledge, Turner, *My Life and The Times* (New York: Harper & Row, 1971).

Ferrer, Eduardo, *Operación Puma* (Miami: International Aviation Consultants, Inc., 1975).

Hunt, Howard, *"Give Us This Day"* (New Rochelle, N.Y.: Arlington House, 1973), for Hunt's personal movements and reactions in Miami.

Johnson, Haynes, *The Bay of Pigs* (New York: Norton, 1964), especially for the Brigade's training and revolt in the Guatemala camps.

McGaffin, William, and Knoll, Erwin, *Anything But the Truth* (New York: Putnam, 1968), contains text of David Kraslow's letter to Clifton Daniel detailing Kraslow's abortive research for the *Miami Herald*.

Meyer, Karl, and Szulc, Tad, *The Cuban Invasion* (New York: Praeger, 1962).

Nixon, Richard M., *Six Crises* (Garden City, N.Y.: Doubleday, 1962), for Nixon's reactions to the presidential debates.

Phillips, David A., *The Night Watch* (New York: Atheneum, 1977).

Pierson, George Wilson, *Yale: The University College, 1921–1937* (New Haven: Yale University Press, 1955), for background on *The Harkness Hoot* and its leaders.

Wise, David, *The Politics of Lying* (New York: Random House, 1973).

Wise, David, and Ross, Thomas B., *The Invisible Government* (New York: Random House, 1964), especially for background of Radio Swan and of the Alabama Air National Guard contingent.

Ibid., *The U-2 Affair* (New York: Random House, 1962).

Articles

Hartford Courant, Dec. 26, 1963, "A Debt Is Owed," by Joseph Alsop.

Life, May 4, 1959, "Fidel's Fine Time in U.S."

Ibid., Oct. 3, 1960, "Boorish Odyssey of K.'s Man from Havana."

The Nation, Nov. 19, 1960, "Are We Training Cuban Guerrillas?"

Newsweek, Apr. 20, 1959, "Bearded Visitor: What's on Castro's Mind?"

Ibid., Apr. 27, 1959, "V.I.P.: Wild About the Beard."

Ibid., May 4, 1959, "V.I.P. with Beard: The Circus."

Ibid., Aug. 23, 1976, "The Mafia: A Swim in the Bay."

The New Yorker, Oct. 8, 1960, "Notes and Comment" ("The Talk of the Town").

The New York Times, Jan. 10, 1961, "U.S. Helps Train an Anti-Castro Force at Secret Guatemalan Air-Ground Base," by Paul P. Kennedy.

Ibid., May 7, 1961, "Anti-Castro Cubans Say CIA Imprisoned Them for 11 Weeks," by Sam Pope Brewer.

Ibid., July 31, 1975, "Maheu Says He Recruited Man for CIA in Castro Poison Plot," by Nicholas M. Horrock.

Ibid., Aug. 9, 1976, "Crime Figure, Linked to Plot on Castro, Found Slain," by the Associated Press.

Ibid., Feb. 25, 1977, "Rosselli Called Victim of Mafia Because of his Senate Testimony," by Nicholas Gage.

Reader's Digest, November 1964, "Cuba, Castro and John F. Kennedy," by Richard M. Nixon.

Time, April 27, 1959, "Cuba: The Other Face."

Ibid., May 4, 1959, "Cuba: Humanist Abroad."

Ibid., Oct. 3, 1960, "Diplomacy: Flight to Harlem."

U.S. News & World Report, May 4, 1959, "A Size-Up of Cuban Leader from Private Talks."

CHAPTER TWO: ESCALATION

Interviews

Alonso, José; Amory, Robert, Jr.; Basulto, José; Beerli, Stanley W.; Bissell, Richard M.; Burke, Arleigh R.; Clifford, Clark M.; Cushman, Robert E., Jr.; Dennison, Robert;

Dillon, Douglas; Douglas, James H.; Drain, Richard; Engler, Jake; García, Eduardo; Goodwin, Richard; Gray, David W.; Inguanzo, Osvaldo; Lansdale, Edward G.; Lemnitzer, Lyman L.; Klein, Herbert G.; Lynch, Grayston; Mann, Thomas C.; Martiínez, Eugenio Rolando; Perez, Silvio; Pruna, Andy; Recarey, Jorge.

Documents

Douglas, James H., May 10, 1976, memorandum to the author on Pentagon reaction to the Cuba project during the Eisenhower administration, also citing his consultation with Defense Secretary Thomas Gates.
Taylor Report, Parts I and II.

Books

Nixon, Richard M., *Six Crises* (Garden City, N.Y.: Doubleday, 1962).

Articles

Harper's Magazine, August 1975, "The Kennedy Vendetta," by George Crile III and Taylor Branch.
Newsday, Sept. 10, 1965, "Ike Speaks Out: Bay of Pigs Was All JFK's," by Earl Mazo.
The New York Times, Oct. 21, 1960, "Kennedy Asks Aid for Cuban Rebels to Defeat Castro," by Peter Kihss.

CHAPTER THREE: REAPPRAISAL AND MOMENTUM

Interviews

Aaron, Annette; Alonso, José; Amory, Robert, Jr.; Bissell, Richard M. Jr.; Bowles, Chester; Bundy, McGeorge; Burke, Arleigh R.; Castro, Fidel; Clark, John A.; Crutchfield, Robert R.; Dennison, Robert; Dunham, Frank C.; Duque, Félix; Engler, Jake; Fickenscher, Edward R., Jr.; Flannery, James E.; Forgy, William J.; Fulbright, J. William; García, Eduardo; Gleichauff, Jay; Gray, David W.; Hilsman, Roger; Kirkpatrick, Lyman B., Jr.; Lynch, Grayston; Noble, Jim; Perkins, Peter; Phillips, David A.; Plank, John; Pruna, Andy; Recarey, Jorge; Sayers, Samuel; Schlesinger, Arthur, Jr.; Searcy, S. S., Jr.; Sopo, Edgar; Sordo, Juan, M.D.; Tirado, Gustavo.

Oral Histories (on file at the John F. Kennedy Library, Waltham, Mass.)

Amory, Robert, Jr.; Bissell, Richard M., Jr.; Bowles, Chester; Burke, Arleigh R.; Kirkpatrick, Lyman B., Jr.; Sorensen, Theodore C.

Documents

Church, Frank, chairman, Select Committee to Study Governmental Operations with Respect to Intelligence Operations, *Alleged Assassination Plots Involving Foreign Leaders*, Senate Report No. 94-465, Nov. 20, 1975 (Washington: U.S. Government Printing Office, 1975).
Central Intelligence Agency, Jan. 27, 1961, "Memorandum for the Director. Subject: Is Time on Our Side in Cuba?" by Sherman Kent, chairman, National Board of Estimates, declassified May 26, 1976.
Ibid., Jan. 30, 1961, Information Report No. 00-A31777796, declassification date unrecorded.
Ibid., March 2, 1961, "Supplement to the Current Intelligence Digest," declassified April 5, 1977.

Ibid., March 10, 1961, Information Report No. CS-2/467,630, declassification date unrecorded.

Ibid., March 10, 1961, "Memorandum for the Director. Subject: Is Time on Our Side in Cuba?" (*supra*).

Ibid., March 13, 1961, Information Report No. CS-3/468,320, declassification date unrecorded.

National Security Council, March 11, 1961, Action Memorandum 31, by McGeorge Bundy, declassification date unrecorded.

Taylor Report, Parts I and II.

United States Air Force, March 17, 1961, Intelligence Report No. 144,512.

Books

Bowles, Chester, *Promises to Keep* (New York: Harper & Row, 1971).

Cosculuella, J. A., *Cuatro Años en la Ciénaga de Zapata* (Havana: Comisión Nacional Cubana de la UNESCO, 1965), contains the best available history and ecology on the invasion area.

Dubois, Jules, *Fidel Castro* (New York, Bobbs-Merrill, 1959).

Hilsman, Roger, *To Move a Nation* (Garden City, N.Y.: Doubleday, 1967).

Matthews, Herbert L., *The Cuban Story* (New York, Braziller, 1961).

Meyer, Karl E. (ed.), *Fulbright of Arkansas* (Washington: Robert B. Luce, Inc., 1963), contains the full text of Fulbright's memorandum on the Cuba project to President Kennedy.

Morison, Samuel Eliot, *Admiral of the Ocean Sea: A Life of Christopher Columbus* (Boston: Little, Brown, 1944; an Atlantic Monthly Press Book). This and the following work contain Columbus' own description of the discovery of the invasion area.

Ibid., *Christopher Columbus, Mariner* (Boston: Little, Brown, 1955; an Atlantic Monthly Press Book).

Morris, William and Mary, *Dictionary of Word and Phrase Origins* (New York: Harper & Row, 1962), for the origin of the term "filibuster."

Schlesinger, Arthur M., Jr., *A Thousand Days* (Boston: Houghton Mifflin, 1965).

CHAPTER FOUR: AT THE WATERSHED

Interviews

Bissell, Richard M., Jr.; Bundy, McGeorge; Bundy, William P.; Castro, Fidel; Catledge, Turner; Cleveland, Harlan; Corona, Ramón; Díaz, Renato; Drain, Richard; Engler, Jake; Fritchey, Clayton; Fulbright, J. William; Goodwin, Richard; Gray, David W.; Kirkpatrick, Lyman B., Jr.; Lundahl, Arthur; Mann, Thomas C.; Meeker, Leonard; Nitze, Paul; Noyes, Charles P.; Pedersen, Richard F.; Phillips, David A.; Plank, John; Plimpton, Francis T. P.; Reston, James; Rostow, Walt W.; Rusk, Dean; Schlesinger, Arthur, Jr.; Sorensen, Theodore C.; Szulc, Tad; Wilson, Donald M.

Oral Histories

Bissell, Richard M., Jr.; Bowles, Chester; Kirkpatrick, Lyman B., Jr.

Documents

Central Intelligence Agency, March 27, 1961, Information Report CS-3/469,391, declassification date unrecorded.

Ibid., March 30, 1961, "Current Intelligence Weekly Summary," declassified April 7, 1976.

Ibid., April 6, 1961, "Current Intelligence Weekly Summary," declassified April 7, 1976.

Ibid., April 6, 1961, Information Report CS-3/470,587, declassification date unrecorded.

Hawkins, Colonel Jack, April 13, 1961, "Precedence Emergency" cable, sanitized version, in *Life*, May 10, 1963, p. 34, with article "We Who Tried," by John Dille.

Schlesinger, Arthur M., Jr., March 31, 1961, "Memorandum for the President. Subject: Howard Handleman on Cuba," and "Memorandum for the President. Subject: Joseph Newman on Cuba."

Ibid., April 5, 1961, "Memorandum for the President. Subject: Cuba," declassified September 12, 1978.

Ibid., April 10, 1961, "Memorandum for the President. Subject: Cuba: Political, Diplomatic and Economic Problems," declassified January 13, 1976.

Taylor Report, Parts I and II.

Books

Catledge, Turner, *My Life and The Times* (New York: Harper & Row, 1971).

Dulles, Allen W., *The Craft of Intelligence* (New York: Harper & Row, 1963).

Kendrick, Alexander, *Prime Time* (Boston: Little, Brown, 1969).

Martin, John Bartlow, *Adlai Stevenson and the World* (Garden City, N.Y.: Doubleday, 1977).

McGaffin, William, and Knoll, Erwin, *Anything but the Truth* (New York: Putnam, 1968), contains the full text of "The Press and National Security," lecture by Clifton Daniel, then managing editor of *The New York Times*, to the World Press Institute at St. Paul, Minn., detailing the role of *The Times* in the Bay of Pigs affair.

Salinger, Pierre, *With Kennedy* (Garden City, N.Y.: Doubleday, 1966).

Articles

The New York Times, April 7, 1961, "Anti-Castro Units Trained to Fight at Florida Bases," by Tad Szulc.

Ibid., April 9, 1961, "Castro Foes Call Cubans to Arms; Predict Uprising," by Sam Pope Brewer.

Ibid., April 11, 1961, "Top U.S. Advisers in Dispute on Aid to Castro's Foes," by James Reston.

Ibid., April 12, 1961, Editorial-page column by James Reston.

Ibid., April 14, 1961, Editorial-page column by James Reston.

CHAPTER FIVE: THE ATTACK BEGINS

Interviews

Alonso, José; Amory, Robert, Jr.; Aragón, Ernesto; Beerli, Stanley W.; Bissell, Richard M., Jr.; Bundy, William P.; Burke, Arleigh R.; Carreras, Enrique; Castro, Fidel; Cleveland, Harlan; Davis, Robert K.; Doster, George R.; Drain, Richard; Engler, Jake; Ferrer, Eduardo; Fritchey, Clayton; Gray, David W.; Lemnitzer, Lyman L.; Maceo, Antonio, M.D.; Manso, Andrés; Mell, Fernández; Morse, Luís; Noyes, Charles P.; Pedersen, Richard F.; Phillips, David A.; del Pino, Rafael; Ponzoa, Gustavo; Pou, Juan; Raymont, Henry; Rusk, Dean; Shoup, David M.; Teegan, Gar; Varona, Antonio de; Villaverde, Rafael; Zuñiga, Mario.

Oral Histories

Amory, Robert Jr.; Bissell, Richard M., Jr.; Kirkpatrick, Lyman, B., Jr.

Documents

Department of State, April 19, 1961, telegram from Adlai Stevenson to Secretary of State, No. 2937, declassified 1976.
Taylor Report, Parts I and II.

Books

Cabell, Charles P., unpublished autobiography.
Hunt, Howard, *"Give Us This Day"* (New Rochelle, N.Y.: Arlington House, 1973).
Johnson, Haynes, *The Bay of Pigs* (New York: Norton, 1964).
Khrushchev, Nikita, *Khrushchev Remembers* (Boston: Little, Brown, 1970).
Schlesinger, Arthur M., Jr., *A Thousand Days* (Boston: Houghton Mifflin, 1965).

Articles

Chicago Sunday Tribune, April 16, 1961, "Sees Bombing and Strafing of Cuban Camp," by Henry Raymont.

CHAPTER SIX: INVASION

Interviews

Alonso, José; Almeida, Juan, M.D.; Artime, Manuel; Basulto, José; Caballero, Víctor; Carreras, Enrique; Castro, Fidel; Clark, John A.; Cleveland, Harlan; Cosculuella, Juan; Crutchfield, Robert R.; Dennison, Robert; Drain, Richard; Dunham, Frank C.; Duque, Félix; Fernández, Ramón José; Ferrer, Eduardo; Fickenscher, Edward R., Jr.; Forgy, William J.; García, Eduardo; Goodwin, Billy; Granda, Raúl; Jimínez, Angel; La Mar, René de, M.D.; López-Estrada, Armando; Lynch, Grayston; Maddock, Edmund J.; Maruri, Angel; Maruri, Ángel, Jr.; McHugh, Godfrey T.; Mejias, Alejandrina; Mejias, Narciso; Mell, Fernández; Moreira, Rafael; Morse, Luís; O'Donnell, Kenneth P.; Oliva, Erneido; Ortiz, Amparo; Pérez, Silvio; Perkins, Peter; del Pino, Rafael; Pou, Juan; Pruna, Andy; Recarey, Jorge; Rivera, Félix; Rostow, Walt W.; Sánchez, Ramiro; Sayers, Samuel; Schlesinger, Arthur, Jr.; Searcy, S. S., Jr.; Shannon, Joseph; Smathers, George; Solís, Raúl; Sopo, Edgar; Sordo, Juan, M.D.; Sueiro, Hugo; Swinbourne, Harry; Teegan, Gar; Tirado, Gustavo; del Valle, Sergio; Villaverde, Rafael.

Documents

Taylor Report, Part I (contains texts of White House message traffic with the invasion beaches) and Part II.

Books

Ferrer, Eduardo, *Operación Puma* (Miami: International Aviation Consultants, Inc., 1975).
Johnson, Haynes, *The Bay of Pigs* (New York: Norton, 1964), contains superb detail of the tank battle and other ground engagements.
del Pino, Rafael, *Amanecer en Girón* (Havana: Instituto Cubano del Libro, 1969).
Rostow, Walt W., *The Diffusion of Power* (New York: Macmillan, 1972), contains detail of White House meetings toward the end and after the battle.
Schlesinger, Arthur M., Jr., *A Thousand Days* (Boston: Houghton Mifflin, 1965).

Articles

Granma, April 21, 1976, "Los Más Significativo Fué la Actitud de los Combatientes; El Derroche de Valor y de Coraje de los Combatientes," by Magali García More. This account of the battle in the daily newspaper of the Central Committee of the Communist Party of Cuba is based on detailed interviews with the principal land commander of the Castro forces, Ramón José Fernández, now Cuban Minister of Education, and contains full texts of some of Castro's principal battle orders.

Life, May 10, 1963, *We Who Tried*, by John Dille, contains details of the tank battle and other ground and aerial action.

Réplica (Spanish-language magazine published in Miami), Aug. 4, Aug. 11 and Aug. 18, 1976, contains a series of eyewitness articles in Spanish by Grayston Lynch of the CIA.

CHAPTER SEVEN: AFTERMATH

Interviews

Bissell, Richard M., Jr.; Crutchfield, Robert R.; Davis, Robert K.; Doster, George R.; Dunham, Frank C.; Ferrer, Eduardo; Flannery, James E.; Franco, Juan Pérez; Lynch, Grayston; Maceo, Antonio, M.D.; Noble, Jim; Plank, John; Ponzoa, Gustavo; Pou, Juan; Powers, David F.; Pruna, Andy; Rostow, Walt W.; Searcy, S. S., Jr.; Taylor, Maxwell D.; Varona, Antonio de.

Books

Castro, Fidel, *Playa Girón—A Victory of the People* (Havana: Editorial en Marcha, 1961), contains Castro's victory speech of April 23, 1961.

Government of Cuba, *Playa Girón: Derrota del Imperialismo*, 4 vols. (Havana: Imprenta Burgay y Cia., 1961).

Phillips, David A., *The Night Watch* (New York: Atheneum, 1977), contains reactions to the defeat at CIA headquarters in Washington.

Sorensen, Theodore C., *Kennedy* (New York: Harper & Row, 1965), contains extraordinary account of President Kennedy's reflections after the event.

Taylor, Maxwell D., *Swords and Plowshares* (New York: Norton, 1972).

Articles

Reader's Digest, November 1964, "Cuba, Castro and John F. Kennedy," by Richard M. Nixon, contains recollections of Nixon's encounters with Dulles and Kennedy at the end of the battle.

CONCLUSION: IT COULD HAPPEN AGAIN

Interviews

Bissell, Richard M., Jr.; Bundy, McGeorge; Burke, Arleigh R.; Duque, Félix; Engler, Jake; Flannery, James E.; Gilpatric, Roswell L.; Gray, David W.; Janis, Irving L.; Kirkpatrick, Lyman B., Jr.; Rostow, Walt W.; Taylor, Maxwell D.

Documents

Bissell, Richard M., Jr., letter to Arthur M. Schlesinger, Jr., Sept. 3, 1965, explaining Bissell's view of the defeat.

McNamara, Robert S., Aug. 30, 1961, "Memorandum for the President," contains
McNamara's views on the responsibility for the defeat.

Taylor Report, Parts I and II.

Books

Bonsal, Philip W., *Cuba, Castro and the United States* (Pittsburgh: University of
Pittsburgh Press, 1971).

Janis, Irving L., *Victims of Groupthink* (Boston: Houghton Mifflin, 1972).

Kirkpatrick, Lyman B., Jr., *The Real CIA* (New York: Macmillan, 1968).

Schlesinger, Arthur M., Jr., *A Thousand Days* (Boston: Houghton Mifflin, 1965).

Taylor, Maxwell D., *Swords and Plowshares* (New York: Norton, 1972).

Articles

Naval War College Review, November–December 1972, "Paramilitary Case Study—
The Bay of Pigs," by Lyman B. Kirkpatrick, Jr.

The Washington Star, "The Bay of Pigs revisited: Former CIA Aide Tells What He'd Do
Differently," July 20, 1965, by Orr Kelly, contains more on Bissell's view of the
defeat.

Index

343

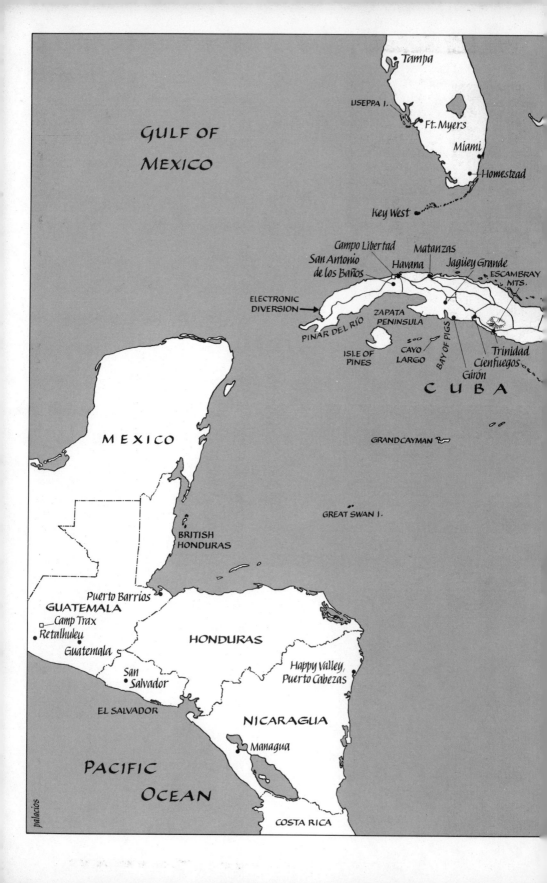